# Abortion before Birth Control

## THE POLITICS OF REPRODUCTION
## IN POSTWAR JAPAN

*Tiana Norgren*

PRINCETON UNIVERSITY PRESS

PRINCETON AND OXFORD

Copyright © 2001 by Princeton University Press
Published by Princeton University Press, 41 William Street,
Princeton, New Jersey 08540
In the United Kingdom: Princeton University Press,
3 Market Place, Woodstock, Oxfordshire OX20 1SY

*Library of Congress Cataloging-in-Publication Data*

Norgren, Tiana, 1970–
Abortion before birth control : the politics of reproduction
in postwar Japan / Tiana Norgren.
p.   cm.— (Studies of the East Asian Institute)
Includes bibliographical references and index.
ISBN 0-691-07004-0 (alk. paper) —
ISBN 0-691-07005-9 (pbk. : alk. paper)
1. Abortion—Japan. 2. Birth control—Government policy—Japan.
3. Family size—Japan. 4. Women—Japan—Social conditions.
5. Japan—Social conditions—1945– I. Title. II. Series.
HQ767.5.J3 N67 2001
304.6′67′0952—dc21        00-066941

This book has been composed in Berkeley Book

The paper used in this publication meets the minimum requirements
of ANSI/NISO Z39.48-1992 (R1997) (*Permanence of Paper*)

www.pup.princeton.edu

Printed in the United States of America

10  9  8  7  6  5  4  3  2  1

10  9  8  7  6  5  4  3  2  1
(Pbk.)

*For my parents, who taught me how to write and how to think*

# Contents

# Illustrations

# Preface

THE DEVELOPMENT of safe and effective contraception methods and abortion procedures has brought about a quiet revolution in human history: the ability to control fertility reliably. As this revolution gained momentum in the twentieth century in conjunction with advances in science, technology, health, and mass communication, urban dwellers in industrialized countries moved rapidly to limit their family size. But more recently it has become clear that rural inhabitants of developing countries also want smaller families. Over the past thirty years, the average number of children per family in developing countries has dropped from about six to about three.[1]

The phenomenon of smaller family size has been attributed to many factors, including economic development, the rise of modern, secular values, radical changes in women's roles and aspirations, urbanization, declines in infant mortality, and family planning programs.[2] But it is clear that the flow of causation goes both ways—for example, that smaller family size was not only a product of economic development, but that it actually spurred economic development as well. Economists David Bloom and Jeffrey Williamson make the argument that one-third to as much as three-quarters of East Asia's "miraculous" economic growth between 1965 and 1990 was the result of an idiosyncratic pattern of rapid demographic transition, whereby the working-age population grew at a faster rate than the overall population, particularly dependent children and the elderly. This phenomenon yielded a "demographic gift," which led to increases in savings and productivity. Bloom and Williamson explain that the number of dependent children declined primarily because of increased contraceptive use, while the working-age population was large because of high birth rates in the previous generation and declines in mortality; the elderly population was small because East Asian countries were emerging from an era when life expectancy was low.[3] They predict that between 1990 and 2025 many Southeast Asian countries with similar demographic profiles and increasing rates of contraceptive use will exchange their "demographic burden" (more dependent children than workers) for a "demographic gift" and experience high rates of economic growth similar to those seen in East Asia decades earlier. Meanwhile, after 2010, "as the bulge in the age distribution works its way through the population," Japan and other East Asian countries will again be burdened by a higher ratio of dependents to workers—this time, elderly dependents rather than children—and experience a 1–3 percent "demographically induced" decline in the gross domestic product (GDP) per capita growth rate.[4]

The causal relationship between smaller family size and changes in women's roles and aspirations has also been reciprocal; that is, changing roles and aspirations have led many women to limit the number of children they bear, but having fewer children has also allowed women to alter their aspirations. The ability to control one's fertility—to determine the number and spacing of children—is a fundamental precondition for achieving many other goals, such as access to higher education, employment outside the home, financial self-sufficiency, and some forms of political participation.[5] Changes in women's roles—primarily women's mass entry into the workforce, and the decreasing number of years that women devote to bearing and rearing children—have had profound effects on the political, social, and economic fabric of countries worldwide. But male behavior, laws, workplace culture, and other large societal institutions are changing at a much slower rate. Hence many countries are beginning to experience wrenching transitions into new, uncharted territory.

In Japan this transition has manifested itself in the form of high rates of postsecondary education for women, increasing female employment, sharp declines in the birth rate, men and women marrying at higher ages, a rapidly growing elderly population, strong resistance to importing immigrant labor, and equally strong resistance to changing the work culture and men's family roles in ways that might make married life and childrearing more attractive to women. How the Japanese will find their way out of this conundrum remains to be seen. What we can see, and what we will see in the chapters that follow, is that many of the trends mentioned above trace their origins to abortion and contraception policies adopted decades ago by political and societal actors who often had very different outcomes in mind.

This book originated many years ago in courses I took with two of my favorite professors, Barney Rubin and Frank Upham, and I am extremely grateful for their early encouragement. My dissertation and I subsequently flourished under the guidance of my advisor, Gerry Curtis, who shares my taste for straightforward, empirically grounded political research. I owe many, many thanks to John Campbell, Jean Cohen, Helen Hardacre, Hiroshi Ishida, Marc Kesselman, Eileen McDonagh, Margaret McKean, Michael Reich, Flip Strum, Frank Upham, an anonymous reviewer for the *Journal of Japanese Studies*, and especially Sheldon Garon, for their truly invaluable comments and suggestions, which, at various stages, pushed me to undertake the necessary but painful process of shaping and refining the analytical and theoretical aspects of this book. Given my shortcomings in these areas, it goes without saying that I take responsibility for any and all deficiencies. I am also grateful to Columbia University, the East Asian Institute at Columbia University, the Fulbright Foundation, Keio University, and the Social Science Research Council for supporting my research. And finally, I should add how fortunate I have been to find such a kindred spirit and intellect in the director of my program at the

Open Society Institute, Ellen Chesler. She has been a wonderful mentor, both academically and professionally.

On the personal side, I would like to thank my friends—Meredith Hyman El Nems, Dave Leheny, Patrice McMahon, Kathy Tegtmeyer Pak, Galia Press, and Erika Weinthal—for keeping me good company during those wonderful, long years of graduate school. Special thanks to Lori Watt and Midori Ashida for collecting materials for me in Japan during the latter stages of this project, and to Alison Tolman and Eleanor Mitch for helping me find and photograph the cover art. I owe the most gratitude to my parents, to whom this book is dedicated, for encouraging my intellectual development and bolstering my self-esteem since I was a small child. And last, but definitely not least, I thank my husband, Chris, who has been my anchor lo these many years, and little Elena, whose birth in 1996 helped focus my attention on the fact that I did not have an indefinite amount of time to finish this project!

Following East Asian practice, Japanese surnames precede given names, excepting those Japanese whose English-language works have been cited. Macrons in Japanese words have been omitted in well-known Japanese words and place names.

# Abbreviations

| | |
|---|---|
| Chūpiren | Chūzetsu kinshi hō ni hantai shi piru kaikin o yōkyū suru josei kaihō rengō; in English, the Women's Liberation Federation for Opposing the Abortion Prohibition Law and Lifting the Pill Ban |
| DSP | Democratic Socialist Party |
| EPCO | Eugenic Protection Consultation Office |
| FDA | Food and Drug Administration |
| FPFJ | Family Planning Federation of Japan |
| IRAA | Imperial Rule Assistance Organization |
| IUD | intrauterine device |
| JAOG | Japan Association of Obstetricians and Gynecologists (Nihon Sanfujinka Gakkai) |
| JMA | Japan Medical Association |
| JCP | Japan Communist Party |
| JFPA | Japan Family Planning Association |
| JSP | Japan Socialist Party |
| LCCA | Law on Control of Contraceptive Appliances |
| LDP | Liberal Democratic Party |
| MHW | Ministry of Health and Welfare |
| MOF | Ministry of Finance |
| Nichibo | Nihon Bosei Hogo Sanfujinkai Kai (formerly Nihon Bosei Hogo I Kyōkai); in English, the Japan Association of Maternal Welfare |
| ob-gyn | obstetrician-gynecologist |
| SCAP | Supreme Command Allied Powers |

Abortion before Birth Control

## CHAPTER ONE

# Introduction

ON MARCH 2, 1998, at the final stage of a review process that had stretched into its eighth year, the Central Pharmaceutical Advisory Council of the Japanese Ministry of Health and Welfare (MHW) again decided to delay approval of the low-dose contraceptive pill and ordered an investigation into the ecological effects of hormonal contraceptives.[1] This was the third time in four decades that the MHW had come close to approving the pill only to back down at the last minute, making it seem increasingly likely that Japan would enter the twenty-first century as the only member of the United Nations that had not legalized the pill. But in January 1999, the MHW hastily approved an erectile dysfunction drug, Viagra, after just six months of deliberation, and on the basis of foreign clinical trial data. This sudden action exposed the MHW to media scrutiny and outraged protests by women's groups, which pointed out the gross disparity between the standards to which the MHW held Viagra and the pill. Bowing to pressure, the Health Ministry finally approved the pill in June 1999, and it went on sale three months later.[2]

In light of this long-term ban on the pill, it may surprise readers to learn that abortion was legalized in Japan in 1948 and became readily available following substantial revisions to the law in 1949 and 1952. The 1949 revision made Japan the first country in the world to allow abortion on socioeconomic grounds, and the 1952 revision eliminated the requirement that women appear before a review committee for permission to have an abortion. This was a marked departure from international norms, as most other countries did not legalize abortion until several decades later—and even in the countries that did make exceptions to save a woman's life or health, abortion was by no means readily available.

Japan's contradictory policies are puzzling, since it seems illogical for a government to, in effect, encourage abortion over contraception. And in fact, what little empirical research has been done on this subject suggests that Japan did have an unusual combination of policies. In a statistical analysis of contraception policy in twenty-nine developed countries, Field found that conservative birth control policies are good predictors of conservative abortion policies, and vice versa.[3] Thus the task of this book is to unravel the puzzle and explain why abortion policy in Japan has been relatively progressive, while contraception policy has been relatively conservative.

Before proceeding any further, however, a brief discussion of the terms *progressive* and *conservative* is in order, because they are such evocative, value-laden terms. For students of American politics, for example, the term *progressive* may conjure up Theodore Roosevelt and the Progressive Era at the turn of the century; the word *conservative* may bring to mind the Reagan revolution of the 1980s and the subsequent rise in religious right-wing influence over American politics in the 1990s. For European and Japanese readers, these terms may elicit other, very different historical and ideological associations. Regardless of nationality, both terms can have either positive or negative connotations, depending on the reader's personal political convictions.

In this book, however, the terms *progressive* and *conservative* are used in a less complicated fashion, and are not intended as shorthand for any larger concepts or agendas. The definitions used here center around a fairly limited notion of receptiveness to change: that is, the propensity of a policymaker or a policy to embrace, or to resist, change. Thus a *progressive* policy is one that makes use of new ideas, opportunities, or institutions to change and improve on the status quo. A *conservative* policy is one that operates within the confines of existing institutions and norms, emphasizing the virtues of tradition and seeking to change as little as possible.

Japanese abortion policy was progressive historically because the Eugenic Protection Law (Yūsei Hogo Hō) effectively decriminalized abortion in 1948 and because doctors interpreted the law loosely, making abortion available on demand—de facto, if not de jure. Technically speaking, of course, the Eugenic Protection Law only established the circumstances under which the Criminal Abortion Law could be superseded (see appendix).[4] This legal approach is different than that of the United States, where abortion is formally legal on demand, but in the broader international context, the Japanese approach is quite common. One-third of all countries in the world today—including the United Kingdom, Australia, and India—now allow abortion on socioeconomic grounds or for reasons of physical or mental health.[5] While the former approach may appear more restrictive on paper—and certainly it does have a greater potential to be restrictive—in practice, abortion is as easily accessible in Japan as in countries where abortion is formally available on demand.[6] As Glendon and others have noted, there is often "a significant discrepancy between a country's legal norms and the practice of abortion it tolerates."[7]

Progressive as Japan's Eugenic Protection Law was for the era in which it was enacted, it must be acknowledged at the outset that it was also retrograde and illiberal in significant ways. Most notably, as its name implies, the Eugenic Protection Law justified legalizing abortion on the basis of a eugenic ideology that had been recently discredited by Nazi abuses. And as we will see in chapter 5, this anachronism was not corrected until 1996, when the law was revised in response to the human rights critiques of feminists and advocates for the disabled. The law was renamed the Maternal Protection Law (Botai Hogo Hō) to reflect the second half of its original rationale, which invoked maternal protection (see Eugenic Protection Law, Article 1). Under current law, an abortion may be performed only before the fetus is viable[8] (Maternal Protection Law, Article 2, Paragraph 2)—though it should be noted that the vast majority of abortions in postwar Japan (90 percent or more) have, in fact, been performed within the first trimester.[9] Abortions may be performed only by a designated physician, and designated physicians must obtain the written consent of the woman and her spouse (Article 3, Paragraph 1).[10] According to Article 14 (Paragraph 1, Items 1–5) of the old Eugenic Protection Law, a woman seeking an abortion qualified if she, her spouse, or a relative had a hereditary physical or mental illness,[11] if either spouse had a nonhereditary mental illness, if either spouse had leprosy, if the pregnancy was the result of rape, or if "the continuation of pregnancy or childbirth [was] likely to seriously harm the mother's health for physical *or economic reasons*" (emphasis added). When legislators revised the Eugenic Protection Law in 1996, however, they removed the first three criteria because of their eugenic content. Thus, under the Maternal Protection Law, only rape and maternal health (physical or economic reasons) are now formally recognized as valid criteria for obtaining an abortion. If the government sought to restrict access to abortion, it could, in theory, force doctors to interpret more narrowly the "economic reasons" clause of Article 4—which has been the reason cited by 99 to 100 percent of Japanese women requesting an abortion throughout the postwar period.[12] But given that right-wing attempts to eliminate the "economic reasons" clause failed in the face of strong opposition both in the 1970s and 1980s (see chapter 5), it seems very unlikely that the government would pursue such a course.

Scholars agree that abortion played a decisive role in the rapid and drastic reduction of the Japanese birth rate in the 1950s (see Figure 1.1), though more recent declines in the birth rate have been attributed to contraception use and later marriage.[13] However, it should be noted that there are no hard and firm figures on the abortion rate for any year in the postwar period, because government statistics are widely regarded as unreliable. This stems from the fact that obstetrician-gynecologists (ob-gyns) have long underreported abortions to avoid paying taxes on the income they generate, a practice made easier by the fact that abortion is not covered by health insurance.[14] Thus, although official figures indicate that more than 1 million abortions were performed per year between 1955 and 1960 (662 to 716 abortions per 1,000 live births), Tsuya estimates that more than 2 million abortions were actually performed per year during that period (1,300 to 1,500 abortions per 1,000 live births).[15] Other researchers estimate that the real abortion rates were as much as 3 or 4 times the official numbers through the 1970s.[16] As for the 1980s and 1990s, while official abortion rates dropped below .5 million per year, Japanese and American researchers believe that the actual abortion rate was still 1.5 to 3 times higher than the official rate.[17] If these estimates are correct, it means that although the abortion rate has definitely declined over time, there are still be-

Figure 1.1. Average total fertility rate of Japanese women, 1920–1998.

tween 750,000 and 1.5 million abortions performed per year (see Figure 1.2). This puts Japan in the low- to mid-range in cross-national comparisons of abortion rates (see Figure 1.3).[18]

If postwar Japanese abortion policy can best be described as progressive, postwar contraception policy must be considered conservative. Japanese contraception policy has been restrictive and slow to change, tending toward maintaining the status quo. For example, Japan's Ministry of Health and Welfare did not approve the intrauterine device (IUD) until 1974, even though IUDs had been in use in other countries for a decade or more.[19] And by the time the MHW finally approved the plastic IUD in 1974, most countries were already replacing plastic IUDs with safer and more effective copper IUDs—which were not approved in Japan until 1999.[20] The most dramatic manifestation of the government's conservative contraception policy, however, is the fact that the MHW did not approve the pill until 1999. For almost forty years, this anti-pill policy denied Japanese couples access to a major method of contraception and fostered reliance on abortion. Given the unfavorable policy environment, Japanese pharmaceutical companies have not yet ventured to apply for approval of more recent contraceptive innovations widely used in many other countries, such as short-acting injectable contraceptives and long-acting subcutaneous contraceptive implants.[21]

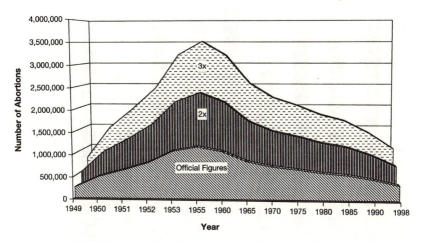

Figure 1.2. Number of abortions in Japan, 1949–1998, official figures and estimates (two and three times official figures).

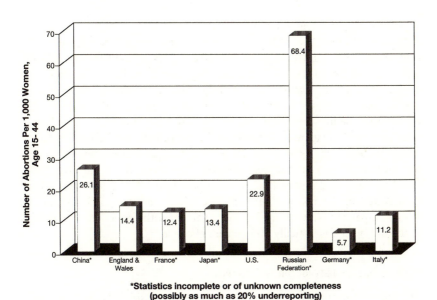

Figure 1.3. Cross-national comparison of abortion rates per 1,000 women, ages 15–44 (1995).

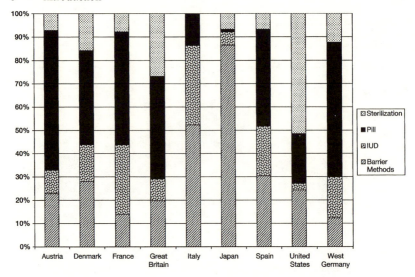

Figure 1.4. Cross-national comparison of contraceptive methods used.

Japan's long-standing pill ban was highly unusual: by 1999, Japan was the only member of the United Nations that had not approved the pill for contraceptive use.[22] Japan's policy on the pill stood in particular contrast to policy in other advanced industrial democracies, where tens of millions of women have been using the pill, legally, for several decades. An average of 30 percent of contraceptors in North America and Western Europe are pill users, and the pill is either the first or second most commonly used contraceptive method in these regions.[23] In Japan, on the other hand, the primary method of contraception is the condom. As of 1998, 78 percent of Japanese contraceptors relied on condoms, 6 percent had been surgically sterilized, 3 percent used IUDs, and 1 percent used oral contraceptives (see Figure 1.4).[24] These figures have varied little in the postwar period.[25] The failure rate for condoms is quite high—12 percent with typical use and 3 percent with perfect use—compared to the pill, which is virtually 100 percent effective.[26]

## Why Abortion before Birth Control?

To return to the original question, then, how can we explain Japan's contradictory abortion and contraception policies? One school of thought holds that Japanese culture provides the answer to this question. Taueber, writing in the late 1950s, argued that there was a cultural basis for acceptance of abortion in Japan because the Japanese traditionally practiced abortion and infanticide, the Japanese made less of an ethical distinction between abortion and contraception, and the Japanese did not share Western religious scruples about abortion.[27] Taueber's sources are dated, but her argument should not be ignored simply for that reason. In fact, contemporary scholars such as LaFleur make similar arguments.[28] In a variation on Taeuber's "lack of Christianity" thesis, LaFleur explains that Japan has been able to avoid the divisive polemics that characterize the Western discourse on abortion because of Buddhist views on the fluidity of life, death, and reincarnation, and because of the Buddhist practice of performing services for the repose of the souls of aborted fetuses (*mizuko kuyō*).[29] Like Taeuber, LaFleur also points out that abortion and infanticide were common practices in Japan historically and that, "in comparison with Europe, there was more latitude and probably also a higher incidence of infanticide in Japan."[30]

There are several problems with cultural explanations of abortion policy and practice. First, regardless of what Japanese attitudes and practices may have been historically, there is no evidence that Japanese attitudes toward abortion in recent times are more tolerant than they are in other industrialized democracies.[31] Second, as a British reviewer of LaFleur's book points out, abortion is less controversial in Northern and Western Europe than it is in the United States.[32] Thus the relatively low-key discussion of abortion in Japan—which LaFleur presents as the consequence of a particularly Japanese religious tolerance of abortion—is actually quite unremarkable in a wider comparative perspective. Finally, cultural explanations of Japan's progressive abortion policy cannot explain why Japanese contraception policy is conservative. For it follows logically that if the Japanese are tolerant of abortion because of their historical practices and religious beliefs, they should also be tolerant of all forms of contraception, given that contraception constitutes a less radical form of intervention in the reproductive process than abortion.

Coleman's research on family planning in Japan points in the direction of noncultural explanations of Japanese abortion and contraception policy. As an anthropologist, Coleman focuses more on individual contraceptive practices and attitudes than on the larger realm of contraception and abortion policy making. He asks why "a country that is ultramodern in so many other respects has a family planning technology that was created in the 1930s,"[33] and he attempts to answer this question primarily through questionnaires and interviews on contraceptive usage, abortion rates, conjugal roles, women's status, and attitudes toward sexuality. But Coleman also explores how doctors, family planning organizations, and other groups have helped create and perpetuate certain patterns of contraceptive behavior in the process of pursuing their own interests. And in doing so, he introduces the notion that Japanese abortion and contraception policy may be the product of politics, not culture.[34]

This book expands on that idea. The argument presented here is that Japan's contradictory abortion and contraception policies are products of very different historical circumstances and, in particular, of very different interest group configurations and dynamics. Medical and family planning interests created Japan's progressive abortion policy during the Allied Occupation, which provided a window of opportunity for innovations of this kind. Doctors and women then defended the policy in the face of a reactionary religious pro-life movement. The explanation for Japan's conservative contraception policy is more complicated, but it, too, can be traced to the confluence of unique historical situations and interest group activity. First, efforts to promote birth control were delayed for ten years after abortion was legalized, because the relevant groups could not reach a consensus on how to promote birth control, or else they had vested interests that militated against promoting birth control. This delay set the tone for a postwar pattern of "abortion before birth control." The pill then appeared at an unfavorable moment historically, when economic recovery and drug-related scandals dominated the public consciousness, and when concerns over the declining birth rate were beginning to surface. More important, while abortion was still illegal or not readily accessible in most other countries when the pill came on the market, in Japan, abortion was legal and easy to access before oral contraceptives were invented. This unusual circumstance led to the creation of groups with a vested interest in abortion, and these groups viewed the pill as a threat to their livelihoods, women's health, and abortion rights.

More recent research by sociologist Joseph Potter confirms the logic of the historical—or what Potter calls the "path dependent"—approach. Potter observes that in most countries an idiosyncratic "contraceptive culture" has evolved over time, in which one or two contraceptive methods predominate over other methods (e.g., condoms in Japan, sterilization in the United States, IUDs and the pill in Egypt). Using Mexico and Brazil as case studies, he seeks to explain why "contraceptive regimes that evolved in one set of circumstances can persist long after they no longer make sense."[35] Potter argues that we should not try to find explanations "solely in terms of deep-seated cultural preferences or the present-day incentive structure." Rather, we should trace the historical chain of often minor and chance events and anomalous laws and practices that, by "the wayward logic of path dependence," get reinforced and magnified over time—by word of mouth among contraceptive users, by medical school and government training programs in the case of Brazil and Mexico, or by interest group politics in the case of Japan—to produce a dominant pattern of contraceptive usage that prevails, often even when it is detrimental to contraceptive users' health, well-being, human dignity, or economic best interests.[36]

## Methods of Analysis

The analytical framework of this book is grounded in the methods of historical scholarship and therefore relies heavily on tracing and evaluating the causes and consequences of political processes over time. The flow of history—the unique events and sequences of events, and the prevailing worldviews of a given time and place—constantly creates and destroys opportunities for an ever changing array of political actors to pursue their agendas. Skocpol's concept of "the feedback effect"—whereby previously established policies affect subsequent policy-making processes both positively and negatively—is particularly helpful in understanding the dynamics of political history.

> As politics create policies, policies also remake politics. Once instituted, policies have feedback effects in two main ways. In the first place, because of the official efforts made to implement new policies using new or existing administrative arrangements, policies transform or expand the capacities of the state. . . . In the second place, new policies affect the social identities, goals, and capabilities of groups that subsequently struggle or ally in politics. . . . According to this political-process approach, a policy is "successful" if it enhances the kinds of state capacities that can promote its future development, and especially if it stimulates groups and political alliances to defend the policy's continuation and expansion.[37]

The feedback effect has been an important factor in postwar Japanese reproduction policy. Laws and ordinances passed in the prewar period strongly influenced the goals and strategies of postwar actors, and consequently played a crucial role in policy outcomes such as the passage of the Eugenic Protection Law and the delay in legalizing and promoting birth control. These postwar policy outcomes produced new feedback effects, such as the creation of the politically active designated abortion providers' group, Nichibo, the counter-mobilization of the anti-abortion religious group Seichō no Ie, and the counter-countermobilization of early feminist groups. These groups have all produced policy ripples of their own. Nichibo, for example, was instrumental in the defeat of the pharmaceutical industry's initial efforts to gain government approval for oral contraceptives in the 1960s, a reversal that has had negative repercussions to the present day. Thus it would be impossible to understand Japan's abortion and contraception policies today without carefully tracing their historical roots.

Methodologically, this book employs an "unequally weighted" comparative approach.[38] This strategy involves conducting in-depth case studies of Japanese reproduction policy, while drawing comparisons with reproduction policy in other industrialized democracies wherever such comparisons are instructive. The main point of this book is to piece together the story of abortion and contraception policy in postwar Japan, but cross-national comparisons often illuminate the forces at work in Japan, and, likewise, the Japanese cases add to our understanding of what is and is not generalizable about the politics of reproduction.[39]

## CHAPTER TWO

# The Politics of Interests

THE RELATIONSHIP between the Japanese state and economic actors has received a great deal of attention, leaving something of a gap in our knowledge about the relationship between the Japanese state and civil society.[1] In particular, the literature underemphasizes the important role that interest groups and citizens' groups play in the Japanese political process, often overemphasizing the power of bureaucrats and the top-down nature of Japanese politics. This neglect of citizen and interest group participation has more than merely academic consequences, for it has contributed to the popular impression that Japan is a simple economic animal, rather than a complex, maturing democracy.

This book paints an alternative picture of Japanese politics, one that depicts interest groups and citizens' groups as key players in postwar abortion and contraception policy making. In these issue areas, bureaucrats have often behaved like "followers" or "referees,"[2] while a variety of groups—medical associations, family planning organizations, pharmaceutical companies, religious groups, women's groups, and groups representing the handicapped and mentally ill—jostled for control over the shape of policy. That interest groups could be key players in Japanese politics should not come as a surprise, for political issues do not grow out of thin air: they are cultivated. And they are often cultivated not by politicians or bureaucrats, but by people who are closer to the ground, and who have very immediate, vested interests in one outcome or another.

The study of interest group politics has occupied a central place in American political thought[3] since the republic's founders pondered the causes, effects, pros, cons, and proper management of "factions." James Madison wrote, in 1778, that the regulation of such factions formed "the principal task of government."[4] And although Madison viewed factionalism as detrimental to the public good, he concluded that the most effective way to lessen the dangers of factionalism was to allow the conflicting interests of a large number of competing groups to check and balance one another in the political arena, thereby decreasing their overall influence.[5]

After World War II Truman, Dahl, and other political scientists incorporated Madisonian thinking into a pluralist theory of interest group politics. In the pluralist view, the American political system has many points of access, participation is open to all, and competition among groups produces a dynamic equilibrium in which no group can predominate for long without provoking other groups to countermobilize.[6] The pluralists have their critics, of course. In general, "pluralism has been criticized as an apology for the pursuit of private interests by public means."[7] Schattschneider questioned the universality and representativeness of the interest group system, asserting that it is biased in favor of the elite.[8] Lowi argued that interest group politics are not necessarily "self-corrective," and that inequalities do, in fact, arise because new groups do not always automatically appear to counterbalance established ones.[9] And according to Olson's now famous theory of collective action, large groups of people with common interests often do not organize to pursue those interests because, if it is possible for potential group members to enjoy goods and services provided by the group without joining or otherwise contributing, then each potential member has little rational incentive to do so.[10] Furthermore,

> members of the general public face high transaction costs in gathering information about interests and in getting and staying organized, all in the face of small per capita gains. . . . [11] Groups whose interests are intense and concentrated . . . are more likely to pay the costs of organizing . . . because the members of groups with concentrated interests get a greater individual payoff from organization.[12]

Broadly speaking, the elitist and pluralist schools reflect two normative streams of thought on the relationship between interest group politics and democracy. In the former view, interest groups corrupt democracy because they represent the interests of some citizens—generally those who are already privileged in other ways—more than others, and often at the expense of others. In the latter view, interest groups play an important and enhancing role in a democracy, affording citizens a form of functional representation tailored more specifically to their interests than geographical representation (i.e., voting). In this view, interest groups also provide important information to legislators and create forums for deliberation on various issues.[13]

As is the case with most academic debates, both pluralists and their critics accurately describe different aspects of political reality because

> different issue areas are home to different configurations of bias. Some generate the interest of a great variety of competing and conflictual interest groups, but other areas witness the mobilization of only one side of an issue. . . . The mobilization of bias can [also] change over time. A single issue area may be altered over the years from a one-sided mobilization of interests to a much more conflictual and multifaceted configuration.[14]

The chapters on Japanese abortion policy in this book perfectly demonstrate this point. Abortion policy making was dominated by one group of doctors for more than a decade after World War II, but, over time, anti-abortion religious groups and family planning groups were provoked to mobilize in order to counter the doctors' influence, in turn leading women and doctors to counter-mobilize to defend access to abortion. The groups that wielded comparatively less political influence in the 1970s—women's groups and handicapped groups—became more powerful in the 1980s and 1990s. Thus we see that a policy-making process that was once quite elitist became increasingly pluralistic over time.

In contrast to the United States, the study of interest groups has not centrally informed scholars' understanding of Japanese politics. While a reasonably sizable, though fragmented, body of case studies on various interest groups in Japan exists,[15] there are few general works on Japanese interest group politics.[16] This inattention to interest groups may result from the popular impression that Japan has a strong state and a weak civil society, but, as we will see in the chapters that follow, this is not an accurate representation of postwar politics.

The prewar period is a different story. Interest groups did exist in prewar Japan, but none were autonomous from government control, and their political influence was limited. This was owing, at least in part, to the fact that parties and politicians were so weak. Gluck explains that politics was "denatured" during the Meiji period, because the elite group of oligarchs who established the Meiji state feared losing power to opposition politicians, and also feared that the unchecked representation of conflicting interests would disunify the country and make it more vulnerable to foreign interference. Therefore they took all possible measures to delegitimize politics. Soldiers, bureaucrats, local officials, and students were barred from engaging in party politics; the Constitution was presented as an imperial gift rather than a political concession that the people had won; and the terms *politics* and *interests* were given a negative cast, while the terms *impartial* and *nonpartisan* (*fuhen futō*) were imparted with positive connotations.[17]

Within this political and ideological structure, interest groups existed only with the government's permission: The government either approved a group—which in many cases had actually been established by the government—or else outlawed it. The groups the government tolerated were strictly controlled. They were often headed by former bureaucrats or men with close ties to incumbent bureaucrats, they were subject to government advisory functions, and most were dependent to one degree or another on government subsidies. But the government did not involve itself in this way solely to monitor and control group activities; it also sought to recruit societal groups to assist in its drives for economic and social management.[18] And prewar interest groups ultimately did play a greater role in implementing government policy than in articulating their own interests—although, as Garon points out, there was often considerable overlap between the interests of the state and those of societal groups. Many groups welcomed, even invited, state intervention, because they saw it as a way to achieve their goals.[19] Tipton concludes that "neither the state nor the social groups . . . in the interwar period emerge as homogenous or monolithic entities, and complexity and ambivalence often characterized state approaches and policies."[20]

There was a brief period in the late 1910s and 1920s when, in tandem with the growth of party politics, interest groups and citizens' groups achieved a greater degree of influence in Japanese politics.[21] But with the rise of the military in the 1930s, the power of politicians and interest groups waned. The government began to suppress even more severely groups and individuals deemed threatening to the sociopolitical order. Many Communist Party members, labor union members, family planning activists, and members of new religions were jailed; their offices and clinics were shut down, their temples smashed. In 1940 the groups that were deemed unthreatening were disbanded as independent organizations and incorporated into a compulsory government-controlled umbrella organization called the Imperial Rule Assistance Association (IRAA), which was modeled after Nazi institutions. The goal of the IRAA was to harness societal groups' manpower—and womanpower—on a large scale for war mobilization campaigns. In the process, groups in civil society lost whatever shreds of autonomy they might have had previously.

After Japan's defeat in war, however, the American-imposed democratic Constitution of 1947 ushered in a new era of state-society relations. While it is true that many prewar institutions and actors continued to exert influence in the postwar era, it is also the case that the Japanese acquired substantial political rights for the first time. These rights included popular sovereignty, universal suffrage, the freedoms of speech and association, and the right to petition and bargain collectively. The new political system effected a sea change in societal groups' ability to gain access to and influence over policy making. According to Garon and Mochizuki:

> In terms of state-society relations, the central feature of postwar Japanese democracy may be that many social groups were able to negotiate social contracts and other agreements with the governing coalition, whereas in the prewar era they could not.[22]

The immediate postwar period witnessed a wave of interest group growth.[23] By 1956 the Japanese media had "discovered" interest groups—or pressure groups (*atsuryoku dantai*), as they were then called—and concluded that these groups were "running wild" in the political arena.[24] On observing the intensity of interest group lobbying before the June 1959 Upper House elections, the *Nikkei shinbun* declared that the era of bureaucratic omnipotence might be giving way to the era of the pressure group.[25] A wide variety of groups, many of which are still active today, were singled out for media attention in the 1950s: for example, the Small and Medium Enterprise Political League

(Chūseiren), the Society of War Bereaved Families (Izokukai), the Japan Medical Association (Nihon Ishikai), the Agricultural Cooperative Association (Nōkyō), the Housewives' Federation (Shufuren), and religious groups such as Sōka Gakkai. As Pempel notes:

> Virtually any social interest that one could imagine is organized in Japan. Although many, particularly the major agricultural, business, and professional associations, retain close ties to government, most are also fiercely independent in the pursuit of their particular vision of the national interest. They organize widely, lobby lustily, endorse or oppose political candidates, and play a major role in the politics of the nation.[26]

The "advocacy explosion" in Japan continued apace over the next several decades.[27] Whereas there were only 11.1 nonprofit associations per 100,000 people in Japan in 1960, by 1991 the number had reached 29.2 per 100,000, edging closer to the U.S. figure of 35.5 per 100,000.[28] Furthermore, group membership is high in Japan. One study of political participation conducted in 1966–67 found that Japan had the highest rate of group membership among the six countries surveyed.[29] Of course, the raw number of groups and the rate of group membership are far from being perfect indicators of interest group power, as many groups do not have political agendas and many group members are inactive. Nevertheless, organized groups have had an indisputable impact on Japanese politics—and not just well-funded business and professional groups either. The grass-roots citizens' movements that mobilized to protest widespread pollution and other threats to the quality of life in the late 1960s and early 1970s succeeded in pressuring the government to produce significant anti-pollution and social welfare legislation, reversing two decades of policy directed almost exclusively toward promoting economic development. Other movements at the time included anti-war, consumer, outcast or *burakumin*, women's, and handicapped liberation movements. The rise of grassroots movements in Japan also helped to usher in an era of liberal mayors and prefectural governors who institutionalized mechanisms for greater citizen participation at the local government level, a lasting legacy.[30]

What caused this advocacy explosion in postwar Japan? Judging from the literature on the United States, it is not a phenomenon that is limited to Japan. The first and probably most important factor is that, in both countries, the economy and the state grew rapidly in the postwar period, with governments vastly expanding public works and social programs. The growth of the welfare state gave groups an incentive to form in order to seek influence over policies pertaining to their interests, and to compete for government work orders and subsidies.[31] Second, the decline of the party system in the United States made group identification more salient to voters.[32] A similar phenomenon may have occurred in Japan, although, in the Japanese case, party organization was weak from the beginning. Third, technological innovations (telephones, photocopiers, computers, and now electronic mail) contributed to the rise of interest groups, making it easier for large numbers of geographically separate individuals with common interests to exchange information. And fourth, pluralists might argue simply that mobilization begets countermobilization.[33]

Japanese interest groups lobby much as interest groups do in other countries: by submitting petitions; organizing letter writing, signature, and telephone drives; distributing leaflets; making political contributions; holding press conferences and public meetings; mobilizing voters; arranging personal contacts with politicians and bureaucrats; suing in the courts; boycotting; propagandizing with sound trucks; marching on political headquarters; holding sit-ins, and occupying buildings. One innovative method that right-wing groups employed in lobbying for the passage of the Era Name Law (Gengo Hō) and the revision of the Eugenic Protection Law was to mobilize local assemblies to pass resolutions in favor of these measures and then to send the resolutions to the national government.[34]

An important difference between Japan and other countries is that religious, racial, ethnic, and class cleavages have less social and political salience, and therefore exert less influence on interest group formation, outlook, and activities. Thus ties with politicians and bureaucrats are particularly important in Japan.[35] According to Tsujinaka's 1988 survey, on average, interest group leaders found lobbying politicians and bureaucrats to be almost equally effective in pursuing their groups' agendas. Across different categories of groups, however, this assessment varied widely. Citizens' groups, labor groups, welfare groups, and professional groups all tended to turn more often to politicians to represent their interests, providing, in exchange, campaign contributions, voter mobilization, and information. Agricultural groups, business groups, and education-related groups, on the other hand, relied more on ties with the bureaucracy, providing in exchange information, assistance in policy implementation, and well-paying *amakudari* (descent from heaven) jobs for retired bureaucrats.[36] There have also been changes over time. Identical surveys conducted in 1980 and 1994 indicated that, overall, there has been a marked decline in contacts between association executives and government ministries, while contacts with politicians have remained stable.[37] This supports the contention made by many students of Japanese politics that, in the last several decades, the balance of power between bureaucrats and politicians has been shifting in favor of politicians.[38]

Over the course of the postwar period, the majority of interest groups have affiliated themselves with the Liberal Democratic Party (LDP), the conservative party that governed Japan without interruption for almost forty years. However, some left-wing groups, including labor and citizens' groups, have consistently affiliated themselves with opposition parties. Professional groups like the Japan Medical Association (JMA) have followed a third pattern, tending to distribute their support more evenly among the ruling and opposition parties (though still favoring the LDP) in an effort to maintain autonomy.[39] In the past, when the opposition Japan Socialist Party (JSP) was more politically viable, other groups also hedged their bets in this manner. There was even a time when big-business interests made contributions to the JSP in an effort to counterbalance labor contributions and deradicalize the party. However, as the JSP's prospects of coming to power became dimmer over the years, most groups saw no reason to continue dividing their support.[40] In the wake of the LDP's overthrow in 1993 and the subsequent upheaval in the Japanese party system in the 1990s, interest groups may be increasingly tempted to support any opposition parties that emerge as viable alternatives to the LDP.

Although Japanese interest groups have many characteristics in common with interest groups elsewhere in the world, some argue that they also have special attributes.[41] The most interesting and important way the Japanese interest group system differs from that of the United States is that Japanese interest groups do not employ professional lobbyists.[42] Instead, Japanese interest groups build close political exchange relationships with politicians. Interest groups provide organizational and financial support, and politicians repay them by acting as internal lobbyists within their parties and the Diet. These politician-lobbyists are often retired or even current officials of the group they represent. According to data from the early 1980s, 30–40 percent of all Japanese politicians either concurrently occupied positions of leadership in an interest group or had done so in the past,[43] making it clear that holding interest group office is one of the primary career paths for aspiring politicians in Japan.[44]

The linked phenomena of politician-lobbyists and dual officeholding can be explained in large part by the structure of institutional incentives incorporated into the Japanese political world. For example, Japanese political parties have never built strong local electoral machines, making the established local networks that many interest groups possess very attractive to politicians seeking ways to mobilize voters. In particular, interest groups are instrumental in helping politicians form and maintain the personal political support groups (kōenkai) that are the mainstay of voter mobilization in Japan. Under the electoral system that was in place until 1994, multimember constituencies forced politicians from the same party to compete with one another, and because politicians from the same party could not present contrasting party platforms, instead they sought to cultivate appeal among voters at a highly personal level through kōenkai.[45] Kōenkai continued to be an important support base for politicians during the political upheaval of the 1990s, because, with new parties constantly forming and dissolving, party identification among voters was weakened even further.

For their part, many interest groups closely involved in politics form auxiliary political organizations devoted exclusively to mobilizing votes, collecting political donations, and conducting other campaign activities. For example, the Japan Teacher's Union, the big labor union Sōhyō, the Japan Medical Association, and many religious groups all have formally separate but affiliated political action committees. One mass membership religious group, Sōka Gakkai, actually moved beyond political action committees to form its own political party in 1964 (the Clean Government Party, or Kōmeitō), further muddying the boundaries between politicians and interest groups. Although Sōka Gakkai maintains that it has no formal, organizational ties with the Kōmeitō, all Kōmeitō politicians are Sōka Gakkai members (often serving simultaneously on Sōka Gakkai's executive board), and the majority of votes for Kōmeitō politicians come from Kōmeitō members.[46]

Sōka Gakkai's political behavior is an anomaly, however. More typical is the Japan Medical Association, a powerful interest group with an offshoot political action group, the Japan Doctors' League (Nihon Ishi Renmei). Steslicke argues that the JMA's political activities have tended to overshadow the group's professional and scientific functions,[47] a proposition borne out by data from the early 1960s and mid-1980s that indicate that the JMA had one of the largest political funds in Japan and was also one of the LDP's biggest contributors.[48] The JMA has been equally, if not more, influential with politicians because of its ability to mobilize voters. In the late 1950s, the JMA boasted that "every doctor carried 100 votes in his medical bag," and Murakawa et al. estimate that the JMA, at its peak, may have commanded as many as 7 million votes.[49]

The JMA has relied more on politicians than bureaucrats to advance its agenda, a pattern typical of professional groups, as mentioned above. Over the years, JMA interests have been represented by both doctor-Diet members (isha giin) and non-doctor, sympathetic Diet members called ikei giin.[50] The JMA is often described as being an unusually proactive and aggressive group, known for its frequent, public head-on collisions with the Ministry of Health and Welfare.[51] Nonetheless, as one of the main representatives of the medical community, the JMA has been incorporated into "institutionalized channels for communication and decision making."[52] It should be noted, however, that in recent years the JMA's political power has declined. This weakening of the JMA stems in part from the death of its powerful and long-standing president, Takemi Tarō (1955–1980), and in part from decreasing membership among doctors.[53]

The extremely close ties between Japanese politicians and interest groups bring us back to questions about the nature of state-society relations in Japan. Many students of Japanese politics subscribe to the view that Japan has a corporatist system of interest representation, though assessments of the degree of corporatization vary.[54] In corporatist systems, such as those found in Latin America and Europe, the public and private spheres interpenetrate each other through "institutional arrangements for linking associationally organized interests of civil society with the decisional structures of the state."[55]

> Ostensibly private and autonomous associations are not just consulted and their pressures weighed. Rather, they are negotiated with on a regular, predictable basis. Their consent becomes necessary for policies to be adopted; their collaboration becomes essential for policies to be implemented.[56]

In short, interest groups and state actors become interdependent in corporatist systems. Interest groups are incorporated into the policy-making and policy implementation structure, guaranteeing them legitimacy, access to government officials, and influence over decisions. State actors, for their part, play a crucial role in defining group interests and activities, and sometimes in the actual formation of groups.[57] Groups are often legally assigned to perform semi-official tasks in place of the government, for which they receive subsidies. For example, the agricultural union Nōkyō performs a variety of functions under the authority of the Agricultural Basic Law,[58] and, as we will see in chapter 5, the Eugenic Protection Law dictates that prefectural medical associations carry out the evaluation and designation of doctors who wish to perform abortions.

There are both pros and cons to corporatist state-society relations. Corporatist arrangements have clear benefits in that they institutionalize channels of communication between state actors and societal groups, promoting efficient exchanges of information, assessments of policy options, and implementation of policy. But the interpenetration and interdependence of public and private spheres does call into question how much autonomy either side can maintain. Interest groups that rely on government subsidies, as many do, clearly have less latitude to criticize government policy or to take independent policy stands. Conversely, politicians who are financially and organizationally beholden to interest groups are less likely to implement policies adverse to the interests of those groups, even if they might benefit the larger public.

There are also several caveats that may be appended to the assertion that the Japanese system of interest representation is, in fact, corporatist. First, very few, if any, interest groups in Japan actually have a true representational monopoly. Even the often cited industrial peak association, the Japan Federation of Economic Organizations (Keidanren), corepresents industry along with other groups, including the Japan Federation of Employers' Associations (Nikkeiren) and the Japan Committee for Economic Development (Keizai Dōyūkai).[59] And, in general, although some policy areas are more corporatized than others, many students of Japanese politics agree that there has been a greater pluralization of interest representation and influence over the course of the postwar period, particularly since the early 1970s.[60] Certainly, the research presented in this book supports that contention. At the same time, it is important to remember that a variation on McKean's and Rosenbluth's observations on state leadership and state strength applies equally to societal groups. Even if a large number of groups are observed to *participate* in the policy-making system, it does not necessarily follow that all those groups have an equal ability to *influence* policy.[61]

The aim of this book is not to prove that interest groups are the most influential political force in Japan, although the case studies that follow do demonstrate that interest groups can be very influential in some issue areas, some of the time. But the case studies—along with the discussion of corporatism above—should also make it clear that power relations between societal actors and state actors are too complicated and fluid to be reduced to a simple formula. The appearances of both the state and society can be deceptive. As Garon points out:

> Most historical accounts of twentieth-century Japan posit a sharp divide between society and a powerful bureaucratic state. Sometimes the people appear to resist the regime; more often they acquiesce, but rarely are they depicted as cooperating actively with the state. . . . [Yet] what appear to be instances of top-down control by the state turn out often to have resulted from demands by nongovernmental groups, which looked to the bureaucracy to advance their agenda.[62]

We shall see a case in point in chapter 5, for while Japanese feminist groups in the 1970s and 1980s often depicted attempts to revise the abortion law as the retrograde policy initiative of conservative state actors, in truth the revision effort was spearheaded by a private religious group that used its political influence to press often reluctant state actors into service. On the other hand, in chapter 6 we learn that Japanese bureaucrats were instrumental in establishing one of the two main "private-sector" family planning organizations in the 1950s.

## CHAPTER THREE

# For the Good of the Nation: Prewar Abortion and Contraception Policy

GROUPS IN civil society (doctors, lawyers, eugenicists, and family planning activists) did attempt to influence abortion and contraception policy during the prewar period, but with mixed success. Some of these groups argued that birth control and abortion should be legalized on the basis of individual considerations—human rights and financial circumstances—but many others defended birth control on eugenic grounds, insisting that its value lay in the national and societal benefits it would produce. For a brief time during the era of "Taishō democracy" in the 1920s, the state tolerated private efforts to promote birth control, but after the military coup and the onset of the Pacific War in the early 1930s, the government adopted eugenic and pronatalist population policies. Family planning activists whose views conflicted with official policy were unable to sustain their movement. Most forms of contraception were banned; birth control clinics were shut down; and some activists were even jailed. On the other hand, the regime incorporated into itself those family planners, doctors, and eugenicists who were sympathetic to—and who in some cases helped to create—its population policies.

Although eugenic and pronatalist population policies were not implemented until the war was well under way, the ideological foundations for these policies had been laid decades earlier. In the fiercely competitive international political environment into which Japan emerged in the late nineteenth century, the elite quickly became interested in the possibility of manipulating the quantity and quality of the population in order to enhance national military strength. Thus a dominant theme in the prewar discourse on population was that, in a country surrounded by danger on all sides, individuals should reproduce—or not reproduce—for the good of the nation. In reality, policies based on these principles had very little effect on reproductive behavior, indicating that they did not appeal to the common man and woman. Nonetheless, statist ideologies left a powerful legacy among the Japanese elite, many of whom still view Japan as "a nation at war in peace," embattled on all sides and vulnerable to every kind of calamity.[1]

## ABORTION AND CONTRACEPTION POLICY BEFORE 1930

Abortion and infanticide (*mabiki*) were common in the Tokugawa period (1603–1868) and in earlier periods.[2] The upper classes and urban dwellers generally had better access to abortion, while poor, rural people resorted more often to infanticide. These practices were sufficiently widespread that they drew the attention of national and local government leaders, who repeatedly condemned them as immoral acts of murder. They further accused their subjects of seeking to deprive the state of future taxpayers, thus laying the groundwork for the statist discourse on reproduction that has dominated the twentieth century. These leaders adopted a variety of positive and negative incentives designed to discourage abortion and infanticide. For example, some local governments distributed allowances for later-order children; others required that all pregnancies be reported. Strict punishments were mandated for infanticide, including execution in some areas, but these were rarely enforced. In 1667 the *shōgun* (military ruler) banned the use of signs to advertise abortion services, and in 1842 a ban on performing abortions was passed as well. However, punitive measures were generally enforced only when the abortion was a consequence of adultery or when the procedure resulted in the woman's death.[3]

Abortion policy under the Meiji government (1868–1912) was an extension of Tokugawa policy. The emperor issued a decree in 1868 banning midwives, the primary practitioners of abortion, from performing abortions.[4] The government then codified abortion as a crime under Japan's first modern penal code, which was enacted in 1880.[5] When the penal code was revised in 1907, the punishments for abortion were made more severe. Women who obtained abortions could be sentenced to as much as a year in jail, while those who performed abortions could be sentenced to as much as seven years of jail time. As mentioned in chapter 1, the Criminal Abortion Law of 1907 (Datai Zai), and indeed the entire penal code of 1907, is still in effect today (see appendix for the full text of the law).

Because Japan's Criminal Abortion Law was modeled after French and German laws grounded in Christian doctrine, some authors have argued that the legal ban on abortion does not reflect Japanese traditions or convictions. These authors maintain that the Japanese were philosophically more tolerant of abortion than Westerners and that the Meiji government criminalized abortion only to appear modern and morally sound to Western governments.[6] Impressing Westerners with Japan's modernity and superior morals was undoubtedly one motivation for passing the Criminal Abortion Law, but this is equally true of many other Meiji policies, including the penal code and the constitution. It would not be fair to say that this was the only, or even the most important, motive for adopting these policies, however. Japan had a long history of pre-Meiji bans on abortion which, though they were not incorporated into a written penal code before the nineteenth century, nevertheless clearly demonstrates that there was a native tradition of criminalizing abortion.

Meiji abortion policy was also motivated in part by the burgeoning concern among the Japanese elite about the relationship between population size and national strength and security. These concerns, which were shared by elites in Europe, are illustrated in the Japanese case by the writings of early nationalists such as Nakabashi Tokugorō, who wrote that a large population was required to become a world power, and Takada Yasuma, who argued that " 'the only weapon that the races of color have against whites is high rates of population increase.' "[7] The statistician Kure Bunsō drew an explicit connection between abortion, population, and national security in a 1907 essay entitled "On Abortion." Kure believed that if Japan did not further increase its territory and population size, it would be overwhelmed by larger, more populous powers. Kure suspected that many of the 150,000 reported stillbirths each year were actually abortions and advocated that the government take measures to prevent such abortions, for

> if we can save 70,000 [fetuses a year from abortion], in ten years we can fight a war. . . . Even in a peaceful war, if we had 700,000 people they would become seeds for gaining influence in Manchuria. Without people, that is to say seeds, we cannot expand. If we do not have a great many people, we cannot develop our national strength.[8]

In 1916 the Home Ministry took up a similar refrain in a report to the Diet explaining the need to fund studies on the state of national health. Home Ministry officials predicted that the birth rate would soon begin to fall in Japan as it had in Western countries and warned that, if Japan's death rate remained high, the combination of the two demographic trends would seriously undermine national military strength.[9] Another Home Ministry document in 1919 discussed the need for serious study of policies designed to increase the birth rate.[10] The first national population census was taken in 1920.[11]

Theories of interracial competition closely associated with theories about population and national security also became popular in Japan around this time, following trends in thinking abroad.[12] Some members of the Japanese elite, like their counterparts elsewhere, came to view eugenics (often called race hygiene, or *minzoku eisei*, after the German *rassenhygiene*) as one way to improve the quality of the race and increase the nation's chances for survival in the midst of Great Power competition.[13] Francis Galton, Charles Darwin's cousin, conceived of the "science" of eugenics in the late nineteenth century. Galton envisioned eugenics as a method for selecting and deselecting human hereditary characteristics in order to improve the quality of a population. In the first half of the twentieth century, many Western countries adopted eugenic policies that involved the use of both pronatalist and anti-natalist measures (primarily sterilization) designed to encourage those deemed genetically "fit" to reproduce while preventing those deemed genetically "unfit" from reproducing.

The categorization of the "fit" and the "unfit" proved fertile ground for racial and class persecution. In all countries, eugenic movements were dominated by professionals from the upper strata of society; most were men. Though some had more compassionate motives, many of these men felt threatened by the leveling social effects of industrialization and urbanization, and worried that they would be overwhelmed by the masses of the poor, uneducated, and racially different, who already reproduced at a greater rate, and who (it was feared) might procreate even more with the introduction of modern social welfare programs and advances in medicine.[14] Eugenicists labeled this phenomenon—whereby the "fit," educated upper classes reproduced at a lower rate, while the "unfit," uneducated lower classes reproduced at a higher rate— "reverse selection." In an effort to avoid reverse selection, eugenicists devised pseudoscientific grounds for sterilizing people they regarded as unfit. In the United States, involuntary eugenic sterilizations were carried out on tens of thousands of women between the 1930s and 1970s. Those who were sterilized were generally poor and were predominantly women, and many were from minority racial groups.[15] In Germany, where the Nazis carried eugenic policies to extremes, hundreds of thousands of handicapped, retarded, and mentally ill people, Jews, gypsies, and other minority groups were sterilized, and, in the later years of the regime, killed outright.

Although the Japanese birth rate did begin to decline gradually after 1920—a trend that continues to the present day—birth rates had been rising steadily for decades up to that point, and death rates had been declining.[16] Thus, in the 1910s, at the same time that some elites started to worry about underpopulation, others became concerned about overpopulation and the social disruption it might cause.[17] Social unrest after World War I (the Rice Riots of 1918, for example) and the worldwide economic depression in the late 1920s underscored these concerns.[18] A foreigner traveling in Japan in 1931 opined that " 'the first subject engaging public opinion in Japan today . . . [is] the population problem.' "[19] It was in this context, and also in the somewhat more liberal political context of the 1920s, that Japan's birth control movement was born, drawing to its ranks feminists, doctors, and labor union activists.

Between 1915 and 1917, Japanese feminists debated the pros and cons of abortion and contraception in the journal *Seitō* (Bluestocking). Harada Satsuki defended abortion as a woman's right; Itō Noe approved of birth control but not abortion, which she viewed as murder; Hiratsuka Raichō endorsed birth control for eugenic reasons, as did many other feminists both in Japan and elsewhere; and the conservative and maternalist Christian feminist (and later nationalist) Yamada Waka abhorred both birth control and abortion.[20] Outside elite and academic circles, however, average Japanese people had little familiarity with birth control. According to a 1950 *Mainichi Shinbun* survey, only 9 percent of all married couples reported having practiced birth control before 1905.[21]

The turning point in the Japanese birth control movement occurred in 1922, when American birth control advocate Margaret Sanger visited Japan and gave a series of lectures.[22] Over the next five years, labor organizers distributed more than fifty thousand copies of Sanger's *Family Limitation* (translated into Japanese) to workers. By 1930 private groups had established sixty to seventy birth control clinics around Tokyo.[23] After the onset of the world depression in the late 1920s, news reports on child abandonment and workers' hardships in Japan multiplied, and the Japanese birth control movement gained more supporters. Municipal governments in Tokyo, Osaka, and other large cities expressed interest in opening birth control clinics for the poor in cooperation with private groups, but it is not clear what became of these initiatives.[24]

As Tipton notes, the national government was ambivalent about family planning. The police monitored the birth control movement closely during the 1920s, but at the same time, activists were allowed a limited range of movement.[25] At an international family planning meeting in 1925, for example, the Japanese representative reported that, on the one hand, family planning advocates were free to speak or write about the theoretical aspects of birth control and to send practical information through the mail; on the other hand, however, all books and pamphlets had to be submitted for government approval before publication, and public speeches on the practical aspects of contraception were banned as injurious to public decency.[26]

In 1931 Abe Isō, Ishimoto (later Katō) Shizue, Majima Yutaka, Hiratsuka Raichō, and others established the Japan Birth Control League, whose goal was to plan and rationalize pregnancy based on principles of maternal protection and eugenics. Thus we see that from the beginning, the Japanese family planning movement was imbued with eugenic ideology—which should not be surprising, given that eugenics was embraced in the West by both right- and left-wing reformers, activists, and radicals.

For readers who have difficulty understanding how progressive, left-wing reformers could have subscribed to such a flawed ideology, a brief review of the historical context in which eugenics emerged may be helpful. As Gordon explains it, eugenics became popular in the nineteenth and early twentieth centuries as part of a broader philosophical reaction against traditional, pre-Enlightenment beliefs about the limitations of human agency. During this period, "all radicalism was imbued with perfectionism." Many left-wing reformers—and others of very different political persuasions—were optimistic that, in the modern era, the problems of humankind could be solved through human engineering. Eugenics was seen as a rational, scientific, and *progressive* response to the problem of undesirable hereditary diseases and characteristics, in much the same way that improvements in sanitation and hygiene were seen as rational, scientific, and progressive. The problem, of course, was that, unlike sanitation and hygiene, eugenics had little basis in science, since eugenicists failed to distinguish between hereditary and acquired characteristics. Eugenicists also failed miserably to grasp eugenics' potential for abuse.[27]

Western feminists—ranging from female socialist doctors in Weimar Germany to the anarchist Emma Goldman to birth control advocate Margaret

Sanger—adopted eugenic arguments "as if they instinctively felt that arguments based solely on women's rights had not enough power to conquer conservative and religious scruples about reproduction."[28] But the feminist embrace of eugenics went deeper than mere rhetorical expedience. Within the turn-of-the-century feminist movement was a powerful strain of "maternalist feminism," which advocated greater societal recognition of the importance of women's childbearing and childrearing roles.[29] In assigning women the important responsibility of producing "quality" children, eugenic ideology dovetailed with maternalist ideology by elevating the status of women.

Like their Western counterparts, many Japanese feminists espoused the Japanese version of maternalism (bosei hogo, or protection of motherhood) and felt that state involvement in the form of eugenic policies was a logical and positive way to achieve public recognition and state support for mothers. Prominent feminists such as Hiratsuka Raichō, Ichikawa Fusae, and Katō (then Ishikawa) Shizue endorsed a variety of eugenic policies. Hiratsuka supported a law that would have prevented venereal disease carriers from marrying. Ichikawa wrote that bearing and rearing children was not just a mother's or a family's duty, but was also the public work of the nation. And in a 1922 Shufu no tomo article, Katō argued that birth control would not only benefit individual mothers, it would also benefit the country as a whole by easing overpopulation, thereby decreasing the possibility of aggressive expansionism and war. Other socialist birth control advocates such as Abe Isō, Yamakawa Kikue, and Yamamoto Senji also approved of eugenic practices.[30]

It is important to understand that these views were not universal in the left-wing community. Katō and Abe were condemned as the " 'cat's paws of the capitalists' " by members of the proletarian birth control movement for supporting the idea that birth control could solve problems of population and food supply, rather than focusing on the fundamental inequity of the distribution of resources.[31] But the most salient philosophical divide was the one within the eugenics camp, because most birth control advocates and feminists were, in fact, eugenicists. Within that group were individualists such as Yamakawa and Yamamoto, who believed that couples should be free—but not forced—to engage in eugenic practices for their own benefit, on a voluntary basis. Then there were feminists such as Hiratsuka, Ichikawa, and Katō, as well as Japan Race Hygiene Association founder Nagai Sen, who, to varying degrees, advocated a top-down, interventionist, nonvoluntary eugenic model that focused as much—or more—on the potential national benefits of such policies.[32]

Interest in eugenics heightened worldwide after 1929 because of the Depression and its staggering socioeconomic implications.[33] Japan was no exception to this trend, although eugenics never gained a popular following in Japan, as it did in many other countries. Its main adherents were professionals and academics, birth control activists, and feminists.[34] In 1925, professionals—70 percent of whom were doctors—formed the Japan Eugenics Association

(Nihon Yūsei Gakkai). In 1930 Dr. Nagai Sen (mentioned above) founded another group called the Japanese Race Hygiene Association (Minzoku Eisei Gakkai), which was also dominated by doctors.[35] In 1935 the government allowed this group to become an incorporated foundation, a designation that carried with it the promise of more intimate relations with the bureaucracy. And indeed, a set of proposals the group made on population policy in 1936 became the blueprint for the government's wartime population policy.[36]

During the brief flowering of the prewar birth control movement some family planning advocates, doctors, lawyers, and feminists also called for abortion law reform. A legal precedent had been established in 1923 allowing doctors to perform emergency abortions to save a woman's life, but criminal prosecutions for abortion still occurred regularly (though few of those prosecuted were doctors).[37] Thus in the same year (1931) that Abe Isō and others organized the Japan Birth Control League, Abe also established the Alliance for Reform of the Anti-Abortion Law (Datai Hō Kaisei Kiseikai). In 1932 feminists Hiratsuka Raichō, Ichikawa Fusae, and Ishimoto Shizue joined the Alliance, bringing with them the support of thirteen women's organizations.[38] The Alliance argued that "it is a woman's right not to bear a child she does not want, and abortion is an exercise of this right," but Alliance members were also clearly influenced by eugenic, financial, and health considerations. The Alliance advocated that abortion be made legal in cases of inferior heredity or leprosy; when the pregnant woman was poor, on public assistance, or divorced; when pregnancy endangered the woman's health; and in cases where pregnancy was the result of rape. In 1934 the Fifth All-Japan Women's Suffrage Congress also adopted resolutions calling for the legalization of birth control and abortion.[39] However, these scattered demands cannot be considered an organized movement—compared, for example, to the 1931 campaign to legalize abortion in Germany, during which left-wing and feminist groups led fifteen hundred rallies across the country—nor did they produce any reaction from the government.[40] Nevertheless, it should be noted that, after the war, some members of the Alliance participated in drafting the law that legalized abortion, and they incorporated almost all the criteria for abortion that the Alliance had recommended in the 1930s.

## JAPAN GOES TO WAR: EUGENICS AND PRONATALISM

Although the police did not actively suppress the family planning movement until the mid-1930s, government tolerance for the movement began to wane in the late 1920s. In 1930 the government Commission on Population and Food Supply Problems (Jinkō shokuryō mondai chōsakai) recommended, among other things, that the government tighten control over the sale of "harmful" birth control devices.[41] Accordingly, later in that same year, the Home Ministry passed an Ordinance for the Control of Harmful Contraceptive Appliances, which banned the sale and display of contraceptive pins, rings, intrauterine devices, and "other contraceptive appliances liable to cause harm."[42] Condoms were not banned, however, as they were valued by the army for prevention of venereal disease. Later on, in 1937, the government also banned publication of written material on birth control.[43]

Developments abroad also had significant effects on Japanese population policy. In a June 1933 speech, Hitler's minister of the interior bemoaned the " 'dismal picture [presented by] Germany's cultural and ethnic decline,' " citing as evidence the million or more " 'feeble-minded' " and " 'inferior' " Germans with hereditary physical and mental diseases. The minister stated that " 'progeny [was] no longer desired' " from these groups, and estimated that a further 20 percent of the population, or 11 million Germans, was undesirable as parents for other reasons. The following month, in July 1933, the Nazi regime implemented its infamous compulsory sterilization law, which was designed to prevent the propagation of " 'lives unworthy of life.' " The Nazis initially planned to sterilize about 1.5 million people, and in fact, this was roughly the number of people sterilized over the course of the next decade, most of them on grounds of "feeble-mindedness."[44] In 1935 the regime also legalized abortion for eugenic reasons. Bock concludes that "never in history had there been a state which in theory, propaganda, and practice pursued an antinatalist policy of such dimensions."[45]

The Nazi regime also implemented a variety of pronatalist policies—as did many other European governments during this era of intense concern about population size. The Nazi policies combined negative and positive incentives. On the one hand, voluntary sterilization was forbidden in order to prevent sabotage by those from whom the state *did* desire progeny. In 1941 the regime also issued a police ordinance banning the import, production, and sale of contraceptive and abortifacient materials. As in Japan, condoms were exempted from the ban.[46] As for positive inducements, the Nazi government offered marriage loans, tax breaks for families with children, monthly state child allowances, and many other perks for those whose genetic stock was deemed desirable.[47]

Eugenicists in Japan were quick to note the changes in German policy and sought to emulate them. A year after the German sterilization law was passed, the Japanese Race Hygiene Society drafted a National Eugenic Protection Bill (Minzoku Yūsei Hogo Hōan), closely modeled on the Nazi law. A sympathetic Diet member sponsored the bill, but it did not pass.[48] The bill was resubmitted in 1937 but again failed upon meeting opposition from pronatalist and right-wing nationalist politicians, who felt that eugenics contradicted the regime's glorification of the family line (kazokushugi) and its exhortation to "Give Birth and Multiply" (umeyo fuyaseyo). Left-wingers opposed the bill because they believed that a sterilization policy would allow the government to avoid the more fundamental issue of equitable distribution of resources. Also in opposition were geneticists, who questioned the premises of eugenics, arguing that more research should be done to distinguish hereditary traits from those caused by social and environmental factors.[49] As noted above, however, members of the Japan Birth Control League—including prominent feminists such as Hiratsuka Raichō—were proponents of eugenics and supported the notion of a National Eugenic Law.[50]

Only when eugenicists persuaded the newly formed Ministry of Health and Welfare to draft and sponsor a bill in 1940 was a law finally passed whose purpose was "to ensure the improvement of the national character by means of preventing an increase in the [number of] persons with a predisposition toward malignant hereditary disease, and promoting an increase in [the number] of persons who have sound constitutions" (Article 1, the National Eugenic Law [Kokumin Yūsei Hō]; see appendix).

The National Eugenic Law allowed for both voluntary and involuntary sterilizations in cases of hereditary mental illness or deficiency, severe hereditary physical deformity, severe and malignant physical ailment, and severe and malignant personality disorder (Articles 3, 4, and 6). The Ministry of Health and Welfare explained that eugenic sterilizations were necessary in order to prevent reverse selection (see Figure 3.1). The Ministry also emphasized the necessity of preventing "race poisons" such as alcoholism, drug abuse, and syphilis.[51]

The initial draft of the National Eugenic Law would also have included a provision specifically permitting eugenic abortions, but the provision was deemed too controversial and was deleted during Diet debate.[52] The provision the Diet included instead spelled out the procedures a doctor should follow before performing an abortion—implying that abortion was legal under some circumstances—but stopped short of explicitly stating that abortion was legal. Thus Article 16 reads:

> Before a doctor performs . . . an abortion, he shall [get] other doctors' opinions on whether or not [the procedure] is necessary. . . . Moreover, said doctor shall submit a report to the administrative office before [he performs such a procedure], as determined by decree. However, these restrictions do not apply in cases where a special emergency operation is required.

In practice, the new procedures were complicated and time-consuming, and doctors were intimidated by the prospect of submitting to state oversight. Consequently, the number of reported abortions declined substantially between 1941 and 1944, from eighteen thousand to eighteen hundred.[53] But the more lasting effect of the abortion provision was to set a legal precedent officially acknowledging the legitimacy of abortion—however obliquely and circumstantially—and that precedent made it much easier for advocates of abortion rights to legalize abortion after the war.

Even with the support of the bureaucracy, however, the National Eugenic Law did not pass without controversy.[54] There was a great deal of debate in

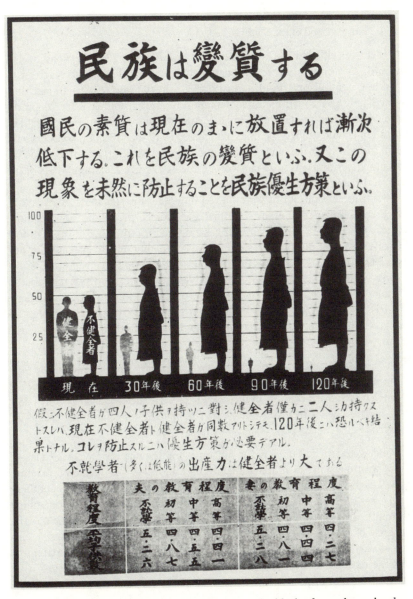

Figure 3.1. "The [Japanese] Race Is Degenerating." The block of text above the chart reads, "If we leave the national character as it is now, it will gradually decline. This is called degeneration. Nipping this phenomenon in the bud is called national eugenic policy." The chart shows two figures on the far left: the left-hand figure, which looks normal, is labeled "fit people" (*kenzensha*); the right-hand figure, which is meant to look like a retarded person, is labeled "unfit people" (*fukenzensha*). The chart demonstrates pictorially that although the number of fit and unfit people is equal at the present time (1941), if left unchecked, the unfit will completely outnumber the fit in 120 years. The text below the chart explains that the unfit have four children for every two children that the fit have, and that the uneducated ("most of whom are feeble-minded") have higher birth rates than fit people.

the Diet over whether the law should permit involuntary sterilizations, and in the end, as a concession to ultranationalists, the Health Ministry agreed to include a compulsory sterilization provision in the law (Article 6) but then immediately postponed its implementation by imperial edict.[55] This compromise emasculated the law, and, indeed, Article 6 was never implemented. The bureaucrats who drafted the bill predicted in 1939 that 300,000 people would be sterilized under the National Eugenic Law, but, in fact, no more than 454 voluntary sterilizations were carried out during the five remaining years of the war, and many applications were turned down.[56]

Sterilization applications were turned down because Japanese officials, unlike their German counterparts, ultimately endorsed pronatalist policies more warmly than anti-natalist ones, emphasizing that the purpose of the National Eugenic Law was not only to sterilize the "unfit" but also to prevent the "fit" from limiting births. Perhaps "undesirable" births were perceived to be less of a threat in Japan because the population was more heterogeneous than that of Germany, and there was less history of persecuting minority groups. Japanese officials believed that "the enemy in [the] population war resides within"— unlike German officials, who saw Jews, gypsies, and other "outsiders" as the enemy—and concluded that

> Fit people undergo sterilization operations, radiation treatments, and other procedures simply for the purpose of contraception: namely, they don't want children, or they have too many children, or they want to preserve their good looks, or they seek to avoid blame for their bad behaviour. This alone [birth control] has caused the decline in the healthy population, so we have banned it.[57]

Policies designed to prevent the "fit" from limiting births were part of a larger set of wartime policies aimed at increasing the overall size of the population, as well as the physical strength and health of the populace. To implement these policies—in particular, to improve the strength of draftees and to combat high mortality rates and diseases such as tuberculosis—the government created the Ministry of Health and Welfare in 1938.[58] Officials in the new ministry embraced their task enthusiastically, affirming the truth of Mussolini's statement that the nations of the world were in the midst of a "population war"[59] (see Figure 3.2), and urging that,

> in order to build the New East Asia today and to fulfill the important mission of managing the continent, a huge population is demanded. Even when this disturbance [the war] is over we cannot stop [because] voices will be raised demanding human resources for the long-term construction [of East Asia].[60]

The government outlined an overarching population policy for the first time at a January 1941 cabinet meeting, announcing that Japan's national population goals were to ensure perpetual population growth; to surpass the rate of increase and quality of populations of other nations; to ensure for the armed

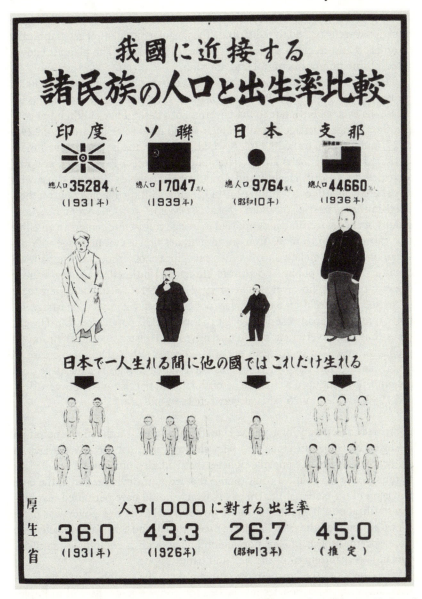

Figure 3.2. "A Comparison of the Populations and Birth Rates of Neighboring Nations." From left, the uppermost chart shows the population of India in 1931 (352 million); the Soviet Union in 1939 (170 million); Japan in 1935 (97 million); and China in 1936 (446 million). The chart below that shows that for every one child born in Japan, five were born in India, three in the Soviet Union, and seven in China. The bottom chart compares the birth rates per 1,000 in the four countries.

forces and the labor force a quantity of personnel sufficient for a high degree of national security; and to redistribute the Japanese population geographically in order to ensure guidance for the peoples of East Asia. The plan also advocated prohibiting birth control and abortion.[61]

Efforts to implement these policies focused overwhelmingly on pronatalist measures. The Population Problems Institute proclaimed that in order to increase the average birth rate to the government's desired five children per couple, the average marriage age for women would need to be lowered from 24.4 to 21, and for men, from 28.4 to 25.[62] Like Germany, the Japanese government instituted marriage loans and preferential tax treatment for married couples, as well as awards for "Healthy and Abundant Households" (that is, those with anywhere from 10 to 20 children).[63] In keeping with the ideology of "motherhood-in-the-interest-of-the-state" (*kokkateki bosei*),[64] patriotic women's youth groups opened government-supported marriage counseling centers in an effort " 'to cause women to move from an individualistic view of marriage to a national one and to make young women recognize motherhood as the national destiny.' "[65] These public and private efforts had little effect on the average citizen's behavior, however. Between 1941 and 1943, when the government promoted promarital and pronatalist policies most vigorously, marriage reporting rates in Japan rose from 8.1 to 10 per 1,000 population, but Havens notes that the government's cash incentives to register marriages promptly probably caused an increase in registration rates rather than an increase in actual marriage rates (Japanese families often waited to register a marriage until the bride had produced a child). The birth rate did not rise at all between 1941 and 1943, and fell by 25 percent between 1944 and 1945.[66]

Compared to Germany, or even the United States, it is clear that the penetration of eugenic ideology in Japan was very shallow, and that there was a lack of political will to enforce eugenic policies, particularly antinatalist ones. This is epitomized by the political compromise that led to the evisceration of the core provision of the National Eugenic Law, which would have permitted involuntary sterilizations. It should be noted, however, that German policy was more the exception than the rule. Fascist regimes in Italy and Spain also rejected the more extreme aspects of Nazi population policy, such as compulsory sterilization and "euthanization" of the sick and handicapped.[67]

Why, then, did the Japanese government go to the trouble of adopting eugenic and pronatalist policies if it lacked the conviction or the will to implement them? It seems likely that the government's wartime population policies were adopted more for symbolic and ideological reasons, with less of an eye toward producing practical results. Eugenics, after all, dovetailed nicely with the established elite ideology of the family-state, which dictated that in all realms of life individuals act for the good of the organic whole. But even if government officials did not wholeheartedly support their own anti-natalist policies, it seems clear that they genuinely wished to increase the quantity and improve the quality of the population through pronatalist policies. These pronatalist policies were part of a broader program of state intervention designed to safeguard and improve public health, and although the pronatalist policies may not have had much effect, other initiatives—such as the establishment of maternal and child health care centers, and the expansion of the national health insurance system—were quite successful. Havens argues that these policies initiated the transformation of the Japanese state into a modern welfare state, a process that was intensifying globally in the 1930s in both fascist and nonfascist countries because of the Depression.[68]

The Japanese government probably could have enforced its pronatalist policies more effectively by dint of sheer coercion, but it chose not to. Such a course would have been too costly not only financially, but also politically. Government officials may have realized that although Japanese citizens were amenable to quite microscopic "social management" of many aspects of their lives, they considered reproductive decisions to be a completely private, family matter.[69] The essence of the problem, however, was that unlike many efforts at social management—such as campaigns to increase household savings—there was a fundamental clash between the interests of the state and those of individual families. For whereas increasing household savings produces benefits for both the individual family and the nation, in an urbanizing, industrializing, consumer society, having many children does not produce benefits for the individual family: in fact, it puts the family at a distinct financial disadvantage. Ultimately, the perks and incentives the Japanese government provided to stimulate births were insufficient to counteract these trends, and the government probably could not have afforded to provide incentives large enough to affect individual behavior to any significant degree.

# Japan Legalizes Abortion: The Intersection of National and Professional Interests

IT WOULD BE impossible to explain the anomalies of Japan's postwar contraception policy without first exploring the forces that have shaped Japanese abortion policy. Abortion was legalized almost ten years before public and private groups began to promote family planning on a wide scale, and much of postwar contraception policy making has been driven by the institutional legacies and interest group imperatives flowing from this prior emphasis on abortion. The "abortion before birth control" phenomenon has had both positive and negative implications for Japanese contraception policy. On the one hand, some contraception policy initiatives succeeded because the government and private groups were alarmed by the high abortion rate; on the other, some policy initiatives failed because groups with vested interests in defending access to abortion believed the initiative would jeopardize abortion-derived income or threaten abortion rights.

This chapter and those that follow revolve around interest group politics. Diet members representing family planning and medical interests sponsored the Eugenic Protection Law that legalized abortion in 1948, and revisions to the law in 1949 and 1952.[1] But these organized interests were able to liberalize Japan's abortion law only because the national political climate was compatible with their goals. They were, after all, proposing a policy change that, at the time, was extremely radical from both the domestic and international perspectives.[2] Noninterest group lawmakers and occupation bureaucrats supported the abortion legislation primarily because they believed that Japan's war-torn economy would never recover unless population growth was curbed.[3] Thus unique historical circumstances produced an intersection of national and professional interests.

## THE EUGENIC PROTECTION BILL OF 1947

After World War II Japan was a defeated country occupied by a foreign army. Stripped of its colonial possessions, its imperial aspirations lay shattered. Twenty percent of all housing was destroyed during air raids (closer to 60 percent in Tokyo and Osaka), and in 1947, four million families were still homeless.[4] The economy was in ruins—about 25 percent of the national wealth had been devoted to the war between 1941 and 1945—and inflation was rampant.[5] Agricultural production declined so severely that in 1946 the finance minister announced that 10 million people were at risk of starving to death, a catastrophe that was averted only by huge imports of American food.[6] Meanwhile, millions of soldiers and civilians were being repatriated from the former colonies, and the birth rate was soaring. Between returnees and the baby boom, the population increased by 11 million people in only five years (from roughly 72 million in 1945 to 83.2 million in 1950).[7]

This combination of factors caused deep concern within both occupation and Japanese government circles. Many feared that the population growth, seemingly out of control, would render Japan incapable of economic recovery, which in turn would jeopardize democratization. These concerns were inextricably intertwined, as demonstrated in the following excerpt from a MacArthur directive:

> With the knowledge that an uncontrolled increase in population in Japan would have a serious effect on the economic situation and would mitigate against the accomplishment of the long-range objective of the Occupation to establish a peaceful, democratic, stable Japan, the Far East Commission, in February 1947, approved the SCAP [Supreme Command Allied Powers] policy of permitting an industrial level equivalent to that of 1930–34 in order to reinitiate the population shift from rural areas to urban centers and provide an incentive for limitation of the size of families and a decrease in the birth rate.[8]

A group of Socialist Party birth control activists, elected to the Lower House of the Diet in 1946, were quick to realize that this crisis consciousness had opened a "window of opportunity" for policy change. Consequently, in December 1947, Representatives Fukuda Masako, Katō Shizue,[9] and Ōta Tenrei introduced a Eugenic Protection Bill (Yūsei Hogo Hōan) to the Diet intended to legalize contraception, eugenic sterilization, and abortion, with the emphasis on physician-supervised contraception. They believed that these measures would help to counteract hereditary disease and the health dangers posed by black market abortions, but they also wanted to give Japanese women some measure of control over their reproductive lives to help them cope with chaotic postwar conditions.[10] When introducing the Eugenic Protection Bill to her colleagues in the Diet Health and Welfare Committee, Katō invoked the plight of the average woman struggling to survive in lean times:

> Many women are lifting their voices [and saying,] "We do not want to have children now." I believe that the voices of today's women [are saying,] "We want to have our beloved children in a little while, once the problems of housing, fuel, and food have eased up."[11]

The purpose the socialists set down in Article 1 of their draft law was "to protect maternal life and health and to prevent the birth of inferior offspring, thereby contributing to the construction of a cultured nation."[12] As the purpose and title indicate, the socialists' Eugenic Protection Bill was a strange mixture of progressive humanitarian measures and repressive, retrograde eugenic measures. Compared to the prewar National Eugenics Law passed only seven years earlier, the Eugenic Protection Bill would have increased individuals' control over their own reproduction in three ways. First, it contained a birth control provision stating that "physicians may freely take steps to [enable patients to] temporarily avoid reproduction."[13] Second, the bill would have increased the number of circumstances under which individuals could seek voluntary sterilizations,[14] whereas the prewar law allowed sterilizations only for a narrow set of eugenic reasons. Finally, the bill provided for legal abortion under a wide range of circumstances, including the following: when pregnancy or childbirth endangered the mother's life or health; when the mother was sickly, poor, or had many children; when pregnancy was the result of rape; or when either spouse or a close relative suffered from alcoholism, mental illness, a physical deformity, or a hereditary illness.[15] On the other hand, however, the bill strengthened provisions for compulsory sterilization, which had been included in the National Eugenic Law but never implemented. The socialists intended to carry out an active program of eugenic sterilization, and their bill would have allowed doctors, judges, and asylum chiefs to recommend that sex criminals and inmates of mental asylums be sterilized "for the public good" (and at public expense). Unlike the National Eugenics Law, however, the Eugenic Protection Bill contained no mechanism for appeal or review of these decisions.[16] In this regard, the socialists made fewer provisions for safeguarding personal liberty and due process than the militarists had—though the militarists, of course, had not included appeal and review mechanisms in the National Eugenics Law to protect individual freedom. Rather, these mechanisms were there to appease ultranationalists, who were concerned that families might be unduly prevented from fulfilling their sacred national obligation to increase and multiply.[17]

Several authors have noted that it was odd for progressive socialists to write such a law, particularly since large portions were borrowed from—and actually strengthened—a law written by the conservative regime that had persecuted them during the war (Ōta and Katō had both been jailed for promoting family planning).[18] In interviews years later, Ōta and Katō—the latter having described herself as more humanist than socialist, more moderate reformer than revolutionary—cited pragmatic reasons for modeling their bill on the National Eugenic Law.[19] Both said essentially that there were few foreign abortion laws to use as models, and given that they were proposing a radical policy change, it was more realistic politically to model the Eugenic Protection Bill on an existing Japanese law.[20] From a practical point of view, that was certainly true. It must be remembered, however, that Ōta, Katō, and Fukuda still subscribed to the eugenic theories they had espoused before the war (which Katō subsequently downplayed).[21] When Katō introduced the Eugenic Protection Bill in 1947, she criticized the military regime's pronatalist policy for trying to force women to have children regardless of the detriment to their health, but she did not criticize the illiberal, discriminatory, or unscientific aspects of the regime's eugenic sterilization policy. On the contrary, she criticized wartime eugenic measures for having been ineffectual in preventing poor heredity because they were overly difficult to implement.[22] Undoubtedly to correct this "problem," the socialists removed from their draft law the appeal and review mechanism found in Articles 9 and 10 of the National Eugenics Law.

On balance, however, the socialists' Eugenic Protection Bill was fairly progressive, certainly when compared to prewar law in Japan, but also compared to laws in other countries, many of which banned birth control, voluntary sterilization, and abortion. In fact, the radical nature of the bill explains, in part, why occupation officials and the socialists' fellow Diet members killed it. There is also evidence that the socialists' legislative initiative failed because their behind-the-scenes consensus building (nemawashi) was insufficient. Moreover, General MacArthur, who had presidential aspirations in the United States, feared losing Catholic political support were he to allow abortion and contraception to be legalized in Japan.[23] Occupation bureaucrats delayed giving permission for the Eugenic Protection Bill to be introduced;[24] and when they finally gave their approval, Japanese lawmakers shelved the bill by refusing to deliberate on it in committee.

## MEDICAL INTERESTS AND THE 1948 EUGENIC PROTECTION LAW

Under ordinary circumstances, the initiative to legalize abortion would almost certainly have ended there, because the socialist family planners were not powerful enough to force legislation through the Diet. As it turned out, however, the socialists were not the only ones interested in legalizing abortion and certain forms of contraception. As early as 1946 the medical community demonstrated its interest in the population problem by organizing symposiums on birth control (which, at the time, was understood to include both contraception and abortion). Articles were also published in medical journals suggesting, for example, that couples with four or more children should be eligible for contraception and abortion.[25] In 1947, four months before Fukuda, Katō, and Ōta introduced their bill in the Health and Welfare Committee, an obstetrician-gynecologist and conservative Upper House representative, Taniguchi Yasaburō,[26] asked the prime minister five questions about the possibility of liberalizing the law on eugenic sterilization, birth control, and abortion.[27] Although there was no communication between the two parties in 1947, during the next session of the Diet in 1948, Taniguchi approached Ōta to say that he would like to help turn the bill into law. But he informed Ōta that he thought parts of the bill were too radical and would need to be revised. Taniguchi also felt that the bill would more easily pass through the Diet if he, rather than Ōta, sponsored it and introduced it in the Upper House.[28]

Taniguchi's revised Eugenic Protection Bill—which ultimately became law—eliminated the birth control provision that had been central to the socialists' draft, thus placing more emphasis on abortion and eugenic sterilization.[29] Since abortion was just as controversial as birth control at the time, one suspects that Taniguchi was more interested in promoting relatively lucrative abortion procedures than in deradicalizing the bill. Taniguchi also eliminated the controversial "financial hardship" provisions of the 1947 bill, giving in to pressure from conservative colleagues who reasoned that Japan should not be the first among "all civilized countries" to allow abortion or sterilization for this reason.[30] Finally, Taniguchi added two stipulations: that only designated doctors (shitei ishi) could perform abortions, and that abortions had to be approved by a Eugenic Protection Committee. Thus the law, as it was initially implemented, did not give individual doctors discretionary power. Before performing an abortion, doctors were required to seek a second opinion from a welfare commissioner or another doctor, and then apply for permission to proceed from the local Eugenic Protection Committee. In most other respects, the 1947 and 1948 bills were similar to each other, and to the prewar National Eugenics Law. Thus, although the Eugenic Protection Law was progressive in that it decriminalized abortion, it did so within a framework of outmoded and potentially repressive eugenic ideology. And while the national goals formulated by Japanese elites had shifted from expansionism and pronatalism to domestic retrenchment and population control, the overarching goal of bringing individuals' reproductive lives into conformity with the national interest remained the same.[31]

Taniguchi and his fellow ob-gyns supported this type of legislation for a variety of reasons, which included safeguarding women's health, protecting and promoting their professional interests, and upholding the national interest. Although all three considerations were undoubtedly salient for ob-gyns, when Taniguchi introduced his revised version of the Eugenic Protection Bill to the House of Councilors in June 1948,[32] he emphasized the national interest almost exclusively, both in terms of eugenics and of the democratic values that would be promoted by protecting maternal health. Taniguchi presumably believed that this line of argument would most appeal to his fellow Diet members, but it should be noted that he was not simply pandering to their biases, for Taniguchi propounded eugenic notions about improving the Japanese race often and enthusiastically in the ensuing years.

In presenting the 1948 Eugenic Protection Bill, Taniguchi discussed the problems of limited resources and overpopulation, maintaining that the pronatalist policy legacy of the former regime was incompatible with the "considerably changed conditions" Japan now faced. Referring to sterilization and abortion, Taniguchi went on to inform his listeners that birth control was one means of addressing these problems but that birth control measures should be designed to discourage the phenomenon of reverse selection (gyakukōta), which would result if "people of comparatively superior classes, thinking of their children's futures, use birth control, and people who are ignorant or of low intelligence do not use it." This in turn would lead to an overall decline in the quality of the Japanese populace (*kokumin soshitsu*).[33] In fact, Taniguchi maintained that the tendency toward reverse selection had already begun to manifest itself, with an increase in the number of "insane and [congenitally] blind persons" and "imbecile child vagrants." He predicted that the Eugenic Protection Law would "prevent the births of 800,000 undesirable elements,"[34] resulting in an overall improvement in the quality of the Japanese people. Or, as Keio University professor Takashi Hayashi asserted:

> By this means [legalizing abortion], the irrational situation will be eliminated in which people give birth to children they do not want and cannot educate. In consequence, 80 percent of our prostitutes and delinquent youths will be eradicated twenty years from now, and Japan will then become a country with people of good quality.[35]

Thus "prevent[ing] the birth of eugenically inferior offspring" was set down in Article 1 as the first half of the Eugenic Protection Law's purpose. In contrast to this extremely illiberal principle, however, the second half of the law's purpose was "to protect maternal health and life." Taniguchi reminded his audience, in highminded but vague language, that although the former regime had encouraged Japanese women to have children regardless of the damage it might do to their health, the new Constitution enshrined respect for human rights, which included maternal protection.[36] Taniguchi and most of his colleagues apparently did not consider that government-sponsored compulsory sterilizations might also constitute a violation of human rights, amounting to what a lone critic called "Hitler's totalitarianism."[37] In short, Taniguchi painted a contradictory picture of a law that would help rebuild Japan by curbing population growth among "undesirables" who were a burden to society, but one that would also support the values of the new democratic regime by allowing women to choose how many children to have. Taniguchi's bill, like the socialists' bill, reflected a schizophrenic view on the appropriateness of state involvement in individuals' reproductive choices.

In less public venues, Taniguchi framed the abortion question differently. For example, he addressed the interests of individual women more directly than he did in the Diet, frankly describing the health risks and exorbitant fees women faced when they underwent illegal abortions, and noting that women, because abortion was illegal, were driven to seek out unqualified abortion providers.[38] But intertwined with such compassionate considerations were more self-interested motives. Understandably, ob-gyns wanted to legalize abortion to preclude the possibility of prosecution under the extant Criminal Abortion Law.[39] Ob-gyns also wanted to establish a monopoly over abortion services, for as long as abortion was illegal, there was no mechanism to exclude non-doctors from the field.[40] Taniguchi and others promoted the establishment of a system of designated abortion providers whereby only doctors certified by the Japan Medical Association (JMA) could legally perform abortions, claiming that such a system was necessary to protect women from dangerous non-physician abortions.[41] However, ob-gyns also wanted to bar doctors in other medical specialties from providing abortions (except in emergencies), maintaining that the many non–ob-gyns who were performing the operation on the black market did not have the requisite training or skill to do so.[42] This suggests that ob-gyns were as concerned about turf protection as they were about women's health or eugenic protection. Others certainly felt this was the case, as demonstrated in the following excerpt from a 1948 letter to the head of SCAP's Public Health and Welfare Section. The letter's author, Yamamoto Tsunekichi, was probably a doctor but not an ob-gyn.

> On this occasion the Welfare Ministry and some influential doctors who are holding a leading position made a system to designate special doctors who are authorized to conduct the operation for intermission of pregnancy. According to this system, even though he is an experienced, skilful doctor, he is prohibited to conduct the aforementioned operation, unless he is a designated doctor. . . . Moreover, in case of conducting this operation, he will be punished as an abortion offence or an offence on injury [a tort]. On the other hand, a designated doctor is never punished even if he is very poor in the tactics. Thus a privileged group of doctors is being made among doctors. I think that it is very undemocratic to make such a system. [sic][43]

Efforts to monopolize the provision of abortions can also be seen as part of a larger, long-term effort by Japanese doctors to gain control over women's health care, primarily by wresting away midwives' birthing practices.[44] To be sure, achieving dominance in women's health care beckoned to Japanese ob-gyns as a lucrative source of income. But it also represented a means to help establish the ob-gyn specialty and, by extension, the medical profession as a whole, as an authoritative, elite body[45]—a phenomenon whose occurrence has been documented in nineteenth-century America, France, and England.[46] As was the case with French and American doctors, Japanese doctors gained government assistance in this process, primarily in the form of legislation biased in their favor.[47] For example, the passage of the Eugenic Protection Law in one stroke accomplished the goal of barring nonphysicians from performing abortions. The 1948 Medical Service Law requiring that hospitals and clinics (including birthing clinics) be supervised by a doctor contributed to the gradual physician takeover of midwives' birthing practices.[48] Further, in the 1960s the JMA pressured the government to alter the rules governing inexpensive public maternal and child health centers, which were staffed primarily by midwives, resulting in their ultimate decline.[49]

It may seem surprising that SCAP was willing to tolerate the resurrection of eugenic policies in Japan, given that the Allied Forces had just fought a war to defeat fascist regimes founded on racist eugenic ideologies. Indeed, this fact did not go unnoticed.[50] Internal memos show that, at different points in the legislative process, officials in SCAP's Legal Section, Government Section, and Public Health and Welfare Section all found the eugenic content and other aspects of the law objectionable and dangerous.[51] At the same time, however, it must be remembered that, in the mid-1930s, thirty American states had compulsory sterilization laws[52] and the American elite's attitude toward eugenics remained ambivalent even after the Nazis had provided overwhelming evidence of its potential for abuse. More to the point, SCAP authorities shared the Japanese elite's view that legalizing abortion and birth control was necessary to control overpopulation, which in turn would help rebuild the economy and prevent a resurgence of militarism. In any event, the Americans were not overly alarmed, as they believed—quite incorrectly, as it turned out—that the Eugenic Protection Law

> has many imperfections which can reasonably be expected will be corrected in the future. . . . As modern contraceptive knowledge is disseminated . . . it is believed that the provisions for abortion will become of little consequence, as they will fall into disuse.[53]

In general, SCAP maintained a low profile in the morally and politically sensitive area of population policy, adopting a posture that Oakley labels "protective neutralism."[54] In other words, although many SCAP officials viewed efforts to legalize birth control and abortion favorably and did not prevent the Eugenic Protection Law from being passed, neither did they advocate legalization publicly or involve themselves in creating legislation. This noninterference can be explained in part by the view that legal abortion would be a temporary phenomenon and also by the view that

> due to its [population policy's] long-range nature, it is not connected with occupation objectives, and any expression of opinion by this Headquarters with regard to general population policy would be interpreted as an unwise imposition of Western ethical, religious or social ideas upon an essentially different Oriental civilization.[55]

Equally compelling for SCAP bureaucrats was the fear that the Catholic Church or the Soviets would accuse the United States of committing genocide if Americans openly defended legalizing birth control and abortion in Japan.[56]

The socialist Diet members (Ōta and Katō in particular) also had reservations about Taniguchi's draft of the Eugenic Protection Law, although for different reasons than SCAP. They believed—correctly—that the conservative doctors had undermined their original legislative intent, which was, first and foremost, to promote birth control and, second, to permit abortion. But, in the end, the socialists agreed to cosponsor the bill, bowing before the pragmatic realization that medical interests had a great deal of influence in the Diet and that, given the dire postwar conditions, if support could not be gained for promoting birth control, then legalizing abortion was the next best option.[57] Katō, for example, reasoned that "to ban abortion will only encourage illegal abortions. I think it is necessary to keep abortion legal for as many reasons as possible, in case of contraceptive failures and ignorance of contraceptive methods."[58] And, like the Americans, the socialists also assumed that the law would only be a temporary measure, and that it would be revised or abolished when the postwar situation normalized.[59]

## REVISIONS TO THE EUGENIC PROTECTION LAW

What neither the Americans nor the Japanese socialists realized, however, was that, in giving designated doctors (who were all ob-gyns) a monopoly over abortion services, the Eugenic Protection Law created an institutionalized incentive for ob-gyns to work to maintain and expand access to abortion—in other words, to protect a mainstay of their livelihood. With a focused agenda and substantial political and financial resources at its disposal, this small, well-organized group of doctors was in an excellent position to take advantage of such an incentive. In a classic demonstration of collective action theory at work,[60] the designated doctors formed an interest group in April 1949, less than a year after the Eugenic Protection Law was passed. The official raison d'être of the designated doctor's group—which was called Nihon Bosei Hogo I Kyōkai,[61] or Nichibo for short (in English, the Japan Association for Maternal Welfare)—was "to compile statistics on maternal protection" (that is, statistics on abortion and sterilization procedures) and "to thoroughly popularize eugenic protection."[62] Unofficially, the group was dedicated to defending and liberalizing the Eugenic Protection Law. Taniguchi organized the group and served as president until his death in 1963. Thus we see in Taniguchi a prime example of the phenomenon discussed in chapter 2: the politician-lobbyist simultaneously holding elected office and serving as an interest group official.

Although Nichibo was nominally a professional association and claimed most practicing ob-gyns as members,[63] in reality it served more as Taniguchi's personal political support group (kōenkai) (see Figure 4.1).[64] Taniguchi also had strong ties with and backing from the large and politically powerful Japan Medical Association—over which he presided from 1950 to 1952—but his core supporters were the ob-gyn members of Nichibo. In exchange for their material and organizational support, Nichibo members gained a committed advocate in the Diet, whose primary legislative agenda was to defend the Eugenic Protection Law and Nichibo's monopoly over providing abortion services—and, wherever possible, to expand Nichibo's powers and otherwise promote its interests, which included increasing access to abortion.[65]

And Taniguchi delivered.[66] In May 1949 he sponsored a successful revision to the Eugenic Protection Law which tacked a clause onto Article 14 that allowed abortions "if the continuation of pregnancy or childbirth is likely to

Figure 4.1. Dr. Taniguchi Yasaburō celebrating his reelection to the Upper House in 1956. In the second paragraph of the accompanying text, Taniguchi writes, "The honor of my election is truly the result of the influential and ardent support of all Nichibo members."

seriously harm the mother's health for physical or economic reasons."[67] Departing rhetorically from abstract notions about eugenics and democracy, Taniguchi argued in the Diet that the revision was necessary for the very concrete reason that "there has been strong demand for [an] economic reasons [clause] since the law was passed" and that "it is necessary to curb the rapidly increasing population."[68] It is probably no coincidence that Taniguchi felt free to change his line of argument at a time when Japan's "population problem" had become the focus of heated and sometimes panicked public discussion.[69] Ōta and Katō did not cosponsor this revision or Taniguchi's subsequent revisions.

The addition of the "economic reasons" clause greatly increased access to abortion, since the other criteria (leprosy, rape, mental illness, and hereditary illness) did not apply to many women. In fact, technically speaking, the "economic reasons" criterion did not apply to many women either, as Taniguchi's official position (which the Ministry of Health and Welfare subsequently wrote into its enforcement regulations) was that it applied only to women who qualified for public assistance under the provisions of the Livelihood Protection Law, and to women who would require public assistance if they had more children.[70] When asked in the Diet if women of "superior character" who had been reduced to "hard living" should also be permitted to have abortions, Taniguchi maintained the eugenically correct position that this should be avoided and that such women should be given as much aid as possible after delivery.[71] In reality, however, doctors and Eugenic Protection Committees never interpreted the "economic reasons" clause that narrowly, and the MHW never enforced its formal regulations.[72] Since the 1949 revision, 99 to 100 percent of Japanese women have cited "economic reasons" on the paperwork that must be filled out when an abortion is performed.[73]

Even though the Eugenic Protection Law effected a radical change in policy, in 1948 there was essentially no debate outside the Diet about whether abortion should be legalized.[74] But by 1949, as the magnitude of Japan's postwar baby boom began to become apparent, there was an explosion of public discussion about Japan's "population problem,"[75] and the question of whether women should be allowed to have abortions for economic reasons—or indeed for any reason—was at the center of the debate. As it happened, Taniguchi succeeded in liberalizing abortion rather easily, both because of the extreme anxiety about the birth rate among Japanese and American officials and because of the political influence of medical interests. Nevertheless, it is worthwhile to examine the arguments against allowing abortion for economic reasons, because these arguments provide clues about what a Japanese abortion debate might have looked like if Japan's defeat in war and total economic collapse had not so biased the outcome.

First, there were religious and moral objections similar to those one encounters in subsequent postwar debates over abortion in Japan and elsewhere. For example, Tanaka Kōtarō—a Catholic politician and prewar progressive who went on to become a Supreme Court Justice—maintained that human beings were not free to dispose of life because it is a gift from God, and that abortion, like suicide, was therefore a sin against the God-given natural order.[76] Tanaka also argued that abortion would ruin women's health, destroy the family, lessen the sanctity of marriage, encourage extramarital affairs and juvenile delinquency, and lead to the spread of venereal disease. Finally, Tanaka maintained that the government should focus on increasing food supplies to accommodate the existing population rather than decreasing the population to accommodate the existing food supplies.[77] It must be remembered, however, that Tanaka's religious faith and his views—for example, that fetuses were living human beings—were in the extreme minority in Japan. The majority view in Japan at the time is probably better represented by Professor Hayashi's response to Tanaka that " 'people should bring up their children by all means, once they give birth to them . . . but it is another thing to destroy embryos. We must not confuse the two.' "[78]

MHW bureaucrats were opposed to the Eugenic Protection Law in general—which is not surprising, given that only a few years earlier they had designed and implemented the military regime's pronatalist policies—and they criticized the proposed "economic reasons" revision from both moral and practical points of view.[79] None were as vehement as the director of the government Institute of Population Problems, who called abortion a crime and said it should not be used as a solution to overpopulation.[80] But in softer language, MHW bureaucrats attacked the law from several angles, pointing out the difficulties inherent in determining who qualified under the "economic reasons" clause, emphasizing that no other country allowed abortion for economic reasons, expressing concern over whether existing manslaughter laws would contravene the "economic reasons" clause, and, finally, reminding politicians of how delicate the abortion issue was from religious and social perspectives.[81] Welfare Minister Miki even went so far as to call for a public hearing on the proposed revision, an unusual proceeding at the time.[82]

Ultimately, however, the bureaucrats at the MHW had limited influence over abortion policy, because they had been so discredited by their unpopular wartime population policies. And they clearly knew they were mistrusted. After delivering a lengthy criticism of the proposed "economic reasons" revision in the Diet, an MHW official begged forgiveness, saying that perhaps he should not have been so outspoken. He went on to reassure the assembled legislators that he understood that the Diet represented public opinion, and that if the revision were passed, he and his fellow MHW officials would faithfully implement it.[83] His hesitance and humility were not misplaced, as the following excerpt from a 1949 letter to the editor demonstrates:

Tojo made the great mistake of strengthening national power by increasing the population. He ordered the people to marry three years earlier and to bear at least five children per couple; and having thus replenished the nation, he led it to defeat. He seemed to have intended to kill as many as half of the people in the war. . . . Although some religionists and moralists absurdly talk about practicing restraint, such a thing is beyond discussion. I believe there is no other way for us Japanese than to carry out abortion. . . . I am convinced that by freely legalizing abortion, Japan can decrease her population from 30 to 40 percent, the quality of her race will improve, and her society will achieve a happier condition.[84]

In contrast to the religious and moral objections described above, other groups opposed liberalizing abortion for political reasons. The Japan Communist Party saw the Eugenic Protection Law as a quick fix. In keeping with its general line that the government should redistribute wealth and improve the Japanese people's living standards—and following logic strikingly similar to that of the Catholic politician Tanaka—the Communists criticized the government for combatting poverty indirectly, by allowing women to have abortions, rather than adopting direct measures to ameliorate poverty and make it possible for families to support children.[85] But it appears that the average person was grateful even for indirect measures, judging from one company employee's letter to the editor, which read: "Frankly speaking, we poor men, far from receiving a cold impression, heartily welcome the formulation of such a humanitarian bill [the Eugenic Protection Law]."[86]

In 1952 Taniguchi sponsored a further revision to the Eugenic Protection Law which eliminated the requirement that women appear before a Eugenic Protection Committee for permission to have an abortion.[87] Taniguchi noted once again that an "imbalance" existed between Japan's economy and its population. He pointed out to fellow legislators that, although contraception was the most desirable way to prevent births, it was necessary to facilitate access to abortion from the standpoint of maternal protection. Because the application process for legal abortions was so complicated, he explained, dangerous and costly black market abortions were still commonplace.[88] Once again, Taniguchi walked a fine line between humanitarianism and turf protection. By this time, though, public discussion of the "population problem" had died down. Therefore, even though the 1952 revision probably exceeded the revision of 1949 in increasing access to abortion, the later revision passed through the Diet in relative obscurity. The new system—which remains in place today—transferred formal decision-making power to individual designated doctors, requiring them to assess the merits of each woman's request for an abortion independently.

The 1952 revision thus consolidated Nichibo's already considerable control over provision of and access to abortion. Taniguchi's manipulation of the Eugenic Protection Law is a good example of how legislation can encourage the formation of interest groups.[89] It also illustrates how

waves of popular enthusiasm surrounding a given issue provide the circumstances for policy makers to create new institutions [such as legislation] to support their programs. These institutions then structure participation and policy making, often ensuring privileged access to the policy process for those who helped set them up.

After public interest and enthusiasm fade, the institutions remain, pushing forward with their preferred policies. These institutional legacies . . . may structure participation so that a powerful subsystem can remain relatively independent of popular control for decades.[90]

Such was the case with the Eugenic Protection Law, whose core provisions remain in effect half a century after the law was put in place, despite substantial revisions in 1996. For example, the law not only gives individual doctors discretionary power over whether a woman may have an abortion, it also privileges doctors as a group by giving prefectural medical associations control over designating which doctors may perform abortions.[91]

At the same time, however, it should be noted that the 1952 revision also eased access to legal abortions for many women who had been reluctant to appear before a committee of strangers. Although Amemiya maintains that the passage of the Eugenic Protection Law and subsequent revisions only sanctioned a practice that was already widespread and did not lead to an appreciable increase in the abortion rate, it is impossible to determine whether this is true.[92] The revisions definitely resulted in an increase in *reporting* of abortions. Government statistics from 1950 show that there was an 85 percent increase in the number of reported abortions a year after the first revision of the Eugenic Protection Law, and a 33 percent increase in 1953, a year after the second revision.[93] But we will never know whether these numbers reflected an actual increase in the abortion rate, or merely reflected the movement of women from illegal, nonreporting abortion providers to those who were legal and reported the abortions.[94] Furthermore, as discussed in chapter 1, government abortion statistics are generally unreliable, because ob-gyns commonly underreport abortions (either to avoid paying taxes or, in some cases, when the patient is a minor or is unmarried). Thus, although there are many indications that abortions were performed on a massive scale,[95] we can never determine the exact abortion rate in the 1950s and 1960s, or whether revisions to the Eugenic Protection Law affected that rate.

This is not to say that designated doctors were motivated solely by self-interest in supporting the Eugenic Protection Law. A great deal of evidence indicates that, as doctors, they were concerned about the health risks posed to women by unsanitary, unprofessional black market abortions, being performed at the time by quasi-qualified and unqualified individuals, such as dentists, otorhynolaryngologists and veterinarians.[96] Whelpton, writing contemporaneously, asserted that

the widespread [notion] that such [illegal] abortions were numerous, that "black market" prices usually were being charged, and that abortions were being performed all too frequently under conditions which resulted in permanently undermining the health of the women (or even in causing death), undoubtedly played an important part in [the passage of the Eugenic Protection Law].[97]

At the same time, however, one cannot ignore the fact that Japan's abortion rates in the 1950s and 1960s were very high and that a small group of designated doctors monopolized the lucrative business of providing abortions.[98] This was "the era in which abortion was profitable."[99] The women's magazine *Fujin kōron* noted in the mid-1950s that the popularity of abortion was increasing rapidly. An official of the Housewives' Federation claimed that it was not uncommon for women to have two, three, even as many as ten abortions, and asserted that young women sought abortions lightly, "like they were going to get a perm."[100] Public health officials and family planning advocates accused designated doctors of "siding with abortion," enriching themselves by providing expensive abortions rather than recommending and selling less profitable contraceptives.[101] While Taniguchi may have genuinely supported measures to promote birth control, many rank-and-file members of Nichibo are reported to have felt that if birth control became popular and the number of abortions decreased, it would "eat up their livelihood" (*meshi o kuiage ni naru*).[102] Some ob-gyns even went so far as to advertise their abortion clinics at family planning conferences.[103]

In conclusion, then, we see that a powerful group of doctors engineered the legalization of abortion and subsequent liberalization of abortion law largely to advance the organizational and financial interests of the group. Japan's total defeat in war caused an intersection of professional and national interests: lawmakers supported the doctors' controversial abortion law because they believed that legalizing abortion was the only way to lower population growth, which in turn would facilitate Japan's paramount goal of economic recovery. Under ordinary circumstances, legislators probably would not have voted to legalize abortion—but then, under ordinary circumstances, doctors probably would not have introduced the legislation in the first place. As we saw in the previous chapter, despite some discussion of lifting the criminal ban on abortion before the war, no law was ever drafted, much less introduced to the Diet for discussion. The doctors and their erstwhile socialist allies strategically chose to introduce the Eugenic Protection Bill when they did, because they recognized that widespread concern about population growth and the economy had created a unique window of opportunity. Such behavior is consistent with Thelen's "dynamic constraints model," in which groups and individuals maneuver strategically within institutions, "acting on 'openings' provided by . . . shifting contextual conditions in order to defend or enhance their own positions."[104] Taniguchi took advantage of this window by presenting the Eugenic Protection Law as a way "to rebuild a cultural Japan and to contribute to the improvement of the people's welfare."[105]

The political dynamics and discourses associated with the legalization and liberalization of abortion in Japan during the occupation were quite different from those seen in other industrialized democracies, most of which legalized abortion in the 1960s and 1970s. First, although doctors have been active in abortion politics in almost all countries,[106] they have acted as lobbyists, not lawmakers. That Taniguchi simultaneously held the president's post at Nichibo and legislative office in the Diet further reinforced doctors' control over an area of policy in which they were already influential.[107] Second, while considerations of national interest have played a role in abortion policy making in other countries (France, for example), rarely have they been so central as in Japan.[108] Conversely, rarely have ethics and religion played so small a role in political debate over legalizing abortion as in Japan. Finally, whereas the women's movement and its agenda have been integral in the process of decriminalizing abortion in other industrialized democracies, in Japan these groups played no part in the effort to legalize abortion and, consequently, had no role in the initial shaping of abortion policy or the discourse surrounding it.[109]

This noninvolvement of the Japanese women's movement cannot be attributed to small size, organizational weakness, or political bias, for the 1940s and 1950s saw a proliferation of left-wing, right-wing, and moderate women's groups with large national memberships. These groups successfully championed a variety of causes, including efforts to protect mothers and children, to keep food prices down, to abolish legal prostitution, to block the revival of the prewar family system, and to promote sanitary measures.[110] Perhaps activist women chose not to participate in abortion policy making in the early postwar period because they justified their political participation through "wifeist, maternalist and guardian-of-the-home arguments," updated versions of the prewar "good wife, wise mother" (*ryōsai kenbo*) ideology.[111] This is not to say that all activist women necessarily opposed abortion: the record shows that, at least before the war, many supported legalizing abortion.[112] Regardless of their personal views, however, it would have been risky for these women to agitate for legalizing abortion, as it could have been interpreted as a rejection of motherhood, thus compromising the foundation of their political legitimacy. Not until the late 1960s and early 1970s did feminist notions of women's rights as individuals begin to infiltrate the Japanese discourse on women's activism, loosening the ideological stranglehold of "good wife, wise mother"—although by no means vanquishing it. This in turn paved the way for women's participation in debates over abortion in the 1970s, 1980s, and 1990s.

What, then, are the implications of the absence of women's participation in early abortion policy making? One perspective holds that it made little difference, that women's interests were served quite well even though few women were involved in the process. For despite the eugenic rhetoric and potentially restrictive provisions of the Eugenic Protection Law, the de facto application of the law since the 1952 revision has essentially made safe, legal abortions available on demand in Japan. Furthermore, Article 1 of the Eugenic Protection Law justified abortion (at least partially) within the maternalist framework favored by activist and other women at the time. In short, the Eugenic

Protection Law conferred substantial health benefits and reproductive rights on women—even though these were largely unintended by-products of a policy-making process informed by considerations of professional control and national interest.

But, in some ways, the lack of female input and the dominance of doctors in the early abortion policy-making process was also detrimental to women's interests. It contributed to the ten-year delay in the effective promotion of birth control techniques and the concomitant overreliance on abortion during the late 1940s, 1950s, and 1960s.[113] There are also more abstract implications to the fact that, without much public debate, Japanese women were *given* abortion rights between 1948 and 1952 rather than having to fight for them, as did many women in the West in the 1960s and 1970s. The liberalization of abortion policy was only possible within the context of the broader SCAP-initiated process of democratization and liberalization, and many have argued that Japan's struggle-free "democratization from above" prevented democratic principles from becoming deeply rooted in the national psyche.[114] Similarly, on a smaller scale, one could argue that the passivity and lack of awareness among Japanese women about matters related to birth control and abortion[115] result in part from their lack of involvement in setting the terms on which abortion and birth control were legalized.

# The Politics of Abortion: Movements to Revise the Eugenic Protection Law (1952–2000)

THE OB-GYNS of Nichibo largely controlled the shape of Japan's early postwar abortion policy, but abortion policy was not destined to remain Nichibo's sole domain, or "policy monopoly."[1] Japan's economic, social, and political environment began to change in the 1950s and 1960s, encouraging a new set of actors to create dialogues over abortion policy where once there had been only monologue. At intervals over the next four decades, the Eugenic Protection Law became the locus of confrontation for groups of doctors, religious people, family planners, feminist and nonfeminist women, and the handicapped. These groups added novel concepts to the vocabulary of the abortion debate, such as fetuses' right to life, women's right to decide whether and when to have children, and handicapped people's human rights.[2] But the entry of these new players did not change—and in fact underscored—the fundamental fact that interest groups have played a critical role in abortion policy making in Japan, with politicians serving as their "agents," and bureaucrats serving as "followers" or "referees."

The fortunes of groups seeking to limit access to abortion and those seeking to defend access fluctuated during this period depending on how well their agendas coincided with larger national issues at a given moment; raw political power and political maneuvering; and the persuasiveness of their respective rhetoric. The basic question over which these groups clashed until the 1980s was whether the existing abortion policy, as embodied by the "economic reasons" clause of the Eugenic Protection Law, should be maintained. But the debate over abortion also flowed into other currents of national discussion—for example, whether Japan should be a country where economic pragmatism displaced other values, or a country where concerns about quality of life, morality, and spirituality also had a place; what the proper role was for women in Japanese society; and what the relationship between state and individual should be in the intimate spheres of life.

## THE ORIGINS OF THE ANTI-ABORTION MOVEMENT

In the late 1950s and early 1960s Japan's rapid economic growth and rapidly declining birth rate became confirmed trends.[3] As soon as Japanese elites realized that Japan was not destined to become an overpopulated Third World country, as many had feared during the early postwar period, they began to fret about the possibility of future labor shortages. The shift in opinion on the nature of Japan's "population problem"—that is, whether the birth rate was "too high" or "too low"—can be tracked quite closely, for, as late as 1956, 86 percent of elite Japanese surveyed by the Japan Family Planning Association replied that family planning was important for Japan's future, and most said that this was the case because Japan was overpopulated.[4] But in 1957–58 medical and family planning newsletters reported that the business world had begun raising questions about the effects of abortion and contraception on the birth rate (which dropped from 4.54 to 2.04 between 1947 and 1957) and the future labor supply.[5] Liberal Democratic Party politicians, ever sensitive to the concerns of their backers in industry, grew increasingly worried about the prospect of labor shortages, and the government began to back away from efforts to promote family planning.[6] Politicians and bureaucrats also became embarrassed that Japan had gained an international reputation as an "abortion paradise" (*datai tengoku*)—that is, a country where abortions could be obtained easily and legally.[7] Thus, although the family planning movement and the nationalist new religion, Seichō no Ie, had both been voicing opposition to abortion and calling for revision of the Eugenic Protection Law since the early 1950s, almost a decade went by before economic, demographic, and political circumstances combined to provide them a "window of opportunity" to press their anti-abortion agenda.

The anti-abortion sentiment was strong within the Japanese family planning movement in the 1950s.[8] A 1954 article in *Kazoku keikaku* condemned abortion as "a barbaric act of sacrificing the health of wives and mothers, and an inhuman deed of killing a tiny life which would otherwise live."[9] In 1958 the head of the Japan Family Planning Federation, Kunii Chōjirō, stated that, in Japan, "family planning is in a struggle against abortion."[10] Another observer remarked in the early 1960s that the family planning movement could more accurately be described as an "abortion prevention movement."[11] The family planners' hostility to abortion and the Eugenic Protection Law sprang from several sources. First, the American birth control activist Margaret Sanger had a strong philosophical influence over the Japanese family planning movement, and, at least in public, Sanger opposed abortion (Sanger's private views on abortion were clearly more nuanced).[12] Second, as noted in the previous chapter, family planners mistrusted ob-gyns, believing they cynically manipulated the Eugenic Protection Law in order to profit from providing abortions—to the detriment of efforts to promote birth control.[13] Finally, Amemiya suggests that, in the late 1950s and early 1960s, birth control advocates were searching for ways to defend themselves against the rising tide of criticism from the business world, which blamed the family planning movement for causing labor shortages.[14]

However, no one in the family planning movement acted on these anti-abortion views until 1958, when Representative Katō Shizue deemed that the time was ripe to mount an attack on the Eugenic Protection Law, which, as we learned in chapter 4, she had had misgivings about since its passage. Katō argued that too many abortions were being performed and called on a multi-party coalition of female Diet representatives (with whom she had successfully fought for the passage of the Antiprostitution Law in 1956) to assist her in attempting to revise the Eugenic Protection Law.[15] Katō proposed that the Eugenic Protection Law be invalidated after a period of three years, during which time birth control would be promoted vigorously. Subsequently, abortion would be allowed strictly on grounds of rape, eugenic considerations, and physical (not economic) damage to the mother's health. Some echoed her call. The Health and Hygiene Section Chief of the Housewives' Federation (Shufu Rengōkai, or Shufuren), for example, deplored the "horrors of abortion" and called for more zealous application of the Criminal Abortion Law.[16] But not everyone in the family planning community agreed. At the 1958 All-Japan Family Planning Conference, where the pros and cons of revising the Eugenic Protection Law became a hot topic of debate, Koya Yoshio and others argued that making abortion more inaccessible would simply drive women to seek out dangerous illegal abortions.[17]

Katō did not gain the cooperation she sought from her female colleagues in the Diet in 1958, but in 1961 she again declared that Japan's abortion rate was "out of control" (nobanashi) and called for the passage of a new law emphasizing maternal health and family planning.[18] Katō held that a fetus was a human life and that the Eugenic Protection Law needed to be revised to conform with the Japanese Constitution's guarantee of human rights for all.[19] In 1962 Katō, pre-war feminist Hiratsuka Raichō, and numerous former and current cabinet ministers founded a Committee to Protect Children's Lives (Kodomo no inochi o mamoru kai), whose organizing statement asserted that abortion was Japan's national shame (kokujoku) and compared the large numbers of abortions being performed to mass murders perpetrated during World War II.[20] In the same year, the Japan Family Planning Association launched the Movement to Cherish Life (Inochi o taisetsu ni suru undō) with the goal of reducing the number of abortions (estimated at the time to be about two million per year) as well as accidental deaths and suicides. The Ministry of Health and Welfare actively supported the movement, as did various social welfare groups, women's groups, and religious groups. The national railway participated by allowing posters that read "Let's Cherish Life More!" ("Motto, inochi o taisetsu ni shiyō") to be posted at rail stations.[21]

In a case of strange bedfellows, the anti-abortion movement in the generally progressive and left-wing family planning world was loosely affiliated with a similar movement organized by the nationalist, right-wing new religion, Seichō no Ie,[22] which had about 1.5 million members in the 1950s and 1960s.[23] Seichō no Ie's spiritual leader, Taniguchi Masaharu (1893–1985), was banned from public speaking and publishing during the occupation because of his support for the wartime regime,[24] but he reentered the political fray as soon as the occupation ended.[25] Over the next several decades Taniguchi involved Seichō no Ie in a variety of right-wing, nationalist causes, including movements to revise the postwar Constitution, to institute a system of state support for Yasu-kuni Shrine, to reinstitute the prewar educational system, to reestablish Foundation Day as a national holiday, and to pass the Era Name Law (Gengo Hō), which provided for the official adoption of a calendar based on the year of the current Japanese emperor's reign.[26]

Taniguchi first voiced his anti-abortion views in 1952 in a ringing denunciation of the Eugenic Protection Law. Taniguchi declared that the law—which he later labeled the "Abortion Promotion Law" and the "Ob-Gyn Protection Law"—gave doctors the freedom to murder, and he exhorted his followers to "Launch a Movement to Save One Million Childrens' Lives."[27] Over the next ten years Taniguchi continued to equate abortion with murder, arguing further that the Eugenic Protection Law was part of an American-imposed "population control policy" which, like the American-imposed constitution, was eroding traditional Japanese values and causing numerous social ills, including murder, suicide, a general trend toward devaluing life, juvenile delinquency, divorce, a decline in sexual morals, a decline in the birth rate, and a labor shortage.[28] He also espoused the view that the spirits of aborted fetuses caused various physical ailments, as well as bedwetting, poor school performance, and job loss, in an effort to get the attention of, or wreak revenge on, their would-have-been siblings and parents.[29]

It was not until the late 1950s, however, that the national circumstances described above provided an "opening" for Seichō no Ie to expand its anti-abortion message to non–Seichō no Ie members.[30] In 1959 Taniguchi renewed his call for revision of the Eugenic Protection Law and charged Seichō no Ie's women's section, the White Dove Committee (Shirohato kai), with organizing a Committee to Protect Children's Lives (Kodomo no inochi o mamoru kai) in order to foster a wider pro-revision movement.[31] Seichō no Ie claims that its members collected 52,000 signatures for a "respect for life" (jinmei sonchō) petition in 1960, and almost 450,000 in 1961. Seichō no Ie submitted both petitions to the Upper and Lower Houses of the Diet, and to the minister of health and welfare.[32] The petition, submitted on September 10, 1961, employed language and imagery that would probably seem familiar to members of the American pro-life movement today:

> It goes without saying that abortion is murder, but parents are murdering their children [nonetheless]. . . . Why is it that this kind of mass murder is occurring openly in our country alone? On top of this carnage, adults are building lives of ease, over [the bodies] of these victims, adults are glorifying the pleasures of the flesh. . . . This is surely a sign of the last days of an age of decadence (mappō sueyo).[33]

The government was initially responsive to the "respect for life" campaigns conducted by Seichō no Ie, family planners, and others. MHW officials announced in 1962 that the ministry was considering revising the Eugenic Protection Law to make the abortion screening system more stringent.[34] And at a cabinet meeting in November 1963 the minister of health and welfare said that he would like to introduce a bill to revise the Eugenic Protection Law at the next session of the Diet. He cited as problems the high number of abortions (which he estimated at twice the reported 900,000), the decline in the birth rate, and the shortage of young workers, and concluded that laissez faire abortion policy fostered a tendency to take life lightly, harmed women's health, and made Japan the target of criticism abroad.[35] Also in 1963, the MHW addressed a sharply worded inquiry to Nichibo, asking whether Nichibo members really followed the rules by applying the economic reasons clause only to women who were receiving public assistance. The MHW asked what Nichibo's leaders thought about the fact that at least one million abortions were being performed per year, and what concrete measures they could suggest to counteract this situation. Nichibo leaders responded angrily that the abortion situation was not "out of control" and that doctors should be left to administer the law independently, albeit more stringently than in the past.[36]

Although the prospect of labor shortages was undoubtedly the main reason the government took an interest in the abortion rate, it should be noted that international criticism of Japan's abortion policy was also a sensitive point. Japan was reentering the world stage after a long period of occupation and reconstruction, and Japan's international reputation was a subject of considerable concern among the elite.[37] Kunii Chōjirō noted in 1964 that it was "something to be ashamed of as a nation" that Japan was known around the world as an "abortion paradise," and commentators frequently referred to the abortion situation as "our national shame."[38] During the 1964 Tokyo Olympics, even the newsletter of the designated abortion providers' group, Nichibo, mentioned the importance of not giving foreign visitors the impression that it was easy to get an abortion in Japan.[39]

For many decades after the Olympics, Japanese actors continued to use international opinion of Japan's abortion policy and international trends in abortion policy to bolster arguments on both sides of the domestic abortion debate. This stands in marked contrast to the abortion debate in the United States, where none of the actors involved appear interested in international opinion of U.S. abortion policy, or in comparing U.S. policies to those elsewhere. But as we will see later in this chapter, elite sensitivity about Japan's international reputation was, in fact, largely responsible for the revision of the Eugenic Protection Law in 1996.

Although the circumstances described above seemed to favor the cause of antiabortion groups, the LDP quickly lost interest in revising the Eugenic Protection Law. Taniguchi Masaharu explained to his followers that the loss of inter-est was the result of a change in administration, which led him to believe that Seichō no Ie had to become directly involved in politics in order to lobby more effectively.[40] But the LDP also backed away from the abortion question in part because it was a "delicate" issue with broad social implications—the type of issue politicians everywhere try to avoid[41]—and in part because of political pressure from Nichibo and the Japan Medical Association.[42]

Although Nichibo was able to fend off the pro-life camp's initial assault, the anti-abortion campaign clearly caught the ob-gyns off guard, forcing them to reassess their group's situation quickly and to delineate a defense strategy. Throughout the 1950s Nichibo leaders promoted the view—and probably gen-uinely believed—that by performing abortions, designated doctors were per-forming a national service. For example, at a Nichibo-sponsored annual service for the repose of the souls of aborted fetuses (mizuko kuyō), group president Taniguchi Yasaburō gave a speech in which he explained that, by implementing the Eugenic Protection Law, designated doctors sought to rebuild the country and improve the people's welfare.[43] The general public may not have thought of Nichibo in quite such positive terms, but nevertheless, during the lean years leading up to Japan's economic recovery, many probably would have acknowl-edged that the group performed a necessary service safely and reliably.

With the upswing of the economy, however, as well as the prospect of labor shortages and the advent of the pro-life movement, Nichibo and the relation-ship between abortion and economic development came to be represented in a very different light. For example, in a 1963 women's magazine article, Profes-sor Yoshida of Meiji University denounced ob-gyns who opposed revising the Eugenic Protection Law as unscrupulous, and claimed that "Japan's economic prosperity was built on the corpses of fetuses" because Japanese housewives, drawn in by advertising, limited the number of children they had so that they could afford to buy consumer goods.[44] While Professor Yoshida was clearly engaging in hyperbole, it should be noted that his statement did have some factual basis. Sociologist Noriko Tsuya draws a similar conclusion (albeit, in much less lurid language) based on statistical and demographic research:

> Fertility decline played a significant role in the overall socioeconomic development of Japan after World War II . . . [and] the dramatic fertility decline from 1950 to the late 1950s was primarily due to decreases in marital fertility rates which were in turn achieved by extensive use of induced abortion and increasing dependence on contraception.[45]

The rapid shift in opinion on the need to curb population growth forced Nichibo's ob-gyn members and their allies to search for new ways to portray their contribution to Japan's well-being. Believing that most Japanese would find adult life more valuable than fetal life, Taniguchi Yasaburō's political suc-cessor, Upper House Representative Marumo Shigesada,[46] suggested emphasizing that revising the law would lead women who could not get abortions to commit suicide. Nichibo's vice president argued similarly that abortion was unavoidable if women were to be guarded from misfortune. He asked what could be done, ultimately, if a woman did not want a child. Would it not be a violation of her human rights to force her to bear a child she did not wish to have? Nichibo board member and Eugenic Protection Law sponsor Fukuda Amano said that revising the law would only drive women to procure illegal abortions, and that, instead of revising the law, a stricter interpretation of the existing law should be imposed and family planning should be promoted.[47]

A few years later the family planning movement also adopted an anti-revision stance, having come to mistrust the motives of both Seichō no Ie and the government for seeking to restrict access to abortion. Kunii Chōjirō wrote in 1967 that revising the Eugenic Protection Law would not lead to an increase in the birth rate because people loved their families more than their country, and that even if having numerous children were in the nation's best interest, most couples felt that having fewer children was in the best interests of their families. For in largely urban, industrial, nonagricultural societies, there is little need for child labor—indeed, children are required to attend school until their mid-teens—transforming children into an expensive luxury rather than a valuable asset. Kunii concluded that the government would do better to analyze the needs and psychology of families living in a modern economy and try to improve their lives through welfare measures, rather than coerce them to have children.[48]

From this time on, family planners consistently voiced opposition to revising the Eugenic Protection Law, often on grounds that Japanese living standards were still sufficiently low to justify abortion for economic reasons. They also noted that Japan would be criticized internationally for trying to increase its population at a time when most countries—including Japan—had signed United Nations resolutions in favor of slowing global population growth. Moreover, representatives of other Asian countries had expressed fear that restrictions on abortion might lead to rapid population growth and renewed Japanese aggression.[49] But perhaps because of their earlier pro-life stance, family planning groups were not nearly as vocal or politically active as other groups in the debate over revising the Eugenic Protection Law.

## The First Effort to Revise the Eugenic Protection Law (1967–1974)

The defection of the family planners and the failure of the White Dove Committee's petition campaign left Seichō no Ie undaunted. Instead, Seichō no Ie regrouped and mounted an eight-year political campaign to revise the Eugenic Protection Law. The designated doctors group, Nichibo (with backing from the JMA), emerged as Seichō no Ie's primary antagonist. Both groups were politically powerful, but neither was powerful enough to ignore the other, forcing them to compromise initially on a draft revision. When the draft was made public, however, a variety of other groups—women's groups, handicapped activists, journalists, opposition politicians, and family planning groups—were galvanized to attempt to block the revision. Although these groups did change the political calculus of the contest over abortion, it is difficult to tell whether their influence was decisive, or whether the revision effort's ultimate failure occurred because medical interests had more established ties with the LDP, thus commanding more money and votes than Seichō no Ie. Regardless, the smaller groups—especially the women's groups—deserve our attention because they engaged Seichō no Ie and other conservatives in novel debates: over abortion, the relationship between the state and the individual, and the role of women in society and the economy.

Seichō no Ie became more directly involved in politics in the mid- to late 1960s in accordance with Taniguchi Masaharu's injunction after the failure of the 1960–61 petition campaign. The religious group formed a political action group in 1964 and set about cultivating conservative LDP politicians (the most noteworthy of whom was Prime Minister Satō),[50] as well as politicians further to the right (such as LDP Representative Tamaki),[51] backing them financially and organizationally in the same way Nichibo had backed Taniguchi Yasaburō and his successor, Representative Marumo. Concretely this meant that, in 1968 and 1969, Seichō no Ie donated money to, and mobilized the vote for, numerous LDP politicians in both Houses of the Diet: of 288 LDP politicians elected to the Lower House in 1969, 142 received support from Seichō no Ie.[52] In exchange, these politicians organized a Diet members' roundtable to discuss revising the Eugenic Protection Law, and in March 1970 they arranged for the LDP Social Policy Committee (*Shakai bukai*) to take up the question. (It should be noted that there was also a sizable, more liberal contingent of LDP representatives who did not favor revising the Eugenic Protection Law, but this group did not voice active opposition at this time.)

Meanwhile, in 1967 Seichō no Ie had formed the League to Revise or Abolish the Eugenic Protection Law (*Yūsei Hogo Hō kaihai kisei dōmei*), in alliance with a small group of Catholic doctors.[53] The League accused ob-gyns of having designed the Eugenic Protection Law only to monopolize the profitable abortion market free from government interference,[54] and reiterated the familiar arguments as to why the Eugenic Protection Law should be revised.[55] But Seichō no Ie also showed signs of increasing political savvy. By heavily supplementing religious and moral rhetoric with reminders about Japan's "national shame," the declining birth rate, and labor shortages, Seichō no Ie drew attention to issues of real concern to politicians.[56] This pragmatic shift in strategy can be seen as the beginning of Seichō no Ie's gradual drift toward compromise with its medical opponents.

Nevertheless, Seichō no Ie's Revision League initially made stringent demands, not only that the economic reasons clause of the Eugenic Protection Law be deleted, but that the approval of two or more doctors be required for an abortion; that the prefectural government, rather than the prefectural JMA, designate doctors; and that abortions be performed only at public hospitals, where oversight would be stricter than at private clinics, which hitherto had dominated the field.[57] These demands, aimed to curtail ob-gyns' independence and professional discretion, evoked an immediate response. In a petition submitted to the Diet in December 1968, Nichibo maintained that relying on the judgment of a designated doctor was the best way to determine whether an abortion should be performed; that if severe restrictions were placed on legal abortion, an increase in illegal abortions would result; and that the only way to prevent abortions was to promote birth control, sex education, and family-friendly measures such as childbirth and child allowances.[58] Elsewhere, Nichibo argued that revising the law would buck the recent trend in other countries toward legalizing abortion.[59] The JMA supported all these positions, having drawn similar conclusions at a meeting in 1966.[60]

Most sources report that career bureaucrats at the MHW were initially opposed to the revision of the Eugenic Protection Law. They preferred instead to encourage Nichibo and the prefectural medical associations to bring the abortion situation under control by disciplining their members privately—a course that would have insulated the MHW from controversy. However, LDP politicians beholden to Seichō no Ie succeeded in pressuring the MHW to adopt a pro-revision stance.[61] In 1968 an MHW White Paper on Public Welfare reported that, because national income had increased, the government was considering eliminating the economic reasons clause of the Eugenic Protection Law. In 1969 the Population Problems Advisory Council urged that it was "necessary to revive the birth rate," and in 1970 the employers' peak organization, Nikkeiren, mentioned that revising the Eugenic Protection Law was a way to prevent future labor shortages. In subsequent years MHW officials repeatedly made the point that Japan was no longer in a state of emergency as it had been when abortion was legalized, and that improved economic conditions rendered the provisions of the law inappropriate to the present day.[62]

Not all bureaucrats towed the party line, however. The head of the MHW's Population Problems Institute responded to the charge that overreliance on abortion had caused the decline in the birth rate by patiently explaining that, although in 1955 abortion was responsible for 70 percent of the birth rate decline, and contraception for only 30 percent, the figures had reversed themselves around 1965 as knowledge of and access to contraception became more widespread. He concluded that restricting access to abortion would not have a great effect on the birth rate and that it would be more effective to improve social conditions for families with children.[63] On another occasion, a representative of the Ministry of Justice contradicted the pro-life argument that abortion was murder. In response to a question about whether the constitutional guarantees of life, liberty, and happiness applied to fetuses, the representative stated that a fetus was considered part of its mother's body until it was born, and was therefore not recognized as a legal person entitled to the human rights protections provided for under the Constitution.[64]

But these kinds of arguments were too dry and factual to carry much weight in an emotionally and ideologically charged debate centering on motherhood, sexual mores, and economic and racial survival. Similarly ineffectual were Nichibo president Moriyama's reminders that the JMA strictly enforced its internal rules governing professional conduct, and that designated doctors were carefully screened and reevaluated every two years. More emotionally compelling for an elite anxious over labor shortages and the general social upheaval of the late 1960s and early 1970s were Seichō no Ie's dire warnings that,

> this mass obliteration of life over the past 20 years has caused a labor shortage, a decline in public morals, a rise in juvenile delinquency, an aging of the population, and a decrease in the population, and if this situation is not corrected, the downfall of the Japanese race is inevitable.[65]

After a "lively" debate in an Upper House Budget Committee meeting in 1970 between politicians affiliated with Nichibo and Seichō no Ie, *Asahi shinbun* reported that sentiment was growing in favor of revising the Eugenic Protection Law.[66]

Nichibo leaders sensed that the political wind was not blowing in their favor. Realizing the impossibility of suppressing discussions about revising the Eugenic Protection Law, they decided to enter into negotiations with Seichō no Ie in order to salvage Nichibo's reputation and retain some measure of control over the terms of a revision, should one be introduced. Seichō no Ie leaders, for their part, were willing to cooperate because Seichō no Ie lacked sufficient influence to force the MHW to introduce a revision in the face of direct opposition from medical interests.[67] Consequently, after much negotiation between 1970 and 1972, the two groups reached an accommodation: medical interests agreed to delete the "economic reasons" clause, provided that they could make revisions of their own, such as adding clauses that would allow abortion if "the continuation of pregnancy or childbirth is likely to seriously harm the mother's *mental* or physical health" (*seishinteki mata wa shintaiteki riyū ni yori*) (emphasis added) and in cases of fetal disease or defect (the so-called fetal provision, or *taiji jōkō*).[68] In a nod to concerns over the declining birth rate, the two groups also agreed to insert into Article 20 an additional duty for Eugenic Protection Consultation Offices, namely, "to . . . give advice and guidance so that women may give birth to their first child at a suitable age"—that age being 22.[69]

Nichibo clearly gained more from the negotiations than its adversary. Seichō no Ie dropped all previous demands except for the deletion of the economic reasons clause, and any substantive effect that might have had was negated by the substitution of the "mental reasons" clause, which gave designated doctors as much interpretive latitude as did the economic reasons clause. Thus Seichō no Ie appeared to founder on the shoals of political compromise during negotiations with Nichibo, and afterward, its anti-abortion campaign, which had begun as a serious effort to ban or limit access to abortion, was gradually transformed into a symbolic act of right-wing protest.

It must not have seemed that way to Seichō no Ie leaders, however, at least initially, for the MHW—playing the role of scribe—promptly drafted a bill to revise the Eugenic Protection Law following the specifications of the two interest groups. The MHW then introduced the bill to the Social Affairs and Labor Committee of the Lower House of the Diet in May 1972. Because of the delays over other controversial bills, discussion of the draft revision was carried over to the next session. LDP politicians promised Seichō no Ie that the bill would be passed by the 1973 Diet, but in 1973 discussion of the bill was once again delayed.[70] At that point, the bill was in danger of becoming void unless a vote was taken to extend discussion of the bill to the next session. The chairman of the Social Affairs and Labor Committee, LDP Representative Tagawa Seiichi, refused to take up the bill for consideration because he opposed the revision; furthermore, he was a long-standing enemy of the ultra-right Seichō no Ie–backed representative Tamaki on the subject of restoring ties with China. So Seichō no Ie's supporters in the LDP arranged to have Tagawa temporarily removed from the chairmanship, and with his replacement presiding, the bill was voted in for extension on the last day of the 1973 Diet session.[71]

By then, opposition political parties, family planning organizations, mainstream women's groups and feminist groups (who were reacting primarily to the proposed removal of the economic reasons clause), and handicapped people's groups (who were responding to the proposed addition of the fetal conditions clause) were submitting petitions, sending telegrams, and staging noisy protests in opposition to government interference—which is how they perceived the revision bill, even though it was strictly a private-sector initiative. MHW bureaucrats were sensitive to such protests because they prompted journalists to write articles accusing the bureaucracy of ignoring the people's will and attempting to revive wartime pronatalist policies.[72] So having never been particularly enthusiastic about the revision in the first place, the MHW started to back away from the bill.[73] As soon as medical interests saw that the political scales were tipping in their favor, they withdrew support for revisions of any kind. Later on, Nichibo president Moriyama even cited the fact that deliberations over the revision had been conducted undemocratically, without adequately listening to the people's opinions—an injustice that apparently had not troubled him in the two years during which Nichibo privately negotiated the fate of the Eugenic Protection Law with Seichō no Ie.[74]

Despite these setbacks, Seichō no Ie–backed politicians managed to get the bill to a vote in the Lower House Social Affairs and Labor Committee in 1974. After a "hasty deliberation" (*supēdo shingi*) of only two days—during which time JMA president Takemi sent a telegram to each member of the committee expressing opposition to the revision—the committee head announced, amid loud booing from opposition party representatives, that the bill was going to a vote.[75] Feminist activists scuffled with guards and shouted protests from the visitors' seats,[76] but the committee voted in favor of the bill, and it subsequently passed from the House of Representatives to the House of Councilors.

For several weeks following this development, the Nichibo newsletter featured nervous speculation about whether the JMA's vote-getting strength surpassed that of Seichō no Ie.[77] But the two LDP politicians representing opposing medical and religious interests (Representatives Marumo and Tamaki) became deadlocked in discussions over a compromise, and the revision bill died before reaching committee discussion in the Upper House.[78] The headline in the next month's issue of the Nichibo newsletter read, "Overwhelming Victory for Representative Marumo!" and the front page showed a grinning Marumo shaking hands with Nichibo president Moriyama.[79]

It is unclear whether Seichō no Ie's campaign to revise the Eugenic Protection Law ever had a real chance of succeeding. On the one hand, there is some evidence that the LDP allowed the revision bill to pass the Lower House only as a symbolic gesture to placate its religious backers, without ever intending to allow it to pass the Upper House and become law.[80] Seichō no Ie's leader, Taniguchi Masaharu, certainly complained afterward that he felt betrayed by the LDP, which he accused of being "materialistic" and easily swayed by other interest groups—this said with no apparent appreciation for the hypocrisy of such a statement.[81] On the other hand, Nichibo and JMA leaders seem to have been genuinely worried at times about whether they could prevent the revision from succeeding. Thus it is possible that some faction of the LDP did seriously intend to try to revise the Eugenic Protection Law at one point, but then lost its will when confronted with the extent of the opposition from within the LDP, the opposition parties, the JMA, and citizens' groups. The Oil Shock of 1973–74 and the subsequent economic downturn probably also contributed to the bill's failure by lessening the elite's sense of urgency about the labor supply.[82]

Until now we have focused on the main plot of the abortion story in the 1960s and 1970s: namely, the struggle between medical and religious interests for control over abortion policy. But there was also a subplot. As Japan Family Planning Association president Kunii noted disapprovingly during the initial debate over abortion in 1970, Nichibo and Seichō no Ie refrained from consulting the true "interested parties" (*tōjisha*)—that is, the housewives and working women who would have been most directly affected by any changes in the law.[83] The two powerful groups tried to rope off a private, backroom abortion policy-making domain, but in a classic demonstration of the pluralist dynamics described by Madison, Truman, Dahl, and others, their efforts had the perverse effect of countermobilizing groups representing housewives and working women, as well as other previously quiescent—even previously nonexistent— groups.[84]

For example, efforts to revise the Eugenic Protection Law invigorated the handicapped people's movement, which had begun to take shape in the late 1960s.[85] These groups organized to protest the proposed fetal conditions clause, which, in their estimation, threatened the lives of handicapped people and strengthened the eugenic component of a law already dangerously influenced by eugenic principles. The most active group was Aoshiba no kai, which represents victims of cerebral palsy. Members of this group petitioned the MHW and the Diet, and demonstrated in front of government buildings, claiming that the fetal conditions clause denied handicapped people the right to exist and promoted prejudice against them. The group argued that rather than eliminating the handicapped before they were born, the government's appropriate role was to create a society in which handicapped people could lead happy, productive lives.[86] News accounts of protesters in wheelchairs essentially accusing the government of trying to kill them must have alarmed LDP politicians, for the fetal conditions clause was quickly deleted from the revision bill as soon as it reached committee deliberation in 1974.[87]

The religious right's anti-abortion movement also helped to shape and strengthen Japan's emerging women's liberation movement (ribu undō), just as, conversely, the Roe v. Wade decision to legalize abortion invigorated the religious right-to-life movement in the United States.[88] Many feminist groups in Japan were formed specifically to protest the proposed revision of the Eugenic Protection Law, while feminist groups already in existence made opposition to the revision a major rallying point.[89] Meanwhile, older, more mainstream women's groups that had never been involved in abortion policy making also came to see reproduction as a political issue in reaction to Seichō no Ie's revision campaign. They voiced opposition to the revision itself, and to the exclusion of women from the abortion policy-making process.[90]

But it was the feminist groups who first came to the fore in the anti-revision movement. According to Ehara, these were generally small, self-contained, exclusive groups, with few connections to organized politics or to other groups in civil society.[91] One of the main feminist groups at the time was Gurūpu Tatakau Onna (The Fighting Women's Group), founded by antiwar activist Tanaka Mitsu and others in 1970. Along with several other feminist groups, Gurūpu Tatakau Onna rented an apartment in the Shinjuku area of Tokyo in 1972 and organized a feminist center, called Ribu Shinjuku Sentā, which grew to be one of the dominant forces in the Japanese feminist movement. The center published a feminist newsletter, Kono michi hitosuji, as well as pamphlets and posters. It also sponsored lectures and teach-ins, provided assistance to battered wives, and organized public demonstrations on various subjects, including the proposed revision of the Eugenic Protection Law.[92]

The other dominant force in the feminist movement was a group called Chūpiren, which was formed specifically in response to the proposed revision of the Eugenic Protection Law. (Chūpiren was an acronym for Chūzetsu Kinshi Hō Ni Hantai Shi Piru Kaikin O Yōkyū Suru Josei Kaihō Rengō, or The Women's Liberation Federation for Opposing the Abortion Prohibition Law and Lifting the Pill Ban.) Chūpiren's primary distinguishing feature was that it alone advocated legalizing oral contraceptives, whereas other feminist groups opposed "the pill" because they viewed it as a potential health hazard and a threat to abortion rights.[93] Chūpiren's style of operation and abortion philosophy also differed from that of Gūrupu Tatakau Onna and the other groups that participated in Ribu Shinjuku Sentā. The groups affiliated with Ribu Shinjuku Sentā, like many European feminist groups, sought to holistically address a wide range of interconnected problems within an overarching Marxist-feminist theoretical framework; they also eschewed the mass media, relying instead on newsletters to communicate their message. Chūpiren, on the other hand, has been described as more closely resembling the American feminist movement by focusing on two or three main issues, attempting to achieve concrete, short-term results, and purposely cultivating media attention as a means of popularizing its views.[94] Although there was some overlap in the various groups' philosophies, the groups associated with Ribu Shinjuku Sentā tended to espouse a more "maternalist" or "societal" brand of feminism, while Chūpiren members tended toward a more "individualist" and rights-oriented feminism.[95]

The individualist, rights-oriented strain of Japanese feminism that emerged during the anti-revision campaign in the 1970s will probably be more familiar to American readers, since the American feminist movement has been dominated by this school of thought. Japanese feminists held that women alone had the right to decide whether to give birth or to have an abortion. Indeed, the slogan "Women Decide Whether or Not to Give Birth!" (*Umu mo umanu mo onna ga kimeru*) was one of the most popular protest slogans at the time. Feminists believed that while commercialism had replaced militarism as the national ideology, government officials continued to pursue a pronatalist policy, viewing women as "baby-making machines" (*ko'umi kikai*) and children as "GNP soldiers." They held that the government had no right to interfere in private reproductive decisions to further national economic goals (or for any other reason). At demonstrations they raised placards that read, "The Government Should Mind Its Own Business!" (*Seifu wa kuchidashi suru na!*) and "Don't Make Women's Wombs into Government Tools!"[96]

This line of reasoning is significant for several reasons. At first glance, the invective against the government appears misdirected, for, as this study makes clear, the impetus for the revision campaign came entirely from the private sector. Most state actors were tools of powerful interest groups, motivated either by the promise of votes and campaign funds (in the case of politicians) or by professional obligation (in the case of bureaucrats). To feminists at the time, however, the religious groups, doctors' groups, politicians, and bureaucrats probably seemed like one homogeneous, elite mass seeking to control women's reproductive capacity. Furthermore, they may have recognized that evoking memories of the unpopular pronatalist policies of the wartime government was a more effective way to attract public sympathy for their cause than attacking interest groups that could wrap themselves in the mantles of professional expertise or religious morality.

More important, though, the individualist feminist rhetoric on abortion is meaningful because it contradicts the more dominant rhetoric of the Japanese feminist movement, the maternalist/societal rhetoric, though feminists sometimes used the two logics interchangeably.[97] According to the maternalist/societal line of reasoning, most women did not have a real choice about whether to give birth or abort. Feminists of this school claimed that women never wanted to have abortions (indeed, Tanaka Mitsu believed that abortion was murder) but that economic and societal conditions forced women to have abortions. These feminists maintained that the government's population policy in the early postwar period coerced women to limit births in order to help resuscitate the economy—ignoring the fact that legalizing abortion had benefited individual women and families as well as the larger economy and society. Regarding more recent years, they cited problems endemic to urban areas where the majority of the Japanese population lived, such as the high cost of housing and food, the small size of apartments, the shortage of landlords willing to rent to families with children, the shortage of day care, the lack of reliable birth control options, and environmental pollution. They then argued that it would be counterproductive for the government to eliminate the economic reasons clause of the Eugenic Protection Law without improving living conditions, as such a measure would only drive women to have illegal abortions. It follows that the rallying cry for these feminists was "Make a Society Where We Can Have Children, Where We Want to Have Children" (Umeru shakai o, umitai shakai o).[98]

Maternalist/societal feminists shared concerns with the burgeoning environmental and consumer movements about the quality of life in Japan,[99] and they were also influenced by Marxist political thought. As we will see in the next chapter, Japan Communist Party politicians contended in the 1940s that if resources were distributed more evenly, women would be free of the financial and other constraints characteristic of capitalist regimes and could have as many children as they wanted, thus obviating the need for birth control and abortion. From the communist viewpoint (which was fundamentally pronatalist), capitalist states prevented women from exercising their "right to maternity."[100] Maternalist/societal feminists shared this view and demanded greater state involvement to achieve a "liveable society"[101] in which women could raise their children—quite the opposite of individualist feminists, who wanted the state to "mind its own business." Indeed, maternalist/societal feminists made a point of distinguishing their vision of the abortion question as part of a larger set of interconnected social problems from Chūpiren's more individualistic, single-issue, rights-based approach.

From a tactical point of view, in the Japanese context, the maternalist/societal argument was unquestionably superior to the individualistic argument. For, as a member of the Fighting Women's Alliance (Tatakau Josei Dōmei) explained, "No one can oppose a slogan like 'Make a Society Where We Can Have Children, Where We Want to Have Children.' "[102] Furthermore, students of Japanese law, politics, and society agree that, generally, the Japanese have not embraced the ideals of liberal individualism and rights as enthusiastically as Westerners have. Even many feminists did not feel comfortable with defining abortion as a right.[103] But, more important, the maternalist/societal argument was successful because it attacked the revisionists' anti-abortion argument on its own terms. Revisionists claimed that it was no longer necessary to allow abortion for economic reasons because the Japanese economy had improved and that, indeed, more young workers would be needed to continue the economic improvement. Maternalist/societal feminists countered that economic and social conditions had not improved sufficiently to justify eliminating the economic reasons clause and called the revisionists' bluff by implying that women would have more children were the government willing to spend enough money to better family living standards. Japanese feminists sought to use the opportunity provided by the revision controversy to make the point to state actors that if the state wished to change women's reproductive behavior, it would have to provide women with benefits in exchange.[104] This dynamic illustrates Shapiro's point about the dual, contradictory nature of the modern welfare state:

> The welfare state institutionalizes dominant elite and professional interests, [but at the same time] the welfare state collects repressed individuals (the poor, minorities, women) into groups and potentially defines common grounds for grievance. The welfare state targets itself for collective action. . . . [Therefore] there are tensions between social-service and social-control functions.[105]

At that time, however, state actors were not yet willing to engage in a dialogue with feminists,[106] a stance embodied by such acts as the physical removal of anti-revision protesters sitting in front of the MHW building and the stubborn silence of an MHW section chief in the face of questions from feminists who besieged his office.[107]

## THE SECOND EFFORT TO REVISE THE EUGENIC PROTECTION LAW (1982–1983)

A second interest group confrontation over abortion policy occurred in the early 1980s. In 1982 the Ministry of Health and Welfare—again prodded by politicians affiliated with Seichō no Ie—announced new plans to delete the economic reasons clause from the Eugenic Protection Law. This announcement was met with vociferous opposition by women's groups across the political spectrum, who mobilized in greater numbers than they had in the 1970s, as well as female politicians, opposition politicians, family planners, and doctors. The anti-revision forces ultimately prevailed by creating a loud public controversy, which persuaded LDP politicians that it would be in the party's best interests electorally to abandon the drafting process—despite the fact that approximately three hundred conservative Diet members (including former prime minister Hashimoto Ryūtarō) had joined the pro-revision Diet Members' Respect for Life League (*Seimei sonchō kokkai giin renmei*) only two months earlier.[108]

Seichō no Ie's leader, Taniguchi Masaharu, renewed his call for abortion law reform in early 1981.[109] Several factors propelled the group to take action at this time. Once again the elite had grown concerned over Japan's birth rate, which had dropped below replacement levels between 1970 and 1980.[110] As was noted both in MHW White Papers in the late 1970s and in a Special Administrative Reform Commission (*Rinji gyōsei kaikaku chōsakai*, or *Rinchō*) report in July 1981, with an ever smaller percentage of the population under age twenty and an ever larger percentage of the population middle-aged or elderly, the Japanese population was aging at an extremely rapid rate, much faster than in other industrialized countries.[111] Moreover, the teen abortion rate had increased slightly during the 1970s, raising elite fears about promiscuity, delinquency, and the general decline of young people's morals.[112] Finally, leadership transitions were rendering Nichibo and the JMA weaker politically—something which Seichō no Ie undoubtedly recognized as advantageous to its cause.[113]

Most important, however, the overall political mood in Japan had turned conservative since the 1970s, when progressive welfare and anti-pollution measures had dominated the public agenda.[114] The conservative LDP won an overwhelming victory in both Houses of the Diet in 1980, ushering in a "new conservative era." In the same year Prime Minister Ōhira's cabinet formulated the Policy to Strengthen the Foundations of the Family (*Katei kiban jūjitsu seisaku*), which reemphasized the traditional family as the basic unit of society and stressed that women's primary role should be that of caregiver for children and the elderly. Perhaps in response to women's increasing entry into the workforce during the 1970s, conservative policy makers discussed giving greater recognition to child care so that women could develop a "professional consciousness as mothers" and "self-confidence and pride as full-time homemakers." Conservatives also advocated the creation of a "Japanese-style welfare society," whereby the Japanese government could avoid the ever expanding welfare outlays that plagued other industrialized nations by relying on the family (read: women) to care for the young, elderly, and sick. These policy statements certainly reflected ideological conservatism, but they also dovetailed with the massive administrative reforms being undertaken at the time, which were aimed at limiting overall government expenditures.[115]

In short, a new window of opportunity had appeared for Seichō no Ie. A conservative, religious Upper House representative, Murakami Masakuni (who had received backing from Seichō no Ie in the 1980 elections), seized that opportunity in the spring of 1982. For the most part, Murakami's views were similar to those put forward by anti-abortion campaigners in the 1960s and 1970s. He claimed that unborn children were being murdered; that Japan had become a "hotbed of free sex;" that the economic reasons clause of the Eugenic Protection Law was no longer valid because of Japan's economic success; that by weighing life against money, the economic reasons clause contributed to the ideology of giving economic growth top priority; and that doctors still underreported abortions in order to avoid taxes.[116] Murakami and other Seichō no Ie affiliates had been making contacts with conservative pro-lifers in the United States, and perhaps in response to these meetings, Seichō no Ie returned to its original emphasis on pro-life rhetoric.[117] But the nationalist rhetoric did not disappear. For example, Murakami argued in his pamphlet, "Why Must We Hurry to Revise the Eugenic Protection Law? In order to Save the Japanese Race from Extinction," and elsewhere, that abortion would lead to the destruction of the Japanese race, as well as to labor shortages and the disintegration of the family.[118]

On March 15, 1982, Murakami stood up in a House of Councilors Budget Committee meeting and sang the following anti-abortion song, which takes its title, "Keihō dai 212-jō," from the section of the penal code that governs criminal abortion:

> Mama! Mama!
> I am the child who missed being born [umaresokoneta kodomo desu].
> I was thrown out all alone
> Without ever having known yummy milk or a warm breast.
> I am a child who cannot become a person.
>
> Mama! Mama!
> Does my voice reach you?
> It's very cold here
> And I'm very scared all alone here
> I want to be near you
> I am the child who missed being born.[119]

Following this dramatic opening, Murakami launched into a lengthy discussion of his anti-abortion views, interrupting himself periodically to seek opinions and information from Prime Minister Suzuki, Health and Welfare Minister Morishita, the justice minister, and others. Using a tactic seen in the 1960s and 1970s, when anti-abortion campaigners made frequent reference to the "national shame" of Japan's international reputation as an "abortion paradise," Murakami sought to marshal international trends and opinions to bolster his argument. He mentioned that, one month previously, he had attended a morning prayer breakfast in Washington, D.C., with President Reagan, and that Reagan, who sought to ban abortion in the United States, also believed that life began at the moment of conception. He described how Nobel Prize winner Mother Theresa, in a visit to Japan in April 1981 (at the invitation of Seichō no Ie), had lamented that Japan suffered from spiritual poverty in spite of its material wealth, as evidenced by the high incidence of abortion.[120] Murakami went on to speak about the Japanese Constitution's guarantee of life, liberty, and happiness (which is ironic since Murakami, as a right-wing politician, had advocated revising the "American-imposed" postwar Constitution); the rise in teen pregnancies and abortions; and the fact that doctors did not apply the economic reasons clause only to women on public assistance, as dictated by MHW directives from the 1950s. He then asked Prime Minister Suzuki and MHW Minister Morishita what they thought about the advisability of eliminating the economic reasons clause from the Eugenic Protection Law.[121]

Prime Minister Suzuki, whom one informant described as "passive" on the abortion question, replied noncommittally that respect for life was important and that he would like to make efforts to gain a national consensus on the subject.[122] Morishita, on the other hand, was a right-wing colleague of Murakami's from the LDP's Religion and Politics Study Group, chaired by the ultraconservative, Seichō no Ie–backed representative Tamaki (who was newly powerful as head of the Upper House Special Committee on Political, Administrative, and Financial Reform). Hashimoto Ryūtarō and the other "dons" of the health *zoku* (policy tribe) had reportedly arranged for Morishita to be appointed as minister of health and welfare as a countermeasure against JMA political influence.[123] So it is not surprising that Morishita replied emphatically that he thought the economic reasons indication for abortion was no longer valid and that he would like to introduce a draft amendment to the Diet.[124]

The *Asahi shinbun* reported that rank-and-file MHW bureaucrats were annoyed by Morishita's comment; after their bitter experiences with the revision attempt in the 1970s, they wanted nothing to do with drafting another revision.[125] Nevertheless, a month later, the MHW dutifully requested that the Central Eugenic Protection Examination Committee (*Chūō Yūsei Hogo Shinsakai*) study the issue.[126] In the meantime, in public statements and interviews, MHW officials adopted the line that Japan was no longer a country where women's health was harmed for financial reasons and, furthermore, that financial matters exceeded doctors' diagnostic abilities.[127] Thus it seems clear that MHW bureaucrats were the obedient, if unenthusiastic, agents of the politician at the head of their ministry, who in turn acted in accordance with the wishes of a powerful private group.

That powerful private group, Seichō no Ie, had actually grown more influential since the 1970s, at least judging by its membership, which increased from roughly 1.5 million to 3.5 million between 1955 and 1980.[128] After Morishita made his public commitment to revising the Eugenic Protection Law, Seichō no Ie stepped up its lobbying activities. As in the past, the group ran pro-life television advertisements, held pro-life rallies and signature drives (the goal was 10 million signatures), and published pamphlets, as well as a book, entitled *Aren't Fetuses Human Beings? (Taiji wa ningen de wa nai ka)*. In Seichō no Ie newsletters, the group's leader, Taniguchi, criticized the materialism of the postwar era, which he felt contributed to disregard for human life. Seichō no Ie newsletters also contained assaults on what the group viewed as nontraditional female roles, attitudes, and practices, as exemplified by an article entitled "What Is the Cause of These Hard-Boiled 'Mothers'? Revising the Eugenic Protection Law Will Restore Motherhood."[129] On July 13, 1982 (the anniversary of the 1948 passage of the Eugenic Protection Law), Seichō no Ie organized a Citizens' Assembly to Appeal for the Dignity of Life and Save the Lives of Fetuses" (Seimei no songen o uttae, taiji no inochi o sukū kokumin no tsudoi), which was attended by about three hundred conservative politicians and representatives of other religious groups. The assembly resolved the following:

> A fetus is a full human being from the moment of conception, and no matter what anyone says, this precious life cannot be taken away. . . . We hear that some people say that abortion is unavoidable in order to protect [maternal] life, and that they emphasize rights and oppose restrictions on abortion. However, this type of argument ignores the fetus's "right to life."[130]

But the most innovative lobbying technique employed by Seichō no Ie was the mobilization of local assemblies to pass pro-revision resolutions and submit them to the government—a technique that right-wing groups, including Seichō no Ie, had used successfully in other efforts.[131] Thus, from the top down, Seichō no Ie created a "grass-roots demand" for revision. According to several sources, these resolutions were often introduced at the last minute and passed with little debate by local assembly members who did not understand the issues at stake and simply thought that "respect for life" sounded positive.[132]

Although Seichō no Ie enjoyed success at the local level initially, it provoked a counterreaction by women, family planners, and doctors. Nichibo doctors, the Japan Ob-Gyn Association, and the JMA were the first to react to Seichō no Ie's political maneuverings. The Nichibo newsletter criticized the exchange between Murakami and Morishita on March 15 as a "put-up job" (*yaochō bentō*) arranged between political cronies. The newsletter also expressed concern that the revision campaign might succeed this time, in part because it was receiving support from powerful politicians such as Hashimoto Ryūtarō, Kanemaru Shin, and Takeshita Noboru, all of whom were members of a Diet members' group (Seiseiren Kokkai Giin Renmei) affiliated with Seichō no Ie's political action group, Seiseiren (Seichō no Ie Seiji Rengō).[133] In opinions and statements in the ensuing months, Nichibo representatives pointed out that in Romania, where abortion was banned in 1966, the birth rate had not risen as the government had intended; instead, the maternal death rate from illegal abortions had increased sevenfold. They also referred to the 1968 Teheran Human Rights Declaration (and similar resolutions passed during the United Nations' Year of the Woman in 1975), which stated that couples have a fundamental human right to decide how many children to have and when to have them, without outside interference. A more direct and rather heavy-handed JMA opinion paper reminded Health and Welfare Minister Morishita that JMA opposition had killed the 1974 bill to revise the Eugenic Protection Law and demanded that Minister Morishita keep in mind the JMA's ongoing opposition to any revisions and "take proper measures."[134]

Nichibo and local JMA chapters mobilized, along with women's groups, to collect anti-revision signatures and pressure local assemblies to adopt anti-revision resolutions.[135] By the end of the revision battle the following year, the anti-revision forces had beaten Seichō no Ie at its own game: as of May 1983, 1.44 million anti-revision signatures had been collected and 226 anti-revision resolutions passed versus 1 million pro-revision signatures and 129 pro-revision resolutions.[136] Anti-revision activists actually persuaded some of the local assemblies that had passed pro-revision resolutions to overturn them and pass anti-revision resolutions—evidence, according to Iwamoto, of the JMA's political influence.[137] Overall, however, the doctors' groups maintained a relatively low profile politically in 1982–83 compared to their activist stance in the 1970s.[138] Confronted with the ongoing decline in the birth rate, the weakness in leadership at Nichibo and the JMA, Seichō no Ie accusations that abortions were a "cash cow" (*doru bako*) for ob-gyns, and the newfound organization and strength of women's groups, leaders of the medical interest groups perhaps decided it would be best to step into the wings.[139]

Women's groups began reacting to Seichō no Ie's revision campaign a few months after the doctors. There were three "hubs" of women's opposition. The first was the Liaison Conference to Block the Revision of the Eugenic Protection Law (Yūsei Hogo Hō "kaisei" soshi renraku kyōgikai), which was organized by the Family Planning Federation of Japan. This liaison group brought together more established and politically well-connected groups—some of which had also participated in smaller-scale anti-revision efforts in the 1970s—such as the Young Women's Christian Association, the Japan Women's Christian Temperance Union, the Society of Japanese Women Physicians, the Japan Midwives Association, the Japan Nurses Association, and the Federation of Health Centers for Mothers and Children.[140] The second hub of women's anti-revision activism centered around a feminist group of more radical political outsiders, the '82 Liaison Group to Block the Revision of the Eugenic Protection Law ('82 Yūsei Hogo Hō kaiaku soshi renrakukai, or Soshiren).[141] Some members of this group had been active in Ribu Shinjuku Sentā and other feminist groups in the 1970s. However, the majority of women who mobilized to oppose abortion law revision in the 1980s had not been active in the 1970s and many had no prior political experience. They were college students, office workers, and housewives involved in community affairs. Across the nation, these women spontaneously formed five thousand or more small, local, grass-roots groups, which comprised the third, and possibly most important, hub of women's anti-revision activism.[142] For it was the widespread mobilization of these ordinary, nonpolitical women, which had not occurred in the 1970s, that eventually signaled to politicians that female voters would not tolerate a drastic curtailment of their access to abortion. As early as August 1982 a female LDP member wrote in the party newsletter *Jiyū Shinpō* that advocating revision of the Eugenic Protection Law could harm LDP support among women voters at the local level.[143]

In general, most of the grounds on which women opposed the revision were familiar from the 1970s. The slogans of Soshiren and other groups again reflected both maternalist/societal and individualist/feminist thought—though, according to one feminist who had also been active in the 1970s, the individualist strain was ascendant in the 1980s anti-revision movement.[144] In successive written statements (*seimeibun*) in 1982 and 1983, Japan Family Planning Federation president Katō wrote that making the abortion law stricter without creating any policies to help prevent unwanted pregnancies would oppress women, and, echoing the maternalist feminists of the 1970s, she called on the government to create an environment in which families could have and raise children easily. Specifically, Katō called for a program of postpartum and post-abortion family planning education, as well as the approval of the low-dose pill and a new type of IUD. Katō also discussed the possible violation of the constitutional separation of church and state that would result were religious teachings inserted into the legislative process.[145] Anti-revision women chided religious groups and politicians that they should consider the human rights of women who were already alive before speaking of the human rights of fetuses not yet born. They also asserted that it was wrong for the government to intervene in an individual woman's decision about whether to have a child, but at the same time they underscored how little choice couples often had in deciding whether to terminate a pregnancy, because economic realities prevented them from having more than two children.[146] One group's petition cautioned the MHW that eliminating the economic reasons clause from the Eugenic Protection Law would cause "social confusion"—a phrase perhaps meant to evoke the prospect of protesters running amok in the streets of Tokyo.[147]

The primary difference between the 1970s and the 1980s was that the theme of abortion law revision as part of an overarching conservative agenda emerged much more prominently in the 1980s. Anti-revision women pointed to welfare cuts and the LDP's efforts to reinforce sex-segregated roles, with "men at work, women in the home," as well as right-wing attempts to revise the Constitution, and Prime Minister Nakasone Yasuhiro's drive to increase the military budget (Nakasone became prime minister in October 1982).[148] Social commentator Higuchi Keiko said that she felt the national mood was returning to the prewar "give birth and multiply" policy, which had sought to produce workers and soldiers for the Empire. Women from anti-revision groups and pacifist groups asserted that the right-to-life argument against abortion was merely a smoke screen for a return to the prewar and wartime policy of "rich country, strong army" (*fukoku kyōhei*).[149] Members of the opposition parties also suggested that the LDP was moving in the direction of reviving wartime policies.[150] Nakasone's active support for revision and his wife's and sister's close connections with Seichō no Ie served to deepen anti-revisionists' suspicions about the nature of the conservative agenda.[151]

When confronted by women on the Committee to Improve the Women's Problems Planning Promotion Conference, MHW officials denied suggestions that the government was pursuing any kind of "population policy" aimed at increasing the birth rate (although, years later, a former MHW bureau chief conceded that stemming the decline in the birth rate was, in fact, part of the government's motivation for considering the revision).[152] MHW bureaucrats also stonewalled questions about whether the MHW had collected data to substantiate its claims that economic reasons were no longer valid, what family planning measures the MHW had adopted since its 1972–74 attempt to revise the Eugenic Protection Law, and how many women were involved in the revision drafting process at the MHW.[153]

The women's anti-revision campaign gained momentum between the late fall of 1982 and the early winter of 1983. In November, approximately eleven hundred people arrived at a Tokyo church to attend an anti-revision meeting sponsored by one of the liaison groups. Meetings were held on the same day in Kyoto, Osaka, and Hiroshima.[154] In late December three female LDP representatives visited MHW Minister Hayashi (who had replaced Morishita when Nakasone took office) and presented him with an anti-revision petition signed by six female LDP representatives. In January twenty-five female Diet members issued a nonpartisan statement opposing revision of the Eugenic Protection Law.[155] Almost every day Hayashi and other officials at the MHW received protest delegations from the Housewives Federation (Shufuren), the Japan League of Women Voters, the Japan Women Lawyers Association, the Japan Women Doctors Association, and many other groups. In early March about one hundred female students began to conduct a hunger strike in front of the MHW building. The *Asahi shinbun* reported that Minister Hayashi—whose mother was involved in anti-revision activities as a leading member of the National Federation of Regional Women's Organizations (Zenkoku Chiiki Fujin Dantai Renraku Kyōgikai, or Chifuren)—"appears to be surrounded by woman power and appears at a loss."[156]

Early on, Hayashi stated that he felt obligated to follow the policy course established by his predecessor, but he was clearly not enthusiastic about the revision personally. More important, he felt that consensus on the need for a revision was lacking, both within the LDP and within society at large.[157] On the same day in mid-March that two thousand people gathered in a driving rain in Tokyo's Yoyogi Park and resolved to oppose pro-revision forces with their voting power in upcoming local and Upper House elections, Hayashi appeared at the LDP Social Policy Committee to demand that the LDP firm its resolve before he proceeded further, a demand he repeated in the same forum two weeks later.[158] At that time it became clear that pro-revision and anti-revision factions within the LDP were no closer to reaching an agreement, and party leaders had grown increasingly mindful of the possibility that the revision controversy could harm the party's support among women voters.[159] Consequently the head of the committee announced:

> We cannot let the Eugenic Protection Law revision issue become a political issue. In order to prevent the rift that has already engulfed the party down to the local assembly level from deepening, I want to freeze the movements on both sides and discuss the issue quietly in a study group.[160]

This announcement effectively froze intraparty debate on the subject, and a few weeks later local LDP chapters were instructed to cease all revision-related activities.[161] Disillusioned with politics, Seichō no Ie disbanded its political action groups and, shortly thereafter, abandoned its anti-abortion campaign. Two years later Seichō no Ie's elderly leader, Taniguchi Masaharu, died, and membership in the group declined drastically, to about 600,000.[162]

Although there were many similarities between the revision battles of the 1970s and 1980s—the focus on the economic reasons clause and many arguments pro and con—there were also important differences. Nichibo continued to defend the existing abortion law in the 1980s but less actively than in the 1970s. Instead, Seichō no Ie's primary antagonists were women, who organized in larger numbers than in the 1970s and represented a broader range of the social and political spectrum. And whereas the small core of radical, left-wing women's liberation activists in the 1970s were the object of media ridicule, public scorn, and government disregard, by the 1980s, because of developments such as the International Year of the Woman in 1975, the press took women's positions more seriously and presented them more sympathetically.[163] This forced politicians and bureaucrats to take them more seriously as well. Thus women had more power to affect the course of policy making in the 1980s, which is particularly noteworthy considering that they were pursuing a liberal agenda within the context of a larger conservative social policy thrust.

Another important, and related, difference between the two conflicts over revising the Eugenic Protection Law was that the policy-making process in the 1970s was largely contained, revolving around backroom negotiations between two powerful interest groups and the politicians representing them. In the 1980s the revision question became a national, publicly discussed issue, and a much wider array of actors with less established political influence were pivotal in determining the outcome.[164] This demonstrates that, at least in the area of abortion policy making, the Japanese political process became more pluralistic over time.

## POSTSCRIPT: THE REVISION OF THE EUGENIC PROTECTION LAW IN 1996

Not until the 1990s did a revision movement finally succeed, resulting in the passage, on June 18, 1996, of the Bill to Revise a Portion of the Eugenic Protection Law and the subsequent promulgation of the renamed Maternal Protection Law (Botai Hogo Hō) on September 26, 1996. But the character and goals of revisionists in the 1990s were very different from those of revisionists in the past. Whereas revision movements in the 1970s and 1980s were launched by a right-wing religious group with strong political connections and were aimed at restricting access to abortion, the impetus for the 1996 revision came from small, politically weak groups of handicapped activists who sought to eliminate the eugenic content of the law. They were aided in their efforts by the strategic mobilization of "outside pressure" (gaiatsu) at international forums and by broader domestic policy initiatives, namely, the 1993 Standard Law for the Disabled (Shōgaisha Kihon Hō) and the government's 1995 plan calling for "the revisions of terms . . . that foster prejudice and discrimination against the handicapped."[165]

Groups representing the handicapped, the mentally ill, and the mentally retarded have long objected to the Eugenic Protection Law, particularly Article 1, which, until 1996, stated that one of the law's purposes was to prevent the birth of the "eugenically inferior," and Article 4, which provided for the involuntary sterilization of the handicapped and mentally ill (see appendix). Although very few people have actually been sterilized under this provision during the postwar period, particularly after the mid-1950s,[166] handicapped activists argued that the law left open the possibility of Nazi-style mass sterilization of those the state deemed "unfit."[167] And there are some documented cases of abuse. In one of the most egregious cases, a doctor in Miyazaki Prefecture castrated an institutionalized, mentally ill boy in 1965 without his parents' permission, without making the proper application to the prefectural Eugenic Protection Committee, and without observing the Eugenic Protection Law's mandate that sterilization should be performed without removing sexual organs (violations of Articles 2, 4, and 5).[168]

In recent years handicapped activists have protested the practice, particularly in institutions, of routinely performing hysterectomies on mentally retarded young women.[169] These activists are part of a larger movement, which originated in Europe and the United States, that advocates for disabled women's right to bear children and be mothers, and argues that all women have the right to waive prenatal screening and give birth to disabled children if they so choose. Handicapped activists fight against the "new eugenics" because they fear that if prenatal screening becomes the norm, society will fault parents who decide not to abort abnormal fetuses, thus rendering the stigma attached to disability even greater. The movement to protect the handicapped also warns of a brave new world in which prenatal screening for disabilities will lead us down the slippery slope to sex screening, and eventually to screening for characteristics—such as intelligence and hair color—that are now considered within the normal range of variation. Members of the handicapped rights movement want prospective parents to know that not all handicapped people are unhappy; they argue that the problem is not disability in itself but rather the societal discrimination disabled people face, and the insufficiency of public assistance for families with disabled children.

The ideological difficulty this left-wing movement faces is that much of its anti-screening, anti-abortion rhetoric—with its emphasis on the inherent value of life and more nuanced understandings of "quality of life"—resembles that of right-wing and religious pro-life groups. For example, the slogan of the German "cripples' movement" (as its members have labeled it) is "Better alive than normal." However, Waldschmidt acknowledges that "the solution to the eugenic dilemma cannot lie in obliging the conservative anti-abortionists and making it women's 'duty to bear disabled children.' " Saxton seeks to differentiate the disabled activists from "violent anti-choice people" by emphasizing that her movement respects women's abilities to assess their own resources and make reproductive decisions independently.[170]

In Japan, feminist groups and groups representing the handicapped first came into contact with each other in the early 1970s, when both were involved in protests against revising the Eugenic Protection Law.[171] Although many members of the two groups are united by a shared Marxist-socialist vision, differences over the abortion issue have always created an underlying tension. Specifically, many feminists believe that women should be able to get an abortion without a doctor's permission and without specifying why they wish to have the procedure. This would allow women to abort for any reason, including fetal defect—which is not permitted under current law. And as discussed above, handicapped rights activists object to the legalization of such abortions as a violation of handicapped people's right to life.[172]

The movement to eliminate the eugenic content of the Eugenic Protection Law originated among small, left-wing feminist groups and handicapped women's groups in the 1990s, and their strategy was quite interesting.[173] Because they were unable to attract attention to their cause at home, groups such as DPI Josei Shōgaisha Nettowāku and Soshiren went abroad, holding forums and workshops at the 1994 International Conference on Population and Development in Cairo and the 1995 U.N. Women's Conference in Beijing, in order to draw the attention of foreign delegates and journalists to the anachronistic, discriminatory, and coercive aspects of the Eugenic Protection Law.[174] In this way they generated outside pressure on the Japanese government to change the Eugenic Protection Law,[175] even though bureaucrats at the Ministry of Health and Welfare were originally opposed to revising the law, fearing that any move in that direction "might widen the debate" to include abortion.[176] In effect, small, left-wing groups used international embarrassment as a fulcrum to accomplish what they were too weak to bring about through domestic lobbying. They also gained intellectual sustenance and ammunition at the Cairo and Beijing conferences from international feminists' arguments that the often coercive, top-down, demographically targeted family planning approach should be replaced with a more holistic, voluntary, and individual-centered paradigm for women's health and social development.

Once the revision movement started to gain momentum, however, more powerful interest groups joined the fray, seeking to use the "strategic opening" presented by the upcoming revision to fulfill their own agendas. A complicated swirl of competing demands emerged, and, in the process, the groups that had initiated the revision movement lost control of it.[177] Women's groups wanted not only to delete the eugenic component of the law, but also to emphasize women's reproductive health and rights rather than maternal protection, to eliminate the Criminal Abortion Law, to make sterilization and abortion available on demand, and to establish national birth control clinics or counseling centers.[178] The smaller, more left-wing handicapped groups shared both the women's groups' goals,[179] while the larger, more mainstream groups representing the handicapped and mentally ill—such as Nihon Shōgaisha Kyōgikai and Zenkoku Seishin Shōgaisha Kazokukai—lobbied only for the elimination of eugenic provisions.[180] Nichibo and the right-to-life group, Seimei Sonchō no Hi Jikkō Iinkai, agreed that the eugenic provisions should be deleted. But Nichibo also expressed renewed interest in a fetal conditions provision, as well as a provision for selective abortions in cases where fertility treatments result in multiple embryos.[181] Pro-life elements still advocated elimination of the economic reasons criteria for abortion and, more broadly, a ban on abortion.[182]

The Social Policy Committee of the LDP undertook the drafting of the revision bill,[183] since politicians and bureaucrats agreed that the revision should be drafted and sponsored by legislators, given that the Eugenic Protection Law was originally a private member bill.[184] Perhaps because committee members sensed, in the rush of interest group activity, the onset of the "wider debate" on abortion which the bureaucrats had predicted, they hurriedly composed the bill in about a month and a half, based on suggestions from Nichibo, Nihon Shōgaisha Kyōgikai, and Zenkoku Seishin Shōgaisha Kazokukai. The women's groups and the smaller handicapped groups that had provided the impetus for the revision movement were not invited to committee meetings[185]—an indication of the limitations of a *gaiatsu* strategy. For *gaiatsu* is a blunt tool: small, politically weak groups can use it effectively to turn attention to an issue, but when it comes to penetrating the decision-making process, *gaiatsu* is no substitute for the membership, resources, and established political connections of larger groups.[186]

In the end, the revision bill was pushed through the Diet in just three days, and the only change made to the law was the one all groups agreed on: elimination of the eugenic component of the law.[187] This outcome disappointed almost all the groups involved (except the handicapped groups), because it did not accomplish their most cherished goals. But it was the only solution that would allow the politicians and bureaucrats to achieve *their* goal—namely, to prevent interest groups from turning the revision process into a contentious national debate on abortion.

It should be noted, however, that Nichibo, women's groups, and anti-abortion advocates continued to press their agendas in the late 1990s. Groups such as Soshiren, Karada to sei no hōritsu o tsukuru onna no kai, and the Professional Women's Coalition for Sexuality and Health (Sei to kenkō o kangaeru josei senmonka no kai) lobbied for abortion and sterilization on demand—as opposed to physician-authorized. Anti-abortion lawmaker Murakami Masakuni, who was active in attempts to revise the Eugenic Protection Law in the 1980s, again called for the elimination of the economic reasons clause of the renamed Maternal Protection Law in February 2000.[188] And Nichibo submitted a petition to the MHW in February 1997 requesting that the law be revised to permit abortions in cases where several doctors deemed a fetal disease or defect to be "incurable and fatal," and to permit abortions on demand in the first twelve weeks of pregnancy.[189] The ob-gyn group then renewed its lobbying efforts in 1999, seeking to add a provision that would allow selective abortions in instances where fertility treatments produce an excessive number of fetuses; to eliminate spousal consent requirements for adults; and to replace "economic reasons" with "psychological reasons" (abortions after twelve weeks would still be "for cause" under Nichibo's proposed revisions).[190]

A particularly significant development was Nichibo's adoption of feminist and human rights rhetoric in arguing for these revisions: its writings were suddenly liberally sprinkled with references to United Nations treaties and phrases such as "women's right to reproductive self-determination." This evoked mixed reactions from Japanese feminists. On the one hand, they exulted that "we are now in an era when even Nichibo is forced to recognize the right to self-determination." On the other hand, they suspected the doctors of only paying lip service to these concepts and so continued to be critical of many aspects of Nichibo's proposed revisions.[191]

It remains to be seen, however, whether Nichibo or any other group will succeed in revising the law further, as several factors militate against such revisions. First, the Japanese government is no longer exposed to international pressure to revise the abortion law, because the eugenic content of the law has been eliminated. Second, handicapped activists oppose the "fetal conditions" provision[192] and have been successful in blocking a similar provision in the past (although a provision for abortion on demand would bypass the fetal conditions issue, at least during the first twelve weeks). And third, allowing abortion on demand would probably necessitate the abolition of the 1907 Criminal Abortion Law to which the Eugenic Protection Law was designed to provide exceptions—a politically controversial move that politicians would surely try to avoid, since anyone advocating its abolition could be represented by opponents as morally lax and "soft" on abortion. As for on-demand sterilization, that is also potentially controversial, given the grave concern over the declining birth rate in many elite circles.[193]

In the decades of contestation over the Eugenic Protection Law, we see once again that interest groups were the leading actors in abortion policy making. On several occasions, economic, social, and political conditions in Japan presented the right-wing religious group Seichō no Ie with the opportunity to mount anti-abortion campaigns, using politicians beholden to the group. Seichō no Ie's efforts to revise the Eugenic Protection Law in turn mobilized doctors and women to defend the status quo, in which they had vested interests. These groups succeeded in defeating revision legislation for two reasons: They commanded more votes than Seichō no Ie, and the majority of the Japanese public was in favor of legal and easily accessible abortion.[194]

Compared to the 1940s and 1950s, Japanese abortion politics during this period bore a greater resemblance to abortion politics in other industrialized democracies. The political antagonism between traditionalist religious groups and feminist women, seen so often in the United States and Europe in recent decades, also emerged in Japan. Much of these groups' rhetoric cleaved along the familiar lines of pro-life versus women's rights. Meanwhile, following a pattern observed in cross-national studies of abortion policy making in the West, most Japanese politicians sought to abstain from, postpone, and depoliticize policy decisions on abortion, acting only under pressure from their interest group clients.[195] One of the main differences between abortion politics in Japan and other countries, however, is that Japanese politicians have been much more successful at containing conflict over abortion than have their peers abroad, who, in many instances, have been unable to prevent the abortion debate from becoming "virulent, divisive, and protracted."[196] Japanese politicians may owe their success to the premium the Japanese place on harmony and avoidance of conflict,[197] or to the influence of Buddhist thought and practices on the Japanese understanding of abortion.[198] More likely, however, the explanation lies in the comparatively small size of the religious opposition to abortion in Japan and its political weakness vis-à-vis other interested groups in society, particularly medical professionals.

In closing, it should be noted that although the empirical evidence shows that the battles over abortion in the 1970s and 1980s were fought among interest groups, average Japanese people—especially women—often viewed them more as battles between state and society over the state's right to interfere in family life. Moreover, they were ambivalent about whether state interference was desirable. On the one hand, women opposed efforts to limit access to abortion, warning the government that they would not cooperate with the revival of pronatalist policies designed to strengthen the economy. On the other hand, however, women urged the government to "Make a Society Where We Can Have Children, Where We Want to Have Children."

State actors have proven ambivalent as well. On several occasions in the 1960s, 1970s, and 1980s, large numbers of politicians and bureaucrats have been persuaded of the need to revise the Eugenic Protection Law—in part for purely political reasons but also because they genuinely believed that restricting access to abortion would raise the birth rate, which they hoped would help sustain economic growth. On each occasion, however, these actors have subsequently retreated from revision efforts. They have also made few attempts to create the "livable society" Japanese women have demanded, in spite of Japan's ever decreasing birth rate. This is most likely because it would be too expensive and would violate the ideal of family-centered welfare that has dominated Japanese policy-making circles since the prewar period.[199] Perhaps, too, government officials recognize that this is one area in which efforts at "social management"[200] have little chance of success. As family planning activist Katō Shizue reportedly told an MHW official: "No matter what policies the government chooses to pursue, not one woman in Japan would decide to have a child because the government says she should."[201]

## CHAPTER SIX

# Abortion before Birth Control: Japanese Contraception Policy (1945–1960)

UNTIL THE MID-1950s contraception policy in Japan was marked by a series of failed initiatives.[1] This was the case in spite of grave concerns on the part of both the Japanese and the occupying Americans that overpopulation might hinder Japan's economic recovery, and in spite of the view expressed by many Japanese—from Prime Minister Yoshida in statements to the Diet to housewives in letters to friends and relatives—that birth control should be part of the solution to Japan's problems. But neither the government nor private groups provided Japanese women with adequate information about contraception. Instead, as we have seen in the previous two chapters, Japanese women were given relatively easy access to safe, legal abortion, so, by default, abortion became the primary means of "birth control" in the initial postwar period. Indeed, in the 1940s and early 1950s, abortion and contraception were popularly understood to be two different forms of "birth control" (*sanji seigen*): only later did the term come to be used exclusively to refer to contraception, as was intended by the Western family planning advocates who coined the phrase.[2]

This chapter seeks to explain the ten-year delay between legalizing abortion and promoting birth control. The hypothesis presented here is that the "abortion before birth control"[3] policy pattern occurred because no group was willing or able to step forward during the occupation to champion birth control in the same consistent, committed fashion in which the designated doctors' group had championed open access to abortion. For doctors, the incentive to provide expensive abortions was greater than to promote inexpensive birth control methods. Women's groups focused their energies on issues that fit within the "wifeist, maternalist, and guardian-of-the-home" framework—and birth control apparently did not fit.[4] Private family planning organizations, which had the strongest incentive to promote birth control, were ineffective politically because of their left-wing allegiances, and ineffective organizationally because of their leaders' personal and philosophical differences. Thus, during the initial postwar period, family planning groups remained small, factionalized, and local. Occupation officials did not include birth control in their public health programs because of international and domestic (American) political constraints. And lack of consensus within the Japanese government over the appropriateness of a government-sponsored birth control program caused public birth control initiatives to be late, limited in scope and resources, and ultimately unsuccessful.

Rather than contraception policy successes, what is notable about the early postwar period is the speed with which government elites discarded their prewar anti–birth control positions while retaining the prewar notion that individual reproductive decisions should be made within the context of the public good. That is, elites continued to ascribe to a reproductive ideology that centered on the national interest, but they now conceived that interest to be economic rather than imperial. The emphasis on eugenics survived the war, however, and, if anything, was probably stronger after the war. Thus, before and during the war, the patriotic and healthy citizen's duty was to give birth and multiply in order to populate the Empire. After the war, however, the duty of patriotic citizens—especially poor, unhealthy ones—was to contracept and even abort for the sake of Japan's economic and racial improvement.

Almost entirely absent from the elite conception of the purposes of birth control was any notion of the needs and desires of individual women, men, and families. Predictably, then, the popular ideology of birth control was very different from the elite version.[5] Though both groups agreed during the 1940s and 1950s that more Japanese people should use birth control, they disagreed about why birth control should be used, who should use it, and when. The average Japanese woman felt that the purpose of birth control was to improve her health and her family's living standards, and she was completely uninterested in what effect her personal decisions might have on the Japanese economy or the overall quality of the Japanese workforce. Given the differences in the daily concerns of each group, it is not surprising that there was such a gulf between elite and popular understandings of contraception. But the concrete result of this dissonance was that elites were unable to design effective policies to promote birth control because they did not know how—or were unwilling—to appeal to the masses in ways that made sense to them. This, along with the interest group factors mentioned above, combined to delay widespread dissemination of birth control until the mid-1950s, when family planning enjoyed a brief moment of national popularity. During this period the Japanese rapidly adopted contraception. But as the economy improved and the prospect of labor shortages arose, government and business elites turned against birth control once more. This set the stage for the politics of interest groups and the logic of "abortion before birth control" to reappear and dominate the debate over oral contraceptives in the 1960s.

## Contraception Policy and Elite versus Popular Ideologies of Birth Control during the Occupation (1945–1952)

Quite soon after the end of the war, in November 1946, an advisory council (*shingikai*) on population policy, organized by the Japanese government, drew up a plan to "control births and produce a better race." According to this plan, abortion and birth control were to be legalized on a voluntary basis, while sterilization was to be made compulsory for sex criminals and those with incurable infectious diseases.[6] But the plan was not implemented, possibly because of a strongly worded memo from an official in the Supreme Command Allied Powers (SCAP) Public Opinion and Sociological Research Section. The memo labeled the council's call for compulsory sterilizations "a revival of Nazi race theories and practices" and "earnestly recommend[ed] that SCAP forbid the Japanese government from undertaking or even entertaining . . . the official formulation of any plans whatsoever to 'control population,' to 'improve the race,' to eliminate or sterilize 'congenitally unfit,' 'incurable criminals,' or any other similar measure."[7]

With or without SCAP intervention, it is unlikely that the Japanese government would have adopted the council's proposals concerning birth control, for throughout most of the occupation period dissension reigned within the Japanese government over what position to take on contraception, and many subsequent recommendations that the government legalize or promote birth control were ignored. Conservative MHW bureaucrats appear to have been unanimously opposed to birth control for the first several years of the occupation, which is understandable given that the MHW was still staffed by the same men who had engineered the government's pronatalist policies during the war. For many years after the war, these men continued to think in pronatalist terms. For example, the head of the MHW's Population Problems Institute wrote in 1946 that "birth control is the equivalent of race suicide."[8] Between 1945 and 1949 successive health and welfare ministers stated that the government had no intention of officially recognizing birth control, both because of the possible ill effects on public morals, and because " 'once the birth rate decreases, it is difficult to recover.' "[9]

But Japan's defeat gave salience to new definitions of the national interest that focused on economic self-sufficiency. Japan's postwar baby boom peaked in 1947, with birth rates remaining almost as high in 1948 and 1949, while the total population increased by 11 million people between 1945 and 1950 (from 72.2 million to 83.2 million).[10] It was estimated that Japan was capable of producing only 80 percent of its food needs independently.[11] Politicians, perhaps by virtue of their profession, adjusted to the altered terrain more rapidly than bureaucrats did, and their views on birth control changed accordingly. In the spring of 1949 Prime Minister Yoshida announced that, although the ideal policy would be to revitalize the economy and so improve Japan's ability to support its population, "in order to surmount the stringent economic times," and because of popular demand for birth control, "it was necessary for the people themselves to fully understand and practice the principles of birth control."[12]

By and large, politicians and other elites came to support birth control because they believed that overpopulation—commonly referred to as "the population problem" (jinkō mondai)—posed a serious obstacle to economic recovery.

The dominant public discourse on birth control at this time was framed in terms of national economic and political interests. For example, the Upper House Welfare Committee's May 1949 draft report on population policy stated that "unless each family is limited to three children or less, national recovery is impossible. . . . [T]he government must as a matter of state policy lower the birth rate through the diffusion of birth control methods."[13] In a foreshadowing of Chinese population policy several decades later, some went so far as to suggest that a legal limit be placed on the number of children a couple could have, with punitive measures for violators.[14]

The notion of birth control as a means of achieving individual ends rarely arose when elites discussed the subject. Even women politicians focused overwhelmingly on birth control's implications for the population problem and the economy—although it is possible that some of these women had individualist or feminist reasons for supporting birth control and merely employed the dominant nationalist rhetoric because it was the most legitimate way to address the subject in public. However, in a 1949 *Shūkan Asahi* interview with twelve pro–birth control women politicians from across the political spectrum, two did openly mention what today would be considered individualist or feminist concerns. Representative Fukuda, a socialist, said she supported birth control because it would lessen women's physical and spiritual burdens, and Representative Oishi of the Shakaku Party favored birth control because she thought it would liberate women. Both also cited the population problem.[15]

The three female Japan Communist Party representatives framed the issue completely differently. They acknowledged the problem of overpopulation and the need for birth control under current political conditions, but they insisted that if Japan became more democratic, then the problem of overpopulation would be solved and there would be no need for birth control.[16] In the Communists' view, the problem was not that there were more people than existing resources could support, but rather that existing resources were maldistributed—improperly directed toward improving industry rather than the people's standard of living. The Japan Communist Party's position on birth control was that a democratic people's government would "guarantee the stabilization of livelihood and . . . work out a policy for the protection of mothers and children, in order to create conditions under which mothers can have children without needless worry."[17]

On the one hand, the Japan Communist Party was the only party at the time advocating that the state serve the needs of individuals through population policy rather than vice versa—which is to be commended. On the other hand, however, the communist philosophy was based on the utopian notion that it is possible to create an economic, social, and political environment in which birth control and abortion are unnecessary, and women can freely choose to have as many children as they wish. The pronatalist subtext was that under these ideal conditions, women would choose to have more children.[18] But as the history of communist countries such as the Soviet Union demonstrates, women resort to contraception and abortion even when resources are distributed more evenly than in the past, either because resources are still inadequate to support large families, or because most women simply do not want numerous children, regardless of the resources available to them.

More in keeping with the dominant views among Japanese elites were the dire warnings of Dr. Warren Thompson, an American demographer and adviser to SCAP who visited Japan for several months beginning in January 1949. The Japanese press gave heavy coverage to Thompson's pronouncements that birth control was Japan's only hope, and that if Japan failed to curb its population growth, the United States might cut off food assistance, or the country might again fall prey to communism or militarism.[19] Thompson's statements also found their way into the international press, prompting Catholics worldwide to protest what they perceived to be SCAP endorsement of birth control in Japan. This led to hasty denials by General MacArthur, who was considering a run for president of the United States at the time and feared losing the Catholic vote. In a memo to the Catholic Women's Club in Japan, and again in an official letter published in the *Nippon Times*, MacArthur stated that population control was not part of the occupation's mandate, that decisions on the subject were to be made independently by the Japanese government, and that Thompson's statements represented his personal views, not those of the occupation.[20] While many attributed SCAP's formal position of noninvolvement in Japanese population policy to MacArthur's fear of Catholic political power,[21] SCAP was also concerned lest any of its policies be associated with Nazi abuses. Gen. Crawford Sams of the Public Health and Welfare Section wrote that any "attempt to force limitation of families [on the Japanese] . . . would place the U.S. and other occupying powers in the position of justifiably being charged with genocide."[22]

At the same time, however, General Sams and others in SCAP agreed with Dr. Thompson that Japan had the potential to become aggressive again if the country remained overpopulated and undernourished.[23] Americans believed that it was crucial to shrink the population and grow the economy in order to achieve their goal of a politically independent, stable, democratic Japan. Thus the occupying Americans joined elite Japanese in seeing the issue of birth control as an issue of national health—the health of the Japanese economy, the health of Japanese democracy—rather than as an issue of individual women's health or happiness. The following excerpt from a draft of MacArthur's 1949 Birth Control Directive shows how inextricably these concerns were intertwined:

> With the knowledge that an uncontrolled increase in population in Japan would have a serious effect on the economic situation and would mitigate against the accomplishment of the long-range objective of the Occupation to establish a peaceful, demo-

cratic, stable Japan, the Far East Commission, in February 1947, approved the SCAP policy of permitting an industrial level equivalent to that of 1930–34 in order to reinitiate the population shift from rural areas to urban centers and provide an incentive for limitation of the size of families and a decrease in the birth rate.[24]

So while SCAP's official position on birth control was neutral—and SCAP never in fact initiated any kind of birth control program or policy of its own—SCAP "encouraged, facilitated, and abetted Japanese activities to promote birth control," rendering SCAP neutrality "interested" or "protective."[25] At the most basic level, this thesis is supported by the fact that occupation authorities did not block the legalization of contraceptives in Japan, as they had in Germany.[26] Also in keeping with theories of behind-the-scenes American influence on Japanese contraception policy are claims that Dr. Thompson convinced Prime Minister Yoshida and other high-ranking decision makers of the need to endorse birth control officially.[27]

Japanese politicians were quick to realize that overpopulation and birth control had serious implications for Japanese independence. As a defeated, over-populated nation, Japan was the ward of another country, dependent on the United States for the basic survival of its citizens. But if population growth could be checked, the economy could be revived and Japan would be self-sufficient again. This in turn would prove that Japan was ready for political independence—so the reasoning went.[28] Consequently Yoshida made a public statement of support for birth control in 1949, and the population problem was subsequently incorporated into the government's list of top ten priorities.[29]

Ultimately, however, there was more talk about birth control during the occupation than actual policy making. Birth control organizations and their representatives in the Diet made the first serious effort to legalize and promote birth control in 1947, but failed because other lawmakers and SCAP—neither of which yet had the crisis consciousness that they would develop by 1949—were uncooperative. In the fall of 1947 the Japan Birth Control League submitted a petition to the Japanese government in favor of legalizing birth control, and also sent representatives to General Sams of Public Health and Welfare to ask for his help.[30] Then a few months later, as we saw in chapter 4, Representatives Fukuda Masako, Katō Shizue, and Ōta Tenrei introduced their ill-fated Eugenic Protection Law draft (Yūsei Hogo Hōan) to the Diet. The socialists intended for the centerpiece of their law to be Article 16 of the draft bill, which provided for physician-supervised contraception.[31] As we know, however, no birth control provisions were included in the physician-sponsored version of the Eugenic Protection Law that was passed in 1948.[32]

In 1949 Representative Taniguchi Yasaburō (the main sponsor of the 1948 bill) proposed several revisions to the Eugenic Protection Law, the most significant of which was the clause that expanded access to abortion by permitting doctors to perform abortions "if the continuation of pregnancy or childbirth is likely to seriously harm the mother's health for physical or economic reasons." This revision passed the Diet, as did another more obscure proposal to add "disseminat[ing] knowledge and giv[ing] guidance concerning proper methods of contraception" to the duties of Eugenic Marriage Consultation Offices, which had previously been required only to offer information on eugenic marriage, heredity, and eugenic protection. Taniguchi sponsored this revision because, like many other politicians and physicians, he was concerned about overpopulation.[33] But his more serious and lasting concern was that the lower classes be given access to birth control in order to prevent reverse selection. For while overpopulation and its relationship to economic growth was decidedly the dominant theme in the public discourse on birth control, an important secondary theme was the eugenic theory of reverse selection—the notion that the quality of the population would diminish if the well-off and well-educated used birth control, and the poor and uneducated did not.

Like the overpopulation/economic growth argument, the reverse selection argument for birth control gave priority to national goals rather than individual needs or desires. In an unpublished paper written in 1948, "How to Solve Our Population Problem," Taniguchi estimated that there were roughly six million poor and physically unfit women of childbearing age in Japan, and argued that these women should be allowed to use birth control and, if birth control failed, to have abortions. "Healthy wives in respectable homes," on the other hand, were "not to be advised to perform birth control." Taniguchi further cautioned in Diet debate that "special attention" be paid to "virgins and widows lest their sexual morality be degenerated." Unconcerned with whether his plan coincided with the wishes or interests of any of these groups of women, Taniguchi concluded that "the adoption of the foregoing measures . . . will easily preclude a rapid increase in population, but prevent our national qualities from deterioration." Taniguchi also believed that birth control should be practiced in line with increases or decreases in the size of Japan's population—that is, that access to birth control should be restricted if population growth slowed, and vice versa.[34] It must be remembered, however, that this understanding of birth control was not unique to conservative male politicians like Taniguchi: two female Japan Socialist Party politicians, in the interview described earlier, mentioned concerns about reverse selection, and Minshu Jiyū Party representative Nakayama Masa (who, as head of the MHW, became Japan's first woman Cabinet member in 1960) said that, although she was in favor of birth control at that time, if the population decreased in the future as a result of birth control, it should be banned.[35]

Ultimately, however, Taniguchi's birth control revision was unsuccessful in encouraging the poor—or any other group in Japanese society—to use birth control. As explained earlier, the "outdated thinkers" who controlled the MHW were opposed to promoting birth control and avoided population-related issues as much as possible.[36] So although the MHW was unable to block the passage of the Eugenic Protection Law revision, it could and did starve the Eugenic Marriage Consultation Offices (later called Eugenic Protection Consultation Offices, or EPCOs) by withholding budget and staff.[37] Legislators tried to get separate budgets for the EPCOs in 1949 and again in 1952, but both times either MHW or Ministry of Finance (MOF) bureaucrats foiled them, leaving EPCO administrators to scrounge what money they could from other welfare programs, which were also underfunded and had little to spare.[38] The result of the MHW's not-so-benign neglect was that although more than one hundred EPCOs were established, they received an average of little over one birth control case per week per office.[39] With proper funding and staff, the EPCOs could have become a progressive national system of birth control clinics; instead, they became a dead letter. A handful of EPCOs are still in operation today, but, for the most part, EPCOs exist only on paper.[40]

So determined were the bureaucrats at the MHW to block access to contraceptives that in 1948, right before the 1930 Home Ministry Ordinance prohibiting harmful contraceptive devices was due to expire, they tried to replace it with an identical law, the draft Law on Control of Contraceptive Appliances (LCCA). The draft law, like the 1930 ordinance, did not criminalize all contraceptives outright, but instead gave the MHW wide latitude to ban any "contraceptive appliances designated by the minister of welfare as liable to cause harm." It also required anyone who wished to manufacture or sell contraceptives to register with the prefectural governor. And under the LCCA, the maximum punishment for manufacturing or selling prohibited contraceptives was two years in jail—whereas under the prewar ordinance it had only been three months.[41] The intent behind attempting to replace the prewar ordinance with the LCCA was clearly to maintain the public's impression that contraceptives belonged in the same category as narcotics and other controlled substances—that is, a category of devices that the government deemed dangerous and kept under close supervision so they could not be easily bought or sold.

As Dower and others have noted, continuity between pre- and postwar institutions and practices was very common,[42] so the MHW's bid to perpetuate prewar birth control policy was not atypical. But in a strange twist, the MHW's attempt to prevent change actually produced the only meaningful contraception policy innovation of the occupation period. For when the draft LCCA came to the attention of SCAP's Narcotic Control Division, it responded by "instructing" the MHW (SCAP rarely exercised its right to issue direct commands)[43] that the prewar ordinance "should become ineffective" and that "no law will be presented to continue the provisions of the ordinance."[44] SCAP directed that contraceptives instead be brought under the authority of the Pharmaceutical Law, which was passed in April 1948 and went into effect in April 1949. Under the new Pharmaceutical Law, certain contraceptives were added to the official list of drugs and devices that could legally be manufactured, advertised, and sold in Japan.[45] This list of approved contraceptives was essentially the same as it would have been under the proposed LCCA—IUDs, for example, were still forbidden. The difference was that under the Pharmaceutical Law, contraceptives were not placed in a special, stigmatized category of "controlled" substances; rather, they were treated like any other drug that could be advertised and sold openly once approved by the MHW.

It is important to note that contraceptives like condoms and diaphragms were not deemed harmful under the prewar ordinance, and hence technically it had never been illegal to manufacture or sell them before or during the war (although it was illegal to advertise them as contraceptives). Nevertheless they were widely *believed* to be illegal. Consequently it was also widely believed that the Pharmaceutical Law "legalized" contraceptives, and this perceived legalization of contraceptives had immediate results. The number of contraceptive device manufacturers increased from seven to seventy-five in the six months after the Pharmaceutical Law went into effect,[46] and sales rose, too: one manufacturer reported a ninefold increase in sales between 1948 and 1949; another reported a fortyfold increase.[47] In November 1949 a group of twenty rubber manufacturers and eighty-seven wholesalers and retailers formed the Japan Contraceptive Device Association, whose stated purpose was to stimulate research on birth control and to promote it.[48] Despite all this early promise, however, the contraceptives industry was plagued by a host of problems. One problem was that the raw materials for contraceptives (primarily spermicidal chemicals and rubber for condoms and diaphragms) were expensive for manufacturers to buy, so supply was limited and consumers were charged high prices. In 1955, a year's supply of birth control cost more than an abortion, which was about five dollars. In addition, government oversight was minimal, leading to poor quality control and an influx of ineffective and dangerous products.[49] These factors undoubtedly made contraceptives seem like an expensive, unreliable, and possibly unsafe gamble compared to the relative cheapness, certainty, and safety of an induced abortion.

Nevertheless, the passage of the Pharmaceutical Law and Dr. Thompson's visit, both in the spring of 1949, generated a great deal of private discussion about birth control. So SCAP's Civil Censorship Detachment, which monitored Japanese public opinion, wrote a report in May 1949 analyzing seven hundred intercepted letters in which the subject of birth control was mentioned. More than half the letters were from housewives. The report is invaluable because it is one of very few sources that documents the views of average people—women in particular—rather than the elite. Unlike elites, who were preoccupied with birth control's usefulness in achieving national goals, pro–birth control letter writers focused almost exclusively on the effects that they hoped birth control would have on their health or their family's standard of living. The censors categorized 81 percent of correspondents as pro–birth control, 7 percent as anti–birth control, and the rest undecided.[50] According to the report, housewives

> advise each other to use contraceptives or to see a doctor about an abortion and explain how children cut into the mother's energy at the expense of her health as well as into the family purse. Many bemoan the fact that they didn't know about birth control sooner.[51]

Nor were the contradictions in elite positions on birth control lost on these correspondents, one of whom found it " 'ironical that the wartime slogan "increase our population" has now been replaced by the national policy of birth control.' "[52] Although the MHW was at pains to dissociate itself from its wartime policies—instructing nurses and midwives, for example, to tell patients that government-sponsored family planning programs were intended to promote maternal and child health, not population control—the average person did not believe that the bureaucrats had changed.[53] One newspaper's editorial announced:

> There is a limit to the role played by the State in respect to birth control . . . [although] in former days, the people did not entertain any doubts about using the term "human resources." Extremely speaking, human beings were regarded as materials.[54]

Another admonished:

> Despite strict criticism of past mistakes, there is a tendency to force the people to follow the Government's opinions again. Some doctors advocate having "two children per couple." [But] it is the right of the people to adopt or reject birth control of their own free will. The Government's duty is to enlighten the people and provide them with conveniences to establish birth control.[55]

The anti–birth control views intercepted by SCAP echoed those voiced by the elite. Of those opposed to birth control, some wrote that contraception went against God or nature, others mentioned concerns about reverse selection, and one correspondent feared that if birth control were legalized, "it [might] bring in an 'age of sexual anarchy as seen among American students.' " They also expressed traditional sentiments such as "children ensure a comfortable old age" and " 'children are poor men's riches.' " Of those who opposed birth control in the *Jiji* survey, 41 percent did so for ideological or religious reasons, 31 percent for social or national reasons (e.g., the need for manpower), 19 percent for moral reasons, and 9 percent for reasons of health. Midwives, who numbered sixty thousand nationally at the time, were opposed to birth control because they feared that the spread of birth control would leave midwives with fewer babies to deliver. The censorship report tells us that "midwives foresee a gloomy future if birth control is the coming thing, although one hopefully remarks that she does not 'think it will prevail easily in Japan.' "[56] This was wishful thinking on her part, however, since surveys conducted by the MHW and *Mainichi shinbun* in 1949 and 1950 showed that roughly 20–25 percent of Japanese were already practicing some form of contraception, and among those who were not yet practicing contraception, 56 percent said they would like to do so in the future. Forty-one percent thought the government should "provide facilities and education to avoid prolificacy [sic]."[57]

In this atmosphere of heightened interest in birth control, Prime Minister Yoshida announced, in April 1949, that he was pro–birth control. In the same month the Cabinet established a second Population Problems Advisory Council, which, in November 1949, submitted the final draft of its recommendations. The council was organized not only because of concern over the economy, but also out of concern for the rapidly increasing abortion rate and the health dangers abortion posed for women.[58] It recommended that, in the ongoing effort to curb overpopulation, birth control should be emphasized over abortion.[59] Specifically the council called for: (1) an increase in the number of personnel at all government health centers and EPCOs, and education concerning family planning and eugenic protection at all national health facilities; (2) the establishment of a separate government agency to be in charge of family planning and eugenic protection projects; and (3) a government program to give birth control information and free birth control to the poor.[60] The council members shared Taniguchi's concerns about reverse selection, as well as the common elite view that birth control and birth control users were tools to be used for solving national problems. The council wrote:

> Under the existing conditions of this country, what is the interest of the nation as a whole should also be a concern of individual families. . . . The national demand to check population growth should find support in the idea of voluntary family planning. . . . [But] under certain circumstances [in the future], increased childbirths may be demanded.[61]

The Population Problems Advisory Council did not focus exclusively on birth control, however. In fact, the council concluded that birth control could not provide an adequate solution to the problem of overpopulation in the short term, and strongly urged the government to direct its energy toward rehabilitating domestic industry—shifting the emphasis from light to heavy industry—and restoring foreign trade.[62] In both pre- and postwar discussions of population policy, the Japanese elite almost uniformly favored industrialization over birth control.[63] But ironically (given the subsequent success of exactly those policies mentioned above), Thompson and others did not believe that industrialization was a viable option for Japan, comparing Japan's postwar prospects with respect to population, natural resources, and productive capacity to those of China and India.[64] A *Shin yūkan* editorial at the time glumly concluded that, although the problem of overpopulation theoretically could be solved through trade and industrialization, "even optimists cannot give any conclusive evidence that there will be a rapid growth of trade and industry in defeated Japan."[65]

But the government did not adopt the council's recommendations on birth control, despite the generally grim outlook for industrial recovery, and despite the MHW's prior statements that its birth control policy would "depend in large measure" on the recommendations of the council.[66] One council member later wrote that there was opposition from within the government and from Diet members representing poor, rural districts who felt the council's plan unfairly targeted their constituents.[67] The council was dissolved in March 1950, and the momentum generated by Dr. Thompson's visit and the passage of the Pharmaceutical Law dissipated.

The momentum did not disappear altogether though, for anxiety over the abortion rate was growing—at least among bureaucrats at the MHW. As the number of reported abortions alone quadrupled between 1949 and 1952,[68] MHW officials came to realize that, by letting birth control initiatives die from neglect, they were contributing to the rise in abortions.[69] On being shown the most recent abortion statistics in 1951, Health and Welfare Minister Hashimoto Ryūgo reportedly shouted: "This is terrible! The Ministry has been careless to neglect this [the abortion situation]."[70] Soon after, Hashimoto announced a Cabinet resolution that information on birth control should be disseminated in an effort to counteract the ill effects of abortion on maternal health.[71] The MHW then drew up a Plan to Promote Conception Control and in June 1952 sent it out to the prefectural governments to be implemented. The plan called once again for the improvement of EPCOs, which was to be accomplished mainly by having midwives and nurses provide group and individual birth control counseling.[72] The introduction of this government-sponsored plan to promote birth control marked the turning point in the MHW's gradual drift away from its wartime anti–birth control position.

The MHW must have coordinated in advance with Representative Taniguchi, the legislative guardian of the Eugenic Protection Law, because in May 1952 Taniguchi sponsored revisions to the Eugenic Protection Law that made it possible for the MHW plan to be implemented. Article 21 mandated the establishment of EPCOs in all prefectures and cities with public health centers; further, Article 15 of the Eugenic Protection Law made it legal for midwives, public health nurses, and nurses to provide birth control counseling, which had previously been restricted to physicians. The midwives and nurses were required to pass a special course in order to receive the prefectural governor's designation as birth control counselors. Three years later, Taniguchi, along with the president of the Midwives Association, Diet member Yokoyama Fuku, sponsored another revision to the Eugenic Protection Law that made it legal for midwives and nurses to sell birth control drugs (presumably spermicides) and devices.[73] It is interesting that all the birth control revisions to the Eugenic

Protection Law were sponsored by Representative Taniguchi, given that the designated abortion providers whom Taniguchi represented as president of Nichibo made little effort to promote birth control in their medical practices.[74] There are two possible explanations for this apparent contradiction. One possibility is that Taniguchi was genuinely interested in promoting birth control but was unable to gain the support of rank-and-file Nichibo members. The other is that Taniguchi had the political savvy to take a pro–birth control position so he could ward off accusations—should they arise—that Nichibo was a group of self-interested abortion mongers. After all, the 1952 birth control revisions went through concurrently with the revision that transferred the power to authorize abortions from Eugenic Protection Committees to individual doctors—a revision that significantly increased access to abortion.

But Taniguchi's birth control revisions again proved fruitless.[75] The 1952 birth control initiative failed to produce the desired results for the same reason—namely, budgetary inadequacy—that had doomed the 1949 attempt to transform EPCOs into birth control clinics. This time it was not the MHW that starved the program: the MHW, after all, had launched it. Rather, the MOF would not give the MHW the budget it requested.[76] According to one estimate, the government's 1952 family planning budget provided for only ¥2 (less than 1¢) per woman of childbearing age.[77] In addition to funding problems, the MHW birth control program also faced a lack of support from all the groups most critical to its success. Birth control field workers—midwives for the most part—lost interest in the program when it became clear that they would receive no payment or only token payment from the government and the people they counseled. As noted in chapter 4, ob-gyns did not cooperate because there was little money to be made by providing birth control compared to the comfortable income furnished by delivering babies and performing abortions. Finally, many of the relevant groups were distrustful of government involvement in promoting birth control.[78] Some leaders of the birth control movement had been jailed or ostracized during the war and were suspicious of the government's attempts to co-opt a movement it had so recently suppressed. Consequently, they did not respond warmly to MHW overtures at administrative guidance. The following excerpt from the government's 1952 Plan to Promote Conception Control is an example of the government's rather heavy-handed approach:

> In carrying out this plan proper cooperation and promotion by . . . voluntary organizations concerned is expected. . . . The MHW will cooperate in the establishment and promotion of voluntary organizations concerned with conception control promotion, at the same time giving guidance to those already established.[79]

An MHW bureaucrat in charge of family planning at the time recalls that at a gathering of welfare commissioners someone shouted at him, " 'During the war you called for us to Give Birth and Multiply [umeyo fuyaseyo], so what's all this now about Don't Give Birth, Don't Multiply [*umu na fuyasu na*]?' "[80] At an MHW-sponsored gathering of health center chiefs in August 1952, the MHW was roundly criticized for its unrealistic thinking on the subject of birth control, and one speaker gave a laundry list of twenty-one reasons why the MHW's proposed birth control program would fail.[81]

Looking back on the occupation period, we see that although there was a great deal of talk about overpopulation and birth control, and although the concern about these subjects appeared genuine, very little happened in terms of educating the Japanese about contraception or making contraceptives widely available. While different political players made intermittent efforts to promote birth control, in the absence of one consistent, committed, well-organized birth control advocate, opposition to birth control won the day, allowing abortion to eclipse contraception. That private family planning organizations were unable to combine forces and provide the necessary advocacy is perhaps the most puzzling of the many events that did not occur during this time. For there were quite a few small birth control groups organized during the 1940s, mostly by people who had been active in the prewar birth control movement.[82] But as Ōta and others point out, many factors mitigated against unification. There were personal struggles for leadership of the birth control movement. There were also philosophical differences among the family planning groups, such as whether the birth control movement's raison d'être should be solving national population problems or protecting individual women's health; whether abortion should be accepted or rejected; whether to promote diaphragms, condoms, or IUDs; and whether the movement should get involved in commercial ventures like selling contraceptives.[83] Some of these subjects remained volatile even after the groups were finally consolidated in 1954. At a national birth control conference in 1958 there was a heated debate over whether the Eugenic Protection Law's abortion provisions should be revised. The head of the Japan Family Planning Association (JFPA) recalls in his memoirs that in 1965 another prominent birth control activist severely criticized the JFPA for its "commercialism," because it relied heavily on sales of contraceptives for income.[84]

## THE FAMILY PLANNING MOVEMENT IN THE 1950s

By the mid-1950s the government and family planning groups were still worried about overpopulation,[85] but they were also increasingly alarmed by the soaring abortion rate. Out of this mutual concern about overpopulation and abortion there arose a merger of private and public initiative in the sphere of birth control policy. The government, realizing that it could not effectively promote birth control by itself, given its failures in the early 1950s, decided to delegate most of the implementation of birth control policy to private groups.[86] This alliance finally accomplished what had previously eluded birth control advocates and policy makers alike: between 1952 and 1961 the percentage of current and once users of birth control rose from 40 percent to 68 percent. Subsequently the percentage of contraceptors continued to rise, leveling off in the early 1980s at around 80 percent.[87] The birth rate also dropped precipitously during this period—faster than it has ever dropped in any country in recorded history—decreasing by half between 1947 and 1957 (see Table 1.1).[88]

In 1954 the government established a permanent Population Problems Advisory Council, which still exists today. Later that year the council presented its conclusions, restating the 1949 council's recommendation that a government family planning agency be established, as well as a program to provide the poor with birth control. The report also recommended that family planning counselors be paid by the government, that efforts be made to gain the cooperation of industry in promoting birth control, and that doctors be obligated to give birth control counseling to abortion patients.[89] The MHW followed the council's advice to the extent of creating a program to give poor women free contraceptives. The government also agreed to pay midwives operating out of EPCOs a nominal fee for birth control counseling (¥100 per visit).[90] Amemiya finds that government-sponsored family planning programs were quite successful in the rural areas where such programs were concentrated,[91] but, overall, the government's efforts to promote family planning remained plagued by difficulties. Government programs did not reach the fast-expanding urban working population; birth control counselors were still underpaid; and case workers had trouble determining who qualified for the government's free contraceptives program.[92] The government's family planning budget continued to be insufficient, again because the MOF refused to meet the MHW's budget requests.[93] Further, the budget that did exist was apparently used ineffectively. For example, half the government's ¥58 million ($161,000, at $1 = ¥360) birth control budget for 1956 was not spent—and in some prefectures, like Miyazaki and Oita, not one *sen* was spent—because the national government gave local governments only one-third of the total funds provided for in the budget, and many local governments were unable to raise the remaining two-thirds as required. The national government funds could not be used without the matching local government funds, leading local governments to label the whole family planning program a "white elephant."[94]

The MHW had more success with an informal birth control initiative it began to pursue around the same time it launched the official program described above. Early in 1954 Hinoue Sadao and his boss, Ozawa Tatsuo, then a section chief in the MHW's Public Health Bureau,[95] asked a friend of Hinoue's if he would establish a private organization to promote birth control. The friend was Kunii Chōjirō, who had founded a successful parasite control movement during the occupation, but who had no expertise in the field of family planning. Hinoue and Ozawa felt compelled to turn to an outsider because the MHW had not gotten the cooperation it requested from established birth control activists during the government's abortive 1952 birth control campaign. MHW bureaucrats must have come to realize that the MHW's pronatalist wartime policies had diminished the ministry's credibility and, in turn, its ability to implement contraception policy directly, for Hinoue and Ozawa informed Kunii that " 'on such a fundamental and private matter [as birth control], the government basically should not force its views upon the people.' " They went on to say, " 'We at the MHW will support you as much as possible. Would you start this voluntary organization?' "[96]

Kunii agreed. He had achieved his goals in the parasite control movement and was eager to tackle this new problem. So in 1954 Kunii formed what came to be known as the Japan Family Planning Association, or JFPA. Apparently none of the parties involved appreciated the irony of government officials asking a private individual to start a "voluntary" organization to carry out the government's agenda because, as we saw in chapter 2, this type of corporatist cooperation between actors from the public and private sectors is not uncommon in Japan. In fact, however, the JFPA was, and is, a truly private organization, even though it was established at the MHW's instigation and has always retained close ties with the ministry. The MHW has provided the JFPA with "moral support," information, and access to government officials over the years, but no funding.[97] Instead, from quite early on the JFPA supported itself by selling and distributing contraceptive supplies (primarily condoms) and teaching materials. The JFPA also started publishing a newsletter, *Kazoku keikaku* (the name was changed to *Kazoku to kenkō* in the 1980s), which is an important source of information on the postwar family planning movement in Japan. But much of the JFPA's income derives from sales.[98]

At the same time that Kunii was forming his birth control group, preexisting groups were also coming together to promote family planning more effectively. In 1953 a visiting U.S. family planning activist urged the leaders of Japan's factionalized birth control groups to join forces and create a national federation of family planning groups, which would in turn be a member organization of the International Planned Parenthood Federation based in London. This outside encouragement seems to have provided the necessary impetus to overcome previous barriers to unification, and in 1954 the Family Planning Federation of Japan (FPFJ) was formed. The FPFJ was established independent of MHW influence and thus might be considered more truly "voluntary" in origin than the JFPA. But the FPFJ soon developed close ties with both the MHW and the JFPA, and, in fact, the two family planning groups now share office space in Tokyo. The FPFJ disseminates information on family planning, conducts research, and engages in fund-raising. The FPFJ also offers the training courses that midwives and nurses are required by law to complete if they wish to receive official permission to provide contraceptive counseling and sell contraceptive devices.[99]

The FPFJ's first act as a newly formed organization was to host the Fifth International Conference on Planned Parenthood in Tokyo in 1955. The theme of the conference was "Overpopulation and Family Planning."[100] This conference was one of the first international gatherings to be held in Japan since Japan had regained independence, and, consequently, ranking politicians and the media paid it a great deal of attention. In addition to the 101 foreign delegates, there were 471 Japanese participants, including the prime minister, the speakers of both Houses of the Diet, the minister of health and welfare, the chairman of the Japan Socialist Party, and the governor of Tokyo.[101] The conference was a turning point for the family planning movement in Japan, for with the recognition it received, the movement gained a legitimacy and momentum it had never had before. A JFPA survey of 573 prominent people in October of the same year showed that 93 percent were either pro–birth control or conditionally pro–birth control.[102] Katō Shizue writes that, although the MHW had looked coldly on the private family planning movement until the mid-1950s (*shiroi me de miru*), after that time the two entered into closer collaboration.[103] In February 1956 MHW officials met with representatives of a host of private organizations—including the JFPA, the FPFJ, the Maternal Protection Association, the Federation of Local Women's Groups (Chiiki Fujin Dantai Rengōkai), the Japan Nurses Association, the Japan Midwives Association, and the Housewives Federation (Shufu Rengōkai)—to ask for their cooperation in the family planning movement. This time the request was taken up enthusiastically. The Housewives Federation, Japan's largest mainstream women's organization at the time, added a family planning consultation room to its Housewives' Hall (Shufu Kaikan) in Tokyo. Four candidates were elected on family planning platforms in the 1956 Upper House elections, including the head of the JFPA and Katō Shizue, who received the largest number of votes in the election (750,000).[104]

Probably the most far-reaching family planning program during this time was an employer-sponsored campaign with some government funding that targeted employees of large companies.[105] This campaign was part of the New Life movement (*Shin seikatsu undō*), which was a diverse collection of public and private initiatives aimed at improving and modernizing daily life, strengthening community ties, and growing the economy. In addition to family planning, the New Life movement included campaigns for health and sanitation, mutual assistance, public morality, attention to time, elimination of wastefulness, and ways to "rationalize family life" through changes in diet, clothing, shelter, household accounts, savings, and social customs.[106]

The Foundation Institute for Research on Population Problems launched the family planning New Life movement in 1953, seeking to promote family planning "on the basis of modern humanitarianism and rationalism."[107] It was the rationalism rather than the humanitarianism that appealed to the many companies that ultimately decided to participate: proponents of the New Life movement claimed that educating workers about birth control would save employers money on family allowances and health costs—and some evidence suggests that it did.[108] Nippon Kōkan, an iron works company with more than 20,000 employees, was the first to join the family planning campaign in 1953; Japan National Railways, with 460,000 employees, joined in 1956; and, by 1958, eighty-two companies—including other large companies such as Toyota—had adopted birth control programs, covering an estimated 1.24 million people.[109] The fact that many workers lived in company housing made it easier to disseminate information on family planning. Employees' wives were asked to organize themselves into small units, and midwives were hired to give them several sessions of practical instruction on different methods of contraception. To bring home the seriousness of the overpopulation problem, family planning instructors showed films such as *The Four Islands [of Japan] Are Sinking*.[110] Some companies, such as Toshiba, bought condoms in bulk and sold them to employees' wives at one-third to one-fifth the retail price.[111]

Union members did initially express reservations about the New Life movement, claiming that corporate family planning projects and other campaigns constituted unwarranted interference in employees' private lives and too closely resembled prewar and wartime austerity programs; that such programs posed unfair competition to similar, "autonomous" (usually union-sponsored) programs; and that they represented a disguised move to reduce workers' family allowances and otherwise "rationalize family life" to conform with the company's needs, without improving workers' poor living standards.[112] Field workers in charge of both government- and corporate-sponsored programs recall that at first they made slow progress attracting people to the movement. Some employees' wives turned birth control counselors away at the door and told them to mind their own business; some angry husbands screamed that if their wives were given contraceptives, they would end up prostituting themselves by the banks of nearby rivers. But by the end of the 1950s most employees and their wives had been won over and enthusiastically embraced the family planning programs and other programs of the New Life movement. The majority of employee households became members.[113] Although corporations clearly adopted New Life movement programs for self-serving reasons, it should be remembered that many of the women and men whom they targeted had reasons of their own to seek control over their reproductive lives, and were undoubtedly pleased to have their employers sanction a practice that had previously been stigmatized. Amemiya suggests that the elite strategy of collapsing family goals into national and corporate economic goals "helped individuals to justify their own actions . . . in terms of an act affecting a community beyond their individual private sphere."[114] Whereas most Americans today would certainly view the New Life movement family planning campaign as a paternalistic intrusion into workers' (and their spouses') private lives, such views were in the minority in Japan. Indeed, the notion that birth control should be solely an individual's or family's concern was considered atavistic at the time. In a 1958 paper the director of the MHW's Institute for Population Problems commented that "there is the *unprogressive* view among some company executives that since family planning is a personal, private matter, companies need not get involved" (emphasis added).[115]

But industry's interest in family planning proved fickle. By 1959–60 the economy was growing rapidly, the unemployment rate had gone down, birth control use was on the increase,[116] and labor shortages suddenly loomed on the horizon. As we saw in chapter 5, business leaders started to speak out against family planning,[117] fearing that declining birth rates and increasing birth control use would lead to continual labor shortages, higher pay for workers, and less profit for employers. Government support for the family planning movement also began to wane as many politicians in the ruling Liberal Democratic Party came to see it as being against the national—and the party—interest. The LDP counted business interests among its chief constituents and owed its long control over the government not only to continued economic growth but also in large measure to support from these interests.[118] In the early to mid-1960s the LDP joined the chorus of voices insisting that low birth rates would hinder economic growth. It was also around this time that the government's family planning budget—never large to begin with—began to stagnate, soon to disappear into obscurity. The short period in which elite Japanese had endorsed birth control in order to spare the economy the burden of excess people came to an end less than twenty years after it had begun.[119]

The family planning movement in the 1950s sprang from two separate streams of state and societal initiative, and although close ties developed between the two, the government delegated most of the responsibility for devising and implementing contraception policy to the private sector. This delegation of authority on the government's part can be interpreted in two ways—either as a concession made from weakness or one made from strength. In other words, the Japanese government either had so little capacity in this sphere of policy that it was forced to yield control over contraception to groups in civil society, or, finding it burdensome to promote birth control, the government strategically ceded all but the most vital elements of control. There is evidence to support both conclusions. For example, the fact that the government tried and failed to carry out its own program to promote birth control in 1952 suggests that it was a concession made from weakness. That the MHW was consistently unable to wrest budgetary commitments for family planning from the Finance Ministry also suggests weakness. On the other hand, it was at the initiative of MHW officials that one of the main private family planning organizations was established. Furthermore, the government retained control over a very crucial aspect of contraception policy making: that is, control over the approval process for contraceptive drugs and devices like the pill and IUD.

Perhaps the most accurate but least satisfying conclusion is that the MHW delegated its authority neither entirely from strength nor weakness. Rather, a mutually beneficial corporatist arrangement seemed to arise between state and societal groups. The MHW made a strategic virtue of necessity and ceded a great deal of control over policy to private groups but, at the same time, shed almost all budgetary and administrative responsibilities. The private family planning groups, for their part, may have lost some autonomy by establishing close ties with the MHW, but in doing so they gained legitimacy and access to policy-making channels. It is important to remember, however, that although the MHW has generally supported the policy line pursued by these groups, they are by no means creatures of the MHW: the flow of information and initiative goes both ways. Ozawa and Hinoue at the MHW may have asked Kunii to form the JFPA but, subsequently, ideas that grew out of Kunii's discussion groups were incorporated into MHW policy.[120] And private family planning organizations are not so dependent on the MHW that they have felt obligated to stifle objections to the ministry's policy decisions. As we shall see in the next chapter, the JFPA and FPFJ have openly criticized the MHW's oral contraceptive policy for various reasons over the last thirty years, whereas pharmaceutical companies—which are subject to MHW regulatory power over every drug they market or wish to market—are less autonomous and thus far more circumspect about voicing criticism of MHW policy.

## CHAPTER SEVEN

# The Politics of the Pill (1955–2000)

UNTIL THE PILL was finally approved in 1999, the ban on oral contraceptives was the defining characteristic of Japan's conservative contraception policy for almost four decades. Just as the combination of a unique historical situation and interest group activity generated Japan's progressive abortion policy in the late 1940s, so, too, did a particular configuration of events and interest groups combine to produce the pill ban in the mid-1960s. In the beginning, anti-pill groups shaped policy on the pill with their efforts to persuade the Ministry of Health and Welfare that their interests coincided with the national interest. Over the next thirty years these groups and new groups then tried—with varying degrees of success—to reshape policy to conform with their changing interests.

Thus the politics of the pill in Japan has been the politics of interest groups. But the politics of the pill has also been merged with—and at times subsumed by—the politics of abortion. For in Japan, unlike most other countries, abortion was legalized and made readily available before the pill was invented. Consequently, discussions of the pill—both pro and con—have often been framed in terms of the pill's possible effects on abortion rates and abortion rights. The pill has also been considered frequently in the context of what effect it might have on national interests such as the birth rate, public health, and public morals. And starting in the 1970s, feminist notions of women's reproductive rights and health began to enter the discourse on the pill.

It should be clear, then, that the question of pill approval in Japan has involved far more than assessments of clinical data. No drug anywhere has been ensnared for as many different reasons or for as long as the pill has in Japan. But political battles over the pill have not absorbed the Japanese public in the way that the abortion wars have absorbed Americans. Instead, what follows is a mostly behind-the-scenes chronicle of how doctors, midwives, family planners, pharmacists, women's groups, and pharmaceutical companies have vied with one another and the state in an effort to mold national reproductive patterns to suit their often conflicting agendas.

Japan's policy on the pill presents an intriguing puzzle. Why did Japan follow such a dramatically different course than that of the vast majority of other countries? Coleman—one of very few academics to address this issue—offers the following explanation for the pill ban.[1] He maintains that the MHW did not approve oral contraceptives, first, because of scares over the ill effects of drugs like Thalidomide and Quinoform in the 1960s; second, because of concerns that the pill might be sold illegally over the counter and misused; third, because of fears that pill use might corrupt the sexual mores of young people, especially women; and fourth, and most important, because the politically powerful obstetrician-gynecologists of the designated abortion providers group, Nihon Bosei Hogo Sanfujinkai Kai, opposed approval.[2] According to Coleman, although Nichibo's official position was that the pill was medically unsafe, its real concern was that pill use might lower the demand for abortions, a mainstay of Nichibo members' incomes.[3] Coleman also points out that family planning organizations and midwives had little incentive to promote the pill, since they derived most of their income from the sales of condoms and diaphragms, whereas the pill, if approved, could only be prescribed and sold by doctors and pharmacists.[4]

Coleman conducted his research in the mid- to late 1970s, so he does not cover developments from the mid-1980s on, but for the period from the 1960s to the early 1970s, Coleman's explanation of the Japanese pill ban is quite accurate. The MHW was, in fact, heavily influenced by opposition from ob-gyn groups, midwives, and family planning groups in the 1960s. And these groups did convey to the MHW concerns over the possibility of prescription drug abuse, sexual disorder, and potential side effects—while keeping their more self-interested concerns to themselves. The problem with Coleman's research is that he does not trace the politics of the pill systematically. For example, he does not explore in any depth the relationship between the Eugenic Protection Law and the interests it spawned, on the one hand, and contraception policy making, on the other. Nor does he explore the initial debate over the pill in the early 1960s, which in many ways established the vocabulary and set the parameters for all subsequent debates over the pill up to the present. Furthermore, he does not discuss changes that began to occur in the 1970s— the hardening of the MHW's anti-pill position, the softening of the doctors' and family planners' anti-pill stance, and the disagreements within the Japanese feminist community over whether the pill should be approved. Even though Coleman's own research pointed in the direction of macrolevel, political factors as an explanation for the idiosyncrasies of abortion and contraception policy in Japan, Coleman chose instead to emphasize microlevel cultural and behavioral factors. In other words, although Coleman started off with a discussion of how various groups helped to create and perpetuate certain patterns of policy and behavior in the process of pursuing their own interests, he ultimately organized his book around surveys and questionnaires on contraceptive usage, abortion rates, conjugal roles, attitudes toward sexuality, and women's status. Thus Coleman's painting of the politics of the pill in the 1960s and 1970s was not sufficiently nuanced, leaving him unable to foresee the marked changes that would occur in the oral contraception drama as it stretched on into the 1980s and 1990s.

For in the mid-1980s, Nichibo, the Japan Association of Obstetricians and Gynecologists, the Japan Family Planning Association, and the Family Planning Federation of Japan all reversed their former positions and petitioned the MHW to allow clinical testing on the low-dose pill.[5] Meanwhile feminist groups, female social commentators, midwives, and Japanese women generally remained suspicious of oral contraceptives and only came to advocate approval grudgingly in the mid-1990s. So while Coleman predicted that the impetus for change would probably arise out of the lobbying efforts of grassroots women's groups rather than elite doctors' groups or family planning organizations, in fact, just the reverse occurred.[6]

Thus it is clear that the reasons for the pill ban have changed over time. From the mid-1980s on, the ban can no longer be attributed to the obstructiveness or undue influence of medical groups or family planners, since these very groups led the fight for approval. Therefore the tasks of this chapter are several: to clarify the reasons for the pill ban in the 1960s and 1970s; to seek an explanation for the pill ban and subsequent approval in the 1980s and 1990s; and to explain why the positions of the various groups involved in the pill debate changed—or stayed the same—over time.

## THE HISTORY AND POLITICS OF THE PILL OUTSIDE JAPAN

In order to put the pill's political journey inside Japan into perspective, it is important to understand the history of the development and introduction of oral contraceptives outside Japan. And it is a rather remarkable history. Between 1951 and 1953, two American birth control advocates (Planned Parenthood founder Margaret Sanger and millionaire suffragist Katherine McCormick) took the unprecedented step of privately commissioning a scientist, Dr. Gregory Pincus, to develop a birth control pill. Sanger and McCormick had corresponded for twenty years about their hopes for a scientific breakthrough in contraception, which both women envisioned as a "fool-proof" contraceptive drug of some kind.[7] The notion was something of a pipe dream, as doctors and scientists had given little thought to what, if any, drug could be used to effect such a radical change in contraceptive technology.

But McCormick's millions[8] induced Pincus to devote his attention to the problem, and in less than ten years he applied recently developed synthetic hormone technology[9] to create a progesterone-based drug that temporarily suppressed ovulation (estrogen was later incorporated after it was discovered that a combination of estrogen and progesterone lessened the incidence of side effects).[10] A colleague of Pincus's first tested the drug on fifty women in Boston in 1954, with good results. Pincus subsequently carried out successful large-scale clinical trials in Puerto Rico.[11]

The outside world first learned about hormonal contraception in 1955, when Pincus presented his research at the annual International Planned Parenthood League Conference, which was held—ironically, considering the pill's subsequent travails—in Tokyo. Pincus was disappointed at the reception his research received: according to one author, "the only noticeable reaction was skepticism."[12] In the JFPA newsletter, *Kazoku keikaku*, the reaction to Pincus's announcement was mixed. Among four Japanese doctors and scientists who gave opinions, one said that new methods of contraception represented scientific progress; another said that if an oral contraceptive drug could be developed that had no harmful side effects, it would be a good thing; a third voiced concerns that widespread use of oral contraceptives would have terrible effects on society; and a fourth was doubtful that oral contraceptives would be on the market any time soon.[13]

This last response was perhaps most typical of the larger international scientific and financial community. Through the late 1950s most observers did not believe that the pill would be marketed as a contraceptive in the near future, even though the U.S. Food and Drug Administration (FDA) approved the synthetic hormone compound Enovid for treatment of gynecological disorders in 1957.[14] An April 1958 *Fortune* magazine article predicted that it would take ten years and clinical data on thousands of women before drugs like Enovid would receive FDA approval as contraceptives.[15] Some even questioned whether there would be any demand for a contraceptive drug—a question that was resolved within two years after Enovid went on the market, by which time half a million American women were using it for unapproved contraceptive purposes.[16]

Encouraged by the drug's popularity, Searle applied to the FDA for permission to market Enovid as a contraceptive. The FDA official in charge of the Searle application later recalled that the FDA was very nervous about approving Enovid as a contraceptive and therefore stipulated the most stringent clinical testing requirements in FDA history.[17] Nevertheless Enovid was duly approved for sale as a contraceptive in May 1960. Between 1961 and 1963 the number of pill users in the United States increased approximately sixfold, from 408,000 to 2.3 million.[18] It is now estimated that 80 percent of women born since 1945 have used the pill at some time. Pharmaceutical companies in Germany, England, and elsewhere began marketing their own brands of oral contraceptives around the same time Searle did, and by 1967 an estimated 12 million women were using oral contraceptives worldwide.[19]

The oral contraceptive drug that Pincus invented changed the lives of millions of women. While several barrier methods of contraception (such as condoms, diaphragms, and spermicides) were available before the pill came on the market, then as now, the failure rate for these methods was quite high: 12 to 21 percent with "typical use."[20] Other commonly cited drawbacks to these methods are that they require application at or near the time of intercourse and, in the case of condoms, that they require the cooperation of the male partner.

The pill, in contrast, is essentially 100 percent effective,[21] does not need to be taken at the time of intercourse, and is entirely female-controlled. It is unlikely that the pill was the cause of such postwar phenomena as increasing rates of female employment and higher education, declining birth rates, and postponement of childbearing, because, in the United States at least, these trends all began to occur in the late 1950s and early 1960s, either before or around the same time the pill was introduced.[22] Nevertheless, the pill undoubtedly facilitated the progress of these trends, enabling women to plan the course of their family and work lives with a greater degree of certainty than had been possible previously.

Not everyone saw the pill as a panacea, however. In the late 1960s and early 1970s some American feminists began focusing on the health risks of the pill, claiming that pharmaceutical companies had concealed the pill's side effects from consumers. Barbara Seaman's 1969 book, *The Doctor's Case against the Pill*, led to Senate hearings on the pill's safety in 1970. In the wake of the Senate hearings and the negative press the pill received as a result, pill use in the United States dropped by 20 percent, but then rose again in the 1980s with the introduction of the low-dosage pill.[23] Feminist criticism spurred drug companies to develop the safer, lower-dosage oral contraceptives and to include explanatory inserts about health risks in all pill packages. In general, the pill controversy led to increased government regulation over medical practice.[24]

Some American feminists have also critiqued the contraceptive philosophy of family planning organizations, drug companies, and governments that promote the use of oral contraceptives. For example, the sociologist Kristin Luker and the historian Linda Gordon have argued that because the pill is a female-controlled method of contraception, it "reinforces the view of birth control as women's responsibility and avoids the discussion and sharing of . . . birth control planning that barrier methods encourage."[25] Gordon further argues that by promoting the pill as a "magic bullet"—the fail-safe technological "cure" for the "illness" of pregnancy—birth control advocates, scientists, and pharmaceutical companies "encourag[e] a passive attitude toward birth control as something bought, not something done."[26] As we will see below, until very recently—with one notable exception in the early 1970s—the predominant view of the pill among Japanese feminists has been similarly negative. Anti-pill feminists maintain that greater emphasis should be placed on barrier methods because they do not pose the health risks that the pill poses, and because, unlike the pill, they promote familiarity with one's body and foster communication between sexual partners. According to Gordon, "when combined with legal abortion as a backup, the diaphragm offers the safest and most effective form of birth control."[27]

While it is true that the pill can have side effects and that the pill rests the burden of contraceptive responsibility on women, the feminist critique of the pill ignores several important facts and ultimately sacrifices practical concerns in favor of idealistic principles. First, just as the pill is associated with certain health risks, so, too, are the pregnancies and abortions that may result from using less effective barrier methods (pregnancy and childbirth are associated with much greater health risks than pill use or abortion).[28] Second, it is unrealistic to assume that because barrier methods such as condoms *require* cooperation between men and women, the necessary cooperation will actually *occur*. For many women, the pill's greater effectiveness in preventing pregnancy is the paramount consideration, while sharing contraceptive responsibility with male partners is of secondary concern. In fact, it seems likely that some women prefer to use the pill precisely because it frees them from having to rely on irresponsible or uncooperative men. Third, it is mistaken to assert that barrier methods necessarily teach women about their bodies or facilitate communication between partners in a way that the pill does not. As Petchesky points out, whether a given type of birth control has positive or negative effects "is not a question intrinsic to its technology or form but is determined by the social relations of its use."[29] Coleman's research on Japan confirms this theory and at the same time contradicts the feminist argument about barrier methods. In Japan, where for decades more than 75 percent of contraceptors have used condoms, Coleman found a comparatively high level of ignorance, embarrassment, and prudishness about matters relating to sexuality, reproduction, and contraception, and a comparatively low level of male-female communication about such matters.[30]

## THE POLITICS OF THE PILL IN THE 1960s (JAPAN)

The process of pill development and approval in Japan was in synchrony with similar processes taking place in other countries until the early 1960s. As in the United States, Japanese pharmaceutical companies obtained approval to market combination estrogen-progesterone drugs for treatment of menstrual disorders in the late 1950s.[31] Searle applied to the FDA for permission to market Enovid as a contraceptive in 1960, just a year before Shio Nogi, Dai Nippon Seiyaku, and Teikoku Zōki Seiyaku made a similar application to the MHW. In response, the MHW set up an Oral Contraception Committee (*Keikō Hininyaku Chōsakai*) within the Central Pharmaceutical Advisory Council (*Chūō Yakuji Shingikai*), or Drug Council, to consider the applications.[32] But in late 1961– early 1962, politics and damaging developments in the pharmaceutical industry began to intrude into the Japanese pill approval process, ultimately derailing what otherwise might have been a smooth progression toward pill approval and causing Japanese contraception policy to diverge irrevocably from contraception policy in other countries.

One factor contributing to the pill's difficulties in this early stage was that there was a feeling of vitality and recovery in the air in the 1960s that made new methods of birth control seem a less urgent priority—quite the opposite of the crisis atmosphere that surrounded the passage of the Eugenic Protection Law that legalized abortion in the late 1940s. Ikeda's income-doubling plan was successfully under way, and the Tokyo Olympics in 1964 showed the world that Japan had recovered from the war. Elites were increasingly focusing their attention on the declining birth rate and the possibility of future labor shortages. Japanese women's groups were not involved in this early debate over whether to approve the pill, presumably for the same reasons that they were not involved in the early debate over abortion (see chapter 4). Therefore, national and professional interests once again shaped policy on an issue that most directly affected women. And the pill ban that resulted from this policy-making process did not have the beneficial unintended "side effects" for women that the Eugenic Protection Law had. Instead, it had the effect of denying Japanese women a major birth control option for the next four decades.

The first event to harm the pill's chances for approval occurred in the spring of 1961, when stories about the illegal sale of sleeping pills to minors began making headlines in Japan.[33] Throughout 1961, and for the next three years, there was a steady stream of reports on comas, accidental deaths, suicides, and crimes resulting from sleeping pill abuse (*suiminyaku asobi*) among trendy young people.[34] The furor over sleeping pill abuse engendered criticism of the MHW's lax oversight of drugs, and this became ammunition for anti-pill forces. They argued that even were the pill approved as a prescription drug, the government would not be able to prevent oral contraceptives from being sold freely and misused, with drastic health consequences. Pill critics also raised the specter of social disorder: uncontrolled access to an extremely effective contraceptive could lead to an epidemic of "free sex" (*sei asobi*) among young people.[35]

Further, in 1961 the Japanese media began to report on the growing number of Thalidomide-induced birth defects in Europe, and "Thalidomide baby" articles became a news staple in Japan for the next several years.[36] Although by far the greatest number of birth defects occurred in Europe, sleeping drugs similar to Thalidomide did cause approximately one thousand Japanese babies to be born with birth defects between 1958 and 1963 (the drug was never approved in the United States).[37] As a result of these domestic and international drug scandals, there developed a widespread sentiment in Japan that the government was not regulating drugs adequately and that the Japanese people were being exposed to a multitude of health dangers. Thus, Reich concludes that "in the early 1960s, while the pill was viewed as the symbol of benevolent scientific progress in the United States, in Japan it was portrayed as the harbinger of sinister social disruption."[38]

In response to the harsh criticism of the government's drug administration, the Oral Contraception Committee overseeing pill applications developed more stringent clinical testing requirements than had been standard in the past.[39] The drug companies complied with these new requirements and presented their results for review in late 1963. The following year officials at the MHW concluded that, as the pill had proven to be effective and to have few side effects, there was no reason not to approve it.[40] This was perhaps not the most enthusiastic endorsement: indeed, an MHW Drug Bureau official was quoted around this time to the effect that even if the pill were approved, he would not want his own wife taking it.[41] Nevertheless, it is clear that in the summer of 1964, on the basis of successful clinical testing, the MHW did intend to approve the pill as a contraceptive[42]—albeit a strictly regulated one.[43] According to a doctor involved in oral contraception research at the time, the Health Ministry told the drug companies informally that the pill would be approved, and, based on this information, they began making preparations for manufacture and sale.[44]

But in the meantime, a political storm was brewing. As early as 1961, family planning activist Katō Shizue (who had moved from the Lower to the Upper House since her Eugenic Protection Law days) voiced strong opposition to oral contraceptives. Addressing the Health and Welfare Minister at an Upper House Committee meeting, Katō explained that scientists had originally hailed atomic energy as scientific progress that would benefit mankind, when in fact it had just the opposite effect. She emphasized that the pill was a completely new kind of drug, and that there were not only questions about its safety and efficacy but about what effects it would have on public morals. Katō commented on the sleeping pill abuse problem and loose government regulation of pharmaceutical sales, and pointedly asked the Health Minister who would take responsibility were the pill to be similarly misused or cause social problems.[45] It is something of a mystery why Katō was opposed to the pill, since she was a friend and disciple of Margaret Sanger, the American family planning activist who commissioned Pincus to develop oral contraceptives. But given the political fault lines in Japan in the 1960s, a progressive socialist like Katō probably saw the possibility of pill approval less as a family planning issue than as yet another example of the ruling Liberal Democratic Party favoring industry's economic interests over the health and safety of the average citizen.

In response to Katō's questions, and to similar questioning a few months later from LDP representative and Japan Midwives Association President Yokoyama Fuku, the Health Minister emphasized that the question of pill approval was being studied carefully, but that if the pill were approved and caused harm to society, he would have to take responsibility himself.[46] The beginning of the pill's political troubles in Japan can be traced to these exchanges, for Japanese bureaucrats—like cautious bureaucrats the world over—fear nothing more than being forced to take responsibility for the consequences of controversial policy decisions.[47]

In the summer and fall of 1964 lobbying by anti-pill interest groups became "quite active" (ugoki wa . . . kanari kappatsu ni natt[a]), since the groups in question believed that the MHW was likely to grant approval imminently.[48] All the following groups came out in opposition to pill approval or else took a "cautious stance" (shinchōron) on the matter: the two main family planning organizations (the FPFJ and the JFPA), the Association of Obstetricians and Gynecologists, the designated doctors' group (Nichibo), the JMA, the Japan Midwives Association, and the LDP's Women's Bureau (whose president, Yokoyama Fuku, was also president of the Japan Midwives Association).[49] Although opposition to the pill among these groups was largely motivated by a desire to protect professional interests, there was also genuine concern about the possible health risks posed by this new type of drug, which was to be taken not by sick people to cure illness but by healthy women to prevent pregnancy. There were questions about what the pill's long-term side effects might be: whether, for example, pill use could render women infertile or otherwise permanently affect their natural hormone balance.[50] University of Tokyo professor and ob-gyn Moriyama Yutaka (who succeeded Dr. Taniguchi as president of Nichibo) voiced the opinion that it was possible for women who used the pill to become masculinized or for babies of pill users to be affected *in utero*.[51] Both the Oral Contraception Committee of the FPFJ and the Hormone Committee of the Association of Obstetricians and Gynecologists published resolutions that more research on the pill's long-term effects was needed and that immediate approval would be premature.[52] FPFJ president Koya Yoshio said that there was no need to hurry to legalize a method of birth control that might have side effects when other kinds of birth control were available and abortion was legal.[53]

It was legitimate for these family planners, midwives, and ob-gyns to express their unselfish concerns about the pill's possible medical and social effects on the commonweal, but it would have been unseemly—and politically damaging—for them to discuss their more self-interested concerns about the pill's possible effects on the birth rate and the demand for condoms, diaphragms and abortions. Consequently one rarely finds references to these less public-minded considerations in written records. But by piecing together the occasional candid quote with interviews after the fact, one begins to get a picture of professionals who felt that their livelihood was being threatened by a new, effective, and easy-to-use form of contraception.

For example, in a mail-in opinion survey on the pill conducted by the JFPA in 1964, the vice president of the Japan Midwives Association wrote that Japan already had the lowest birth rate in the world, and that because Japanese people love new things, everyone would rush to use the pill if it were approved, and soon the future of the Japanese race and nation would be jeopardized.[54] This assessment may seem overblown, but it does accurately reflect the midwives' fears concerning their rapidly eroding childbirth practice—which, in reality, was being threatened more by ob-gyns than by the declining birth rate.[55] Midwives also controlled the condom and diaphragm business, often selling for the JFPA and other family planning organizations, which generated much of their revenue through such sales.[56] The midwives and, by association, the family planners, feared losing contraception business to doctors if the pill were approved, since they assumed that the pill would be popular and knew it would require a doctor's prescription.[57]

The midwives need not have worried on that score, however. The ob-gyns were uninterested in the contraception business because it was not particularly lucrative and was associated with lower-status practitioners (i.e., midwives and social workers). Ob-gyns also believed that because drugs were not tightly regulated, it would be difficult for them to properly supervise pill use[58]—that is, it would be difficult for them to achieve and enforce a monopoly over the prescription and sale of pills. Most important, many of the ob-gyn members of Nichibo and the Japan Association of Obstetricians and Gynecologists saw the pill as a potential threat to their abortion and childbirth practices, on the assumption that pill use would lower both the abortion rate and the birth rate.[59] Of the thirty-two ob-gyns who replied to the JFPA mail-in survey, only three agreed that the MHW should approve the pill.[60]

Thus, as one journalist wrote in early 1965, "it seems that the only ones who are anxiously awaiting [pill] approval now are the drug companies."[61] All other relevant interest groups were opposed.[62] These groups were motivated to one degree or another by self-interest, but in explaining their opposition to the pill they skillfully emphasized the public and national interest, representing themselves as guardians of those interests. At the same time they played on the fears of MHW bureaucrats, who dreaded being blamed for future health or social problems. This anti-pill lobbying technique is epitomized by a July 1964 meeting between the Oral Contraception Committee of the FPFJ and representatives from the MHW's Drug Bureau and Drug Council. During the course of the meeting, members of the Oral Contraception Committee demanded to know why the MHW had not waited for groups like theirs to submit opinions on the pill. They cited the problem of sleeping pill abuse and suggested that the pill would cause similar juvenile delinquency. They asked what would happen to the babies of women who unknowingly became pregnant and continued to take the pill, conjuring up images of deformed Thalidomide babies. They claimed that Japan had the lowest birth rate in the world and questioned whether it was necessary to approve this "perfect" form of birth control, which would lower the birth rate even more. They argued that with a drug that had such potentially strong effects on public morals, the quantity and quality of the population, and the future of Japan's economy, it would be inappropriate to base an approval decision solely on narrow medical and pharmacological criteria. They asked the MHW bureaucrats: Is there some pressing social reason why the pill has to be approved so quickly? And who will take responsibility if the pill is approved and has unexpected medical or social side effects?[63]

In the face of this kind of pressure, the MHW caved. Had it remained a simple matter of assessing clinical tests, the MHW would have approved the pill as a matter of routine. But because it was a "sensitive issue," the MHW hesitated to give approval,[64] and, in the end, the anti-pill groups succeeded in cultivating an aura of expert knowledge and public-mindedness that was too compelling for the MHW to ignore. The pharmaceutical companies, left to occupy the moral low ground as self-serving profit seekers, could not compete. It must be remembered, too, that the pharmaceutical industry was coming from a position of lesser political influence to begin with, at least compared to the doctors, who were at the peak of their postwar political power in the 1960s.[65] According to widespread rumor, the anti-pill victory was clinched when Prime Minister Satō Eisaku—a social conservative who opposed abortion and who had called on Japanese women to bear more children[66]—contacted MHW officials the day before the Drug Council was due to hand down its decision and asked that pill approval be put on hold.[67] The decision-making process was duly suspended, and, although the Drug Council's Oral Contraception Committee was not dissolved until 1966, no verdict on the pill was ever announced.[68]

## THE "PILL DEBATE" IN THE 1970s

After the drug companies' bid for pill approval failed in the mid-1960s, the pill went dormant as a political issue until the early 1970s. The first sign that the pill was reentering the political stage occurred in December 1971 when the Ministry of Health and Welfare issued a set of regulations to the Private Broadcasters Federation stating that no programs or commercials should deal with the subject of oral contraceptives and that the words *the pill* and *oral contraceptives* should not be mentioned on the air.[69] On April 1, 1972, the MHW designated the therapeutic pill a prescription drug, and two months later a general recall removed the pill from pharmacy shelves, where it had been available previously without a prescription.[70] These measures were clearly intended to suppress public discussion of the pill and to keep women from using the therapeutic pill for birth control purposes, but it is unclear whether they were taken in response to any particular trend or event, such as increased media coverage of the pill or increased sales of therapeutic pills for off-label contraceptive use. Ogino speculates that the government, which had been sued repeatedly in the 1960s for health damage caused by Thalidomide and Quinoform, may have acted in an attempt to preempt pill-related lawsuits.[71]

Whatever incited the MHW to take this course, the attempt to suppress public discussion of the pill failed. In 1973 and 1974 the pill became a hot topic in newspapers, in professional newsletters, in women's magazines, and at demonstrations. A "pill debate" (*piru ronsō*) even erupted in the Diet in the spring of 1973.[72] And women were taking the pill in increasing numbers as well. There were ten different kinds of hormonal compounds on the market that could be used for contraceptive purposes, and drug companies actually increased production between 1972 and 1974: sales were estimated at ¥20 to ¥40 billion per year ($56 to $111 million).[73] Demand was such that, in November 1973, one company's product sold out in Tokyo.[74]

The new interest in oral contraceptives was caused by Seichō no Ie's attempts to revise the Eugenic Protection Law. The proposed revisions introduced the possibility that abortion rights might be curtailed in the near future, and this in turn made widening the range of birth control options a more urgent priority for some groups—although not necessarily the groups one might expect. Family planners and mainstream women's organizations stayed on the sidelines of the debate, and, with the exception of one pro-pill feminist group called Chūpiren, most Japanese feminist groups believed that the pill was dangerous to women's health and represented a threat to abortion rights. Instead, the pill's main proponents in the 1970s were two professional groups—ob-gyns and pharmacists—who were vying with each other for control over the right to distribute the pill. A few politicians also advocated lifting the pill ban, both in order to lower the abortion rate, which they continued to regard as a national embarrassment, and to make restrictions on abortion more palatable to the public. But most bureaucrats opposed the pill on the grounds that it had dangerous side effects for which they did not wish to be held responsible.

It is not surprising that mainstream women's groups avoided the pill debate, given that, with a few exceptions, these groups had never been very active in contraception or abortion policy making.[75] However, it is less clear why family planners absented themselves from the debate. Katō Shizue did give the pill a qualified endorsement in 1974, remarking that, although she would personally choose another method of birth control, she thought it was necessary for the pill to be approved in order to promote birth control widely.[76] Otherwise, the record is almost entirely devoid of reference to the family planning community's position on the pill in the 1970s.[77] It seems likely that, as in the 1960s, family planners refrained from advocating the pill because of ongoing concerns about side effects and because of the business relationship between family planning groups and midwives.

With the advent of the women's liberation movement (ribu undō), as the feminist movement was called in the 1970s, we see feminists attempting to insert the vocabulary of women's rights and women's interests into the contraception policy-making process for the first time. A guiding principle of the feminist movement was that women should be allowed to make decisions about their bodies and their reproductive lives without outside interference. Indeed, many Japanese feminist groups were formed around this time in order to combat efforts to restrict access to abortion. At first glance, then, one might logically assume that feminist groups would have also advocated lifting the pill ban, since women must have access to a range of contraceptive methods as well as abortion in order to control reproduction.

But, in fact, most members of the *ribu* movement did not believe that lifting the pill ban would serve women's interests. For one thing, American feminists had recently provoked Senate hearings on the pill's safety with their claims that oral contraceptives had not been adequately tested and that they had dangerous side effects which drug companies were concealing from consumers.[78] These claims seemed valid to many Japanese feminists, some of whom had tried using the pill and experienced various negative side effects.[79] Japanese feminists suspected that Japanese drug companies and doctors were conspiring with the government to legalize the pill and reap profits without regard for women's health. They also feared that if the pill were approved, it would help justify limiting access to abortion. This was not such a far-fetched notion, as some bureaucrats and politicians did publicly discuss making restrictions on abortion contingent on approval of the pill and the IUD, so as not to force women into desperate situations. But feminists turned the chain of causality around and claimed that proposals to restrict abortion were actually aimed at boosting sales of oral contraceptives. Ribu Shinjuku Sentā leader Tanaka Mitsu asked, "Behind the clamor for banning abortion, isn't the goal to try to sell the pill?"[80] And as demonstrated by the following quote from the Executive Committee to Block the Revision of the Eugenic Protection Law, even more elaborate conspiracy theories were circulating in the feminist community.

> [Given that] there are no reliable methods of birth control now, if the ban on the pill is lifted, it's obvious that women will snap it up. Since the pill has already become a prescription drug, the doctors and the drug companies are both making money. Also, lifting the pill ban would break the movement opposing the Eugenic Protection Law revisions and improve the government's image, so it would kill four birds with one stone. Isn't the government conspiring with doctors and drug companies, watching for a time to lift the pill ban? And with the opposition to the Eugenic Protection Law revisions on the agenda now, isn't the MHW holding the possibility of lifting the pill ban in reserve?[81]

The pill was also a distasteful subject for many Japanese feminists because it was a favorite cause of the radical feminist group Chūpiren. In general, Chūpiren was quite different from the rest of the movement philosophically (see chapter 5). Chūpiren particularly antagonized and mortified other feminists because its splashy (*hade na*), publicity-seeking protest activities attracted a great deal of media attention (and ridicule), leading the general public to believe that Chūpiren was representative of the larger *ribu* movement.[82] Chūpiren is of particular interest here because it was the first group of women in Japan to advocate legalizing oral contraceptives actively and therefore represents a subcurrent in the Japanese discourse on the pill that should not be ignored. Of course, the concerns of the average pro-pill Japanese woman were probably more mundane than those of Chūpiren members, who had a penchant for idealistic diatribes peppered with Marxist and feminist jargon. But Chūpiren's message cannot have been completely off-putting or obscure because soon after the group formed, it began receiving five to ten letters a day from housewives, students, and office workers who wanted to take the pill and were seeking information on how to get it.[83]

Chūpiren was an acronym for *Chūzetsu kinshi hō ni hantai shi piru kaikin o yōkyū suru josei kaihō rengō*, or The Women's Liberation Federation for Opposing the Abortion Prohibition Law and Lifting the Pill Ban. Chūpiren came into being at the 1972 Women's Liberation Convention (*Ribu Taikai*) in Tokyo. During the convention, Chūpiren's future leader, Enoki Misako, broke with the feminist group Urufu Kai in a dispute over her right to sell pamphlets entitled "Lift the Pill Ban!" (*Piru o kaikin se yo!*) under the Urufu Kai name. Urufu Kai members claimed that the pamphlets misrepresented the group's position as enthusiastically pro-pill.[84] Among generally small, anonymous feminist groups, Chūpiren quickly became notorious throughout Japan for its militancy, as well as for its members' revolutionary ensemble, which consisted of pink helmets, and sometimes sunglasses and towels over the mouth.

Enoki herself is a rather enigmatic figure. Former Urufu Kai member Akiyama Yōko has written the only detailed description of Enoki and Chūpiren, but Akiyama is clearly biased against Enoki, so her testimony is not completely reliable. Akiyama seeks to depict Enoki as a shady character, informing readers that Enoki was a pseudonym (her real name was Katayama); that she was a pharmacology major in college; that she lived with (but was not married to) a well-to-do ship's doctor in a fancy apartment; that it was unclear what kind of work she did, if any; and that, at consciousness-raising meetings, she "did not really open her heart as others did." According to Akiyama and others, many non-Chūpiren feminists believed that Chūpiren was not a "real" feminist group, but rather a front of some kind. They suspected that Chūpiren had connections with politicians and that it received funding from drug companies interested in selling oral contraceptives.[85]

Chūpiren may well have been connected with the pharmaceutical industry and politicians in some way,[86] but it seems unlikely that Chūpiren was a mere front organization, given the variety of causes in which it was involved and its tactical and philosophical sophistication. For example, in 1972 Chūpiren protested the commodification of women at a beauty contest. And in 1974 Chūpiren organized a Committee to Keep Women from Crying Themselves to Sleep (*Onna o nakeneiri shinai kai*). The purpose of the committee was to aid isolated and powerless women, and committee members conducted several highly publicized demonstrations at the offices of men who had beaten or divorced their wives.[87] Although it is unclear how many demonstrations actually occurred, they clearly caught the Japanese public's attention, as informal interviews reveal that many middle-aged Japanese people still remember them today. This type of activity would probably be considered shocking in the United States even now, in an era when the feminist movement is well established and there is a great deal of openness about divorce and domestic violence. In Japan, where divorce and domestic violence were taboo subjects until quite recently, and where public humiliation is arguably a more serious affair than in the United States, it is difficult to imagine how outrageous and offensive Chūpiren must have seemed twenty-five years ago—even against the backdrop of heightened radical leftist activism at the time.

Chūpiren was primarily active in the causes from which its name derived—that is, opposing the Eugenic Protection Law revisions and the pill ban. Chūpiren's position on the pill was that

> the freedom to choose [whether] to have children is a basic right of women, and for women to protect their right *not* to have children, the pill is the only method of contraception that they can control themselves.[88] (emphasis added)

Chūpiren members argued that birth control should come before abortion because abortions could be dangerous; that the pill was used all over the world and was recognized as safe and effective; and that therefore the Drug Bureau should approve the pill for sale under the supervision of pharmacists (i.e., without a prescription) in order to protect women from the health dangers presented by abortion.[89] To promote its views, Chūpiren held seminars on the pill at college campuses and demonstrated in front of the Ministry of Health and Welfare and elsewhere. For example, on October 23, 1973, thirty pink-helmeted Chūpiren members stormed uninvited into a meeting of midwives and public health nurses (who opposed the pill), charged up to the stage, and argued loudly with audience members for about an hour over whether the pill ban should be lifted. Nurses and midwives in the audience maintained that the existing methods of birth control in Japan were perfectly adequate, but Chūpiren members got the last word in as they marched out of the auditorium, shouting to the assembled group that it was responsible for two million abortions.[90]

Things might have gone differently between Chūpiren and the rest of the Japanese *ribu* movement had Enoki not adopted a combative attitude toward other feminist groups, especially Ribu Shinjuku Sentā (which at the time was the largest feminist group other than Chūpiren).[91] Enoki's abrasive personality raised many hackles—including those of other Chūpiren members, a large body of whom left the group in 1974 in protest against her autocratic style.[92] This defection led to the gradual disbanding of the group, for the last one hears of Enoki is that she organized the Japan Women's Party and ran unsuccessfully for the Lower House in 1977. Subsequently she disappeared from the public eye.[93]

Enoki Misako and Chūpiren present intriguing contradictions. On the one hand, Enoki was too much the loner in a culture oriented toward the group and too radical even for her fellow radicals. On the other hand, she was energetic, creative, and ahead of the times in understanding the potential power of using the media to forward a cause. While her dramatic gestures played into media efforts to portray the feminist movement as laughable, she did at least bring the movement and its ideas to the public's attention. Even Akiyama, whose portrait of Enoki is generally negative, concedes that media coverage of Chūpiren had some effect in appealing to public opinion on the pill and abortion issues.[94] But the antigovernment tactics of Chūpiren and other feminist groups did not endear them to politicians and bureaucrats, and the lack of political connections, combined with the internal divisions within the *ribu* movement, doomed to failure whatever influence feminists might have had over the outcome of the pill debate.

Ob-gyns and pharmacists filled the contraception policy-making niche that Japanese feminists left vacant. Both professional groups agreed, conditionally, that the pill should be approved as a contraceptive, but they differed over which group should be allowed to prescribe and sell the pill. Ob-gyns and pharmacists were in competition over the pill because, unlike most other countries, Japanese law allows doctors to sell the drugs they prescribe. This practice gives doctors a financial incentive to fill their own prescriptions, which in turn gives them a functional monopoly over the sale of prescription drugs. Indeed, Japanese pharmacists do not fill doctors' prescriptions as often as pharmacists do in other countries, forcing them to rely more heavily on selling nonprescription drugs and sundries.[95]

As we saw above, ob-gyns had already gained control over the therapeutic pill when it was designated a prescription drug. But the pill-as-contraceptive had not yet received approval, and consequently the Health and Welfare Ministry had not decided whether it would be a prescription or nonprescription drug. While it might seem a foregone conclusion that the contraceptive pill would become a prescription drug since the therapeutic pill had been so designated, pharmacists clearly felt that it would be worthwhile to test the waters. Perhaps they reasoned that if conservative forces succeeded in revising the Eugenic Protection Law and restricting access to abortion, the government could be persuaded of the need to make the most reliable form of birth control available over the counter. The pill presented a reliable and lucrative source of potential income to both pharmacists and doctors, as it reportedly cost ¥1,500–¥3,000 per month in the mid-1970s (roughly $4–$8 per month), which was considered quite expensive.[96]

One of the most ardent proponents of the pill was Japan Socialist Party Representative Suhara Shōji, a pharmacist by trade. It was Suhara who instigated what the newspapers dubbed the "pill debate" in the Diet. Over the course of ten months between April 1973 and January 1974 Suhara repeatedly asked MHW officials to tell him whether the pill was going to be approved and, if not, to explain why. Suhara laid out multiple rationales for why the pill ban should be lifted. He cited Japan's high abortion rate and claimed that the pill would lower it; he compared the failure rates of other types of contraceptives to the pill's high level of effectiveness; he argued that there were no medical problems with the pill, only political ones, and that, in any event, it was normal for drugs to have minor side effects; and he underlined the fact that Japan, Turkey, and the two Koreas were the only countries where the pill was not legal, while in many other countries the pill was the most popular form of birth control.[97] Suhara's position was that the pill should be approved as a contraceptive and that it should be freely available in drugstores under the supervision of pharmacists.[98]

While other Diet members argued in favor of the pill in 1973–74, none attacked the subject with as much vigor, in as much detail, or as repeatedly as did Representative Suhara. Rather, they were content to make brief and general comments: for example, if limits were to be placed on access to abortion, adequate measures should be taken to promote contraceptives such as the IUD and the pill; and if the pill was legal in other advanced countries, Japan should legalize it, too.[99] Several factors suggest that Suhara's agenda went beyond simple humanitarianism: his specific insistence that the pill be made available without a prescription; his diatribe against the high-handedness of MHW paper-pushers (kanryōteki dokuzen) deciding to designate the therapeutic pill as a prescription drug;[100] the fact that he sustained his inquiries about the pill for almost a year when others only addressed the subject in passing; and the fact that Suhara himself was a pharmacist. In short, it seems likely that, in exchange for lobbying for the pill, Suhara was receiving funding from pharmacists or pharmaceutical companies or both.

Ob-gyns also had an incentive to lobby for the pill because they expected to lose some portion of their income derived from abortions if the Eugenic Protection Law was revised. But members of the designated abortion providers group, Nichibo, had a prior, stronger interest in maintaining open access to abortion, and they also had doubts about whether they would be able to enforce a physician monopoly over pill sales. So Nichibo adopted contradictory positions to cover both possible outcomes of the abortion conflict: if access to abortion remained relatively unrestricted, Nichibo did not want the pill to be approved; but if abortions became more difficult to obtain, Nichibo wanted the pill to be approved as a prescription drug in order to ensure a physician monopoly over sales.

Consequently, at the same time that Nichibo was advocating pill approval and arguing that the pill should be available only with a doctor's prescription and regular checkups,[101] it was also reinvoking many of the same anti-pill arguments it had employed in the 1960s.[102] Furthermore, Nichibo president Moriyama Yutaka—who was not personally in favor of the pill[103]—stressed that ob-gyns should give priority to promoting the IUD before promoting the pill, because the IUD lent itself more readily to physician control.[104] Moriyama explained that under the lax system of drug administration in Japan, even were the pill designated a prescription drug, it would be impossible for doctors "to supervise pill use properly." In Moriyama's view, the benefit of IUDs was that it was impossible (and illegal) for a woman to use an IUD without having a doctor insert it.[105]

Nichibo's divided attitude toward the pill was paralleled at the MHW, where there were internal divisions over whether the pill should be approved. At a Diet committee meeting, Representative Suhara elicited a pro-pill response from the Medical Affairs Bureau chief, who said: "When you consider the pill's effectiveness and the fact that it is widely used internationally, as well as the abortion situation in this country . . . I certainly say that we should think of ways to actively introduce [the pill]."[106] But the Drug Bureau chief disagreed and urged that the matter be resolved "cautiously and bureaucratically"—undoubtedly an attempt to signal to the Medical Affairs Bureau chief that the pill was not his turf and that he should refrain from further comment. This exchange provoked the minister of health and welfare to reprimand the two bureau chiefs publicly, reminding them that "the MHW should present a united front."[107]

After Suhara again pressed the pill question in late 1973 and early 1974, Prime Minister Tanaka announced that, although the government had no intention of approving the pill as a contraceptive because of safety concerns, it was not forbidden by law to use approved drugs for nonapproved purposes.[108] The Drug Bureau chief, for his part, reminded doctors that if they prescribed the therapeutic pill for birth control purposes, they—not the MHW—would be held responsible for any health problems that might result.[109] This "informal legalization" of the high-dose pill—equivocal, hypocritical, and cowardly as it was—apparently satisfied MHW bureaucrats, as it achieved informal resolution of the pill question without actually approving the pill, thus absolving the MHW of responsibility for overseeing the pill-as-contraceptive and bringing to an end the embarrassing questions in Diet committee meetings.[110]

The outcome of the "pill debate" of the 1970s mirrored the relative power of the groups involved. The politically stronger Nichibo won, ultimately getting everything its members wanted. On the one hand, ob-gyns retained the authority to prescribe and sell the therapeutic pill and received informal permission to prescribe it for birth control purposes; on the other hand, the pill was not formally approved as a contraceptive, and access to abortion was not restricted. The politically weaker pharmacists lost the political contest over the pill, and the nascent feminist groups were not even able to enter the contest in any meaningful way. But it was ordinary women who were hurt most, because the government's refusal to grant formal approval meant that the pill's status remained ambiguous. Few doctors were willing to prescribe it, and most women were either scared to use it or did not know it existed.[111] This meant that, for all intents and purposes, the range of birth control options did not expand in the 1970s, leaving women to continue relying on condoms and the rhythm method, with abortion as a backup. As in the 1960s, professional interests and bureaucratic timidity dictated the contours of Japanese contraception policy.

## THE POLITICS OF THE PILL IN THE 1980S AND 1990S

At a Social Policy and Labor Committee meeting during the "pill debate" in 1973–74, Drug Bureau chief Matsushita commented that a birth control pill with fewer side effects and the same level of effectiveness would be most desirable.[112] The remark proved prophetic, for not long afterward just such a pill was developed in the West. The second generation of birth control pills had substantially lower doses of estrogen and progesterone, and fewer side effects than the first generation, but was just as effective in preventing pregnancy.[113] Doctors in Europe and the United States began prescribing the low-dose pill in the late 1970s and early 1980s, and by the mid-1980s the high-dose pill had been largely phased out in the West. But in Japan, a small number of women continued to use the high-dose therapeutic pill for contraception through the late 1990s—despite Japanese researchers having completed successful clinical trials on the low-dose pill in the late 1980s—because the MHW refused to grant approval to the low-dose pill.

In the mid-1980s the positions of some of the key players from past battles over the pill shifted. Ob-gyns and family planners came to endorse the pill. Some feminists started to advocate legalizing the pill, arguing that even though they would not choose it as a contraceptive method, other women should have the opportunity to decide whether to do so. Meanwhile, the MHW opposed the pill with increased determination for both new and old reasons. The positions of other groups did not change. The pharmaceutical industry continued to lobby for the pill, a bit more aggressively than in the past. Midwives, facing the ongoing decline of their profession, still opposed the pill. And the majority of ordinary Japanese women still feared the pill's side effects and expressed little interest in using it. In this chapter of the pill's political progress, national interests (as interpreted by the MHW) came to have greater influence over policy than professional interests, and women's interests began to receive consideration in a way they never had before.

The political configuration surrounding the pill reversed itself in the mid-1980s, and professional groups that had opposed government efforts to approve the pill in the past found themselves in the position of lobbying a reluctant Health Ministry to approve the pill. For, over the course of twenty years, both ob-gyns and family planners had evolved from an anti-pill position to a pro-pill position.[114] The most straightforward explanation for this turnabout is the one given by the ob-gyn and family planning groups: namely, that two decades had elapsed in which millions of women throughout the world used first the high-dose pill and then the low-dose pill without dire health consequences, dissipating concerns about the pill's safety. Also, by the mid-1980s, both groups had undergone generational changes, allowing younger, less conservative members—many of whom had trained in the West—to redefine interests and priorities.[115] Less straightforward explanations focus on the fact that the birth rate and abortion rate had gone down considerably, diminishing the persuasiveness of arguments that the pill posed a threat to childbirth and abortion practices, and possibly making contraceptive prescriptions seem more attractive as a steady source of income.[116]

Thus, ironically, the same ob-gyn and family planning groups that had contributed to stigmatizing the pill in the minds of politicians, bureaucrats, and the public in the mid-1960s, twenty years later petitioned the MHW to set in motion the testing and approval process for the low-dose pill. An article on the new generation of pills first appeared in the Nichibo newsletter in September 1981, and in September 1985 Nichibo and the Japan Association of Obstetricians and Gynecologists (JAOG, or Nihon Sanfujinka Gakkai) both submitted a petition to the Drug Bureau at the MHW requesting permission to conduct clinical trials of the low-dose pill. The petition stated that oral contraceptives had been in common use in many countries for the last thirty years, and that the new, low-dose pill was safer and more reliable than the high-dose pill.[117] Family Planning Federation of Japan (FPFJ) president Katō Shizue submitted a similar petition four months later in January 1986, acknowledging that although the FPFJ had opposed the pill in the past, its position had changed because numerous studies in other countries had proven the pill's safety and effectiveness, and because the hormone content of oral contraceptives had been greatly reduced.[118]

In February 1986 the MHW organized a study group on the low-dose pill composed of ob-gyns, pharmaceutical experts, and specialists in basic medicine.[119] Almost a year later, in December 1986, the study group concluded that clinical trials on the low-dose pill's safety and efficacy should indeed be performed, and in April 1987 the MHW issued testing guidelines.[120] Shortly afterward, family planning and ob-gyn groups began conducting trials with funding from pharmaceutical companies. The trials were successful, and in 1990–91 nine different domestic and foreign drug companies applied for permission to manufacture or import the pill.[121] These applications were forwarded to the Combination Drug Committee (Haigōzai Chōsakai) of the MHW's Drug Council, which was to evaluate the applications and make a recommendation to the Drug Bureau.

Thus far, the MHW had proven cooperative and even appeared to regard the pill favorably.[122] Newspaper and magazine articles in 1991 predicted that the low-dose pill would soon be approved and that it would go on sale by the spring of 1992.[123] Drug companies, ob-gyns, and family planners also expected the pill to be approved.[124] But in a surprise shift reminiscent of similar events in 1964, the Drug Council decided in late February 1992 that "ongoing deliberations" (*keizoku shingi*) on the pill were necessary, essentially freezing the approval process. Several weeks later, in March, the Council announced its decision to pharmaceutical companies and the media, explaining that the freeze was intended to safeguard public health, as pill use could decrease condom use and lead to the spread of AIDS.[125] The Council's decision came on the heels of a report two months earlier from the MHW's AIDS Surveillance Committee which showed that the number of HIV-infected people in Japan had increased by two and half times the number in the previous year. The report also indicated that most of the HIV infections had been contracted through heterosexual sex and cited fears that pill approval would lead to a decrease in condom use and an increase in the number of HIV infections.[126] Drug Bureau representatives said that it would be difficult to approve the pill until a cure for AIDS was discovered or until using condoms to prevent AIDS became common practice among the Japanese people.[127]

All the parties involved in the approval process claim that the Drug Council's announcement was "a bolt from the blue" (*nemimi ni mizu*).[128] Some speculate that the rapid policy shift resulted from internal divisions within the MHW similar to those that occurred in the 1970s.[129] Others point out that it may never be clear exactly what happened, because Drug Council deliberations, like those of many other government advisory councils, are closed.[130] This means that no one other than bureaucrats and Council members are privy to the Council's proceedings—not the public, not industry or professional groups, not even interested politicians.[131] And because Drug Council members are chosen by the MHW, they cannot be considered truly independent.[132] Thus government advisory councils are often closed loops that render bureaucrats less accessible to outside influence, enabling them to make decisions secretly and to stonewall outside inquiries when they choose to do so.

Many believe that the AIDS issue merely provided a convenient excuse, and that the real reason MHW bureaucrats refused to lift the pill ban was the fear that pill use would further lower Japan's already low birth rate.[133] In 1990 the so-called "1.57 shock" revealed that Japanese women had given birth to only 1.57 children on average in 1989—a record low at the time—though the birth rate has dropped even further since, to 1.38 as of 1998.[134] According to one academic ob-gyn, "there [was] so much fear of the population aging in the future that there [was] an atmosphere that a stop should be put to all things related to birth control."[135] Iwamoto concurs and argues that the pill freeze was actually part of a succession of policies aimed at putting a brake on the declining birth rate.[136]

Regardless of whether the Health Ministry froze the pill approval process for public health reasons (to prevent the spread of AIDS) or for "national health" reasons (to stem the decline in the birth rate), it is clear that the MHW considered the pill question in light of the national interest rather than the interests of individual women and families. By denying women the option of using the pill for the sake of what the MHW construed to be the greater good, the MHW perpetuated a paternalistic pattern of reproduction policy making in which the interests of individuals have been subordinated to national or professional interests or both. Furthermore, the MHW's understanding of the national good did not have a solid scientific foundation. For example, a World Health Organization study demonstrated that pill use is not related to the spread of AIDS. More recent research has revealed that the chlamydia infection rate among Japanese women is generally between 5 percent and 10 percent—and as high as 20 percent among fifteen to nineteen year olds in some areas. The prevalence of this sexually transmitted disease indicates that couples use condoms inconsistently, which in turn suggests that condom use cannot fully explain Japan's low AIDS rate.[137] The MHW's biased and unscientific approach to the pill has exposed untold numbers of Japanese women to the health risks of unwanted pregnancies and abortions, which are significantly higher than any of the health risks associated with the low-dose pill. The ban on the low-dose pill also forced hundreds of thousands of Japanese women who wished to take the pill to continue taking the high-dose pill, even though it has more side effects and was discontinued in other countries in the early 1980s.[138]

After the Drug Council's announcement, pro-pill interest groups mounted a campaign to restart the pill approval process. In past episodes of abortion and contraception policy making, some interest groups had been able to convince politicians and bureaucrats that their interests coincided with the national interest. But when they clashed with the MHW over the question of pill approval in the 1990s, for the first time they were unable to reach an accommodation. Representatives of Nichibo, the Japan Association of Ob-Gyns, and both family planning organizations met with MHW officials and also sent them opinion papers and petitions throughout 1992 and 1993. The ob-gyns and family planners attacked the MHW's position from every angle. They tried to draw on their authority as experts and scientists, emphasizing that the Drug Council had found merit in several years' worth of Japanese clinical data proving the pill's safety and effectiveness. They also pointed to research demonstrating that there was no causal relationship between pill use and the spread of AIDS. They made humanitarian arguments: that approving the pill could help lower the abortion rate; that the damage to women's health caused by abortions and the high-dose pill should be considered a "public health matter" on a par with

AIDS; and that women should have the freedom to choose from the widest possible range of contraceptive options because it is a basic human right to decide when to have children and how many to have. They tried to evoke national embarrassment, reminding the MHW that the pill was in common use in almost every other country in the world and that no other country had banned the pill in order to prevent AIDS. They even attempted sarcasm, suggesting that, according to the MHW's logic, the IUD should be banned also, since it did not protect people from getting AIDS.[139] But the ob-gyns' and family planners' arguments and tactics—all so effective in the 1960s and 1970s—were to no avail in the 1990s.

The pharmaceutical companies also took the offensive after the Drug Council's announcement, and in a much more visible and organized fashion than they had done in the past. For while the low-dose pill was by no means their largest project, nevertheless, these companies had collectively spent approximately $100 million on clinical trials[140] and expected to tap into a market worth anywhere from $500 million to $5 billion.[141] They formed an Oral Contraceptives Liaison Committee with representatives from all nine companies in order to share information and present a united front to the government.[142] Nippon Organon, by all accounts the most active among the nine companies in fighting the pill ban,[143] went even further and engaged the lobbying services of Japan Socialist Party Representative Yokomitsu Katsuhiko, who, like Representative Suhara in the 1970s, addressed the pill question more frequently and in more depth than his peers.

In Diet committee exchanges and written opinions submitted to the Cabinet and the MHW,[144] Yokomitsu reproduced almost verbatim arguments set forth in internal Organon documents written beforehand.[145] Yokomitsu was personally interested in the pill because he believed that were the pill approved, it might lower the abortion rate.[146] But because he was representing a pharmaceutical company whose primary interest was in getting the pill approved, he used any and all possible arguments. On the one hand, Yokomitsu propounded the pro-life sentiment that abortion is "cruel" and "nips a new life in the bud" and that the pill should be approved in order to protect the dignity of life. But Yokomitsu also used the rhetoric of family planners and feminists, arguing, for example, that the number of birth control options should be increased to ensure that all children were wanted children and that the 13 percent of Japanese women who wished to use the pill should have access to this female-controlled birth control method so they might exercise their human right to control their own reproductive lives.[147]

Some executives at other drug companies and those knowledgeable about the pharmaceutical industry expressed a low opinion of Organon's lobbying; they claimed it may have actually hindered the pill's progress because bureaucrats dislike interest groups using politicians to pressure them.[148] However, this was a risk Organon felt it could afford to take. An Organon executive explained that Organon was free to lobby more actively than other companies because it has a limited product line in Japan, whereas its counterparts with larger product lines feared that antagonizing the MHW on the pill issue might affect unrelated drug approval processes in the future.[149]

In any event, Yokomitsu's lobbying did not have much effect. The MHW rebuffed all Yokomitsu's inquiries as one year of "ongoing deliberations" stretched into a second, third, and fourth year. When Yokomitsu wrote in 1995 that the public had a right to know why the pill had not been approved after all this time, the bureaucrats replied blandly that they could not reveal the council's deliberations because it might compromise the council's fairness and impartiality. In response to Yokomitsu's assertion that the Japanese people needed access to a wide range of birth control options, the MHW retorted that the Japanese people had access to a variety of birth control methods which, if used correctly, were "adequately effective."[150] The ob-gyns and family planners fared little better: when representatives of the four groups met with Health and Welfare Minister Niwa on May 12, 1993, to present a petition, he told them that, while he personally agreed that lifting the pill ban and preventing AIDS were two separate issues, the public was fearful of AIDS, women were fearful of the pill, and not all women's groups agreed that the pill should be approved.[151]

Upper House Representative Dōmoto Akiko has argued that pressure from women on reproductive rights issues could have had an effect on policy,[152] but the majority of ordinary Japanese women expressed little interest in using the pill—a fact the MHW made good use of in maintaining its anti-pill position. In surveys taken in the 1990s, at most only 13 percent of Japanese women said that they would want to use the pill if it were approved. As of 1998, 54 percent of women surveyed said that they would not want to use the pill were it approved, and 35 percent said they did not know. Of those who said they would not use the pill, 72 percent cited concerns about side effects, a number that has remained fairly consistent since 1986.[153] Indeed, the pill acquired such a negative reputation in Japan over the years that one pro-pill gynecologist asserted in 1999 that " 'it's easier for a Japanese woman to come out and say she's had an abortion than to say she's on the pill' "—a strange state of affairs, perhaps, from the Western, and particularly the American, point of view, but not so surprising given what we learned in the preceding chapters on Japan's abortion policy.[154]

According to Ogino:

> The most important reason why the pill is so unpopular in Japan is the widespread fear of side effects from taking synthetic hormones daily for a long period. . . . [Many women feel] a sense of "unnaturalness" regarding the pill . . . [and] prefer the methods that interfere least with the natural rhythms of the woman's body.[155]

It should be noted, however, that the fear of side effects and feelings of unnaturalness do not extend to other drugs: Japan is the second largest pharmaceutical market in the world and has the second highest per capita consumption of pharmaceuticals. Indeed, "overutilization of medicine has been a serious health hazard as well as a financial problem for [Japanese] consumers."[156] Given that the Japanese enthusiastically embrace a whole pharmacopoeia of drugs—many with potential side effects equal to or greater than those of the pill—it seems clear that fears concerning the pill's side effects are the result of the barrage of negative attention the pill has received from health professionals and the media over the course of several decades, rather than of some generalized Japanese aversion to drugs. Thus, ironically, it appears that even after doctors and family planners reversed their position on the pill, they were unable to overcome the anti-pill bias created by their own past public relations and lobbying successes.

But midwives, female social commentators, and feminists were also responsible for biasing women's views of the pill. In articles with titles like "Is the Low-Dose Pill Really Women's Ally?" midwives argued that the pill destroyed the body's natural rhythms by artificially putting women into a constant state of pseudo-pregnancy (an argument that is ironic, given anthropological research demonstrating that women's natural state during most of human history pre–birth control was, in fact, a nearly constant state of pregnancy, with premodern women experiencing approximately 75 percent fewer menstrual cycles during a lifetime than modern women. Contraceptive researchers argue that the "incessant ovulation" and menstruation of the modern era translates into increased incidence of anemia and some forms of cancer.[157]) They also cited the newfound concerns about the pill promoting AIDS, as well as old, familiar concerns about the pill turning women into sex objects and placing the burden of contraceptive responsibility on women.[158] Social commentator and feminist Jansson Yumiko echoed these views in newspaper columns and on television, maintaining that she viewed even the low-dose pill as a potential health risk.[159]

As for other Japanese feminists, initially they either opposed the pill outright or else took a neutral position.[160] However, the attitude of many Japanese feminists gradually evolved in the 1990s toward what might be described as reluctant or grudging advocacy for the pill. For example, Uno of the Osaka Women's Center wrote in 1992 that it would be better to approve the low-dose pill than to have women continue using the more dangerous high-dose pill. The group Onna no Karada to Iryō o Kangaeru Kai stated that the range of birth control options should be increased, and Asia Josei Kaigi and some members of Soshiren took the position that the pill should be approved so that individual women could weigh the health risks for themselves and decide whether to use it.[161] Even groups like Nihon Joseigaku Kenkyūkai and Nihon Fujin Kaigi, which did not favor the pill as a form of birth control, criticized the government for putting public health before women's health.[162]

And in 1996–97, for the first time since Chūpiren lobbied for the pill more than twenty years earlier, two small groups emerged that were unequivocally pro-pill. In 1996 Repro de Genki no Kai was formed, and in 1997 a group of doctors and other professionals organized the Professional Women's Coalition for Sexuality and Health (Sei to Kenkō o Kangaeru Josei Senmonka no Kai).[163] The latter group was guided by the Programme of Action laid out at the International Conference on Population and Development in Cairo in 1994, which included calls for women's empowerment, comprehensive, quality reproductive health care, and informed consent. Citing statistics that only 36 percent of pregnancies in Japan are wanted or planned, that 40 percent of all births are mistimed or unwanted, and that one in four married women have had at least one abortion in their lifetime, the Coalition concluded that,

> deprived of modern effective contraceptives, Japanese women cannot choose the timing of childbearing. . . . Obviously, Japanese women are not enjoying their reproductive rights declared in Cairo in September 1994.[164]

To remedy this situation, the Coalition lobbied for approval of the pill and other modern contraceptives, as well as on-demand sterilization, the elimination of the Criminal Abortion Law, the formulation of policies to prevent sexually transmitted diseases, sex education in the schools, research on sexual and reproductive health, and the introduction of informed consent and other reforms to the Japanese health care system, including the establishment of a new women's health care system that would move beyond the "maternal protection" paradigm. This last was aimed at taking advantage of the planned reorganization of the Japanese bureaucracy, which is supposed to occur by 2001, in order to create a Women's Health Bureau within the new Ministry of Labor and Welfare.[165]

Between 1995 and 1997 there were strong indications that the government would approve the low-dose pill. After the resumption of active deliberations on the question of pill approval in April 1995, important milestones included: the Drug Council's determination in September 1995 that widespread availability of oral contraceptives had not contributed to the spread of HIV infection in other countries;[166] Health and Welfare Minister Kan Naoto's July 1996 announcement that the Drug Council would very likely approve the low-dose pill in 1997;[167] the Drug Council's February 1997 conclusion that low-dosage birth control pills are safe and effective; and the Public Health Council's June 1997 recommendation that the low-dose pill be approved in conjunction with efforts to increase public education on sexually transmitted diseases.[168] Despite all these indicators, however, pill advocates remained skeptical that the pill would actually be approved because of the ministry's record of last-minute reversals in the past.[169] And, as it turned out, they were correct. On March 2, 1998, the Drug Council postponed pill approval indefinitely by ordering that studies be conducted on the possible environmental effects of the pill, as well as the relationship between the pill and uterine cancer.

According to Ashino, the MHW was "rescued" from approving the pill by an environmental group called the Kanto Network to Stop Dioxin Pollution (Tomeyō Dioxin Osen Kantō Nettowāku). This group submitted a petition to the MHW in December 1997 requesting that the ministry "proceed cautiously" in its deliberations on the pill because of the possibility that pill users' urine, when released into the environment, might cause hormonal imbalances in animals and humans.[170] This theory was presumably extrapolated from American and European research documenting decreasing sperm counts, rising rates of testicular cancer, and rising incidences of genital malformation and feminization among male human and animal populations in certain areas. However, the scientists in question have identified the estrogen-like breakdown products of various industrial pollutants—detergents, pesticides, and PCBs—as the most likely cause of these phenomena, not the pill.[171] Given that no research conducted over the last ten years presents the pill as a possible cause of hormonal imbalances, and given that the MHW would ordinarily pay scant attention to the demands of such a small environmental group, it seems clear that the MHW, or some group within the MHW, was grasping at straws, willing to adopt the flimsiest of excuses in order to delay pill approval.

At the end of March 1998, FPFJ president Katō Shizue submitted a new petition calling for the speedy approval of the low-dose pill.[172] The Professional Women's Coalition for Sexuality and Health also started lobbying in earnest after the March 2 meeting, holding press conferences and sending out information kits on the pill and on reproductive health and rights to seventy politicians, MHW bureaucrats, members of the Drug Council, and the media. However, the political "opening" for pro-pill groups did not occur until almost a year later when, on January 25, 1999, the Health Ministry announced that it had approved the impotency cure, Viagra®. The decision was based on foreign clinical data and a scant six months of Drug Council deliberations on the safety and effectiveness of the drug.[173] The contrast between the Health Ministry's unusually hasty approval of Viagra and its decades of foot-dragging about the pill starkly exposed the sexist and unscientific nature of the decision-making process at the MHW and provoked an immediate outcry from Japanese feminist groups, women politicians, and the media.[174] Given that most drugs take considerably longer than six months to gain approval in Japan, and given that drug companies are generally required to perform clinical tests in Japan even if there is existing foreign data (as was the case with the low-dose pill), it would be difficult to overstate the gross disparity between the standards to which the MHW held Viagra and those to which it held the pill. Though the MHW justified its haste by explaining that black market Viagra sales had already resulted in some deaths in Japan,[175] it goes without saying that the Health Ministry never evinced this kind of concern about the health of women who used the therapeutic high-dose pill for off-label contraceptive purposes. As one journalist put it, the two decision-making processes "highlight the extent to which Japan remains a society dominated by men—elderly men willing to license a pill for their own benefit, but who seem scared of giving young women control over their fertility and sexuality. Japan remains a male gerontocracy."[176]

Finally shamed into action, on March 3, 1999, the Drug Council announced that the low-dose pill was safe and effective, and formally approved it three months later, on June 2.[177] The pill went on sale on September 2, 1999. However, the pill prescription guidelines the government endorsed—which were written by the two ob-gyn associations, the Japan Family Planning Association, the Japan Society of Fertility and Sterility, and the Japanese Association for Infectious Diseases—were quite stringent. They require pill users to visit a doctor every three months for a pelvic examination and undergo tests for sexually transmitted diseases and uterine cancer. In the United States and Europe, in contrast, an annual examination is standard for pill users. Reich points out that these guidelines are likely to serve as a barrier to access, since Japanese women do not visit gynecologists as regularly as women in many Western countries do, and they are more squeamish about pelvic exams. More to the point, though, the pill is not covered by health insurance, so women must pay for the pill themselves, as well as the frequent checkups, which represents a significant expense: between $550 and $950. Further, the requirement for frequent checkups clearly gives a signal to women—most of whom already distrust the pill after being bombarded with misinformation about it for decades—that the pill is a dangerous drug to use. And, in fact, one year after the pill was approved, only 100,000 Japanese women of childbearing age—less than half of 1 percent—had gotten prescriptions for the low-dose pill.[179] Although groups such as the Professional Women's Coalition seek to persuade the MHW to enact more moderate prescription guidelines, the professional groups that wrote the guidelines have far more influence with the Health Ministry. This means that over the next several years, if the pill becomes more popular—as it probably will, despite the strict guidelines—pro-pill groups may be forced to waste valuable time and energy fighting to ease prescription guidelines, when their resources would be better spent on lobbying for new contraceptive and early abortion technologies, as well as the revamping of the women's health care system.

## Conclusion

This chapter highlights the central fact that interest group influence over policy on the pill has been less consistent over time than interest group influence over abortion policy. Early on, interest groups—especially doctors' groups—played a decisive role in shaping pill policy, first overriding MHW plans to approve the high-dose pill in the 1960s, and then fashioning a doctor-friendly policy on the pill in the 1970s. But in the 1980s and 1990s, after these same groups reversed their position on the pill, they found that their ability to manipulate the bureaucracy was severely diminished.

There are several possible overlapping explanations for this development. One of the most important parts of the explanation lies in the tremendous loss of political influence that the JMA experienced in the early 1980s after the death of its powerful and well-connected president, Tarō Takemi, a blow that has been compounded by declining rates of membership over the last two decades (see chapter 2). Thus, over time, doctors lost much of their ability to bully the government into compliance—a phenomenon, incidentally, that has affected all professions in all industrialized democracies over the last several decades.[180] Equally important is that women—the pill's logical key constituency—long refrained from lobbying for the pill. And even after a few women's groups began to adopt a more positive and proactive stance on lifting the pill ban, the scope of women's mobilization around the pill issue was essentially nonexistent compared to women's efforts to block revision of the Eugenic Protection Law in the early 1980s. As for other interested groups (midwives, family planning advocates, pharmacists, and pharmaceutical companies), none came close to having the kind of political power that doctors once had or that women potentially have.

There are also structural, institutional factors that have affected interest groups' ability to shape the pill's fate in the 1980s and 1990s. Two important ones are that the MHW controls the selection of Drug Council appointees and is also able to keep the proceedings of the Drug Council secret from the public, and even from interested politicians. This allows the Ministry to isolate itself from outside influences when it chooses to do so. Abortion policy, in contrast, is controlled by the legislative branch, which is more susceptible to interest group influence.[181] But this explanation only begs the question: Why did the MHW avail itself of its institutional buffers in the 1980s and 1990s but not in the 1960s and 1970s? One surmises that the MHW was emboldened by the weakening of doctors' political power in the 1980s. It is also possible that the delay in approving the low-dose pill was influenced to some degree by the marked, overall slowdown of the drug approval process in Japan, which began in the mid-1980s.[182] Most important, though, the birth rate "crisis" continued to deepen from the 1960s on, with birth rates dropping relentlessly every year. Japan, Italy, and Spain now have the lowest birth rates in the industrialized world, and the extent of elite nervousness on this subject cannot be underestimated.[183]

Thus, at the end of the twentieth century, Japan approved a forty-year-old contraceptive technology—with prescription guidelines almost guaranteed to make Japanese women hesitate to use it—while other countries embraced contraceptive implants, contraceptive injections, emergency contraception, and medical abortion. It will undoubtedly be many years before these new technologies are introduced in Japan, absent a major mobilization of Japanese women. And as this chapter makes clear, such a mobilization is unlikely in the near future. The Japanese government has ratified several U.N. conventions on reproductive rights and women's rights, and in 1996 launched its own National Plan of Action for Promotion of a Gender-Equal Society by the Year 2000, but clearly, given the way the government handled the pill approval process, it is not yet prepared—nor does it probably understand how—to match rhetorical commitments with action.[184] The Japanese people have been badly served by their government, as well as by interest groups and the media, all of which have pursued their own agendas with little regard for individual needs, reproductive health and rights, or accurate and even-handed information. The story of the pill in Japan is a story without heroes.

## CHAPTER EIGHT

# Conclusion

HUMAN AFFAIRS are seldom orderly enough to accommodate "conclusive" conclusions. As the preceding chapters amply illustrate, history and politics are a glorious mess, full of surprising alliances and unexpected consequences. That said, two important themes can be teased out of the story of abortion and contraception policy in postwar Japan. One of these themes is the underrecognized activity and importance of interest groups and citizens' groups in Japanese politics. Chapters 4 and 5 reveal that the influence of interest groups has been particularly marked in the area of abortion policy making. But it would be premature to declare a societal "victory" over the state, for chapters 6 and 7 show that interest groups had more ambiguous and sometimes cooperative ties with the state in early birth control policy making and that interest group influence over pill policy declined after peaking in the 1960s and 1970s. Thus it is clear that the state-society relationship is a highly fluid, changeable entity designed to frustrate any definitive pronouncements on its character.

Another significant theme, or question, that surfaces in this book is, What is the nature of "progressive" or "liberal" thought in Japan, particularly with respect to the collective versus the individual good? How familiar or unfamiliar does the progressive-conservative divide in Japan look to a Western observer? And what have been the practical consequences of eugenic and nationalistic ideologies for reproductive health and rights in Japan? Readers will undoubtedly agree that ideology is even murkier and less amenable to definitive pronouncements than the state-society relationship, but it is worth exploring nonetheless.

The preceding chapters paint a picture of interest groups that get where they want to go by skillfully harnessing the larger political, social, and economic forces around them, just as good sailors harness wind and water to propel their little boats. Interest groups have, in many cases, taken the initiative in making reproduction policy and have often been able to convince or compel state actors to cooperate in implementing their agendas. But why have interest groups been able to affect reproduction policy—especially abortion policy— more than other political actors? Admittedly this question sets up something of a false dichotomy between state and societal groups, since much of the influence that medical and religious interests have exercised in this area has flowed from close, mutually beneficial, and synergistic relationships with politicians. In particular, we have seen how Taniguchi Yasaburō, the doctor who led the drive to legalize abortion, seamlessly fused the roles of interest group leader and politician. Yet there is also some truth to the notion that interest groups have been more active in this policy area than state actors, particularly bureaucrats. Part of the explanation may lie in what Margaret McKean has identified as the Japanese bureaucracy's inability or reluctance to resolve issues that fall into the regulatory, moral, or symbolic realms of policy, as opposed to the distributive or redistributive realms.[1] In this view, citizens' groups and interest groups have filled the leadership vacuum left by a bureaucracy unwilling or unable to take initiative on such complicated, morally charged, and potentially controversial issues as abortion and contraception—issues that cannot be reduced to monetary formulas during the budget-making process.

However, some Japanese academics and activists would dispute the notion that state actors so tamely conceded the field to societal groups. They would argue that state actors in the postwar period have regarded women much as they did in the prewar period, as mere "baby-making machines" to be switched on and off according to changes in the national interest. In this view, variations in the national interest can be used to explain variations in reproduction policy: During the Pacific War, the state promoted pronatalist policies and suppressed abortion and birth control in order to expand the Empire; after the war, the state legalized abortion and contraception in order to shrink the population and facilitate economic recovery; and when it became clear, starting in the 1960s, that Japan's economy was no longer in jeopardy and that a labor shortage loomed, the state tried to modify reproduction policy again by banning the pill and attempting to curtail access to abortion. Ishii, Iwamoto, and others argue that policies such as the continuing ban on voluntary sterilizations, the maintenance of the Criminal Abortion Law, and the shortening of the legal abortion period are further proof of the state's efforts to preserve control over reproduction and increase the birth rate.[2]

This book certainly provides evidence that state actors have often conceived of reproduction in nationalist or statist terms, as something that individuals should either engage in or refrain from in accordance with larger economic and political goals. Many government officials—both bureaucrats and politicians— would probably translate statist ideology into policy to a greater extent if they could, for there is great concern among elites that the declining birth rate and the aging of the population will lead to labor shortages, high taxes, and a heavy welfare burden that will ultimately cripple the Japanese economy. But there is a huge gap between elite rhetoric and what can actually be accomplished in the intimate realm of reproduction. Witness a 1990 statement by Hashimoto Ryūtarō (then finance minister and subsequently prime minister), who opined that the increase in higher education among women was a primary cause of declining birth rates and suggested that the government therefore alter its policy of enabling all students to attend college. Hashimoto's comments provoked a public outcry, and his chief Cabinet secretary was asked if the government intended to return to its wartime policy of exhorting women to "Give Birth and Multiply." He replied ruefully that " 'it isn't such an easy matter to get Japanese women to bear children for us.' "[3] No changes were made in education policy.

Thus it is clear that, regardless of what they might wish they could do, state actors are constrained—and know they are constrained—from adopting overtly discriminatory or coercive measures by the realities of democratic government. (And, in fact, this book demonstrates that even in the prewar period, when the political environment was decidedly undemocratic, the Japanese government failed utterly to raise birth rates.) For the most part, the driving force behind abortion and contraception policy making has been the self-interest of organized groups. These groups have skillfully—and opportunistically—maneuvered within and manipulated changing historical circumstances and ideologies, including the statist ideology of reproduction, in order to further their agendas.

However, societal actors in Japan have not always maneuvered and manipulated: at times, they themselves have succumbed to the allure of ideologies that promote collective over individual interests. And while this is not surprising in the case of right-wing conservatives, it may at first seem puzzling that it has also been true of some left-leaning birth control advocates and feminists, particularly in the prewar and occupation periods. Though some did oppose coercive eugenic policies and argue that individuals should be free to undergo sterilization on a purely voluntary basis, many of their peers supported coercive eugenic policies in the name of the national interest. Immediately after the war, socialist birth controllers actually sought to strengthen provisions for involuntary sterilization, "for the public good."

Given the tremendous emphasis on protecting individual freedom and minority rights in Western—particularly Anglo-American—liberal thought, the Western reader might initially question whether twentieth-century Japanese liberals and progressives were really all that liberal or progressive, or perhaps conclude that the lines of ideological cleavage in Japan were substantially different than in the West. This would be a flawed comparison, however, for, in the United States at least, there has always been a great gulf between the ideal of Lockean liberalism that looms so large in the national mythology, on the one hand, and the actual historical track record, on the other.[4] In fact, many Western liberals and left-wing activists embraced eugenics as enthusiastically as some of their Japanese counterparts did in their quest to find solutions to social ills, and were likewise blinded to eugenics' potential for abuse. The point here is not to make excuses for the Japanese, but merely to place them in the appropriate international and historical context.

What have the practical consequences of eugenic and nationalistic ideologies been for reproductive health and rights in Japan? In the very narrowest sense—that is, if one measures actual outcomes against desired consequences—these ideologies have had little effect, as noted above. Even during the most mobilized, collectivized period of the Pacific War, eugenic and nationalist policies failed to achieve either higher birth rates among the "fit" or lower birth rates among the "unfit." The same held true after the war, when provisions for involuntary sterilization were strengthened—though the postwar situation is more complicated, since the Eugenic Protection Law probably *did* contribute to lowering birth rates, though not within the eugenic sterilization framework that its authors had envisioned. In other words, birth rates were lowered across the board, not just among those whom lawmakers deemed "unfit," and they were lowered initially through the use of abortion, not sterilization, with 99 percent of women citing economic, rather than eugenic, reasons. Subsequently contraception (primarily condoms) became widespread enough to explain a larger percentage of fertility decline than abortion, but sterilization never became a popular method of contraception in Japan (see Figure 1.4), either for eugenic or maternal health reasons.

One positive and unintended consequence of these ideologies was that Japanese women gained easy—as opposed to highly regulated and restricted—access to safe and legal abortion much earlier than women in other countries, thereby avoiding many of the mental, physical, familial, and economic hardships associated with unwanted pregnancy and childbirth. But the early legalization of abortion in turn had the unintended and perverse effect of delaying the introduction of birth control. And even after birth control began to gain wider acceptance in the late 1950s, the early legalization of abortion continued to exert a negative "feedback effect"[5] on the pill approval process. The limited range of birth control options available in Japan exposed Japanese women to a variety of health risks—most notably, the risk of unplanned pregnancy, which stood at 40 percent of all pregnancies in 1995.[6] In sum, eugenic and nationalistic ideologies benefited women in unexpected ways early on by giving them easy access to safe abortions; but, in more recent decades, the costs flowing from these ideologies—that is, the limited access to the most reliable and effective forms of contraception, and the concomitant increased risk of unintended pregnancy—have probably outweighed the benefits.

What does the story of reproduction policy making tell us about civil society in Japan and, more broadly, about the state of Japanese democracy? For one thing, it demonstrates that, after World War II, elements in society gained more leverage over the state than they had before the war. The case of abortion policy making, in particular, suggests that civil society in Japan is more robust than is often acknowledged in the academic literature and the popular press. And since the strength of civil society is often cited as one of the indicators of the health of a democracy, it is tempting to conclude that Japan has a healthy democracy—or at least a healthier democracy than many give it credit for having.

Such a conclusion would tell only part of the story, however, for while the power of state actors is checked by that of societal actors, the reverse is also true. This is most strongly evident in the fact that over the course of a decade in the 1980s and 1990s, the Ministry of Health and Welfare successfully stonewalled medical and family planning groups seeking to gain approval for the low-dose pill. It is also evident in the fact that MHW officials initiated the creation of one of the main private family planning organizations, the Japan Family Planning Association. With respect to this kind of state-society relationship, Garon asks:

> Is it possible to speak of the proliferation of community groups as a manifestation of grass-roots democracy when so many got their start, or at least maintained themselves, due to official encouragement, outright subsidies, and governmental co-ordination?[7]

And he answers:

> Postwar Japan would seem to present an enigma. It is a polity whose democratic institutions and firm guarantees of civil liberties coexist with a broad-based commitment to managing society. . . . Perhaps the true genius of the Japanese state lies in its ability to marry the currents of democratization and social management.[8]

Setting aside for the moment the larger—and fundamentally unanswerable—question of state versus societal power, one must also consider the narrower issue of interest group power vis-à-vis that of other groups in civil society. For civil society consists of more than just interest groups; it also includes the large mass of individuals and families who are not members of any organized group. Women, in particular, have interests with regard to abortion and contraception policy—whether or not they articulate them—because these policies affect their lives so intimately. But as collective action theory teaches us, the interests of large, geographically dispersed groups with diverse concerns, few resources, and little incentive to organize tend to be subordinated to those of small, well-organized groups with focused agendas and financial and political resources at their disposal. Japan is no exception to this rule, and, as a result, women have not been as well represented as professional and religious groups in the abortion and contraception policy-making arena.

This underrepresentation of women lends weight to the view that interest groups corrupt democracy because they represent some people more than others and because, even within the interest group community, some groups are able to influence policy more than others.[9] But the situation in Japan has not been totally static: From the early 1970s on, groups representing women's interests, broadly speaking, began to compete with professional and religious groups for "voice" in abortion and contraception policy making.[10] And while their lobbying activities have had mixed results and much remains to be desired, nevertheless, they have gradually widened the scope of representation and begun to legitimize the concept of *women's* interests—as opposed to the traditional concept of mothers' and wives' interests—in the Japanese political world. The Japanese women's movement, in turn, has been bolstered and legitimized over the last twenty-five years by new currents of thinking that have emerged in various United Nations forums on family planning, women's health, and human rights (see chapter 5).

Thus it seems that in Japan, as in Europe and the United States, "the fundamental contribution of the modern women's movement was its ability to alter the 'universe of political discourse.' "[11] It is no longer acceptable, as it was in the early 1970s, for the Japanese media and government officials to publicly ridicule feminist demands for equal treatment and reproductive autonomy. As we saw in chapter 5, one indication of women's increased political power is the fact that the government and the designated abortion providers group, Nichibo, have gone so far as to adopt feminist and human rights rhetoric in recent years, calling for revisions to the Eugenic Protection Law and the Maternal Protection Law in the name of women's right to self-determination and handicapped people's human rights.[12] Of course, one suspects that the majority of male, middle-aged, and older Health Ministry officials and ob-gyns have little innate understanding or appreciation of the histories, goals, and possible long-term implications of the movements to whose ideologies they are now forced to pay lip service. Nevertheless the adoption—some would call it co-optation—of the feminist and human rights language definitely represents progress, even though real life improvements lag far behind rhetorical gains. For every United Nations resolution, White Paper, and law that uses this rhetoric will provide groups in society with a potential tool to effect change.

# Criminal Code, Section 29: Criminal Abortion (1907)
## [EXTANT]

### Article 212 (Abortion)

When a pregnant woman aborts using medicinal or other methods, she shall be sentenced to not more than one year of penal servitude.

### Article 213 (Consensual Abortion)

A person who performs an abortion [on a woman after being] commissioned by, or obtaining the consent of said woman shall be sentenced to not more than two years of penal servitude. If, as a result [of the abortion], said woman is injured or killed, the person [who performed the abortion] shall be sentenced to not less than three months, and not more than five years of penal servitude.

### Article 214 (Abortion by a Professional)

A physician, midwife, pharmacist, or druggist who performs an abortion [on a woman after being] commissioned by, or obtaining the consent of said woman shall be sentenced to not less than three months, and not more than five years of penal servitude. If, as a result [of the abortion], said woman is injured or killed, the person [who performed the abortion] shall be sentenced to not less than six months, and not more than seven years of penal servitude.

### Article 215 (Nonconsensual Abortion)

*Paragraph 1.* A person who performs an abortion [on a woman] without being commissioned by, or obtaining the consent of said woman shall be sentenced to not less than six months, and not more than seven years of penal servitude.

*Paragraph 2.* An attempt to commit the crime [described in] the preceding paragraph shall be punished.

### Article 216 (Resulting Aggravation)

A person who commits the crime [described in] the preceding paragraph and, as a result, injures or kills the woman shall be punished [for] battery in accordance with the severity [of the injury].

All translations are by the author.

# National Eugenics Law (1940)
## [ABOLISHED 1948]

### Article 1

The purpose of this law shall be to ensure the improvement of the national character by means of preventing an increase in the [number of] persons with a predisposition toward malignant hereditary disease and promoting an increase in [the number] of persons who have sound constitutions.

### Article 2

Under this law, "eugenic operations" shall be defined as operations or treatments to be prescribed by order that render reproduction impossible.

### Article 3

*Paragraph 1.* When a person suffers from one of the following diseases, and medical experience [suggests] that there is a particularly marked danger that said person's children or descendents will suffer from the same disease, said person may undergo a eugenic operation in accordance with this law. However, these restrictions do not apply if said person is recognized, at the same time, to have a particularly excellent constitution.

*Item 1.* Hereditary mental illness
*Item 2.* Hereditary mental deficiency
*Item 3.* Severe and malignant hereditary personality disorder
*Item 4.* Severe and malignant hereditary physical ailment
*Item 5.* Severe hereditary deformity

*Paragraph 2.* In cases where persons who are married to each other each have or had blood relatives within the fourth degree of consanguinity who suffer, or who suffered, from one of the diseases [listed] in the preceding paragraph, if medical experience [suggests] there is a particularly marked danger that future offspring will suffer from the same disease, [then] the preceding paragraph [applies]. (This includes [people who], even though they are not registered [as married], are married de facto.)

*Paragraph 3.* [In cases where] persons have or had children who suffer, or who suffered from one of the diseases [listed] in the first paragraph, if medical experience [suggests] that future offspring will suffer from the same disease, [then] the first paragraph applies.

### Article 4

*Paragraph 1.* A person who [qualifies] to undergo a eugenic operation in accordance with the provisions of the preceding article may file an application for the eugenic operation. In such cases, if said person has a spouse, it is required that his or her consent be obtained. (This includes people who are not registered [as married], but who are married de facto. This applies throughout.) If said spouse has not reached thirty years of age, or is feeble-minded, [then] it is required that the consent of the parents of the household be obtained. ([If] said person entered his or her spouse's household through marriage, it shall be the spouse's parents. This applies throughout.)

*Paragraph 2.* When a person who [qualifies] to undergo a eugenic operation in accordance with the provisions of the preceding article is *non compos mentis*, the parents of the household may file an application for a eugenic operation, regardless of the provisions of the preceding paragraph. However, if said person has a spouse, the spouse as well as the parents of the household may file the application.

*Paragraph 3.* If the spouse cannot be found/is unknown or cannot express his or her wishes, in cases where Paragraph 1 [applies], the consent of the parents of the household shall replace that of the spouse; in cases where the proviso in the preceding paragraph [applies], only the parents of the household shall be able to file an application.

*Paragraph 4.* In cases where, in accordance with the provisions of the three preceding paragraphs, the consent of the parents of the household is required, or said parents file an application, if one of the parents cannot be found/is unknown, is deceased, has left the house, or cannot express his or her wishes, the consent or application of the other parent will be sufficient. If both parents cannot be found/are unknown, are deceased, have left the house, or cannot express their wishes, [the consent or application] of the guardian [shall replace the consent or application of the parents of the household]. If the guardian cannot be found/is unknown or cannot express his or her wishes, or if there is no guardian, [the consent or application] of the family head [shall replace the consent or application of the parents of the household]. If the family head cannot be found/is unknown, is a minor, or cannot express his wishes, the consent or application of a family council shall replace the consent or application of the parents of the household. However, in accordance with the provisions of Paragraph 2, guardians and family councils may not file applications.

## Article 5

*Paragraph 1.* With regard to persons who [qualify] to undergo eugenic operations in accordance with the provisions of Article 3, Paragraph 1, and who are in [protective] custody, are receiving hygienic guidance, or are [undergoing] examination and treatment: according to the Mental Hospital Law, directors of hospitals (including substitute mental hospitals, as provided for in Article 7 of said law) or health centers, and doctors designated by decree may obtain the consent of the person in question and file an application for a eugenic operation. In such cases, if the person in question has a spouse, it is required that his or her consent also be obtained. If the spouse has not reached thirty years of age, or is feeble-minded, [then] it is required that the consent of the parents of the household also be obtained.

*Paragraph 2.* In cases where an application for a eugenic operation is filed in accordance with the provisions of the preceding paragraph, if the person in question is *non compos mentis*, the consent of the parents of the household shall replace that of the person in question.

*Paragraph 3.* The provisions of Paragraphs 3–4 of the preceding article shall apply to cases [described] in the two preceding paragraphs.

## Article 6

In instances where, for example, a person who [qualifies] to undergo a eugenic operation in accordance with the provisions of the preceding paragraph has a particularly malignant disease, or said person's spouse suffers from the same disease, if it is recognized that in order to prevent inheritance of the disease it is necessary, for the public good, [to perform a eugenic operation], an application for a eugenic operation may be filed, [along with] the reasons [such application is being filed], even if it is not possible to obtain the necessary consents in accordance with the provisions of the preceding paragraph.

## Article 7

*Paragraph 1.* Applications for eugenic operations shall be [addressed] to local governors, as determined by decree.

*Paragraph 2.* The medical certificate of the person in question, an examination certificate concerning [said person's] heredity, and a doctor's certificate [confirming that] said person understands that the eugenic operation will render reproduction impossible shall accompany the application [described] in the previous paragraph. (If the person in question is *non compos mentis*, [the eugenic operation shall be explained] to the parents of the household. However, if the person in question has a spouse, [the eugenic operation shall be explained] to [both] the spouse and the parents of the household.)

*Paragraph 3.* The provisions of Article 4, Paragraphs 3–4, apply to cases [described] in the preceding paragraph.

## Article 8

*Paragraph 1.* When a local governor receives an application for a eugenic operation, he will decide whether to authorize the operation.

*Paragraph 2.* Before making the decision [described] in the preceding paragraph, local governors shall solicit the opinion of the local Eugenic Investigation Commission [hereafter referred to as EIC].

*Paragraph 3.* When the local governor has made the decision [described] in Paragraph 1, in accordance with the provisions of Articles 4–5, [the following persons] shall be notified: the persons who may file an application for a eugenic operation, and [any] persons whose additional consent must be obtained for the application.

## Article 9

*Paragraph 1.* Should [any] person notified [of the governor's decision] in accordance with the provisions of Paragraph 3 of the preceding article have an objection to the decision [described] in the same article, he or she may make a statement to the Minister of Health and Welfare.

*Paragraph 2.* Statements, as [described] in the preceding paragraph, may not be made after thirty days have elapsed since notification of the decision. (In the case of persons who did not receive notification, [statements may not be made] after the decision [has been made].)

*Paragraph 3.* If the Minister of Health and Welfare deems that there are reasons [allowances] should be made, he may receive [statements] even after the time period [described] in the preceding paragraph has elapsed.

## Article 10

*Paragraph 1.* In cases where the Minister of Health and Welfare receives a statement, as [described] in the preceding article, if he deems the statement to be groundless, he shall reject it; if he deems the statement to have grounds, he shall revoke the local governor's decision and decide whether to authorize a eugenic operation.

*Paragraph 2.* Before rejecting [a statement], revoking [a governor's decision], or making a decision [as to whether a eugenic operation should be authorized], the Minister of Health and Welfare shall solicit the opinion of the central EIC.

*Paragraph 3.* The provisions of Article 8, Paragraph 3 apply to the rejections, revocations, and decisions [described] in Paragraph 1.

## Article 11

*Paragraph 1.* In accordance with the provisions of Articles 4–5, the [following persons] may submit a statement of fact or opinion, orally or in writing, to either the central or a local EIC: persons who may file an application for a eugenic operation, and [any] persons whose additional consent must be obtained for the application.

*Paragraph 2.* If the Minister of Health and Welfare or a local governor deems it necessary for the central or local EIC's investigation, the person who [qualifies] to undergo a eugenic operation may be required to appear before the Investigation Commission and state the facts, or the doctor's medical certificate may be obtained, as determined by decree, and in accordance with the provisions of Article 3.

## Article 12

Bylaws concerning central and local EICs shall be established by imperial edict.

## Article 13

*Paragraph 1.* When the decision to authorize a eugenic operation has been confirmed, the person who [qualifies] to undergo a eugenic operation in accordance with the provisions of Article 3 shall undergo a eugenic operation, as determined by decree.

*Paragraph 2.* The eugenic operation shall be performed by a doctor designated by decree, in a location designated by decree, in accordance with the Health and Welfare Minister's or a local governor's orders.

*Paragraph 3.* The doctor who performs the eugenic operation as provided for in the previous paragraph shall give the local governor a progress report, as determined by decree.

## Article 14

Expenses related to eugenic operations shall be [defrayed] as determined by imperial edict.

## Article 15

Operations or radiation procedures [meant] to render reproduction impossible may not be performed without cause.

## Article 16

*Paragraph 1.* Before a doctor performs an operation to render reproduction impossible, a radiation procedure, or an abortion, he shall [get] other doctors' opinions on whether [the procedure] is necessary, except in cases that are in accordance with the provision of Article 13. Moreover, said doctor shall submit a report to the administrative office before [he performs such procedures], as determined by decree. However, these restrictions do not apply in cases where a special emergency operation is required.

*Paragraph 2.* In cases where a report has been [submitted as described] in the preceding paragraph, if the administrative office deems it necessary, the designated doctor may be required to [give] his opinion again.

*Paragraph 3.* In cases where the proviso in Paragraph 1 [applies], if an operation to render reproduction impossible, a radiation procedure, or an abortion is performed without a report being submitted, a report shall be submitted to the administrative office, as determined by decree.

## Article 17

When he or she intends to marry, a person who has undergone a eugenic operation shall notify [his or her prospective spouse] of that fact upon request.

## Article 18

Persons who violate the provisions of Article 15 and perform operations to render reproduction impossible or radiation procedures shall be sentenced to not more than one year of penal servitude or be required to [pay] a fine not exceeding ¥1,000. If, as a result [of the operation], the [patient] is killed, [said person] shall be sentenced to not more than three years of penal servitude.

## Article 19

*Paragraph 1.* If [any of the following persons] disclose secrets they learn in the course of performing their duties, they shall be sentenced to not more than six months of penal servitude or be required to [pay] a fine not exceeding ¥1,000: members of central and local EICs; their assistants; present or former public officials involved in investigating or performing eugenic operations; and their assistants.

*Paragraph 2.* If one anticipates being accused of the crime [described] in the preceding paragraph, one cannot discuss it.

## Article 20

Persons who violate the provisions of Paragraph 1 or Paragraph 3 of Article 16 and do not submit a report, or submit a false report, shall be sentenced to [pay] a fine not exceeding ¥100.

## Bylaws

The effective date of this law and each of its provisions shall be determined by imperial edict.

## References

Summary of the Mental Hospital Law, Law #25, proclaimed March 27, 1920: If a Cabinet minister deems it necessary, a public or private mental hospital that has been deemed appropriate may, in accordance with the provisions of Article 1, be substituted for an established mental hospital during a designated period, [once] consent has been obtained [from said public or private mental hospital]. In such cases, the provisions of Articles 2 and 5 shall apply.

# Eugenic Protection Law (1948)
## [ABOLISHED 1996]

### CHAPTER 1. GENERAL PROVISIONS

### Article 1 (Purpose)

The purpose of this law is to prevent the birth of eugenically inferior offspring, and to protect maternal health and life.

## Article 2 (Definitions)

*Paragraph 1.* Under this law, a "eugenic operation" shall be defined as an operation that renders reproduction impossible without removing the sexual organs; eugenic operations are to be prescribed by order.

*Paragraph 2.* Under this law, "artificial interruption of pregnancy" [hereafter, "abortion"] shall be defined as the artificial discharge of a fetus and its appendages during the period when the fetus cannot sustain life outside the mother's body.

CHAPTER 2. EUGENIC OPERATIONS

## Article 3 (Physician Authorized Eugenic Operations)

*Paragraph 1.* A physician may perform eugenic operations on persons to whom one of the following items applies, once said physician has received the consent of the person in question, and, if said person has a spouse, the consent of said person's spouse. (This includes people who are not registered as married but who are married de facto. This applies throughout.) However, this does not apply with respect to minors, mentally ill persons, or mentally deficient persons.

Item 1. If the person in question or that person's spouse has a hereditary psychopathic disorder, hereditary physical ailment, or hereditary deformity, or said spouse is mentally ill or mentally deficient

Item 2. If a blood relative within the fourth degree of consanguinity of the person in question or that person's spouse has a hereditary mental illness, hereditary mental deficiency, hereditary psychopathic disorder, hereditary physical ailment or hereditary deformity

Item 3. If the person in question or that person's spouse suffers from leprosy and is likely to infect offspring

Item 4. If pregnancy or childbirth is likely to endanger the mother's life

Item 5. If the mother already has several children, and her health is likely to deteriorate markedly with each birth

*Paragraph 2.* In the cases described in Items 4 and 5 of the preceding paragraph, a eugenic operation may also be performed on the spouse, in accordance with the provisions of said paragraph.

*Paragraph 3.* With respect to the consent mentioned in Paragraph 1, when the spouse cannot be found, or cannot indicate his or her wishes, the sole consent of the person in question shall be sufficient.

## Article 4 (Applications for Eugenic Operations for Which an Investigation Is Required)

In cases where, as the result of his or her examination, a physician confirms that a person suffers from one of the ailments listed in the appendix to this statute, and recognizes that in order to prevent hereditary transmission of the disease it is necessary, for the public good, to perform a eugenic operation, said physician shall apply to the metropolitan, Hokkaido, or prefectural Eugenic Protection Commission [hereafter, EPC] for a judgment on the appropriateness of performing a eugenic operation.

## Article 5 (Eugenic Operation Investigations)

*Paragraph 1.*   When a metropolitan, Hokkaido, or prefectural EPC receives an application, as provided for in the preceding article, in addition to notifying the person to be operated on that said application has been received, said EPC shall investigate whether the case meets the requirements provided for in the preceding article and, based on said investigation, shall determine the appropriateness of performing a eugenic operation. Said EPC shall then notify the applicant and the person to be operated on of its decision.

*Paragraph 2.*   When a metropolitan, Hokkaido, or prefectural EPC determines that it is appropriate to perform a eugenic operation, said EPC shall ask the opinion of the applicant and concerned parties and then appoint a physician to perform the eugenic operation, and notify the applicant, the person to be operated on, and the physician in question of that appointment.

## Article 6 (Application for Reinvestigation)

*Paragraph 1.*   When, in accordance with the provisions of Paragraph 1 of the preceding article, a person receives the metropolitan, Hokkaido, or prefectural EPC's decision that he or she should undergo a eugenic operation, should that person have an objection, he or she may apply to the Public Health Commission for a reinvestigation within two weeks of the date on which he or she was notified of the decision.

*Paragraph 2.*   The spouse, parent, guardian, or assistant of a person who receives such a decision may also apply for a reinvestigation.

*Paragraph 3.*   Applications for reinvestigation provided for in the previous two paragraphs shall go through the metropolitan, Hokkaido, or prefectural EPC which made the decision that a eugenic operation should be performed. In such cases, said EPC shall submit pertinent opinions to the Public Health Commission.

## Article 7 (Reinvestigation of Eugenic Operations)

When the Public Health Commission receives an application for reinvestigation as provided for in the preceding article, in addition to notifying the physician [appointed to] perform the operation of this development, said Commission shall once again weigh the appropriateness of performing a eugenic operation, on the basis of an investigation. Said Commission shall then notify the following persons of its decision: the applicant, the person to be operated on, the metropolitan, Hokkaido, or prefectural EPC in question, and the doctor appointed to perform the operation.

## Article 8 (Statements of Opinion concerning Investigations)

The applicant provided for in Article 4, the person to be operated on, and that person's spouse, parent, guardian, or assistant may submit an oral or written statement of fact or opinion concerning the investigation provided for in Article 5, Paragraph 1, or the reinvestigation provided for in the preceding article, to either the metropolitan, Hokkaido, or prefectural EPC in question or the Public Health Commission.

## Article 9 (Filing a Suit)

Persons dissatisfied with the Public Health Commission's decision may file a suit for its cancellation.

## Article 9, Part 2 (Procedure for Disputation)

Persons dissatisfied with a decision that a eugenic operation should be performed, as provided for in Article 5, Paragraph 1, may only dispute matters provided for in Article 6 or the preceding article.

## Article 10 (Performance of Eugenic Operations)

When there are no objections to the decision that the performance of a eugenic operation is appropriate, or when either the original decision or a reinvestigation of the original decision has been conclusively settled, the physician provided for in Article 5, Paragraph 2 shall perform the eugenic operation.

## Article 11 (Defrayment of Costs)

*Paragraph 1.* Expenses related to eugenic operations performed in accordance with the provisions of the preceding article shall be paid by the metropolis, Hokkaido, or the prefecture in question, as prescribed by Cabinet order.

*Paragraph 2.* The National Treasury shall defray the expenses provided for in the previous paragraph.

## Article 12 (Eugenic Operations on Mentally Ill Persons, etc.)

With regard to persons suffering from mental illnesses or mental deficiencies other than those hereditary conditions listed in Items 1 and 2 of the appendix: In cases where a physician has the consent of the protector provided for in Article 20 (where the guardian, spouse, parent, or assistant acts as protector) or Article 21 (where the city, town, or village head acts as protector) of the Mental Health Law (1950, Law #123), said physician may apply to the metropolitan, Hokkaido, or prefectural EPC for a judgment on the appropriateness of performing a eugenic operation.

## Article 13

*Paragraph 1.* When a metropolitan, Hokkaido, or prefectural EPC receives an application, as provided for in the preceding article, said EPC shall investigate whether the person in question suffers from one of the mental illnesses or mental deficiencies provided for in the preceding article, and whether performing a eugenic operation is necessary for the protection of the person in question. On the basis of said investigation, said EPC shall then determine the appropriateness of performing a eugenic operation, and notify the applicant and the person giving consent (mentioned in the previous article) of its decision.

*Paragraph 2.* When, as provided for in the preceding paragraph, a physician has received the decision that performing a eugenic operation is the appropriate course to follow, said physician may perform the eugenic operation.

## Chapter 3. Protection of Motherhood

## Article 14 (Physician-Authorized Abortion)

*Paragraph 1.* A physician designated by his or her prefectural medical association (a corporate juridical body) may perform abortions on persons to whom one of the following items applies, once said physician has received the consent of the person in question and that person's spouse. (Such physicians will hereafter be referred to as "designated physicians.")

> *Item 1.* If the person in question or that person's spouse has a mental illness, mental deficiency, psychopathic disorder, hereditary physical ailment or hereditary deformity
>
> *Item 2.* If a blood relative within the fourth degree of consanguinity of the person in question or that person's spouse has a hereditary mental illness, hereditary mental deficiency, hereditary psychopathic disorder, hereditary physical ailment or a hereditary physical deformity
>
> *Item 3.* If the person in question or that person's spouse suffers from leprosy
>
> *Item 4.* If the continuation of pregnancy or childbirth is likely to seriously harm the mother's health for physical or economic reasons
>
> *Item 5.* If pregnancy results from rape due to assault, coercion, or inability to offer resistance or refusal

*Paragraph 2.* With respect to the consent mentioned in the preceding paragraph, when the spouse cannot be found, cannot indicate his wishes, or is deceased, the sole consent of the person in question shall be sufficient.

*Paragraph 3.* When the person who will undergo the abortion is mentally ill or mentally deficient, the consent of the protector provided for in Article 20 (where the guardian, spouse, parent, or provider acts as protector) or Article 21 (where the city, town, or village head acts as protector) of the Mental Health Law may be regarded as the consent of the person in question.

## Article 15 (Practical Guidance about Contraception)

*Paragraph 1.* Other than physicians, no one but persons appointed by the metropolitan, Hokkaido, or prefectural governor shall professionally offer practical guidance about birth control methods that employ contraceptive devices that the Minister of Health and Welfare has designated for women's use. However, no one other than a physician shall professionally insert intrauterine devices.

*Paragraph 2.* Midwives, public health nurses, and nurses who have completed a short training course authorized by the prefectural governor in accordance with the standards established by the Minister of Health and Welfare may be appointed by the governor as provided for in the preceding paragraph.

*Paragraph 3.* In addition to matters provided for in the preceding two paragraphs, necessary matters related to governors' designation or authorization shall be prescribed by Cabinet order.

## Chapter 4. Metropolitan, Hokkaido, and Prefectural Eugenic Protection Commissions

## Article 16 (Metropolitan, Hokkaido, and Prefectural Eugenic Protection Commissions)

Metropolitan, Hokkaido, and prefectural Eugenic Protection Commissions [EPCs] shall be established under the supervision of Metropolitan, Hokkaido, and prefectural governors in order to conduct investigations into the appropriateness of eugenic operations.

## Article 17

Deleted.

## Article 18 (Organization)

*Paragraph 1.* The EPC shall be composed of no more than ten members.

*Paragraph 2.* When there is a particular need for it, a temporary member may be appointed to the EPC.

*Paragraph 3.* Governors shall appoint members and temporary members from among physicians, welfare commissioners, judges, public prosecutors, national and municipal government officials in related administrative offices, and other learned and experienced persons.

*Paragraph 4.* EPC members shall elect one person from among themselves as chairman.

*Paragraph 5.* Concerning remuneration and compensation for EPC members, the provisions of Article 203 (remuneration and compensation) of the Local Autonomy Law (1947, Law #617) shall apply.

## Article 19 (Delegated Matters)

Except for those matters provided for in this law, necessary matters concerning the administration of the EPC—such as members' terms of office and chairmen's duties—shall be prescribed by order.

Chapter 5. Eugenic Protection Consultation Offices

## Article 20

Eugenic Protection Consultation Offices [hereafter, EPCOs] shall be established to offer advice about eugenic marriage, to promote the dissemination and improvement of necessary knowledge about heredity and eugenic protection, and to disseminate knowledge and give guidance concerning proper methods of contraception.

## Article 21 (Establishment)

*Paragraph 1.* Metropolises, Hokkaido, and prefectures, as well as cities with public health centers, shall establish EPCOs.

*Paragraph 2.* The EPCOs described in the preceding paragraph may be attached to public health centers.

*Paragraph 3.* The state may subsidize a portion of the expenses necessary to establish and operate the EPCOs described in Paragraph 1, as prescribed by Cabinet order.

## Article 22 (Approval of Establishment)

*Paragraph 1.* When a person other than the state, a metropolis, Hokkaido, a prefecture, or a city with a public health center wishes to establish an EPCO, he or she shall obtain approval from the Minister of Health and Welfare.

*Paragraph 2.* The EPCOs described in the preceding paragraph shall have doctors and equipment necessary for examinations, in accordance with the standards established by the Minister of Health and Welfare.

*Paragraph 3.* Should an EPCO (described in Paragraph 1) no longer meet the standards [described] in the preceding paragraph, the Minister of Health and Welfare may revoke said EPCO's license. In such a case, the Minister of Health and Welfare shall have an official conduct a hearing to give said EPCO's founder an opportunity to explain his or her case.

## Article 23 (Exclusive Use of Name)

According to this law, entities that are not EPCOs shall not use the characters "Eugenic Protection Consultation Office," or characters that resemble the aforementioned in their names.

## Article 24 (Delegated Matters)

Except for those matters provided for in this law, necessary matters concerning EPCOs shall be prescribed by order.

## CHAPTER 6. REPORTING, PROHIBITIONS, ETC.

## Article 25 (Reporting)

When a physician or designated physician performs eugenic operations or abortions in accordance with the provisions of Article 3, Paragraph 1; Article 10; Article 13, Paragraph 2; or Article 14, Paragraph 1, said physician shall sum up the results of operations performed that month and submit a report to the Metropolitan, Hokkaido, or prefectural governor describing the reasons for performing the operations by the tenth day of the following month.

## Article 26 (Notification)

A person who has undergone a eugenic operation shall notify his or her prospective spouse to that effect before the marriage takes place.

## Article 27 (Preservation of Privacy)

Persons involved in investigating eugenic operations, persons who perform abortions or eugenic operations, and employees of EPCOs shall not divulge secrets they learn in the course of their work. The same shall [apply] even after retirement.

## Article 28 (Prohibitions)

No one shall, without cause, perform an operation or an X ray for the purpose of rendering reproduction impossible, other than in cases provided for in this law.

## CHAPTER 7. PENAL REGULATIONS

## Article 29 (Violations of Article 15, Paragraph 1)

Persons who violate the provisions of Article 15, Paragraph 1 shall be sentenced to pay a fine not exceeding ¥500,000.

## Article 30 (Violations of Article 22)

Persons who violate the provisions of Article 22 and open an EPCO without obtaining a license from the Minister of Health and Welfare shall be sentenced to pay a fine not exceeding ¥300,000.

## Article 31 (Violations of Article 23)

Persons who violate the provisions of Article 23 and use the characters "Eugenic Protection Consultation Office," or characters that resemble the aforementioned, in their organization's name shall be sentenced to pay a correctional fine not exceeding ¥100,000.

## Article 32 (Violations of Article 25)

Persons who violate the provisions of Article 25 and either do not submit a report, or submit a false report, shall be sentenced to pay a fine not exceeding ¥100,000.

## Article 33 (Violations of Article 27)

Persons who violate the provisions of Article 27 and divulge secrets without cause shall be sentenced to not more than six months penal servitude or be required to pay a fine not exceeding ¥300,000.

## Article 34 (Violations of Article 28)

Persons who violate the provisions of Article 28 shall be sentenced to not more than one year of penal servitude or be required to pay a fine not exceeding ¥500,000. If this violation leads to someone's death, then the sentence shall be not more than three years of penal servitude.

BYLAWS

## Article 35 (Effective Date)

This law shall become effective sixty days after it is promulgated (September 11, 1948).

## Article 36 (Abolition of Related Laws)

The National Eugenics Law (1940, Law #107) is abolished.

## Article 37 (Continued Validity of Penal Regulations)

Even after this law becomes effective, the law mentioned in the preceding article shall remain valid with regard to the application of penal regulations to violations committed before the current law became effective.

## Article 38 (Exceptions for Reports)

The provisions of Article 25 shall not apply in cases where a report was submitted in accordance with the provisions of the Minister of Health and Welfare's 1946 Order #42 (provisions concerning reports on stillbirths).

## Article 39 (Medical Supplies Necessary for Guidance about Birth Control)

*Paragraph 1.*  Until July 31, 1995, only those persons who have been appointed by a prefectural governor in accordance with the provisions of Article 15, Paragraph 1, may sell medical supplies and devices that are necessary for contraception, and that have been designated by the Minister of Health and Welfare, to persons receiving practical guidance about contraception. This applies regardless of the provisions of Article 24, Paragraph 1, of the Pharmaceutical Law (1960, Law #145).

*Paragraph 2.*  A governor may revoke a person's appointment in accordance with the provisions of Article 15, Paragraph 1, if one of the following items applies to that person.

> *Item 1.*  In cases where the provisions of Article 43 of the Pharmaceutical Law apply to medical supplies designated by the Minister of Health and Welfare in accordance with the provisions of the preceding paragraph: if the person in question has sold medical supplies that have not passed clinical tests, as provided for in said article
>
> *Item 2.*  If the person in question has professionally sold medical supplies other than those designated by the Minister of Health and Welfare in accordance with the preceding paragraph
>
> *Item 3.*  In addition to the preceding two items, if the person in question has professionally sold medical supplies to persons other than those receiving practical guidance about contraception

*Paragraph 3.*  When a governor seeks to discipline someone in accordance with the provisions of the preceding paragraph, said governor shall inform the person in question of the grounds for discipline and conduct a public hearing. Moreover, said governor shall inform the person who is to be disciplined of the date and place of the hearing not less than one week before it occurs, and shall request the presence at the hearing of the person in question or that person's representative. However, if the person in question or that person's representative does not respond to the hearing, without good cause, then the governor may proceed with the disciplinary action in accordance with the provisions of the preceding paragraph, without conducting a public hearing.

## APPENDIX

### (Related to Article 4 and Article 12)

> *Item 1.*  *Hereditary Mental Illnesses*: schizophrenia; manic-depression; epilepsy

*Item 2.* *Hereditary Mental Deficiency*

*Item 3.* *Serious Hereditary Psychopathic Disorders*: seriously abnormal sexual desires; serious criminal tendencies

*Item 4.* *Serious Hereditary Physical Ailments*: Huntington's chorea; hereditary spinal ataxia; hereditary cerebellar ataxia; progressive muscular atrophy; progressive muscular dystrophy; myotonia; congenital musculorom atonia; congenital cartilaginous malformation; albinism (leukosis); ichthyosis; multiple soft neurofibroma; sclerosis nodosum; epidermolysis bullosa hereditaria; hereditary porphyria; hereditary hyperkeratosis of the palm or sole; hereditary atrophy of the optic nerve; retinitis pigmentosa; total color blindness (achromatopsia); hereditary retinoblastoma; blue sclera; hereditary hearing impairment or hereditary deafness; hemophilia

*Item 5.* *Extreme Hereditary Deformities*: lacerated hand or foot; congenital bone defect

# Maternal Protection Law (1996)
## [EXTANT]

CHAPTER 1. GENERAL PROVISIONS

### Article 1 (Purpose)

The purpose of this law is to establish rules for sterilization operations and artificial interruption of pregnancy [hereafter, "abortion"] in order to protect maternal health and life.

### Article 2 (Definitions)

*Paragraph 1.* Under this law, a "sterilization operation" shall be defined as an operation that renders reproduction impossible without removing the sexual organs; sterilization operations are to be prescribed by order.

*Paragraph 2.* Under this law, "artificial interruption of pregnancy" shall be defined as the artificial discharge of a fetus and its appendages during the period when the fetus cannot sustain life outside the mother's body.

CHAPTER 2. STERILIZATION OPERATIONS

### Article 3

*Paragraph 1.* A physician may perform sterilization operations on persons to whom one of the following items applies, once said physician has received the consent of the person in question and, if said person has a spouse, the consent of said person's spouse. (This includes people who are not registered as married but who are married de facto. This applies throughout.) However, this does not apply with respect to minors.

Item 1. If the person in question or that person's spouse suffers from leprosy and is likely to infect offspring

Item 2. If pregnancy or childbirth is likely to endanger the mother's life

Item 3. If the mother already has several children, and her health is likely to deteriorate markedly with each birth

Paragraph 2. In the cases described in the preceding paragraph, a sterilization operation may also be performed on the spouse, in accordance with the provisions of said paragraph.

Paragraph 3. With respect to the consent mentioned in Paragraph 1, when the spouse cannot be found, or cannot indicate his or her wishes, the sole consent of the person in question shall be sufficient.

## CHAPTER 3. PROTECTION OF MOTHERHOOD

### Article 4 (Physician-Authorized Abortion)

Paragraph 1. A physician designated by his or her prefectural medical association (a corporate juridical body) may perform abortions on persons to whom one of the following items applies, once said physician has received the consent of the person in question and that of the person's spouse. (Such physicians will hereafter be referred to as "designated physicians.")

Item 1. If the person in question or that person's spouse suffers from leprosy

Item 2. If the continuation of pregnancy or childbirth is likely to seriously harm the mother's health for physical or economic reasons

Item 3. If pregnancy results from rape due to assault, coercion, or inability to offer resistance or refusal

Paragraph 2. With respect to the consent mentioned in the preceding paragraph, when the spouse cannot be found, cannot indicate his wishes, or is deceased, the sole consent of the person in question shall be sufficient.

### Article 5 (Practical Guidance about Contraception)

Paragraph 1. Other than physicians, no one but persons appointed by the metropolitan, Hokkaido, or prefectural governor shall professionally offer practical guidance about birth control methods that employ contraceptive devices that the Minister of Health and Welfare has designated for women's use. However, no one other than a physician shall professionally insert intrauterine devices.

*Paragraph 2.* Midwives, public health nurses, and nurses who have completed a short training course authorized by the prefectural governor in accordance with the standards established by the Minister of Health and Welfare may be appointed by the governor as provided for in the preceding paragraph.

*Paragraph 3.* In addition to matters provided for in the preceding two paragraphs, necessary matters related to governors' designation or authorization shall be prescribed by Cabinet order.

## CHAPTER 5. REPORTING, PROHIBITIONS, ETC.

### Article 6 (Reporting)

When a physician or designated physician performs sterilization operations or abortions in accordance with the provisions of Article 3, Paragraph 1; or Article 4, Paragraph 1, said physician shall sum up the number of operations performed that month and submit a report by the tenth day of the following month to the metropolitan, Hokkaido, or prefectural governor describing the reasons for performing the operations.

### Article 7 (Notification)

A person who has undergone a sterilization operation shall notify his or her prospective spouse to that effect before the marriage takes place.

### Article 8 (Preservation of Privacy)

Persons involved in investigating sterilization operations and persons who perform abortions or sterilization operations shall not divulge secrets they learn in the course of their work. The same shall [apply] even after retirement.

### Article 9 (Prohibitions)

No one shall, without cause, perform an operation or an X ray for the purpose of rendering reproduction impossible, other than in cases provided for in this law.

## CHAPTER 6. PENAL REGULATIONS

### Article 10 (Violations of Article 5, Paragraph 1)

Persons who violate the provisions of Article 5, Paragraph 1, shall be sentenced to pay a fine not exceeding ¥500,000.

## Article 11 (Violations of Article 9)

Persons who violate the provisions of Article 9 shall be sentenced to not more than one year of penal servitude or be required to pay a fine not exceeding ¥500,000. If this violation leads to someone's death, then the sentence shall be not more than three years of penal servitude.

### BYLAWS

## Article 12 (Effective Date)

This law shall become effective three months after it is promulgated (September 26, 1996).

# Notes

1. The Alan Guttmacher Institute, ed., *Hopes and Realities: Closing the Gap between Women's Aspirations and Their Reproductive Experiences* (New York: The Alan Guttmacher Institute, 1996), p. 23.

2. See, e.g., ibid.

3. David E. Bloom and Jeffrey G. Williamson, "Demographic Transitions and Economic Miracles in Emerging Asia" (Cambridge, Mass.: National Bureau of Economic Research Working Paper 6268, November 1997), pp. 4, 9–11, 17.

4. Ibid., pp. 9–10, 18–19.

5. Of course, advances in literacy, civil and political rights, and societal attitudes and practices related to women are equally fundamental preconditions, though they are not the focus of this book.

## Chapter One
### Introduction

1. *Mainichi Daily News*, December 5, 1997; January 6, 1998; *Watashi no karada kara* (formerly *Soshiren nyūsu*), April 29, 1998. See chapter 7 for a more detailed discussion of the controversy over "environmental hormones" in Japan.

2. See, e.g., *Mainichi shinbun*, June 3, 1999; *U.S. News & World Report*, July 5, 1999, p. 41; *Medical Industry Today*, September 7, 1999.

3. Marilyn Jane Field, *The Comparative Politics of Birth Control* (New York: Praeger, 1983), pp. 32–33, 182–83.

4. According to the letter of the law, anyone who deviates from these criteria may be prosecuted for criminal abortion. Prosecutions for criminal abortion are extremely rare, though there was one case that went before Japan's Supreme Court as recently as 1988. The case involved a late-term fetus that was aborted but born alive. Ishii Michiko, "Yūsei Hogo Hō ni yoru datai gōhōka no mondaiten," *Shakai kagaku kenkyū* 34:4 (1982): 153; "Gyōmujo datai, hogosha iki chishi, shitai iki hikoku jiken," *Saikō saibansho keiji keireishū* 42:1–6 (January–July 1988). For a summary and analysis of the case, see Nakatani Kinko, "Datai ni yori shussei saseta mijukuji o hōchi shita ishi to hogosha iki chishizai no seihi," *Jūrisuto rinji zōkan: Shōwa 63 nendo jūyō hanrei kaisetsu* 935 (1989). Because prosecutions are so rare, many commentators call the Criminal Abortion Law a "dead letter," but others note that, by leaving the law on the books, legislators hold in reserve the potential to restrict access to abortion in the future. Yasuko Tama, "The Logic of Abortion: Japanese Debates on the Legitimacy of Abortion as Seen in Post–World War II Newspapers," *U.S.–Japan Women's Journal* 7 (1994): 16; Kinko Nakatani, "The Status of Abortion in Japan and Some Issues," *Keio Law Review* (1985): 14; Ogino Miho, "Jinkō ninshin chūzetsu to josei no jiko ketteiken," in Hara Hiroko and Tachi Kaoru, eds., *Bosei kara jisedai ikuseiryoku e* (Tokyo: Shinyōsha, 1991), p. 138.

5. Forty percent of countries allow abortion on demand, without restriction as to reason. In 26 percent of countries worldwide, abortion is either prohibited or permitted only to save the woman's life (Center for Reproductive Law and Policy, "The World's Abortion Laws 1999" [map]).

6. In fact, given the prevalence of nonlegal barriers to access in the United States, such as shortages of providers and anti-choice harassment at women's health clinics, I suspect it is generally *easier* to get an abortion in Japan.

7. Mary Ann Glendon, *Abortion and Divorce in Western Law* (Cambridge, Mass.: Harvard University Press, 1987), p. 13; Evert Ketting and Philip van Praag, "The Marginal Relevance of Legislation Relating to Induced Abortion," in Joni Lovenduski and Joyce Outshoorn, eds., *The New Politics of Abortion* (London: Sage, 1986), pp. 154, 156–57, 162.

8. The Japanese Health Ministry has shortened the legal abortion period several times in the last two decades in accordance with medical advances in sustaining premature infants, from twenty-eight weeks to twenty-four weeks in 1976, twenty-four to twenty-three weeks in 1978, and twenty-three to twenty-two weeks in 1991. The MHW vice minister makes these changes via *tsūtatsu* (directives). The legal abortion period in the United States is also based on fetal viability, but most industrialized democracies limit abortion to the first trimester (twelve weeks) of pregnancy (Stanley K. Henshaw and Evelyn Morrow, *Induced Abortion: A World Review* [New York: The Alan Guttmacher Institute, 1990], pp. 27–31).

9. Statistics and Information Department, Japanese Ministry of Health and Welfare, *Heisei gonen yūsei hogo tōkei hōkoku* (Tokyo: Kōseishō Daijin Kanbō Tōkei Hōkokubu, 1994).

10. This last provision is not strictly enforced. The phrasing of the law in terms of "the person in question and that person's spouse" (*honnin mata wa haigūsha*) leaves the legal status of abortion for the unmarried in a gray area, although it is not specifically prohibited.

11. Hereditary illnesses included, for example, muscular dystrophy, color blindness, deafness, and hemophilia.

12. See *Yūsei hogo tōkei hōkoku, 1993* (Tokyo: Kōseishō Daijin Kanbō Tōkei Jōhōbu, 1994), p. 23.

13. Nakagawa Kiyoshi, "Toshi nichijō seikatsu no naka no sengo: minshū ni totte no jinkō ninshin chūzetsu," in Narita Ryūichi , ed., *Kindai nihon no kiseki: toshi to minshū* (Tokyo: Yoshikawa Kobunkan, 1993), p. 274; Robert Hodge and Naohiro Ogawa, *Fertility Change in Contemporary Japan* (Chicago: University of Chicago Press, 1991), p. 47; Michiko Ishii, "Yūsei Hogo Hō ni yoru datai gōhōka no mondaiten," *Shakai Kagaku Kenkyū* 34, no. 4 (1982): 113.

14. Samuel Coleman, *Family Planning in Japanese Society* (Princeton, N.J.: Princeton University Press, 1983), p. 4. First trimester abortions cost between ¥60,000 and ¥140,000; second trimester abortions, between ¥140,000 and ¥240,000 (interview with Ashino Yuriko, Deputy Executive Director, Family Planning Federation of Japan, January 10, 1995). Underreporting of abortions is common in other countries as well, though for different reasons. In France and Italy, for example, the number of abortions performed in a hospital or other facility may not exceed a certain percentage of all operations performed, leading doctors to stop reporting abortions performed after the quota has been reached (Ketting and van Praag, "The Marginal Relevance of Legislation," p. 165).

15. Noriko Tsuya, "Proximate Determinants of Fertility Decline in Postwar Japan," in The Population Problems Research Council, The Mainichi Papers, ed., *The Population and Society of Postwar Japan—Based on Half a Century of Surveys on Family Planning* (Tokyo: Mainichi Newspapers, 1994), pp. 116–23. The problem with Tsuya's study is that she only estimates underreporting for abortions performed on married women. Abortions performed on unmarried women are thought to go unreported at a higher rate than those performed on married women, so it is safe to assume that the degree of underreporting for all abortions is higher than Tsuya estimates (Coleman, *Family Planning in Japanese Society*, p. 6).

16. Nakagawa cites a report by Muramatsu and Ogino of the National Public Health Hospital which estimated that although 1 million abortions were reported in 1953, the actual number was between 1.8 and 2.3 million (Nakagawa, "Toshi nichijō seikatsu no naka no sengo," p. 274). See also Minoru Muramatsu, "Estimation of Induced Abortions, Japan, 1975," *Bulletin of the Institute of Public Health* 27:2 (1975); Minoru Muramatsu and Jean van der Tak, "From Abortion to Contraception: The Japanese Experience," in Henry P. David et al., eds., *Abortion in Psychosocial Perspective: Trends in Transnational Research* (New York: Springer, 1978), pp. 145–67.

17. Mariko Jitsukawa and Carl Djerassi, "Birth Control in Japan: Realities and Prognosis," *Science* 265 (August 19, 1994); *Mainichi Daily News*, November 5, 1996; personal communication from Midori Ashida, former secretary of the Professional Women's Coalition for Sexuality and Health, December 1999.

18. Until the mid-1980s the majority of abortions were performed on married women in their late twenties, thirties, and forties, but since 1985 the percentage of abortions obtained by married women has dropped below 50 percent of the total, while the percentage of abortions obtained by unmarried women in their teens and early twenties has increased. Thus the demographics of abortion in Japan may be moving in the direction of other industrialized democracies, where a large percentage (often the majority) of abortions are obtained by teenagers (Coleman, *Family Planning in Japanese Society*, p. 5); Miho Ogino, "Abortion and Women's Reproductive Rights: The State of Japanese Women, 1945–1991," in Joyce Gelb and Marian Lief Palley, eds., *Women of Japan and Korea: Continuity and Change* (Philadelphia: Temple University Press, 1994), pp. 74–76; and Tsuya, "Proximate Deterrents of Fertility Decline," p. 117.

19. See *Population Reports* 7:3 (May 1979). In fact, IUDs first became available in Japan in the mid-1930s, when a Japanese doctor (Ōta Tenrei) invented a gold and gold-plated IUD design. They were subsequently outlawed by the military government.

20. Japanese researchers have performed successful clinical tests on copper IUDs over the last twenty-five years, but the MHW only began considering whether to approve the copper IUD in 1994 (*Women's Health and Sexuality* 2 [February 1998]); personal communication from Midori Ashida, former secretary of the Professional Women's Coalition for Sexuality and Health, December 1999.

21. Interview with Wagatsuma Takashi, International Medical Center, International Medical Cooperation Bureau, November 17, 1994.

22. *Financial Times*, February 27–28, 1999.

23. E. Ketting, *Contraception in Western Europe: A Current Appraisal* (Park Ridge, N.J.: Parthenon, 1990), p. 81; United Nations Department for Economic and Social Information and Policy Analysis, Population Division, *World Contraceptive Use Chart, 1994*, 1994. The IUD is a popular birth control method in Europe, but the IUD use rate

in the United States is very low (2 percent) because of lawsuits against IUD manufacturers in the 1970s and 1980s.

24. The Population Problems Research Council, The Mainichi Papers, ed., *The Future of the Family: Beyond Gender, Summary of the Twenty-fourth National Survey on Family Planning* (Tokyo: The Population Problems Research Council, *Mainichi Shinbun*, 1998), p. 42. It should be noted, however, that not all aspects of Japanese contraception usage are completely atypical. For example, the sterilization rate in most of Western Europe is as low as it is in Japan (less than 10 percent on average). In Great Britain and the United States, however, 25 percent or more of all contraceptors rely on sterilization. There is also a high rate of sterilization in developing countries (Ketting, *Contraception in Western Europe; World Contraceptive Use Chart, 1994*).

25. The percentage of Japanese contraceptors reporting sterilization as their method of birth control has fluctuated between 4 percent and 10 percent since 1955; IUD use peaked around 9 percent between 1973 and 1977; and pill use peaked around 3 percent between 1975 and 1979 (The Population Problems Research Council, *The Population and Society of Postwar Japan*, p. 80).

26. The phrase "typical use" refers to the rate of accidental pregnancy during the first year of method adoption (not necessarily for the first time) among typical couples; the phrase "perfect use" refers to the rate of accidental pregnancy during the first year of method adoption (not necessarily for the first time) among couples who use the method perfectly, that is, both consistently and correctly (*Contraceptive Technology Update* 17:2 [February 1996]: 14). Also, according to Ogino, most couples actually use condoms in conjunction with the rhythm method (i.e., only during "dangerous" periods in the woman's cycle). Ogino claims that this combination of methods accounts for the high marital abortion rate because it is susceptible to miscalculations, which may in turn lead to unplanned pregnancies (Ogino, "Abortion and Women's Reproductive Rights," pp. 76, 78).

27. Irene B. Taeuber, *The Population of Japan* (Princeton, N.J.: Princeton University Press, 1958), pp. 272, 278, 282–83.

28. Some Japanese make this type of argument, too. For example, during my interview with former MHW Public Health Bureau Chief Miura Daisuke (June 7, 1995), Miura claimed that the Eugenic Protection Law passed easily because of Buddhist notions of rebirth, and because the Japanese practiced infanticide (*mabiki*) in the past. For a discussion of historical morality concerning abortion, see also Ogino, "Jinkō ninshin chūzetsu to josei no jiko ketteiken," p. 119.

29. LaFleur argues that *mizuko kuyō* provides a socially acceptable ritual outlet for women who have aborted (and their partners) to acknowledge their pain and guilt, and to gain release without being condemned (William LaFleur, *Liquid Life: Abortion and Buddhism in Japan* [Princeton, N.J.: Princeton University Press, 1992], pp. xiii–xiv, 26–29, 196–97, 216). However, Hardacre argues that *mizuko kuyō* "is a minority phenomenon rejected by the majority of religious institutions in Japan, [and] we would be very much mistaken to gloss it simply as 'Japan's way of dealing with abortion.'" Even when *mizuko kuyō* was at its peak of popularity, only an estimated 20 percent of women who had abortions performed services. Furthermore, many temples and shrines will not perform the services, at least in part because they view *mizuko kuyō* as crass capitalization on people's fears. The services are performed for a fee, and the popular press and some *mizuko kuyō* practitioners have promoted the notion that if a woman does not

perform *mizuko kuyō* after an abortion, both she and her living children could be subject to spirit attacks (*tatari*) by the aborted fetus (Helen Hardacre, *Marketing the Menacing Fetus in Japan* [Berkeley: University of California Press, 1997], pp. 17, 81–100, 190–96, 209).

30. LaFleur, *Liquid Life*, chap. 6 and p. 205.

31. In opinion polls taken in Japan at two-year intervals from 1963 to the present, in 1965, 16 percent of those surveyed approved of abortion unconditionally, 62 percent approved conditionally, and 15 percent disapproved; in 1975, the figures were 9 percent, 68 percent, and 11 percent; in 1984, 16 percent, 66 percent, and 13 percent; and in 1994, 26 percent, 55 percent; and 10 percent (The Population Problems Research Council, *The Population and Society of Postwar Japan*, pp. 222–396; Mainichi Shimbunsha Jinkō Mondai Chōsakai, ed., Atarashii Kazokuzō o Motomete [Tokyo: Mainichi Shimbunsha, 1994], p. 69). In opinion polls taken in the United States at irregular intervals from 1975 to 1995, in 1975, 21 percent of Americans surveyed felt that abortion should be legal under any circumstances; 54 percent, that it should be legal under certain circumstances; and 22 percent, that it should be illegal in all circumstances; in 1983, the numbers were 23 percent, 58 percent, and 16 percent; and in February 1995, the numbers were 33 percent, 50 percent, and 15 percent (The Gallup Organization, 1975–95). If one combines the categories of those who favor access to abortion conditionally and those who favor access to abortion unconditionally, it becomes clear that the proportion of both Americans and Japanese who favor access to abortion in some form has basically remained constant for the last several decades, and that these numbers are roughly equivalent in the United States and Japan. The same can be said for the proportion of Americans and Japanese who do not favor access to abortion.

32. Ian Reader, "Review of *Liquid Life*," *The Journal of Japanese Studies* 21:1 (winter 1995): 196–97. The United States is very unusual in terms of the extent of mobilization around the issue of abortion, the political power of both pro-choice and pro-life forces, the "rights talk" in which the American abortion debate is framed, and the actual provisions for abortion under the law (Glendon, *Abortion and Divorce*; Mary Ann Glendon, *Rights Talk* [New York: The Free Press, 1991]).

33. Coleman, *Family Planning in Japanese Society*, p. 3.

34. Ogino also comes close to this notion with her observation that decisions about reproduction are important not only for women but also for men, families, communities, the state, religious groups, and doctors (Ogino, "Jinkō Ninshin Chūzetsu to Josei," p. 110).

35. Joseph E. Potter, "The Persistence of Outmoded Contraceptive Regimes: The Cases of Mexico and Brazil," *Population and Development Review* 25, no. 4 (December 1999): 704–6, 732.

36. Ibid., 704–5, 708–14, 731–32.

37. Theda Skocpol, *Protecting Soldiers and Mothers: The Political Origins of Social Policy in the United States* (Cambridge, Mass.: Harvard University Press, 1992), pp. 41, 58–59.

38. Skocpol uses a similar approach, which she has labeled a "comparatively informed case study" (ibid., p. 61).

39. The data presented here were gathered from a variety of sources. Both English- and Japanese-language primary and secondary sources were picked over to piece together the puzzle: documents from the Allied Occupation stored at the National Archives (which used to be located in Suitland, Maryland, but were subsequently moved

to the University of Maryland); newspaper clipping collections and transcriptions of Diet committee debates at the National Diet Library in Tokyo; and newsletters from in-house libraries of various Japanese interest groups and citizens groups. Statistics gathered by the Japanese and U.S. governments, the United Nations, and private organizations provided key comparative data on variables such as reproductive and contraceptive practices and trends in health personnel. The *Mainichi shinbun*'s bi-annual opinion survey on family planning, which has been conducted at regular intervals since the 1950s, was particularly useful in developing a picture of the average person's views on family planning and related subjects. Interviews with interest group and citizens group members, politicians, bureaucrats, and journalists fleshed out the decision makers' perspective. Finally, readers who are interested in women and politics or reproductive rights should be aware that the library at the National Women's Education Center in Musashi Ranzan, Japan, is an invaluable resource. Also please note Mizoguchi Akiyo et al.'s three excellent edited volumes of primary sources from the heyday of the Japanese feminist movement in the 1970s (*Shiryō Nihon ūman ribu shi*).

CHAPTER TWO
THE POLITICS OF INTERESTS

1. Cohen and Arato define civil society as "a sphere of social interaction between economy and state, composed above all of the intimate sphere (especially the family), the sphere of associations (especially voluntary associations), social movements, and forms of public communication" (Jean Cohen and Andrew Arato, *Civil Society and Political Theory* [Cambridge, Mass.: MIT Press, 1992], p. ix).

2. For the concept of the state as follower or referee, see Margaret McKean, "State Strength and Public Interest," in Gary D. Allinson and Yasunori Sone, eds., *Political Dynamics in Contemporary Japan* (Ithaca: Cornell University Press, 1993).

3. Mark P. Petracca, "The Rediscovery of Interest Group Politics," in Mark P. Petracca, ed., *The Politics of Interests: Interest Groups Transformed* (Boulder, Colo.: Westview, 1992), p. 4.

4. James Madison, Alexander Hamilton, and John Jay, *The Federalist Papers* (New York: New American Library, 1961 [1788]), pp. 78–79.

5. Ibid., pp. 82–83.

6. David Truman, *The Governmental Process* (New York: Knopf, 1951), pp. 509–10, 513–14; Robert Dahl, *Who Governs?* (New Haven: Yale University Press, 1961). See also V. O. Key Jr., *Politics, Parties and Pressure Groups* (New York: Crowell, 1958).

7. Petracca, "The Rediscovery of Interest Group Politics," p. 5.

8. E. E. Schattschneider, *The Semisovereign People: A Realist's View of Democracy in America* (Hinsdale, Ill.: Dryden, 1975), pp. 30–35.

9. Theodore Lowi, *The End of Liberalism: The Second Republic of the United States* (New York: Norton, 1979), p. 57.

10. Mancur Olson, *The Rise and Decline of Nations: Economic Growth, Stagflation, and Social Rigidities* (New Haven: Yale University Press, 1982), pp. 18–19.

11. Frances McCall Rosenbluth, "Financial Deregulation and Interest Intermediation," in Allinson and Sone, *Political Dynamics in Contemporary Japan*, p. 114.

12. Jane Mansbridge, "A Deliberative Theory of Interest Representation," in Petracca, *The Politics of Interests*, p. 47.

13. Ibid.

14. Frank Baumgartner and Bryan Jones, *Agendas and Instability in American Politics* (Chicago: The University of Chicago Press, 1993), p. 175.

15. See, e.g., John Campbell, "Compensation for Repatriates: A Case Study of Interest-Group Politics and Party-Government Negotiations in Japan," in T. J. Pempel, ed., *Policymaking in Contemporary Japan* (Ithaca: Cornell University Press, 1977); Aurelia George, "The Japanese Farm Lobby and Agricultural Policy-making," *Pacific Affairs* 54:3 (fall 1981); Margaret McKean, *Environmental Protest and Citizen Politics in Japan* (Berkeley: University of California Press, 1981); Kenneth Ruoff, "Reviving Imperial Ideology: Citizens' Movements from the Right," paper presented at the Annual Meeting of the Association for Asian Studies, Honolulu, April 1996; William Steslicke, *Doctors in Politics: The Political Life of the Japan Medical Association* (New York: Praeger, 1973); Donald Thurston, *Teachers and Politics in Japan* (Princeton, N.J.: Princeton University Press, 1973); Frank Upham, *Law and Social Change in Postwar Japan* (Cambridge, Mass.: Harvard University Press, 1987); James White, *The Soka Gakkai and Mass Society* (Stanford: Stanford University Press, 1970).

16. Aurelia George's 1982 monograph is probably the most comprehensive and in-depth treatment of the subject in English, while, in Japanese, Tsujinaka Yutaka's *Rieki Shūdan* is often cited (Aurelia George, "The Comparative Study of Interest Groups in Japan: An Institutional Framework," Australia-Japan Research Centre Research Paper No. 95, December 1982; Tsujinaka Yutaka, *Rieki Shūdan* [Tokyo: Tokyo Daigaku Shuppansha, 1988]).

17. Carol Gluck, *Japan's Modern Myths: Ideology in the Late Meiji Period* (Princeton, N.J.: Princeton University Press, 1985), pp. 72, 246.

18. Takeshi Ishida, "The Development of Interest Groups and the Pattern of Political Modernization in Japan," in Robert Ward, ed., *Political Development in Modern Japan* (Princeton, N.J.: Princeton University Press, 1968), p. 302; George, "The Comparative Study of Interest Groups in Japan," p. 63.

19. Sheldon Garon, *Molding Japanese Minds: The State in Everyday Life* (Princeton, N.J.: Princeton University Press, 1997), pp. 6, 16.

20. Elise Tipton, "Introduction," in Elise Tipton, ed., *Society and the State in Interwar Japan* (New York: Routledge, 1997), p. 4.

21. Ibid., p. 3; Hitoshi Abe et al., *The Government and Politics of Japan* (Tokyo: University of Tokyo Press, 1994), p. 47; Ishida, "The Development of Interest Groups," pp. 305–12; Tsujinaka, *Rieki Shūdan*, p. 58. The era of party rule is actually dated from 1918 to 1932.

22. Garon and Mochizuki define a social contract as "a political exchange relationship between the state and social groups that is mediated by interest organizations and that establishes public-policy parameters that endure over time. Typically the social groups use their market and political power to extract policy concessions from the state, while the state adopts such policies in exchange for their support . . . [which may take the form of] direct electoral backing . . . restraints on collective action and a general acceptance of the socioeconomic order" (Sheldon Garon and Mike Mochizuki, "Negotiating Social Contracts," in Andrew Gordon, ed., *Postwar Japan as History* [Berkeley: University of California Press, 1993], pp. 145–47).

23. Tsujinaka, *Rieki Shūdan*, p. 58; Abe et al., *The Government and Politics of Japan*, p. 47. Almost half of all the interest groups surveyed in a 1978 study had been estab-

lished within ten years of the end of the war (Frank Jacob Schwartz, "Shingikai: The Politics of Consultation in Japan," unpublished dissertation, Harvard University, Cambridge, Mass., 1991), p. 110.

24. Steslicke, *Doctors in Politics*, pp. 4–5.

25. *Nikkei shinbun*, February 7, 1959, cited in Taguchi Fukuji, *Shakai shūdan no seiji kitai* (Tokyo: Miraisha, 1969), p. 158.

26. T. J. Pempel, "Prerequisites for Democracy," in Takeshi Ishida and Ellis Krauss, eds., *Democracy in Japan* (Pittsburgh: University of Pittsburgh Press, 1989), pp. 27–28.

27. I borrow the term *advocacy explosion* from Petracca, "The Rediscovery of Interest Group Politics," p. 14.

28. Tsujinaka, *Rieki Shūdan*, pp. 12–17.

29. Ibid., p. 21.

30. Abe et al., *The Government and Politics of Japan*, 1994, pp. 185–87.

31. Baumgartner and Jones, *Agendas and Instability*, pp. 176–77; Petracca, in Petracca, ed., 1992, pp. 23–24; Steslicke, 1973, p. 241; Taguchi, 1969, p. 158.

32. Petracca, "The Rediscovery of Interest Group Politics," p. 26.

33. Ibid., pp. 24, 27.

34. See Ruoff, "Reviving Imperial Ideology," and chapter 5 of this book.

35. Tsujinaka, *Rieki Shūdan*, p. 36.

36. Ibid., pp. 119–20.

37. Yutaka Tsujinaka, "Interest Group Structure and Regime Change in Japan," Maryland/Tsukuba Papers on U.S.–Japan Relations, November 1996, pp. 43–47.

38. See note 60, below.

39. Tsujinaka, *Rieki Shūdan*, pp. 126–27. See also Taguchi, *Shakai Shūdan no seiji kitai*, p. 164; and Steslicke, *Doctors in Politics*, p. 234.

40. George, "The Comparative Study of Interest Groups in Japan," pp. 28–35.

41. See, e.g., Ishida, "The Development of Interest Groups," pp. 317, 331; and Murakawa Ichirō et al., eds., *Gendai no seiji katei* (Tokyo: Gakuyō Shobō, 1982), p. 170.

42. Tsujinaka, *Rieki Shūdan*, p. 126.

43. The phenomenon of dual office holding dates to the prewar period and occurs at both the national and local levels. It is more prevalent in the Upper House than the Lower House. This discrepancy may reflect the fact that the Upper House was originally designed to represent the interests of different occupational groups (George, "The Comparative Study of Interest Groups in Japan," pp. 9–13; Tsujinaka, *Rieki Shūdan*, p. 13).

44. The bureaucracy and local elected offices are other common career routes for Japanese politicians. In addition, a substantial number of Japanese politicians are "hereditary" politicians—that is, they have inherited their fathers' Diet seats and personal support groups (*kōenkai*) (Curtis, *The Japanese Way of Politics*, p. 235).

45. George, "The Comparative Study of Interest Groups in Japan," pp. 14–17; Peter Cheng, "Japanese Interest Group Politics," *Asian Survey* 30:3 (March 1990): 253–54.

46. Sōka Gakkai is a Buddhist new religion whose members are primarily urban and middle or lower-middle class. Estimates of membership over the last several decades have varied between eight million and fifteen million. Sōka Gakkai first entered politics in 1955, successfully running candidates on an independent ticket in prefectural and local elections. The group then ran candidates for the Upper House for the next few years and, in 1960, formed a political action committee called the Kōmei Seiji Renmei. After the party was formed in 1964, the Kōmeitō first ran candidates for the Lower

House in 1967 and has since commanded a small though consistent percentage of the opposition vote. The party platform has centered on efforts to combat political corruption and pollution, and to promote peace and social welfare policies. See Arvin Palmer, *Buddhist Politics: Japan's Clean Government Party* (The Hague: Martinus Nijhoff, 1971), pp. 12–15, 24, 32–33, 61; White, *The Soka Gakkai and Mass Society*, pp. 61–80.

47. JMA politicking in the postwar period has centered around two main issues: health insurance policy and the separation of medical treatment from the preparation and sale of medicine (*iyaku bungyō*) (Steslicke, *Doctors in Politics*, pp. 35, 46, 55, 62–63).

48. Ibid., pp. 119–20; Murakawa et al., *Gendai no seiji katei*, p. 179; Stephen J. Anderson, *Welfare Policy and Politics in Japan: Beyond the Developmental State* (New York: Paragon, 1993), p. 124.

49. Taguchi, *Shakai Shūdan no seiji kitai*, p. 194; Murakawa et al., *Gendai no seiji katei*, p. 179; Anderson, *Welfare Policy and Politics in Japan*, 1993, p. 124.

50. For example, in 1960 fourteen doctors were elected to the Lower House (six were LDP members and eight were JSP members) (Taguchi, *Shakai shūdan no seiji kitai*, p. 191). In 1981 there were eighteen *ikei giin* distributed among the LDP, JSP, JCP, and Kōmeitō (Murakawa et al., *Gendai no seiji kitai*, p. 181).

51. Steslicke, *Doctors in Politics*, p. 82; Taguchi, *Shakai Shūdan no seiji kitai*, pp. 188–90; Murakawa et al., *Gendai no seiji katei*, 1982, p. 172.

52. William Steslicke, "The Japanese State of Health," in Edward Norbeck and Margaret Long, eds., *Health, Illness, and Medical Care in Japan* (Honolulu: University of Hawaii Press, 1987), pp. 56–57.

53. In 1970 at least 75 percent of all physicians were members of the JMA, but as the number of private clinic owners (formerly the mainstay of JMA membership) declined and the number of salaried hospital employees increased, the percentage of physicians joining the JMA also decreased, to 65 percent in 1981 (Steslicke, *Doctors in Politics*, p. 56; Anderson, *Welfare Policy and Politics in Japan*, pp. 126–27). In fact, a similar phenomenon is occurring in the American Medical Association (AMA). The rate of membership in the AMA peaked at about 90 percent in the 1960s and then declined over the next several decades, to about 40 percent in 1997. The average age of JMA and AMA members is now also much higher because few younger doctors are joining these organizations (*New York Times*, December 2, 1997).

54. For example, Pempel and Tsunekawa explain that both state and societal groups in Japan worked to establish corporatist relations as a response to Japan's perceived vulnerability in a hostile international environment, hoping that such arrangements would promote order, national unity, and economic success. But Pempel and Tsunekawa differentiate Japan from many of the corporatist systems in Europe, because organized labor plays an important role in most European state-society coalitions, whereas Japanese corporatism, they argue, is "corporatism without labor" (T. J. Pempel and Keiichi Tsunekawa, "Corporatism without Labor? The Japanese Anomaly," in Philippe Schmitter and Gerhard Lembruch, eds., *Trends toward Corporatist Intermediation* [Beverly Hills: Sage, 1979]).

55. Schmitter's more often cited definition describes corporatism as "a system of interest representation in which the constituent units are organized into a limited number of singular, compulsory, noncompetitive, hierarchically ordered and functionally differentiated categories, recognized or licensed (if not created) by the state and granted

a deliberate representational monopoly within their respective categories in exchange for observing certain controls on their selection of leaders and articulation of demands and supports" (Philippe Schmitter, "Still the Century of Corporatism?" in Schmitter and Lembruch, *Trends toward Corporatist Intermediation*, pp. 9, 13).

56. Philippe Schmitter, "Interest Intermediation and Regime Governability in Contemporary Western Europe and North America," in Suzanne Berger, ed., *Organizing Interests in Western Europe: Pluralism, Corporatism, and the Transformation of Politics* (Cambridge: Cambridge University Press, 1981), p. 295.

57. George, "The Comparative Study of Interest Groups in Japan," p. 44.

58. Ibid., pp. 46–49.

59. Ibid., pp. 56–58.

60. Ibid., p. 59; Tsujinaka, "Interest Group Structure and Regime Change in Japan," pp. 53, 57. For the related argument that, in the early 1970s, power gradually began to transfer from bureaucrats exclusively to a broader range of elites, especially *zoku* politicians, resulting in increased, though still circumscribed, pluralism, see T. J. Pempel, "The Unbundling of 'Japan, Inc.': The Changing Dynamics of Japanese Policy Formation," *The Journal of Japanese Studies* 13:2 (summer 1987); Gary Allinson, "The Structure and Transformation of Conservative Rule," in Gordon, *Postwar Japan as History*, pp. 136–44; Gerald Curtis, *The Japanese Way of Politics* (New York: Columbia University Press, 1988), epilogue; Steslicke, *Doctors in Politics*, p. 229; McKean, "State Strength and Public Interest," p. 103; and Michio Muramatsu and Ellis Krauss, "The Conservative Policy Line and the Development of Patterned Pluralism," in Kozo Yamamura and Yasukichi Yasuba, *The Political Economy of Japan*, vol. 1 (Stanford: Stanford University Press, 1987).

61. McKean, "State Strength and Public Interest," pp. 72–104; Rosenbluth, "Financial Deregulation and Interest Intermediation," pp. 107–29.

62. Sheldon Garon, *Molding Japanese Minds: The State in Everyday Life* (Princeton, N.J.: Princeton University Press, 1997), pp. 16–17.

CHAPTER THREE
FOR THE GOOD OF THE NATION

1. Garon, *Molding Japanese Minds*, p. 8.

2. Ishii cites a Heian period (794–1185) poem dedicated "to the woman who aborted her child when she visited her lover's hometown" as evidence that abortion was practiced even before the Tokugawa period. Ishii, "Yūsei Hogo Hō ni yoru datai gōhōka no mondaiten," 1982, p. 118.

3. Irene B. Taeuber, *The Population of Japan* (Princeton, N.J.: Princeton University Press, 1958), pp. 29–32; Ishii, "Yūsei Hogo Hō ni yoru datai gōhōka no mondaiten," p. 118. For a description of various measures taken to prevent abortion and infanticide in the Tokugawa and early Meiji periods, see also Ryoichi Ishii, *Population Pressure and Economic Life in Japan* (London: P. S. King and Son, 1937), pp. 33–36.

4. Ogino Miho, "Jinkō ninshin chūzetsu to josei no jiko ketteiken," in Hara Hiroko and Tachi Kaoru, eds., *Bosei kara jisedai ikuseiryoku e* (Tokyo: Shinyōsha, 1991), p. 112.

5. Between 1883 and 1908, 10,455 people were found guilty of abortion. For a detailed description of the 1880 law, see Ishii, "Yūsei Hogo Hō ni yoru datai gōhōka no mondaiten," pp. 118–19.

6. See, e.g., Ōta Tenrei, *Nihon sanji chōsetsu shi—Meiji, Taishō, Shōwa shoki made* (Tokyo: Nihon Kazoku Keikaku Kyōkai, 1969); Ishii, "Yūsei Hogo Hō ni yoru datai gōhōka no mondaiten," p. 118.

7. Ishii, *Population Pressure and Economic Life in Japan*, p. 39; Kozy K. Amemiya, "The Road to Pro-Choice Ideology in Japan: A Social History of the Contest between the State and Individuals over Abortion," unpublished dissertation, University of California, San Diego, Calif., 1993, p. 101.

8. Kure Bunsō, "Datai ron," *Kokka igaku zasshi* 239 (1907), reprinted in Ichikawa Fusae, ed., *Nihon fujin mondai shiryō shūsei*, vol. 6 (Hoken) (Tokyo: Domesu Shuppan, 1978), pp. 118–19, 124.

9. Hiroshima Kiyoshi, "Gendai nihon jinkō seisakushi kōron: jinkō shishitsu gainen o megutte (1916–1930)," *Jinkō Mondai Kenkyū* 154 (1981): 48.

10. Ibid., 49–50.

11. Taeuber, *The Population of Japan*, p. 365.

12. Zenji Suzuki, "Geneticists and the Eugenics Movement in Japan," *Japanese Studies in the History of Science* 14 (1975): 159.

13. Takagi Masashi, "Senzen nihon ni okeru yūsei shisō no tenkai to nōryokukan, kyōikukan—sanji seigen oyobi jinkō seisaku to no kankei o chūshin ni—" *Nagoya Daigaku Kyōikugakubu Kiyo (Kyōiku Gakka)* 40 (1993): 41. Eugenic theories were first introduced to Japan in the late nineteenth century but did not gain a serious following until the 1920s (Suzuki, "Geneticists and the Eugenics Movement in Japan," pp. 157, 160).

14. Paul Weindling, "Fascism and Population in Comparative European Perspective," in Michael S. Teitelbaum and Jay M. Winter, eds., *Population and Resources in Western Intellectual Traditions* (Cambridge: Cambridge University Press, 1989), pp. 108–12; Jeremy Noakes, "Nazism and Eugenics: The Background to the Nazi Sterilization Law of 14 July 1933," in R. J. Bullen, H. Pogge von Strandman, and A. B. Polonsky, eds., *Ideas into Politics: Aspects of European History, 1880–1950* (Totowa, N.J.: Barnes & Noble, 1984), pp. 77–79.

15. According to Bock, involuntary sterilization was legal in thirty states. Between 1907 and 1930, eleven thousand people were sterilized, and between 1930 and 1964, fifty-three thousand. Most were sterilized on grounds of feeblemindedness (Gisela Bock, "Racism and Sexism in Nazi Germany: Motherhood, Compulsory Sterilization, and the State," in Renate Bridenthal et al., eds., *When Biology Became Destiny* [New York: Monthly Review Press, 1984], p. 280). Saxton's numbers are different: she claims that more than two hundred thousand women were sterilized during this period (Marsha Saxton, "Disabled Women's View of Selective Abortion: An Issue for All Women," *Journal of the American Medical Women's Association* 54, no. 1 (1999): 26.

16. Noriko Tsuya, "Proximate Determinants of Fertility Decline in Japan after World War II," unpublished dissertation, University of Chicago, 1986, pp. 7–9.

17. *Asahi shinbun*, May 15, 1949.

18. Toshinobu Kato, *The Development of Family Planning in Japan with Industrial Involvement* (New York: United Nations, 1978); Ishii, "Yūsei Hogo Hō ni yoru datai gōhōka no mondaiten," p. 125.

19. Elise K. Tipton, ed., *Society and the State in Interwar Japan* (New York: Routledge, 1997), p. 47.

20. Miho Ogino, "Abortion, Contraception, and Feminism: Reproductive Politics in Modern Japan," paper presented at the Annual Meeting of the Association for Asian

Studies, Chicago, March 1997; Sharon Sievers, *Flowers in Salt: The Beginnings of Feminist Consciousness in Modern Japan* (Stanford: Stanford University Press, 1983), pp. 183–84. For some of the original texts of the feminist debates on abortion and contraception, see Suzuki Naoko, ed., *Shiryō sengo bosei no yukue* (Tokyo: Domesu Shuppan, 1985). Other prominent feminists involved in the birth control movement in the 1920s included Ishimoto (later Katō) Shizue, Oku Mumeo, and Yamakawa Kikue.

21. Tipton, *Society and the State in Interwar Japan*, pp. 51–52.

22. For more detail on the Sanger visit, see Ellen Chesler, *Woman of Valor: Margaret Sanger and the Birth Control Movement in America* (New York: Simon and Schuster, 1992); Elise Tipton, "Birth Control and the Population Problem," in Tipton, *Society and the State in Interwar Japan*, pp. 42–59.

23. Amemiya, "The Road to Pro-Choice Ideology in Japan," pp. 119–21, 129; Ishii, *Population Pressure and Economic Life in Japan*, p. 239.

24. One source reports that the cities did open clinics despite opposition from the national government, whereas another account relates that the national government successfully pressured city governments to abandon their plans (Fujime Yuki, "Senkanki nihon no sanji chōsetsu undō to sono shisō," *Rekishi Hyōron* 430 [February 1986]: pp. 88–91; Ishii, *Population Pressure and Economic Life in Japan*, p. 239).

25. Tipton, *Society and the State in Interwar Japan*, p.4.

26. Iso Abe, "The Birth Control Movement in Japan," in Margaret Sanger, ed., *International Aspects of Birth Control* (New York: The American Birth Control League, 1925), pp. 73–74.

27. Linda Gordon, *Woman's Body, Woman's Right: Birth Control in America* (New York: Penguin, 1990), pp. 83, 87–88, 121, 128.

28. Ibid., pp. 112, 219; Atina Grossmann, *Reforming Sex: The German Movement for Birth Control and Abortion Reform, 1920–1950* (New York: Oxford University Press, 1995), pp. 70–71.

29. Offen uses the terms *familial* or *relational* for this type of feminism. "Familial" feminists, according to Offen, call for equality between the sexes while stressing that the importance of women's distinct roles (primarily childbearing and childrearing) must be acknowledged and supported by society (Karen Offen, "Defining Feminism: A Comparative Historical Approach," *Signs* 14 [1988]): 119–57.

30. Ishizaki Nobuko, "Seishoku no jiyū to sanji chōsetsu undō—Hiratsuka Raichō to Yamamoto Senji," *Rekishi Hyōron* 503 (March 1992): 96; Elise K. Tipton, "Birth Control and the Population Problem in Prewar and Wartime Japan," *Japanese Studies Bulletin* 14, no. 1 (1994): 57–59; Ōbayashi Michiko, "Sanji chōsetsu undō to yūsei shisō," *Nihon Fujin Mondai Konwakai Kaihō* 46 (1987).

31. Tipton, "Birth Control and the Population Problem," p. 56; Ōbayashi, "Sanji chōsetsu undō to yūsei shisō," pp. 3–4.

32. Ōbayashi, "Sanji chōsetsu undō to yūsei shisō," p. 10; Ishizaki, Seishoku no jiyū to sanji chōsetsu undō," p. 98.

33. Noakes, "Nazism and Eugenics," p. 84.

34. Noma Shinji, "Kenzen naru Dainihon Teikoku," *Hisutoria* 120 (September 1988): 45.

35. Suzuki, "Geneticists and the Eugenics Movement in Japan," pp. 158, 160–62; Julie Rousseau, "Quantity and Quality: The Politics of Eugenic Discourse in Imperial Japan," unpublished M.A. essay, Columbia University, Department of History, 1990, p. 8.

36. Rousseau, "Quantity and Quality," pp. 2, 20–21.

37. Amemiya, "The Road to Pro-Choice Ideology in Japan," p. 116; Ishii, "Yūsei Hogo Hō ni yoru datai gōhōkau no mondaiten," pp. 121–23.

38. Interestingly, however, Ishizaki claims that, because Raichō had complicated views on abortion and birth control, she never mentioned her involvement in the Alliance in her writings at the time or subsequently (Ishizaki, "Seishoku no jiyū to sanji chōsetsu undō," pp. 93–94).

39. Ogino, "Abortion, Contraception, and Feminism"; Ōta Tenrei, *Nihon sanji chōsetsu 100-nen shi* (Tokyo: Shuppan Kagaku Sōgō Kenkyūjo, 1976), p. 345; Amemiya, "The Road to Pro-Choice Ideology in Japan," pp. 124–25.

40. Atina Grossmann, "Abortion and Economic Crisis: The 1931 Campaign against Paragraph 218," in Renate Bridenthal et al., eds., *When Biology Became Destiny* (New York: Monthly Review Press, 1984), p. 74.

41. The commission was organized in reaction to the 1918 rice riots, the progress of the birth control movement, changes in U.S. immigration laws that banned Japanese entry, and the 1927 financial panic (Hiroshima, "Gendai nihon jinkō seisakushi kōron," pp. 50–52).

42. WNRC RG No. 331, Box No. 9425, "Eugenics" file, SCAP, PHW Section, Administrative Branch, Subject File. To get around the ban on contraceptives, activists advertised and sold spermicides as drugs for the prevention of venereal disease; contraceptives were also advertised as "cures" for menstrual disorders (Katō Shizue, *Aru josei seijika no hansei* [Kyoto: PHP Kenkyūjo, 1981], p. 152); Miyahara Shinobu, "Kazoku keikaku to tomo ni ayunda michi—Katō Shizue-san intabyu," *Josanpu Zasshi* 44, no. 10 (1990).

43. Ōta, "Nihon sanji chōsetsu 100-nen shi," pp. 352–53.

44. Bock, "Racism and Sexism in Nazi Germany," p. 276; Gisela Bock, "Antinatalism, Maternity, and Paternity in National Socialist Racism," in Gisela Bock and Pat Thane, eds., *Maternity and Gender Politics: Women and the Rise of the European Welfare States, 1880–1950s* (New York: Routledge, 1991), pp. 235–36.

45. Bock, "Antinatalism, Maternity, and Paternity," p. 240.

46. Atina Grossmann, "The Debate That Will Not End: The Politics of Abortion in Germany from Weimar to National Socialism and the Postwar Period," in Manfred Berg and Geoffrey Cocks, eds., *Medicine in Nineteenth- and Twentieth-Century Germany: Ethics, Politics, and Law* (Cambridge: Cambridge University Press, 1994).

47. Bock, "Antinatalism, Maternity, and Paternity," pp. 242–43; Weindling, "Fascism and Population," pp. 114–15.

48. Hirose Yoshi, "Yūsei Hogo Hō ni tsuite," *Nihon Ishikai Zasshi*, 109, no. 12 (June 15, 1994): 1899.

49. The 1934 bill was not discussed in the Diet until the 1935 session (Hiroshima Kiyoshi, "Gendai nihon jinkō seisakushi kōron [2]: Kokumin Yūsei Hō ni okeru jinkō no shitsuseisaku to ryōseisaku," *Jinkō Mondai Kenkyū* 160 (1982): 73; Noma, "Kenzen naru Dai Nihon Teikoku," pp. 53–54).

50. Ogino, "Abortion, Contraception, and Feminism."

51. *Shūhō* 151 (September 6, 1939): pp. 7–11.

52. Ishii, "Yusei Hogo Hō ni yoru datai gōhōka na mondaiten," p. 128.

53. Ōta Tenrei, *Datai kinshi to Yūsei Hogo Hō* (Tokyo: Keieisha Kagaku Kyōkai, 1980), p. 154; Hiroshima, "Gendai nihon jinkō seisakushi kōron (2)," pp. 68–69. A series of

articles on abortion in the Japanese medical journal *Nihon iji shinpō* in 1941 discussed the need for doctors to refrain from performing abortions for "social reasons" in order to support the war effort (Amemiya, "The Road to Pro-Choice Ideology in Japan," p. 147).

54. Ōta, *Datai Kinshi to Yūsei Hogo Hō*, p. 150.

55. Rousseau, "Quantity and Quality," pp. 28–30; Noma, "Kenzen naru Dai Nihon Teikoku," pp. 56–57.

56. Eighty-four more operations were performed during the two years after the war when the law was still in effect (Kōseishō Gojūnen Shi Shuiinkai, ed., *Kōseishō Gojūnen Shi*, vol. 1 [Tokyo: Chūō Hōki, 1988], p. 350; Ōta, *Nihon sanji chōsetsu shi*, p. 158; Ishii, 1982, p. 128).

57. Kōseishō, "Kokumin Yūsei Hō Kaisetsu," *Shūhō* 244 (June 11, 1941): 4, 10.

58. Kōseishō Gojūnen Shi Shuiinkai, *Kōseishō Gojūnen Shi*, pp. 395, 405. The National Strength Law (Kokumin Tairyoku Hō) of 1940 introduced specific measures designed to improve the physical health and strength of the nation's youth, and to reduce the mortality rate.

59. *Shūhō* 244 (June 11, 1941): 2–3.

60. Ibid., 151 (September 6, 1939): 5.

61. Ibid., (February 12, 1941); (February 19, 1941); Kōseishō Imukyoku, ed., *Isei hyakunen shi* (Tokyo: Gyōsei, 1976), p. 272; Taeuber, p. 367.

62. *Shūhō* 245 (June 25, 1941): 26–27.

63. Taeuber, *The Population of Japan*, p. 368; Rousseau, "Quantity and Quality," p. 64.

64. Yoshiko Miyake, "Doubling Expectations: Motherhood and Women's Factory Work under State Management in Japan in the 1930s and 1940s" in Gail Lee Bernstein, ed., *Recreating Japanese Women, 1600–1945* (Berkeley: University of California Press, 1991), p. 271.

65. Thomas Havens, "Women and War in Japan, 1937–45," *American Historical Review* 80, no. 4 (October 1975): 927.

66. Ibid.: 928.

67. Weindling, "Fascism and Population," p. 107.

68. Thomas Havens, *Valley of Darkness: The Japanese People and World War Two* (New York: Norton, 1978), p. 47; Weindling, "Fascism and Population," p. 110.

69. Garon, *Molding Japanese Minds*, pp. 3–22.

CHAPTER FOUR
JAPAN LEGALIZES ABORTION

1. It should be noted that the Eugenic Protection Law was unusual in this respect, as 85 percent of all legislation between 1945 and 1975 was written and introduced to the Diet by government ministries (T. J. Pempel, *Policy and Politics in Japan: Creative Conservatism* [Philadelphia: Temple University Press, 1982], p. 17).

2. Many countries (including most states in the United States) did make exceptions to their criminal abortion laws to save the life or health of the mother, but this did not mean that abortion was easily accessible.

3. For the view that the legalization of abortion served the interests of the state, see Marumoto Yuriko, "Josei no karada to kokoro—dataitsumi, Yūsei Hogo Hō, Boshi

Hoken Hō o megutte," *Jūrisuto Zōkan Sōgō Tokushū* 39 (summer 1985); Taniai Noriko, *Namida no senkyo—dokyumento Yūsei Hogo Hō* (Tokyo: Shio Shuppansha, 1978), p. 80; and Amemiya, "The Road to Pro-Choice Ideology in Japan," p. 153.

4. Hane, *Modern Japan*, p. 341; *Proceedings of the House of Representatives Health and Welfare Committee*, no. 35 (February 1, 1947): 274.

5. Takafusa Nakamura, *The Postwar Japanese Economy: Its Developments and Structure* (Tokyo: University of Tokyo Press, 1981), pp. 14–15, 21–22.

6. Amemiya, 1993, "The Road to Pro-Choice Ideology in Japan," p. 156; Hane, *Modern Japan*, pp. 341–42.

7. Boshi Eisei Kenkyūkai, ed., *Boshi hoken no omo naru tōkei* (Tokyo: Boshi Hoken Jigyōdan, 1994), p. 18.

8. U.S. National Archives, WNRC, RG No. 331, Box No. 9344, "Birth Control" file, SCAP PHW Section, Administrative Division, Nursing Affairs and Health Statistics. For a similar view, see also Warren Thompson, "The Need for a Population Policy in Japan," *American Sociological Review* 15, no. 1 (February 1950): 32.

9. Katō was elected to the House of Representatives twice, and then to the House of Councilors four times between 1946 and 1974.

10. *Proceedings of the House of Representatives Health and Welfare Committee*, No. 35 (February 1, 1947): 273–74.

11. Ibid., p. 274.

12. Ibid., p. 272.

13. Article 16, Eugenic Protection Bill, in ibid., p. 273.

14. These circumstances were essentially the same as those under which abortion could be sought.

15. Articles 3 and 12, Eugenic Protection Bill, in *Proceedings of the House of Representatives Health and Welfare Committee*, No. 35 (February 1, 1947): 272–73.

16. Section 3, Compulsory Sterilization, Eugenic Protection Bill, in ibid., p. 273.

17. Rousseau, "Quantity and Quality," p. 65.

18. Saitō Chiyo, "Mienai 'michi'—Yūsei Hogo Hō no keifu o tazunete mita koto kangaeta koto," *Agora* 28 (June 1983): 52; Miyahara Shinobu, "Kazoku keikaku to tomo ni ayunda michi—Katō Shizue-san intabyū," *Josanpu Zasshi* 44, no. 10 (1990); "Kono hito ni kiku: Katō Shizue san," *Agora* 28 (June 1983): 178; Amemiya, "The Road to Pro-Choice Ideology in Japan," p. 179.

19. Tipton, "Birth Control and the Population Problem," pp. 56–57, 60.

20. Saitō, "Mienai 'michi,' p. 52; "Kono hito ni kiku: Katō Shizue san," p. 178.

21. Taniai, *Namida no senkyo—dokyumento Yūsei Hogo Hō*, pp. 80–83.

22. *Proceedings of the House of Representatives Health and Welfare Committee*, No. 35 (February 1, 1947): 273.

23. Deborah Oakley, "The Development of Population Policy in Japan, 1945–1952, and American Participation," unpublished dissertation, University of Michigan, Ann Arbor, 1977, pp. 224, 226–27; Katō Shizue, *Aru josei seijika no hansei* (Kyoto: PHP Kenkyūjo, 1981), pp. 153–56; Ōta Tenrei, *Datai kinshi to Yūsei Hogo Hō* (Tokyo: Keieisha Kagaku Kyōkai, 1980), p. 164; Saitō, "Mienai 'michi,' " pp. 54–55; Helen Hardacre, *Marketing the Menacing Fetus in Japan* (Berkeley: University of California Press, 1997), p. 56.

24. Ōta, *Datai Kinshi to Yūsei Hogo Hō*, pp. 164, 166.

25. Nishiuchi Masahiko, *Nihon no boshi hoken to Moriyama Yutaka: Subete no haha to ko ni hoken to iryō no onkei o* (Tokyo: Nihon Kazoku Keikaku Kyōkai, 1988), p. 217.

26. In 1947 Taniguchi was a member of the conservative Progressive Party (Shinpotō); he became a member of the Liberal Democratic Party (LDP) in 1956.

27. Taniguchi posed his questions on August 20, 1947; the socialists introduced their bill on December 1, 1947 (Nishiuchi, *Nihon no boshi hoken to Moriyama Yutaka*, p. 214).

28. Ōta, *Datai Kinshi to Yūsei Hogo Hō*, p. 170. Taniguchi also referred to the socialists' draft bill as "extremely progressive" (*kiwamete shinpoteki*) (Taniguchi Yasaburō and Fukuda Masako, *Yūsei Hogo Hō kaisetsu* [Tokyo: Kenshin Shuppan, 1948], p. 85).

29. The sponsors for the Eugenic Protection Law were Fukuda Masako, Katō Shizue, and Ōta Tenrei of the Japan Socialist Party; Ōhara Hirō of the Kyōdō Party; Nakayama Toshihiko, Takeda Kiyo, Takenaka Shichirō, Taniguchi Yasaburō, and Sakakibara Tōru from the Japan Democratic Liberal Party; and Fujimori Shinji from the Ryokufūkai (another conservative party). All the sponsors except Katō and Takeda were doctors (Ōta, Datai Kinshi to Yūsei Hogo Hō, p. 171).

30. Taniguchi and Fukuda, *Yūsei Hogo Hō kaisetsu*, p. 110; Takahashi Katsuyo, "Yusei Hogo Hō un'ei ni okeru todōfuken ishikai no yakuwari," *Nihon Ishikai Zasshi* 90, no. 1 (July 1, 1983): 17; and *Proceedings of the House of Representatives Health and Welfare Committee*, no. 18 (June 28, 1948), p. 3.

31. See, e.g., Amemiya, "The Road to Pro-Choice Ideology in Japan," p. 177; Ogino Miho, "Jinkō ninshin chūzetsu to josei no jiko ketteiken," in Hara Hiroko and Tachi Kaoru, eds., *Bosei kara jisedai ikuseiryoku e* (Tokyo: Shinyōsha, 1991), p. 118.

32. There is some evidence that Taniguchi resurrected the socialists' bill at the urging of SCAP Public Health and Welfare Section Chief Gen. Crawford Sams, who favored legalizing abortion to curb population growth but who had not wanted to give the socialists a legislative victory because their party was the minority party and because he viewed them as anti-occupation (Oakley, "The Development of Population Policy in Japan," pp. 198, 201–2, 226).

33. *Proceedings of the House of Councilors*, June 19, 1948, as translated in *The Official Gazette Extra* 51 (June 23, 1948): 14–17; Taniguchi's speech cited in Ogino, "Jinkō ninshin chūzetsu to josei no jiko kettei-ken," p. 118; and in Oakley, "The Development of Population Policy in Japan," pp. 234–35.

34. October 1948 paper by Taniguchi Yasaburō entitled "How to Solve Our Population Problem" (WNRC, RG No. 331, Box No. 9332, "Eugenic Protection Law" file, SCAP PHW Section, Administrative Division, Publications File).

35. *Asahi shinbun*, May 15, 1949.

36. *Proceedings of the House of Councilors*, June 19, 1948, as translated in *The Official Gazette Extra* 51 (June 23, 1948): 14–17; Taniguchi's speech cited in Ogino, "Jinkō ninshin chūzetsu to josei no jiko ketteiken," p. 118; and in Oakley, "The Development of Population Policy in Japan," pp. 234–35.

37. *Tokyo Mainichi shinbun*, May 11, 1949.

38. Taniguchi and Fukuda, *Yūsei Hogo Hō kaisetsu*, pp. 30, 35–38, 48.

39. Taniai, *Namida no senkyo-dokyumento Yūsei Hogo Hō*, p. 68; Amemiya, "The Road to Pro-Choice Ideology in Japan," p. 183. In a cross-national study of abortion policy, Githens and Stetson note that it is often the case that doctors press for more liberal abortion legislation because they are concerned about legal challenges (Marianne Gi-

thens and Dorothy McBride Stetson, eds., *Abortion Politics: Public Policy in Cross-Cultural Perspective* [New York: Routledge, 1996], p. xii). Although it is not clear how many of these cases were actually prosecuted, a study of 590 cases of professional criminal abortion in Japanese provincial courts between 1927 and 1931 shows that only about 10 percent of defendants were doctors (Ishii, "Yūsei Hogo Hō ni yoru datai gōhōka no mondaiten," p. 120).

40. Ogino concurs in this assessment, stating that "the fact that 8 out of 10 Diet members who introduced the bill were physicians suggests that the law was designed to protect the professional interests of legitimate ob-gyns" (Ogino, "Abortion and Women's Reproductive Rights, p. 72).

41. Taniguchi and Fukuda, *Yūsei Hogo Hō kaisetsu*, pp. 37–38.

42. *Sanfujinka no sekai* 1, no. 2 (1949).

43. Translation of a December 1948 letter from Yamamoto Tsunekichi, Nihonbashi, Tokyo, to General Sams, Chief of Public Health and Welfare Section, WNRC, RG No. 331, Box No. 9425, "Eugenics" file, SCAP, PHW Section, Administrative Branch, Subject File.

44. This involved both the direct process of taking over deliveries and the indirect process of reducing the overall number of births by sponsoring legislation to increase access to abortion. For example, Rep. Inoue Natsue asked the government to devote resources to retraining midwives in light of the fact that the 1949 revision to the Eugenic Protection Law would reduce the number of childbirths and threaten midwives' livelihood (*Proceedings of the House of Councilors*, May 13, 1949, reproduced in *The Official Gazette Extra* 26 [May 14, 1949]: 13, WNRC, RG No. 331, Box No. 2508).

45. Reproductive health issues were an important part of the JMA's early postwar agenda. For example, the JMA formed a committee to explore revision of the National Eugenics Law from the standpoint of the medical profession in July 1947, and birth control and abortion were major topics of discussion at the third annual meeting of the JMA in 1949 (Amemiya, "The Road to Pro-Choice Ideology in Japan," p. 166; *Tokyo Times*, May 15, 1949).

46. According to Petchesky, in the United States "prior to the mid-twentieth century, if there was a state policy on population and fertility, it was created not directly by the state apparatus but by emerging elites [in the American Medical Association] who sought control over the dispensing of private reproductive health care and the state's backing to legitimate that control" (Rosalind Pollack Petchesky, *Abortion and Woman's Choice: The State, Sexuality, and Reproductive Freedom* [Boston: Northeastern University Press, 1990], pp. 78–79, 124–25). In his research on France in the nineteenth century, McLaren finds that gaining a monopoly over women's health care represented a means for French doctors to establish the medical profession as an authoritative, elite body (Angus McLaren, *Sexuality and Social Order* [New York: Holmes & Meier, 1983], pp. 44–45, 63). Similarly, English doctors sought to reform abortion law in the nineteenth century out of a mixture of concern for women's health and a desire to consolidate the status of the profession (Donald Kommers, "Abortion in Six Countries: A Comparative Legal Analysis," in J. Douglas Butler and David F. Walbert, eds., *Abortion, Medicine, and the Law*, 4th ed. [New York: Facts on File, 1992], p. 317).

47. Amemiya, "The Road to Pro-Choice Ideology in Japan," pp. 175–76; William Steslicke, "The Japanese State of Health: A Political-Economic Perspective," in Edward

Norbeck and Margaret Lock, eds., *Health, Illness, and Medical Care in Japan* (Honolulu: University of Hawaii Press, 1987), p. 43.

48. Ōbayashi Michiko, *Josanpu no Sengo* (Tokyo: Keisō Shobō, 1989), pp. 251, 265. In 1947, 92.1 percent of births were attended by midwives, and only 3.5 percent were attended by physicians. Midwives' share of deliveries decreased to 71.5 percent in 1957 and further decreased to 32.7 percent in 1964; meanwhile, physicians' share of deliveries increased to 25.1 percent in 1957 and then to 66.6 percent in 1964. This trend persisted over time so that by 1990, midwives were attending the minority of births— only 2 percent—and physicians attended the rest (*Maternal and Child Health in Japan*, compiled under the supervision of the Maternal and Child Health Division, Children and Families Bureau, Ministry of Health and Welfare [Tokyo: Mothers' and Children's Health and Welfare Association, 1992], p. 60). The number of midwives in Japan has also declined dramatically during the postwar period, from 55,356 in 1955 to 22,690 in 1992 (Boshi Eisei Kenkyūkai, ed., *Boshi Hoken no omo naru tōkei*, p. 114).

49. Margaret Powell and Masahira Anesaki, *Health Care in Japan* (New York: Routledge, 1990), pp. 109–11.

50. For example, as early as 1946, SCAP Public Opinion researcher Herb Passin wrote:

> I have read with the utmost alarm an article on the front page of the *Nippon Times*, dated Nov. 6, 1946, on a "Plan Drawn Up to Control Population Through Eugenics.". . . One of the very first steps taken by the Nazis after their seizure of political power in Germany was the establishment of a government controlled program of eugenic "race improvement.". . . In Japan, likewise, racialism has been a strong element in the intellectual history of the nation, and a main theoretical support of militarism and ultra-nationalism. . . . I do not think the Japanese fully realize the implications of a systematic eugenic program. They may not even have racialist ideas uppermost in their minds, but the possibilities are all there in favor of a revival or at least support for racialist elements with the slackening of our authority here. . . . This innocent appearing eugenic program is a sign of a profound lack of understanding of the principles and developments of modern Western science, and evidence of the profound hold that tribal racialism still exerts over the Japanese people.

(November 7, 1946, Check Sheet, WNRC, RG No. 331, Box No. 9425, "Eugenics" file, SCAP PHW, Administrative Division, Subject File, memo from Herb Passin, Public Opinion and Sociological Research).

51. For example, even though SCAP officials noted that the Eugenic Protection Law's exclusion of the right of appeal to a court was unconstitutional, they did not force the law's sponsors to add a proper appeal mechanism. See May 11, 1948, Memo by Alfred Oppler, Chief, Courts and Law Division, WNRC, RG No. 331, Box No. 9322, SCAP PHW Section, Administrative Division, Publications File, "Eugenic Protection Law" File. For other objections to the Eugenic Protection Law, see, e.g., PHW Memo to Government Section, June 25, 1948, WNRC, RG No. 331 Box No. 2203, Government Section, Central Files Branch, National Diet Reports File. It would have been highly unusual for SCAP authorities to take direct action to quash the Eugenic Protection Law, since SCAP's general policy was to fulfill its agenda via indirect channels and leave everyday governance to Japanese bureaucrats and lawmakers (see, e.g., Hane, *Modern Japan*, pp. 244–45).

52. Thomas Shapiro, *Population Control Politics: Women, Sterilization, and Reproductive Choice* (Philadelphia: Temple University Press, 1985), p. 36.

53. Public Health and Welfare memo to Diplomatic Section, October 24, 1949, p. 6, WNRC, RG No. 331, Box No. 9344, "Birth Control" File, PHW Section, Administrative Division, Nursing Affairs and Health Statistics.

54. Oakley, "The Development of Population Policy in Japan," p. 201.

55. Legal Section memo to Government Section, June 10, 1948, WNRC, RG No. 331 Box No. 2203, Government Section, Central Files Branch, National Diet Reports File.

56. Oakley, "The Development of Population Policy in Japan," p. 225.

57. Ōta, *Datai kinshi to Yūsei Hogo Hō*, p. 170; Katō, *Aru josei seijika no hansei*, pp. 156–57; Oakley, "The Development of Population Policy in Japan," p. 229.

58. *Mainichi shinbun*, May 17, 1949.

59. Ōta, *Datai kinshi to Yūsei Hogo Hō*, p. 171; Miyahara, "Kazoku keikaku to tomo ni ayunda michi," p. 178; interview with Ashino Yuriko, Deputy Executive Director, Family Planning Federation of Japan, April 24, 1995. Evidently many doctors involved in politics also passed the Eugenic Protection Law with the understanding that it was a temporary, emergency measure (Takemi Tarō, " 'Keizaiteki riyū' wa sakujo subeshi," in Nihon Kyōbunsha, ed., *Taiji wa ningen de nai no ka: Yūsei Hogo Hō no gimonten*" [Tokyo: Nihon Kyōbunsha, 1982] p. 86).

60. See chapter 2.

61. Nichibo changed its Japanese name to *Nihon Bosei Hogo Sanfujinkai Kai* in 1994.

62. See *Bosei hogo i hō* 1, no. 1 (July 1949).

63. Currently roughly 16,000 ob-gyns practice their profession in Japan, and about 13,500 of them are members of Nichibo. The number of ob-gyns and Nichibo membership has remained relatively constant throughout the postwar period. Thus, although the overall number of physicians and physicians per capita has increased greatly in the last fifty years, the ob-gyn specialty has shrunk. From 1955 to 1965, 12–14 percent of doctors specialized in obstetrics and gynecology, but by 1975 that number had dropped to 7 percent and has continued to decrease slowly ever since (Minoru Muramatsu, "Fertility Control in the Postwar Years—an Overview," in The Population Problems Research Council, The Mainichi Papers, ed., *The Population and Society of Postwar Japan—Based on Half a Century of Surveys on Family Planning* [Tokyo: The Mainichi Newspapers, 1994], p. 94; Powell and Anesaki, *Health Care in Japan*, p. 208; Boshi Eisei Kenkyūkai, ed., *Boshi hoken no omo naru tōkei*, p. 114). One ob-gyn cites the decrease in the birth rate to explain the declining percentage of doctors choosing the ob-gyn specialty (interview with Wagatsuma Takashi, International Medical Center, International Medical Cooperation Bureau, November 17, 1994).

64. See, e.g., the comments of a member of the Tokushima chapter of Nichibo, who wrote in 1967 that Nichibo was originally nothing more than Taniguchi's electoral support base (*senkyo botai*) (*Bosei hogo i hō*, March 1967). JMA president Takemi Tarō also referred to Nichibo as Taniguchi's *senkyo botai* (Takemi, "Keizaiteki riyū wa sakujo subeshi," p. 86). The JMA was also extremely politicized (Steslicke, *Doctors in Politics*, pp. 35, 62).

65. For concrete evidence of Nichibo's role as Taniguchi's *kōenkai*, see the organization's newsletter, *Bosei hogo i hō*, between 1949 and 1963, when it was dominated by news of Taniguchi's election campaigns and legislative efforts related to the Eugenic Protection Law. The newsletter has been called *Nichibo i hō* since 1974.

66. Taniguchi may have taken the initiative in May because Prime Minister Yoshida came out in favor of birth control in April (Oakley, "The Development of Population Policy in Japan," p. 237). Taniguchi actually proposed seven revisions in 1949, but the most important one was the addition of the economic reasons clause. For the other seven revisions, see *Proceedings of the House of Councilors Health and Welfare Committee*, no. 18 (May 6, 1949): 1–4.

67. Taniguchi apparently wanted to specify further that the mother's health included both psychological and physical health, because he felt that providing for harm to physical health alone would make the law difficult to apply; however, he did not have enough time to make further revisions (Ishii, "Yūsei Hogo Hō ni yoru datai gōhōka no mondaiten," p. 142).

68. *Proceedings of the House of Councilors Health and Welfare Committee*, no. 18 (May 6, 1949): 1. See also *The Official Gazette Extra*, 26 (May 14, 1949).

69. See chapter 6 for an examination of the occupation-era discourse on population.

70. *Proceedings of the House of Councilors Health and Welfare Committee*, no. 18 (May 6, 1949): 2; *The Official Gazette Extra*, 26 (May 14, 1949); *Mainichi shinbun*, June 17, 1949.

71. *Proceedings of the House of Councilors Health and Welfare Committee*, no. 18 (May 6, 1949).

72. See, e.g., Tama, who cites a February 1949 *Kyōto shinbun* article in which the head of a Eugenic Protection Committee says that a fairly loose legal interpretation of "the health of the mother" will probably be applied (Tama, "The Logic of Abortion": 13).

73. See *Yūsei hogo tōkei hōkoku, 1993* (Tokyo: Kōseishō Daijin Kanbō Tōkei Jōhōbu, 1994), p. 23.

74. For reasons that are unclear, the newspapers barely covered the story (Tama, "The Logic of Abortion," 12, 14). Therefore, the public presumably did not know the law had been passed.

75. P. K. Whelpton, "The Outlook for the Control of Human Fertility in Japan," *American Sociological Review* 15, no. 1 (February 1950): 36.

76. A like-minded colleague held that the population problem should not be addressed through government policy but instead should be "left to Nature" (*Proceedings of the House of Councilors Health and Welfare Committee*, no. 18 (May 6, 1949); *The Official Gazette Extra* 26 (May 14, 1949): 13; *Tokyo Mainichi shinbun*, May 11, 1949; *Asahi shinbun*, May 15, 1949.

77. *Proceedings of the House of Councilors Health and Welfare Committee*, no. 18 (May 6, 1949); *The Official Gazette Extra* 26 (May 14, 1949): 13; *Tokyo Mainichi shinbun*, May 11, 1949.

78. *Asahi shinbun*, May 15, 1949.

79. Although they were unable to prevent the passage of the Eugenic Protection Law, MHW bureaucrats did what they could to oppose it, delaying issuing guidelines to implement the law and publicly emphasizing that abortion was still illegal (Oakley, "The Development of Population Policy in Japan," p. 236; *Fujin shinbun*, March 7, 1949). See also a May 21, 1948, Medical Services Division memo which notes that the Eugenic Protection Bill "meets with opposition from the Welfare Ministry" (WNRC, RG No. 331, Box No. 9322, "EPL" file, SCAP PHW, Administrative Division, Publications File).

80. Amemiya, "The Road to Pro-Choice Ideology in Japan," p. 188.

81. *Proceedings of the House of Councilors Health and Welfare Committee*, no. 18 (May 6, 1949): 4; Oakley, "The Development of Population Policy in Japan," pp. 236–240.

82. Oakley, "The Development of Population Policy in Japan," pp. 238–40. Outshoorn tells us that, cross-nationally, abortion laws are often passed through unusual procedures (Joyce Outshoorn, "The Stability of Compromise: Abortion Politics in Western Europe," in Githens and Stetson, *Abortion Politics*, pp. 157–58).

83. *Proceedings of the House of Councilors Health and Welfare Committee*, no. 18 (May 6, 1949): 4.

84. *Tokyo Times*, May 19, 1949, in WNRC, RG No. 331, Box No. 379x;y (March–June 1949), Asst. Chief of Staff, G-2, Allied Translator and Interpreter Service.

85. Ishii, "Yūsei Hogo Hō ni yoru datai gōhōka no mondaiten," 142.

86. *Jiji Shimpō*, May 19, 1949, in WNRC, RG No. 331, Box No. 379x;y (March–June 1949), Asst. Chief of Staff, G-2, Allied Translator and Interpreter Service.

87. Taniguchi also sponsored two other, less important revisions to the law at this time. See *Proceedings of the House of Councilors Health and Welfare Committee*, no. 21 (March 25, 1952).

88. Ibid., p. 1; *Bosei hogo i hō*, April 1952; May 1952; Ishii, "Yūsei Hogo Hō ni yoru datai gōhōka no mondaiten," 147.

89. Petracca, "The Rediscovery of Interest Group Politics," p. 24. The Eugenic Protection Law spurred the formation of local chapters of both the Japan Ob-Gyn Association and Nichibo because an informal rule specified that, to become a designated doctor, one first had to become a member of the local ob-gyn association (*Nichibo i hō*, August 1983).

90. Frank Baumgartner and Bryan Jones, *Agendas and Instability in American Politics* (Chicago: University of Chicago Press, 1993), p. 83.

91. Ōta points out that giving the JMA control over certification of designated doctors is problematic because membership in the JMA is no longer compulsory (as it was before the war), introducing the possibility that nonmembers applying for certification may be treated unfairly (Ōta, *Datai Kinshi to Yūsei Hogo Hō*, p. 280).

92. Amemiya, "The Road to Pro-Choice Ideology in Japan," pp. 196–97.

93. Official abortion statistics show that 264,104 abortions were reported in 1949; 489,111 in 1950; 805,524 in 1952; and 1,068,066 in 1953 (The Population Problems Research Council, *The Population and Society of Postwar Japan*, p. 116).

94. *Nihon Kazoku Keikaku Fukyūkai* newsletter, August 1958, reprinted in *Bosei hogo i hō*, October 1958.

95. For example, a 1955 *Fujin Kōron* survey showed that about half of all women in their twenties and thirties had had an abortion (Nakagawa, "Toshi nichijō seikatsu no naka no sengo," p. 275). Tama also calculates that in 1955 half of all women of reproductive age had had an abortion (Tama, "The Logic of Abortion," 18).

96. Ōta Tenrei, *Nihon sanji chōsetsu 100-nen shi* (Tokyo: Shuppan Kagaku Sōgō Kenkyūjo, 1976), p. 359.

97. Whelpton, "The Outlook for the Control," p. 38.

98. Taniguchi stated in 1949 that abortions cost about ¥1,500 or, at most, ¥2,000 (*Proceedings of the House of Councilors Health and Welfare Committee*, no. 18 [May 6, 1949]: 4). But according to a May 14, 1950, article in *Mainichi shinbun*, an MHW survey

found that people thought abortions were unreasonably costly and that the fee should be capped at ¥1,500—indicating that many ob-gyns must have charged more than that amount.

99. Nishiuchi, *Nihon no boshi hoken to Moriyama Yutaka*, p. 236.

100. Nakagawa, "Toshi nichijō seikatsu no naka no sengo," p. 276; *Nihon Kazoku Keikaku Fukyūkai* newsletter, August 1958, reprinted in *Bosei hogo i hō*, October 1958.

101. Nishiuchi, *Nihon no boshi hoken to Moriyama Yutaka*, p. 236; *Nihon Kazoku Keikaku Fukyūkai* newsletter, August 1958, reprinted in *Bosei hogo i hō*, October 1958; "Kono hito ni kiku: Katō Shizue san," 174–75.

102. Nishiuchi, *Nihon no boshi hoken to Moriyama Yutaka*, pp. 236–37.

103. *Asahi shinbun*, January 13, 1956.

104. Kathleen Thelen, cited in Sven Steinmo et al., eds., *Structuring Politics: Historical Institutionalism in Comparative Analysis* (Cambridge: Cambridge University Press, 1992), p. 17. Immergut describes a similar phenomenon in which "strategic openings" are created by "veto points" that "emerge, disappear, or shift location" as a result of changes in exogenous conditions (Ellen Immergut, cited in Steinmo et al., *Structuring Politics*, p. 7). See also McAdam and Eisinger for the earlier concept of "political opportunity structure" (McAdam, *Political Process and the Development of Black Insurgency, 1930–1970*, pp. 40–43; Peter K. Eisinger, "The Conditions of Protest Behavior in American Cities, *American Political Science Review* 67 [1973]: 11–28).

105. *Bosei hogo i hō*, March 1956.

106. James Mohr, *Abortion in America* (New York: Oxford University Press, 1978); Gordon, *Woman's Body, Woman's Right*.

107. Thus Japanese abortion policy fits the "doctor-controlled" model in Stetson's typology of woman-controlled, doctor-controlled, and state-controlled abortion policy. Stetson found that abortion policy in the former Soviet Union was also controlled by doctors (Dorothy McBride Stetson, "Abortion Policy Triads and Women's Rights in Russia, the United States, and France," in Githens and Stetson, *Abortion Politics*, pp. 112–13.

108. The French elite's concerns over depopulation and "race suicide" led to the establishment of a number of laws and programs to protect mothers and children but also resulted in increasingly severe legal treatment of abortion. This trend culminated in the 1942 Vichy law that labeled abortion a crime against society, the state, and race, and made it an act of treason punishable by death (Karen Offen, "Body Politics: Women, Work, and the Politics of Motherhood in France, 1920–1950," in Bock and Thane, *Maternity and Gender Politics: Women and the Rise of the European Welfare States, 1880s–1950s*, p. 140; Jane Jenson, "Changing Discourse, Changing Agendas: Political Rights and Reproductive Policies in France," in Mary Fainsod Katzenstein and Carol McClurg Mueller, eds., *The Women's Movements of the United States and Western Europe: Consciousness, Political Opportunity, and Public Policy* [Philadelphia: Temple University Press, 1987], p. 75). See also Anne Cova, "French Feminism and Maternity: Theories and Policies, 1890–1918," in the same volume; Karen Offen, "Depopulation, Nationalism, and Feminism in Fin-de-Siècle France," *American Historical Review* 89 (June 1984); and Alisa Klaus, "Depopulation and Race Suicide: Maternalism and Pronatalist Ideologies in France and the United States," in Seth Koven and Sonya Michel, eds., *Mothers of a New*

*World: Maternalist Politics and the Origins of the Welfare State* (New York: Routledge, 1993).

109. However, Katō Shizue should be given credit for trying to be a voice for women in her 1947 speech in the Diet Health and Welfare Committee, in which she represented abortion in a maternalist light as a means of ensuring that mothers could give adequate care to the children they already had. It was also at Katō's suggestion that the All-Japan Women's Congress included a demand that abortion and birth control be legalized in its 1934 yearly resolutions. This was an isolated incident, however. Abortion and birth control were not part of the regular agenda of the Congress nor did the Congress actively pursue legalization beyond making the resolution. See Yuko Nishikawa, "Feminist Rhetoric and War Mobilization of Women," and Miho Ogino, "Abortion, Contraception, and Feminism: Reproductive Politics in Modern Japan," papers presented at the Annual Meeting of the Association for Asian Studies, Chicago, Ill., March 1996.

110. Kathleen Uno, "Death of 'Good Wife, Wise Mother'?" in Andrew Gordon, ed., *Postwar Japan as History* (Berkeley: University of California Press, 1993), pp. 308–10, 317.

111. Ibid., pp. 307–8, 319; Garon, *Molding Japanese Minds*, pp. 181–82, 186.

112. Ogino, "Abortion, Contraception, and Feminism."

113. Although abortion is generally very safe, still it is an invasive surgical procedure that can pose health risks, particularly to women who have had more than one abortion.

114. John Dower, *Embracing Defeat: Japan in the Wake of World War II* (New York: Norton, 1999), p. 71.

115. Coleman, *Family Planning in Japanese Society*; and Ogino, "Jinkō ninshin chūzetsu to josei no jiko ketteiken," p. 133.

CHAPTER FIVE
THE POLITICS OF ABORTION

1. Baumgartner and Jones, *Agendas and Instability in American Politics*, pp. 6–9.

2. Baumgartner and Jones write that "the creation and maintenance of a policy monopoly is intimately linked with the creation and maintenance of a supporting policy image. In those cases where monopolies of control have been established, there tends to be a single understanding of the underlying policy question" (ibid., p. 26). The policy monopoly begins to break down when new groups introduce competing understandings of the policy question and gain adherents in the policy-making arena.

3. It is widely recognized that American military procurements for the Korean War were instrumental in reviving the Japanese economy in the 1950s. With respect to the declining birth rate, one sees discussions of how the declining birth rate will produce an aging population forty to fifty years later as early as 1960 (*Kazoku keikaku*, May 1960).

4. *Kazoku keikaku*, October 1956.

5. *Bosei hogo i hō*, September 1957; *Kazoku keikaku*, January 1958; Noriko Tsuya, "Proximate Determinants of Fertility Decline in Japan after World War II," unpublished dissertation, University of Chicago, 1986, p. 20.

6. See, e.g., *Bosei hogo i hō*, April 1960.

7. As Amemiya notes, the origins of the sobriquet "abortion paradise" are unclear (Amemiya, "The Road to Pro-Choice Ideology in Japan," p. 262).

8. Nurses and midwives also joined the anti-abortion camp. In the case of midwives, their opposition to abortion sprang in part from the fear that abortions were threatening both their childbirth and their contraception business (Ōta, *Datai kinshi to Yūsei Hogo Hō*, 1980, p. 280).

9. *Kazoku keikaku*, March 1954, cited in Amemiya, "The Road to Pro-Choice Ideology in Japan," p. 231. *Kazoku keikaku* ran features on the ill effects of abortion throughout the 1950s.

10. *Kazoku keikaku*, November 1958.

11. Ibid., November 1961.

12. See Chesler, *Woman of Valor*.

13. *Kazoku keikaku*, November 1961. The adversarial feeling was apparently mutual, for in a 1964 speech to members of the JMA, JMA president Takemi Tarō referred sarcastically to the formidable attacks on designated doctors by "the famous grannies in the Japan Socialist Party" (*yūmei na shakaitō no obāsangata*). (*Bosei hogo i hō*, February 1964).

14. Amemiya, "The Road to Pro-Choice Ideology in Japan," p. 262.

15. For a discussion of the political campaign to pass an antiprostitution law, see Garon, *Molding Japanese Minds*, pp. 196–205. See chapter 3 of the same book for a discussion of prewar movements to abolish legal prostitution.

16. *Nihon Kazoku Keikaku Fukyūkai* newsletter, August 1958, reprinted in *Bosei hogo i hō*, October 1958.

17. *Kazoku keikaku*, November 1958.

18. Ibid., August 1961; Ōta, *Datai Kinshi to Yūsei Hogo Hō*, p. 274.

19. Ibid., August 1961.

20. *Bosei hogo i hō*, May 1962.

21. *Nihon keizai shinbun*, July 29, 1962.

22. Taniguchi founded Seichō no Ie in 1929 as an offshoot of Ōmotokyō. Seichō no Ie assimilates the beliefs of many different religions including Shintō, Confucianism, and Christianity, but its philosophy centers around spiritualism, psychoanalysis, and questions about the existence of the soul before birth and after death (Inoue Nobutaka et al., eds., *Shinshūk yō jiten* [Tokyo: Kōbundō, 1990], p. 79; Helen Hardacre, *Marketing the Menacing Fetus in Japan* [Berkeley: University of California Press, 1997], pp. 73–75).

23. Even when it reached a peak of 3.5 million members in the late 1970s, Seichō no Ie was a relatively small group compared to the large and politically active religious group Sōka Gakkai, which claimed 8 million members at that time (Hardacre, *Marketing the Menacing Fetus*, p. 74; Daniel Metraux, *The Soka Gakkai Revolution* [Lanham, Md.: University Press of America, 1994], p. 24).

24. Amemiya, "The Road to Pro-Choice Ideology in Japan," p. 258.

25. Taniguchi first advocated political involvement in 1953 (Seichō no Ie Honbu, ed., *Seichō no Ie 40-nen shi* [Tokyo: Nippon Kyōbunsha, 1970], p. 488).

26. For a discussion of the latter two movements, see Kenneth Ruoff, "Reviving Imperial Ideology: Citizens' Movements from the Right," paper presented at the Annual Meeting of the Association for Asian Studies, Honolulu, Hawaii, April 1996. In general, see Seichō no Ie Honbu, ed., *Seichō no Ie 40-nen shi*; and Seichō no Ie Honbu, ed., *Seichō no Ie 50-nen shi* (Tokyo: Nippon Kyōbunsha, 1980).

27. *Shirohato*, July 1952; August 1962. The July 1952 tract was reprinted in *Shirohato*, November 1982.

28. Amemiya, "The Road to Pro-Choice Ideology in Japan," p. 259; Seichō no Ie Honbu, ed., *Seichō no Ie 40-nen shi*, p. 492.

29. Hardacre, *Marketing the Menacing Fetus in Japan*, p. 75; *Shirohato*, January 1966.

30. Amemiya concurs with this view ("The Road to Pro-Choice Ideology in Japan," p. 260).

31. It is not clear whether this was the same committee as the one mentioned above in which Katō and others were involved, or whether there were two committees with the same name.

32. Seichō no Ie Honbu, ed., *Seichō no Ie 40-nen shi*, p. 493; *Bosei hogo i hō*, June 1961; *Shirohato*, February 1962.

33. "Heiwa no konpon to naru mono: umare kuru seimei o yutaka ni sodateyo," pamphlet edited and published by Seichō no Ie Shirohato Kai. For a reproduction of this pamphlet, see Ōta, *Datai Kinshi to Yūsei Hogo Hō*, pp. 271–73.

34. *Asahi shinbun*, June 3, 1962.

35. *Sankei shinbun*, November 6, 1963; *Bosei hogo i hō*, November 6, 1963. The Health and Welfare Minister's focus on reducing the number of abortions complemented the larger "people building" policy initiative (*hitozukuri seisaku*) that Prime Minister Ikeda undertook in 1962 in response to projected labor shortages. The goal of this policy was to improve the overall quality of the Japanese population by improving the health of children and pregnant women, preventing physical handicaps, increasing physical strength, and preventing delinquency (*Kazoku keikaku*, February 1963). In keeping with the government's policy, the family planning movement shifted its emphasis from "quantity" (lowering the birth rate) to "quality" (the quality of the population) in the early 1960s, promoting "The Movement to Bear a Good Child" and "The Movement to Bear No Unfortunate Children" (Amemiya, "The Road to Pro-Choice Ideology in Japan," pp. 243–50). The family planning movement was also active in pushing for the passage of the 1965 Mother and Child Health Law (Boshi Hoken Hō), which instituted various preventive health measures for pregnant women and infants. See *Kazoku keikaku*, 1964–65.

36. Ōta, *Datai Kinshi to Yūsei Hogo Hō*, pp. 275–76.

37. It should be noted that Japanese elite sensitivity to international trends in social policy and international criticism of Japanese social policy was also evident before the war. See, e.g., Garon, *Molding Japanese Minds*, chapter 3. This sensitivity probably flowed from the Japanese elite's sense of urgency about the need for Japan to catch up with the West as a military and industrial power.

38. *Bosei hogo i hō*, May 1962; *Kazoku keikaku*, August 1964. Japan became known as an "abortion paradise" because so many women from the United States and Europe (where abortion was illegal) traveled to Japan to get abortions. See, e.g., Tama, "The Logic of Abortion," p. 18. This practice caused a scandal in 1967, when the Japanese papers learned that a Tokyo ob-gyn had sent the following letter (written in English) to hospitals and doctors in the United States:

> As the Artificial Abortion is lawful in Japan and we keep our patients' records strictly confidential, we have been treating Western patients, residents or visitors successfully for many years. Some of our patients flew back to America on the next day of their arrival here, with relief and satisfaction.
>
> Serving the public like lawyers or doctors, you might be asked for your advice on these

matters by your clients, their families or friends. In such case, simply let her fly to Tokyo and leave the rest to us. Your introduction will be appreciated and 10 percent of the patient's payment for operation fee will be paid to you as your introduction fee. (*Yūkan Asahi*, March 7, 1967).

39. *Bosei hogo i hō*, August 1964.

40. *Shirohato*, July 1965.

41. Ōta, *Datai kinshi to Yūsei Hogo Hō*, p. 278; Githens and Stetson, *Abortion Politics*, p. xi.

42. For example, the November 1962 edition of the designated doctors' newsletter records a speech given by Upper House Representative Dr. Marumo Shigesada in which he thanks Nichibo members for their support, promises to defend their position on the Eugenic Protection Law (i.e., that the law should not be revised), and speculates on what arguments would be most effective in defending that position (*Bosei hogo i hō*, November 1962).

43. Nichibo sponsored *mizuko kuyō* services on a regular basis from 1952 until at least 1988. See, e.g., *Bosei hogo i hō*, March 1956; August 1982; July 1983; and October 1988; *Kazoku keikaku*, August 1961.

44. *Fujin Kōron* article, cited in *Bosei hogo i hō*, May 1963.

45. Tsuya, "Proximate Determinants of Fertility Decline," p. 227. Fewer children per family benefited the economy in a number of concrete ways: families were left with more money for spending and savings; women could enter the workforce, which held labor costs down; and the government was able to keep welfare expenditures at a minimum (Amemiya, "The Road to Pro-Choice Ideology in Japan," p. 370).

46. Former Lower House Representative Tagawa Seiichi described Representative Marumo negatively as someone who was seen by other Diet members as having been "bought" by the JMA (interview with Tagawa Seiichi, February 15, 1995).

47. *Bosei hogo i hō*, November 1961; August 1962; and November 1962. In an interesting parallel to the Japanese case, abortion law in England also came to be interpreted much more loosely with the passage of time than had been originally intended. When confronted with proposals to circumscribe the circumstances under which abortion was allowed (thus circumscribing doctors' decision-making latitude), English doctors, like Japanese doctors, protested vigorously and suggested that abuses could be corrected through stricter administration of existing law (Kommers, "Abortion in Six Countries," p. 319).

48. *Kazoku keikaku*, July 1967.

49. *Asahi shinbun*, June 13, 1972; May 11, 1973; May 19, 1973, and May 25, 1973.

50. On different occasions Satō commented that it was "scandalous" that Japan was known abroad as an abortion paradise, that there was a trend toward too many abortions, and that he wanted the Eugenic Protection Law to be enforced more strictly. At times Satō drew a connection between abortion and the labor shortage, but at other times he insisted that his position on the Eugenic Protection Law sprang from a desire to prevent social disorder and inculcate respect for life (*Asahi shinbun*, March 15, 1967; *Kazoku keikaku*, March 1967; *Proceedings of the House of Councilors Budget Committee Meeting* no. 4 [April 4, 1972], 23). Satō's predecessor, Prime Minister Ikeda, was also sympathetic to the pro-life cause: one of his slogans was, "To make a great nation, first make people" (Tama, "The Logic of Abortion," 1994, p. 18).

51. Former representative Tagawa described Tamaki as an "ultraconservative" and a "lone wolf" in the political world (interview with Tagawa Seiichi, February 15, 1995).

52. Amemiya, "The Road to Pro-Choice Ideology in Japan," pp. 267–68.

53. *Bosei hogo i hō*, January 1967; Amemiya, "The Road to Pro-Choice Ideology in Japan," p. 265. The League published two volumes on the Eugenic Protection Law, the second of which was in the form of a running debate with Nichibo on different points related to abortion and the law. See Inoue Shiden, *Yūsei Hogo Hō kaisei o meguru mondai to iken* (Tokyo: Yūsei Hogo Hō Kaihatsu Kisei Dōmei, 1968–69).

54. Amemiya, "The Road to Pro-Choice Ideology in Japan," pp. 266–67.

55. I.e., that abortion was murder, that the abortion situation was out of control, that it harmed women's mental and physical health, that the law had lowered sexual morality and devalued life, and so on (*Bosei hogo i hō*, March 1969; Moriyama Yutaka, "Yūsei Hogo Hō to jinkō mondai," *Sanfujinka no sekai* 25, no. 9 [1973]: 47).

56. *Bosei hogo i hō*, March 1969; *Asahi shinbun*, June 4, 1972.

57. *Bosei hogo i hō*, June 1969.

58. *Asahi shinbun*, July 14, 1970.

59. *Bosei hogo i hō*, December 1968.

60. Unsurprisingly, 97 percent of rank-and-file Nichibo members surveyed in 1969 concurred with these views (*Bosei hogo i hō*, August 1970; Ishii, "Yūsei Hogo Hō ni yoru datai gōhōka no mondaiten," pp. 156–57; *Asahi shinbun*, August 22, 1970).

61. *Bosei hogo i hō*, June 1967; *Asahi shinbun*, June 4, 1972; *Nihon keizai shinbun*, June 9, 1973; Amemiya, "The Road to Pro-Choice Ideology in Japan," p. 269.

62. *Ampo* 17 (summer 1973): 17; *Asahi shinbun*, July 14, 1970; June 13, 1972; Watashitachi no ima o tō kai, ed., *Zenkyōtō kara ribu e—Jūgoshi nōto 8 sengoken* (Tokyo: Impakuto Shuppansha, 1996), p. 262.

63. *Asahi shinbun*, July 14, 1970.

64. *Proceedings of the House of Councilors Budget Committee*, no. 13 (April 2, 1970): 12.

65. *Asahi shinbun*, July 14, 1970.

66. Ibid.

67. Amemiya, "The Road to Pro-Choice Ideology in Japan," pp. 273–74.

68. The fetal defect clause would have allowed for abortions "in cases where it is recognized that there is a marked possibility that the fetus has a disease or defect that will cause serious mental or physical disability (*sono taiji ga jūdo no seishin mata wa shintai no shōgai no genin to naru shitsubyō mata wa kekkan o yūshite iru osore ga ichijirushii to mitomerareru mono*). See *Bosei hogo i hō*, May 1972.

69. This was really a symbolic gesture, as Eugenic Protection Consultation Offices had long been defunct.

70. Seichō no Ie Honbu, ed., *Seicho no Ie 50-nen shi*, pp. 533–34.

71. Interview with Tagawa Seiichi, February 15, 1995; Amemiya, "The Road to Pro-Choice Ideology in Japan," p. 282.

72. See, e.g., *Asahi shinbun*, June 4, 1972.

73. *Nihon keizai shinbun*, June 9, 1973.

74. *Bosei hogo i hō*, May 1973; Moriyama Yutaka, "Yūsei Hogo Hō to ichibu kaisei mondai," *Sanfujinka no sekai* 27, no. 2 (1975): 5–6.

75. The opposition parties opposed the revision for several reasons: They felt it would endanger women's health by driving them to seek out expensive, illegal abortions; it went against international trends toward liberalizing abortion laws and attempting to limit population growth; the mental health clause could be applied strictly or liberally, according to the doctor's or the government's whim; they felt that the fetal conditions clause would foster discrimination and human rights violations by allowing prenatal culling of those deemed socially and economically unfit, and lastly, because they believed that a revival of pronatalist legislation could lead to a revival of militarism. See *Proceedings of the House of Representatives Social Affairs and Labor Committee*, no. 28 (May 22, 1974): 15–37; no. 29 (May 23, 1974), pp. 3–33. For a summary, see Ishii, "Yūsei Hogo Hō ni yoru datai gōhōka no mondaiten," pp. 158–59. Several weeks after these deliberations the JSP drew up its own revision draft called "The Law Concerning Birth Control, Abortion, and Sterilization" (*Jutai chōsetsu, jinkō ninshin chūzetsu oyobi hinin shujutsu ni kansuru hōritsu*). This draft's primary modification to the Eugenic Protection Law was that it would have made abortion and sterilization available at the individual's request (on demand), rather than with the doctor's permission (*Agora* 19 [October 31, 1978]: 228–32.

76. *Asahi shinbun*, May 24, 1974.

77. It was estimated that Seichō no Ie commanded 1.4 million votes, which accords with estimates of the group's membership at the time. According to retired LDP representative Tagawa, the JMA was more powerful and had more members than Seichō no Ie (*Nichibo i hō*, June 1, 1974; June 8, 1974; interview with Tagawa Seiichi, February 15, 1995).

78. *Asahi shinbun*, May 29, 1974.

79. Ibid., July 1, 1974.

80. Ibid., May 19, 1973; Ishii, "Yūsei Hogo Hō ni yoru datai gōhōka no mondaiten," p. 160.

81. Seichō no Ie Honbu, ed., *Seichō no Ie 50-nen shi*, pp. 533–34.

82. Ishii, "Yūsei Hogo Hō ni yoru datai gōhōka no mondaiten," p. 160; Amemiya, "The Road to Pro-Choice Ideology in Japan," pp. 282–83.

83. *Asahi shinbun*, July 14, 1970.

84. See chapter 2.

85. For a history of one of the larger handicapped groups, the National Liaison Conference for the Handicapped People's Liberation Movement (Zenkoku Shōgaisha Kaihō Undō Renraku Kaigi, or Zenshōren), see Zenshōren Zenkoku Jimukyoku, ed. and pub., *Zenshōren Kessei Taikai Hōkokushū* (Osaka, 1977), esp. pp. 267–72.

86. *Asahi shinbun*, May 14, 1973; see also *Ampo* 17 (summer 1973), for an account in English.

87. Handicapped people's groups built on their newfound political muscle in later years, successfully lobbying the government for anti-discrimination legislation and policies designed to improve living conditions for the handicapped in the 1980s and 1990s.

88. See Kristin Luker, *Abortion and the Politics of Motherhood* (Berkeley: University of California Press, 1984).

89. Some of the groups active at this time were Chūpiren, Chūnen Ribu "Akai Rokugatsu," Fujin Minshū Kurabu, Gurūpu Tatakau Onna, Himoji (The Scarlet Letter), Sabetsu o Tatakau Ajia Afurika Fujin Kaiku, Shūdan S.E.X., Tatakau Josei Dōmei (The Fighting Women's League), and Tokyo Commune. In 1973 twenty-five women's liberation

groups formed the Committee to Prevent the Revision of the Eugenic Protection Law (Yūsei Hogo Hō Kaiaku Soshi Jikkō Iinkai) (*Asahi shinbun*, May 11, 1973; May 12, 1973; May 14, 1973; May 19, 1973; *Nihon keizai shinbun*, May 12, 1973).

90. Marumoto Yuriko, "Josei no karada to kokoro—Datai Zai, Yūsei Hogo Hō, Boshi Hoken Hō o megutte," *Jūrisuto Zōkan Sōgō Tokushū* 39 (summer 1985): 150; Miho Ogino, "Abortion and Women's Reproductive Rights: The State of Japanese Women, 1945–1991," in Joyce Gelb and Marian Lief Palley, eds., *Women of Japan and Korea: Continuity and Change* (Philadelphia: Temple University Press, 1994), pp. 88–89. Some of the mainstream women's groups that petitioned the government were the National Liaison Council of Local Women's Groups (Chifuren), the University Women's Association, the Japanese League of Women Voters, the Japan Nurses Association, the Young Women's Christian Association, and the women's sections of labor unions such as Sōhyō, Nikkyōso, Jichirō, and Zendentsū (*Asahi shinbun*, June 13, 1972).

91. Yumiko Ehara, "Japanese Feminism in the 1970s and 1980s," *U.S.–Japan Women's Journal, English Supplement* 4 (1993): 50.

92. The *Asahi shinbun* recorded *Gurūpu Tatakau Onna*'s fifty-person, women-only demonstration on International Antiwar Day, October 21, 1970, as the day the Japanese women's liberation movement was launched. Some of the other feminist groups that helped found Shinjku Ribu Sentā were Shūdan S.E.X., Tokyo Commune, Himoji (The Scarlet Letter), and Tatakau Josei Dōmei (The Fighting Women's League) (Mizoguchi Akiyo, Saeki Yoko, and Miki Soko, eds., *Shiryō Nihon ūman ribu shi*, vol. 1 [1969–1972] [Kyoto: Shōkadō, 1992], p. 209; Mizoguchi et al., eds., *Shiryō Nihon ūman ribu shi*, vol. 2 [1972–75], [Kyoto: Shōkadō, 1994], p. 58).

93. Chūpiren's philosophy and activities with respect to the pill are described in greater detail in chapter 7.

94. Mizoguchi et al., *Shiryō Nihon Ūman ribu shi*, vol 2, pp. 188–208; Watashitachi no ima o tō kai, *Zenkyōtō kara ribu e*, p. 268.

95. The two types of feminism described here correspond closely to what Offen identifies as "familial" or "relational" feminism, on the one hand, and "individualist" feminism, on the other. According to Offen, "familial" feminists in countries like France and Germany call for equality between the sexes while stressing that the importance of women's distinct roles (primarily childbearing and childrearing) must be acknowledged and supported by society. The "individualist" feminist, more characteristic of England and the United States, supports equality between the sexes on the basis of universal human rights, and emphasizes independence and self-realization (Offen, "Defining Feminism"). Several authors have noted this type of split in the Japanese feminist movement; Taniai also notes that the split in Japanese feminist thought in the 1970s mirrors the split among Japanese feminists in the 1920s. See, e.g., K. Inoue, "Ūman ribu no shisō," in Tanaka Sumiko, ed., *Josei kaihō no shisō to kōdō, sengohen* (Tokyo: Jiji Tsūshinsha, 1975); Akiyama Yōko, "Enoki Misako to Chūpiren—'ribu shishi nōto' yori—" *Joseigaku Nenpō* 12 (October 1991): 109; Taniai Noriko, *Namida no senkyo—dokyumento Yūsei Hogo Hō* (Tokyo: Shio Shuppansha, 1978), p. 205.

96. *Nihon keizai shinbun*, June 12, 1972; *Asahi shinbun*, June 13, 1972; May 12, 1973; May 22, 1974; *Yomiuri shinbun*, March 26, 1974; Mizoguchi et al., *Shiryo Nihon ūman ribu shi*, vol. 2, pp. 31, 158, 168, 178. Some attempts to establish pronatalist policies at the local level were made around this time. For example, the governor of Kagoshima Prefecture gave an order (*gōrei*) in 1970 to start a third child movement in the prefec-

ture. His initiative met with resistance from housewives, who said that housing conditions, low salaries, and nuclear families made it impossible for most families to have more than two children (*Asahi shinbun*, August 27, 1970).

97. This point is demonstrated by the following excerpt:

> The LDP says the people's living standards have improved, so economic reasons are outdated, but with pollution, high real estate prices, etc., many couples can't have children even if they want to. . . . The revision is also an attempt to kill two birds with one stone by returning women to the home and acquiring a labor force at the same time. . . . [But] whether to have kids or not is absolutely a choice to be made between the two parties involved. Who would have children just for the good of the nation?

(From a May 26, 1972, Women's Liberation Front [*Onna kaihō sensen*] article; reprinted in Mizoguchi et al., *Shiryō Nihon ūman ribu shi*, vol. 2, p. 143.)

98. *Nihon keizai shinbun*, June 12, 1972; *Asahi shinbun*, June 13, 1972; July 2, 1973; Mizoguchi et al., *Shiryō Nihon ūman ribu shi*, vol. 2, pp. 154–55, 178; "Kono hito ni kiku: Tanaka Mitsu san," *Agora* 28 (June 1983): p. 190.

99. See Margaret McKean, *Environmental Protest and Citizen Politics in Japan* (Berkeley: University of California Press, 1981).

100. See Dorothy McBride Stetson, "Abortion Policy Triads and Women's Rights in Russia, the United States, and France," in Githens and Stetson, *Abortion Politics*, pp. 99–100. For a discussion of a related subject—pronatalism among European socialists—see Jay M. Winter, "Socialism, Social Democracy, and Population Questions in Western Europe, 1870–1950," in Michael S. Teitelbaum and Jay M. Winter, eds., *Population and Resources in Western Intellectual Traditions* (Cambridge: Cambridge University Press, 1989).

101. *Asahi shinbun*, June 13, 1972.

102. Watashitachi no ima o tō kai, ed., *Zenkyōtō kara ribu e*, p. 217.

103. "Kono hito ni kiku: Tanaka Mitsu san," *Agora* 28 (June 1983): 190. As one of the founders of the feminist group S.E.X. explained, although "women decide [whether] to have an abortion, it is not a right" (Watashitachi no ima o tō kai, ed., *Zenkyōtō kara ribu e*, p. 215). For a lengthy discussion of Japanese feminists' views on the concept of rights and the concept of rights in Japanese culture, see Amemiya, "The Road to Pro-Choice Ideology in Japan," pp. 358–66.

104. For a discussion of prewar women's groups' cooperation with state actors in the pursuit of benefits for women, see Garon, *Molding Japanese Minds*, chapter 4.

105. Thomas Shapiro, *Population Control Politics*, pp. 21–22.

106. Ehara, "Japanese Feminism in the 1970s and 1980s," p. 52.

107. *Asahi shinbun*, May 12, 1973; May 16, 1973.

108. Ibid., February 9, 1983. By the end of March, 303 LDP representatives had joined, comprising fully 70 percent of LDP members (Amemiya, "The Road to Pro-Choice Ideology in Japan," p. 350). Only 75 LDP members joined the anti-revision Diet Members' League to Promote Maternal Welfare (*Bosei no fukushi o suishin suru giin renmei*) (*Asahi shinbun*, March 24, 1983).

109. See *Shirohato*, February 1981; September 1981; October 1981.

110. See Figure 1.1. The total fertility rate declined from 2.13 to 1.75 (Boshi Eisei Kenkyūkai, ed., *Boshi hoken no omo naru tōkei* [Tokyo: Boshi Hoken Jigyōdan, 1994], p. 104).

111. Iwamoto Misako, "Jinkō ninshin chūzetsu seisaku ni okeru kettei, hikettei, meta-kettei: 1980 nendai nihon no nitōri no kēsu o chūshin ni," *Gyōsei* (May 1993): 121; Amemiya, "The Road to Pro-Choice Ideology in Japan," p. 317.

112. The number of abortions performed on teens rose from about fifteen thousand in 1972 to about twenty-two thousand in 1981. These numbers are very low by international standards (though they were almost certainly underreported), but nevertheless they were seen as cause for concern in Japan (*Asahi shinbun*, September 18, 1982; *Mainichi shinbun*, July 23, 1982).

113. The JMA's politically powerful president, Takemi Tarō, retired in 1981, and Representative Marumo, champion of the doctors' anti-revision position in the 1970s, became terminally ill and died in 1981 (*Nichibo i hō*, July 1, 1982; Iwamoto, "Jinkō ninshin chūzetsu seisaku," p. 125).

114. There was also a conservative political mood abroad, at least in England and the United States, where Thatcher and Reagan—both ultraconservatives—had recently been elected to highest office.

115. Iwamoto, pp. 120–22; group interview with *Soshiren* members, June 20, 1995; *Mainichi shinbun*, July 23, 1982.

116. *Asahi shinbun*, August 30, 1982; *Mainichi shinbun*, July 23, 1982; "Yūsei Hogo Hō no kaisei o naze isoganakereba naranai ka—nihon minzoku o shimetsu e no michi kara sukū tame ni—" pamphlet published by Murakami Masakuni; reprinted in "Yūsei Hogo Hō kaiaku soshi no tame no kiso shiryō," published by Zenkoku Aoshiba no Kai Sōrengokai; provided to author by *Aoshiba no Kai* with no date of publication. According to Murakami, ob-gyns were on the National Tax Administration Agency's top five list of tax evaders. Powell and Anesaki report that owners of private hospitals rank second only to pachinko parlor operators in volume of undeclared taxable income (Powell and Anesaki, *Health Care in Japan*, p. 203).

117. *Shirohato*, August 1981; Fujin Kyōdō Hōritsu Jimusho, ed., *Ima naze Yūsei Hogo Hō o kaiaku ka?* (Tokyo: Rōdō Kyōiku Sentā, 1983), p. 26; Iwamoto, "Jinkō ninshin chūzetsu seisaku," p. 121. The difference between Murakami and hardcore pro-lifers in the United States is that pro-lifers in the United States often oppose contraception as well as abortion, whereas Murakami felt that contraception would solve the problems that banning abortion would create (*Mainichi shinbun*, July 23, 1982).

118. *Mainichi shinbun*, July 23, 1982.

119. *Proceedings of the House of Councilors Budget Committee Meeting*, no. 8 (March 15, 1982): 2. The song is also reprinted in Taniai, *Namida no senkyo*. A version of this song also appeared in the early 1970s. See Mizoguchi et al., *Shiryō Nihon ūman ribu shi*, vol. 2, p. 154.

120. See *Shirohato*, October 1982; November 1982.

121. *Proceedings of the House of Councilors Budget Committee Meeting*, no. 8 (March 15, 1982): 3–6.

122. Interview with Nozaki Sadahiko, former Mental Health Section Chief, Public Health and Hygiene Bureau, MHW, during the 1982–83 revision process, February 21, 1995; *Proceedings of the House of Councilors Budget Committee Meeting*, no. 8 (March 15, 1982): 3.

123. Morishita was also reportedly known as a troublemaker within the LDP (*Asahi shinbun*, August 30, 1982; Iwamoto, "Jinkō ninshin chūzetsu seisaku," pp. 121–23).

124. *Proceedings of the House of Councilors Budget Committee*, no. 8 (March 15, 1982): 4–5; *Nihon keizai shinbun*, March 15, 1982.

125. *Asahi shinbun*, March 16, 1982; Amemiya, "The Road to Pro-Choice Ideology in Japan," p. 351. MHW representatives were evasive when asked if the MHW was undertaking the revision voluntarily or at the prompting of the LDP ("Yūsei Hogo Hō no dōkō ni tsuite," transcript of a March 25, 1983, meeting between the *Fujin Mondai Kikaku Suishin Kaigi Jōkyō Kaizen Iinkai* and representatives of the MHW, produced by the Women's Issues Room of the Prime Minister's Secretariat, p. 9).

126. *Asahi shinbun*, June 20, 1982.

127. Ibid.; *Mainichi shinbun*, July 23, 1982; "Yūsei Hogo Hō no dōkō ni tsuite," transcript of a December 20, 1982, meeting between the *Fujin Mondai Kikaku Suishin Kaigi Jōkyō Kaizen Iinkai* and MHW representatives, produced by the Women's Issues Room of the Prime Minister's Secretariat, p. 14.

128. Hardacre, *Marketing the Menacing Fetus*, p. 74.

129. *Shirohato*, August 1982; November 1982.

130. *Shirohato*, December 1982; Iwamoto, "Jinkō ninshin chūzetsu seisaku," p. 123; *Asahi shinbun*, July 14, 1982.

131. See Ruoff, "Reviewing Imperial Ideology."

132. Amemiya, "The Road to Pro-Choice Ideology in Japan," pp. 329–33; *Asahi shinbun*, August 30, 1982; group interview with *Soshiren* members, June 20, 1995.

133. *Nichibo i hō*, April 1982; May 1982; July 1982; November 1982; *Asahi shinbun*, June 20, 1982; August 30, 1982; Fujin Kyōdō Hōritsu Jimusho, ed., *Ima naze Yūsei Hogo Hō o kaiaku ka?*, pp. 19–20.

134. *Nichibo kenkai* (opinion), June 24, 1982; *Nichibo seimei* (statement), August 5, 1982; *Yomiuri shinbun*, November 9, 1982; JMA *ikensho* (opinion paper) submitted to the Health and Welfare Minister, November 24, 1982.

135. *Asahi shinbun*, August 30, 1982; Iwamoto, "Jinkō ninshin chūzetsu seisaku," p. 125.

136. *Kinkyū nyūsu* 3 (May 25, 1983).

137. Taniai, *Namida no senkyo*, pp. 126–45; Iwamoto, "Jinkō ninshin chūzetsu seisaku," p. 125.

138. Amemiya, "The Road to Pro-Choice Ideology in Japan," p. 308; Iwamoto, "Jinkō ninshin chūzetsu seisaku," p. 129.

139. *Asahi shinbun*, June 20, 1982; August 30, 1982.

140. Amemiya, "The Road to Pro-Choice Ideology in Japan," pp. 342–43, 345.

141. This group was originally organized to oppose efforts to revise the postwar Constitution (Iwamoto, "Jinkō ninshin chūzetsu seisaku," p. 126; Amemiya, "The Road to Pro-Choice Ideology in Japan," pp. 342–43). A variety of groups were involved in this coalition, including anti-pornography groups, groups struggling against workplace discrimination, groups involved in women's causes in the Third World, consumer groups, handicapped groups, and groups opposed to military bases.

142. Iwamoto, "Jinkō ninshin chuzetsu seisaku," p. 125; Amemiya, "The Road to Pro-Choice Ideology in Japan," pp. 340, 345–46; *Asahi shinbun*, June 30, 1982.

143. Iwamoto, "Jinkō ninshin chuzetsu seisaku," p. 127.

144. *Asahi shinbun*, March 14, 1983; Watashitachi no ima o tō kai, *Zenkyōtō kara ribu e*, 217.

145. *Kazoku keikaku*, August 1982; March 1983. This shift in Katō's views on abortion (her third reversal in the postwar period) may have been influenced by the 1968 United Nations resolution in Teheran, the 1973 *Roe v. Wade* decision in the United States, and the general trend toward legalizing abortion in the West in the 1970s (Amemiya, "The Road to Pro-Choice Ideology in Japan," pp. 343–44).

146. *Mainichi shinbun*, July 23, 1982; *Asahi shinbun*, January 29, 1983; March 10, 1983.

147. Complaint against the Partial Revision of the Eugenic Protection Law, November 4, 1982, submitted by the Action and Liaison Committee of the Assembly of Seven Women's Groups (*Nana Fujin Dantai Gikai Katsudō Renraku Iinkai*).

148. *Asahi shinbun*, July 17, 1982.

149. Ibid., June 20, 1982; *Yomiuri shinbun*, November 9, 1982; Sensō e no Michi o Yurusanai Onnatachi no Saitama Shōkai, ed., *Onna ni wa umenai toki mo aru* (Tokyo: Gogatsusha, 1982), pp. 47, 59–61.

150. *Asahi shinbun*, January 29, 1983.

151. Interview with Nozaki Sadahiko, former Mental Health Section Chief in the MHW's Public Health and Hygiene Bureau, February 21, 1995; Iwamoto, "Jinkō ninshin chūzetsu seisaku," p. 125.

152. For example, in a December 20, 1982, meeting between the Fujin Mondai Kikaku Suishin Kaigi Jōkyō Kaizen Iinkai and MHW representatives, one woman expressed concern that wartime pronatalist policies would be revived, recalling with dismay that during the war the MHW had given a mother of eighteen children a prize for fecundity. The MHW representative replied that the ministry was not considering any kind of population policy ("Yūsei Hogo Hō no dōkō ni tsuite," transcript of the aforementioned meeting, pp. 27–28, produced by the Women's Issues Room of the Prime Minister's Secretariat; interview with Miura Daisuke, former head of the MHW's Public Health and Hygiene Bureau, June 7, 1995).

153. Yūsei Hogo Hō no dōkō ni tsuite," transcript of December 20, 1982 meeting, produced by the Women's Issues Room of the Prime Minister's Secretariat, pp. 27–28; Yūsei Hogo Hō no dōkō ni tsuite," transcript of March 25, 1983 meeting, produced by the Women's Issues Room of the Prime Minister's Secretariat, pp. 11–12, 21.

154. *Asahi shinbun*, November 4, 1982.

155. Ibid., December 28, 1982; January 14, 1983.

156. Ibid., January 14, 1983; March 10, 1983; Izumi Kusano and Keiko Kawasaki, "Japanese Women Challenge Anti-Abortion Law," *Ampo* 15, no. 1 (1983).

157. Interview with Miura Daisuke, former head of the MHW's Public Health and Hygiene Bureau, June 7, 1995; interview with Nozaki Sadahiko, former Mental Health Section Chief in the MHW's Public Health and Hygiene Bureau, February 21, 1995.

158. *Asahi shinbun*, March 14, 1983; March 24, 1983.

159. Group interview with Soshiren members, June 20, 1995.

160. *Asahi shinbun*, March 24, 1983.

161. Amemiya, "The Road to Pro-Choice Ideology in Japan," pp. 351–52.

162. Hardacre, *Marketing the Menacing Fetus*, p. 76.

163. Tama, "The Logic of Abortion," p. 24; Ehara, "Japanese Feminism in the 1970s and 1980s," p. 51. Soshiren members speculate that the deradicalization of the feminist movement and the fact that more women had entered the workforce also contributed

to women being taken more seriously in the 1980s (group interview with Soshiren members, June 20, 1995).

164. Interview with Nozaki Sadahiko, former Mental Health Section Chief in the MHW's Public Health and Hygiene Bureau, February 21, 1995; group interview with Soshiren members, June 20, 1995.

165. *Asahi shinbun*, February 14, 1996; www.jaog.or.jp, p. 2.

166. The number of involuntary, physician-initiated sterilizations decreased from 1,362 in 1955 to 513 in 1965, to 82 in 1975, to 11 in 1985, to 0 in 1991. A total of 16,520 involuntary sterilizations were performed between 1949 and 1994 (Kōseishō Daijin Kanbō Tōkei Hōkokubu, ed. and pub., *Yūsei hogo tōkei hōkoku* [Tokyo, 1993], p. 31).

167. *Soshiren nyūsu*, September 1997.

168. *Asahi shinbun*, March 7, 1966. An interesting, if peripherally related fact is that sex change operations violate the Eugenic Protection Law because, at least with men, the procedure involves removing the sexual organs and sterilizing the patient. This violates both Article 2, which requires that sexual organs be left intact, and Article 28, which forbids doctors from sterilizing patients without due cause (see appendix). A Tokyo doctor who performed sex change operations in the mid-1960s was prosecuted under the Eugenic Protection Law (*Mainichi shinbun*, October 6, 1965). For discussions of the so-called Blue Boy Case, see *Bessatsu jūrisuto* 33 (1971): 258–61; *Hanrei taimuzu* 280 (1972): 88–94; *Bessatsu jūrisuto* 50 (1976): 202–3; and *Bessatsu jūrisuto* 57 (1978): 76–77.

169. *Zenshōren* 93 (February 20, 1990); *Mainichi Daily News*, June 19, 1993; *Soshiren nyūsu*, September 1997.

170. Marsha Saxton, "Disabled Women's View of Selective Abortion: An Issue for All Women," *Journal of the American Medical Women's Association* 54, no. 1 (1999): 26–28; Anne Waldschmidt, "Against Selection of Human Life—People with Disabilities Oppose Genetic Counselling," *Issues in Reproductive and Genetic Engineering* 5, no. 2 (1992): 157, 163.

171. See, e.g., Mizoguchi et al., *Shiryō Nihon ūman ribu shi*, pp. 22–24.

172. *Fukushi rōdō* 21 (special edition on the Eugenic Protection Law revision) (December 1983); Iwamoto, "Jinkō ninshin chūzetsu seisaku," p. 127; Kozy Amemiya, "Choice by Whom and for Whom: A New Alliance of Pro-Choice Women and Disabled People for Reproductive Rights in Japan," paper presented at the Annual Meeting of the Association for Asian Studies, Honolulu, Hawaii, April 13, 1996; Watashitachi no ima o tō kai, *Zenkyōtō kara ribu e*, 215, 226.

173. *JAOG News*, July 1996; *Soshiren nyūsu*, April 1996.

174. The April 1996 issue of *Soshiren nyūsu* refers to *gaiatsu* generated by *Josei Shōgaisha Nettowāku* member Asaka Yūho at the 1994 Cairo Population Conference. The October 1995 issue describes a workshop on the Eugenic Protection Law held by handicapped people's and women's groups at the 1995 Beijing Women's Conference. Approximately one hundred people attended, two-thirds non-Japanese. See also the discussion of the "Artificial Interruption of Pregnancy Law of Japan" on the Nichibo website (in English or Japanese) at www.jaog.or.jp, p. 2.

175. This was a conscious strategy. For example, at a meeting sponsored by the *DPI Josei Shōgaisha Nettowāku* on June 2, 1995, at the Nakano Ward Women's Hall, group

members specifically said that they would try to generate outside pressure on the Japanese government at the Beijing Conference because the government is "susceptible to outside pressure" (*gaiatsu ni yowai*). Other groups in Japan clearly have the same idea, since it is not uncommon for Japanese groups to travel to the United States or take out full-page advertisements in major U.S. newspapers to explain their cause and to try to generate *gaiatsu*. See, e.g., Kenneth Ruoff, "Mr. Tomino Goes to City Hall: Grass-roots Democracy in Zushi City, Japan," in Joe Moore, ed., *The Other Japan* (Armonk, N.Y.: M.E. Sharpe, 1996), p. 330.

176. *JAOG News*, July 1996.

177. For a detailed discussion of the political process leading up to the revision, see Mariko Jitsukawa, "Making of the Law of the Protection for Mothers' Bodies: A Case Study on How Women's Issues Are Dealt with in the Japanese Political Process," Ph.D. Kenkyūkai Conference, International House of Japan, Tokyo, July 9, 1996.

178. *Soshiren nyūsu*, October 1996. In addition to Soshiren, women's groups include Boshi Hoken Hō Kaiaku ni Hantai Suru Onnatachi Ōsaka Renrakukai, Josei to Kenkō Nettowāku, and Karada to Sei no Hōritsu o Tsukuru Onna no Kai.

179. In addition to DPI Josei Shōgaisha Nettowāku, these groups include Nihon Nōsei Mahisha Kyōkai Zenkoku Aoshiba no Kai Sōrengōkai (Aoshiba no Kai) and Zenkoku Shōgaisha Kaihō Undō Renrakukai. See, e.g., " 'Yūsei Hogo Hō' kanzen teppai o motomeru yōbōsho," petition submitted by Aoshiba no Kai to the Ministry of Health and Welfare Mental Health Section, January 26, 1996.

180. See, e.g., "Yūsei Hogo Hō no minaoshi ni tsuite no yōbōsho an," draft petition to be submitted by *Nihon Shōgaisha Kyōgikai* to the Ministry of Health and Welfare, January 1996.

181. *Yomiuri shinbun*, April 18, 1996. This revision was first discussed in 1993 (*Nichibo i hō*, March 1993).

182. *Soshiren nyūsu*, April 1996; *Seimei sonchō nyūsu*, June 1996.

183. The LDP Social Policy Committee formed a group to study revising the Eugenic Protection Law in December 1995.

184. *JAOG News*, July 1996.

185. See Representative Dōmoto Akiko's comments on the exclusion of women from the drafting process, House of Councilors Financial Settlement Committee, September 12, 1996. See also *Soshiren nyūsu*, June 1996, for the roster of those who attended an LDP Social Policy committee meeting. These groups did have opportunities to meet with opposition politicians and MHW officials (including high-ranking ones like MHW Minister Kan Naoto) to ask questions, but they were not included in the actual drafting process.

186. This seems to confirm Campbell's point that "only conservative politicians and what might be seen as 'establishment' interest groups are represented [in the policy-making process]; others—such as opposition politicians and labor or other left-of-center groups—are generally excluded from the system" (John Campbell, "Democracy and Bureaucracy in Japan," in Takeshi Ishida and Ellis Krauss, eds., *Democracy in Japan* [Pittsburgh: University of Pittsburgh Press, 1989], p. 126).

187. In concrete terms, this involved changing the title and purpose of the law, deleting all articles providing for involuntary and voluntary sterilization and abortion on grounds of physical disability, mental illness, or retardation, and replacing the term

*eugenic operation* (*yūsei shujutsu*) with the term *sterilization procedure* (*funin shujutsu*). Since almost no sterilizations or abortions have been performed on eugenic grounds for the last twenty to thirty years, the revision will have little effect on actual practice. The leprosy provisions of the Eugenic Protection Law were deleted in accordance with the abolition of the Leprosy Prevention Law (Rai Yobo Hō, 1907), effective April 1, 1996 (*Soshiren nyūsu*, April 1996).

188. *Soshiren nyūsu*, March 2000.

189. Ibid., October 1996; December 1996; March 1997; April 1997; "Piru to josei no kenkō" (kentō shiryō), Sei to kenkō o kangaeru josei senmonka no kai, November 1998.

190. *Asahi shinbun*, February 28, 1999; *Soshiren nyūsu*, April 1999; August 1999.

191. *Soshiren nyūsu*, April 1999; August 1999; October 1999.

192. The following women's groups and handicapped groups all sent formal protests to Nichibo in March 1999: Soshiren Watashi no Karada Kara; DPI Josei Shōgaisha Nettowāku; Karada to Sei no Hōritsu o Tsukuru no Kai; Yūsei Shisō o tō Nettowāku; and Aoshiba no Kai (ibid.). And as of July 1999, Nichibo had, in fact, decided to put aside efforts to add a "fetal conditions" clause to the law in favor of its other two, less controversial proposed revisions (*Asahi shinbun*, July 18, 1999).

193. For example, in January 1999 a group of lawmakers from the LDP, Kōmeitō, and other parties drafted "A Basic Law to Take Countermeasures against the Declining Birth Rate" (Shōshika Shakai Taisaku Kihonhō), though it is unclear whether it will ever progress beyond the draft stage. A few months later the prime minister established a Cabinet committee to promote policy responses to the declining birth rate (*Soshiren nyūsu*, May 1999; June 1999; *Mainichi shinbun*, May 21, 1999).

194. See, e.g., Tama, who writes that the Japanese came to regard abortion as a vested right ("The Logic of Abortion").

195. Lovenduski and Outshoorn, *The New Politics of Abortion*, pp. 2–3; Githens and Stetson, *Abortion Politics*, p. xi.

196. Lovenduski and Outshoorn, *The New Politics of Abortion*, p. 4.

197. Pharr notes that "the notion that conflict is desirable—that, like bitter medicine, it is ultimately good for body and soul, and for the state itself—is profoundly alien to Japanese. . . . Even protesters voicing social concerns are apt to see conflict as negative, disruptive, and regrettable" (Susan Pharr, *Losing Face: Status Politics in Japan* [Berkeley: University of California Press, 1990], p. 207).

198. LaFleur, *Liquid Life*.

199. The government did establish a system of child allowances in the early 1970s but only after making a series of compromises with opposing business interests (Stephen J. Anderson, *Welfare Policy and Politics in Japan: Beyond the Developmental State* [New York: Paragon House, 1993], pp. 102–4).

200. For a discussion of "social management," see Garon, *Molding Japanese Minds*, chapter 1.

201. Miyahara Shinobu, "Kazoku keikaku to tomo ni ayunda michi—Katō Shizue san intabyū—" *Josanpu zasshi* 44, no. 10 (October 1990): 49. This assertion is at least partially borne out by a 1990 survey in which 70 percent of female respondents stated that government pronatalist policies would have no effect on their reproductive decision making (*Mainichi Daily News*, July 8, 1990).

CHAPTER SIX
ABORTION BEFORE BIRTH CONTROL

1. Oakley comes to a similar conclusion, stating that "the period of initiation and discussion was much more prolonged for birth control/population than for other policy issues. . .[and] birth control/population policy was marked by long periods between policy adoption and policy implementation" (Oakley, "The Development of Population Policy in Japan," pp. 299–300).

2. For example, a *Nihon keizai shinbun* editorial from April 22, 1949, stated, "As everybody knows, there are two methods of birth control—contraception and abortion." See also *Yomiuri shinbun*, December 27, 1948; Ōta *Nihon sanji chōsetsu 100-nen shi*, p. 403; Nakagawa, "Toshi nichijō seikatsu no naka no sengo," p. 279; Nishiuchi Masahiko, *Nihon no boshi hoken to Moriyama Yutaka: Subete no haha to ko ni hoken to iryō no onkei o* (Tokyo: Nihon Kazoku Keikaku Kyōkai, 1988), pp. 216–17; P. K. Whelpton, "The Outlook for the Control of Human Fertility in Japan," *American Sociological Review* 15, no. 1 (February 1950): 37; and Irene B. Taeuber, *The Population of Japan* (Princeton, N.J.: Princeton University Press, 1958), p. 272. It should be noted that although voluntary and compulsory sterilization were legal under the Eugenic Protection Law, sterilizations could only be performed for reasons of hereditary illness and maternal health; furthermore, sterilization was not widely understood to be, or promoted as, a form of birth control.

3. Others have noted this pattern. See, e.g., Mariko Jitsukawa and Carl Djerassi, "Birth Control in Japan: Realities and Prognosis," *Science* 265 (August 19, 1994): 1048. Although Jitsukawa and Djerassi are incorrect in saying that contraceptive marketing was legalized in 1952, since it was in fact legalized in 1948, they are essentially correct when they argue that "the four year lag between the availability of legal abortion (1948) and the approval of contraceptive marketing (1952) proved to be critical in Japanese acceptance of abortion as a key component of birth control." For while contraceptives were technically legal before the mid-1950s, they were not promoted or widely accepted until then.

4. Kathleen Uno, "Death of 'Good Wife, Wise Mother'?" in Andrew Gordon, ed., *Postwar Japan as History* (Berkeley: University of California Press, 1993), pp. 307–8, 319. See chapter 4 for a more detailed discussion of this theory.

5. I derive the concept of elite versus popular ideologies from Carol Gluck, *Japan's Modern Myths: Ideology in the Late Meiji Period* (Princeton, N.J.: Princeton University Press, 1985).

6. *Nippon Times*, November 6, 1946.

7. November 7, 1946, Check Sheet, WNRC, RG No. 331, Box No. 9425, "Eugenics" file, SCAP PHW, Administrative Division, Subject File, memo from Herb Passin, Public Opinion and Sociological Research.

8. Ōta, *Nihon sanji chōsetsu 100-nen shi*, p. 370.

9. Shikiba Ryūzaburō, *Sanger fujin den to sanji chōsetsu tembō* (Tokyo: Taigensha, 1947), p. 313, cited in Toshinobu Kato, *The Development of Family Planning in Japan with Industrial Involvement* (New York: United Nations, 1978), p. 7; Oakley, "The Development of Population Policy in Japan," pp. 355, 380; Amemiya, "The Road to Pro-Choice Ideology in Japan," p. 192.

10. Amemiya, "The Road to Pro-Choice Ideology in Japan," pp. 154–55.

11. Oakley, "The Development of Population Policy in Japan," p. 150.

12. WNRC, RG No. 331, Box No. 2508, *The Official Gazette Extra*, no. 21, the Fifth Session of the National Diet, May 7, 1949, p. 8; *Nippon Times*, April 15, 1949.

13. *Mainichi shinbun*, May 31, 1949.

14. *Yomiuri shinbun*, April 9, 1949; *Mainichi shinbun*, May 9, 1949.

15. *Shūkan asahi*, May 29, 1949.

16. Ibid. Ōta notes that Japanese Marxists had opposed population control arguments since before the war (Ōta, *Nihon sanji chōsetsu 100-nen shi*, p. 371). For a description of the Taishō debate between nationalist Takada Yasuma and socialist Kawakami Hajime on the population problem, see Amemiya, "The Road to Pro-Choice Ideology in Japan," pp. 101–2.

17. *Akahata*, June 3, 1949.

18. For a discussion of a related subject, socialist pronatalist thought in Europe before World War II, see Jay Winter, "Socialism, Social Democracy, and Population Questions in Western Europe: 1870–1950," in Michael S. Teitelbaum and Jay M. Winter, eds., *Population and Resources in Western Intellectual Traditions* (Cambridge: Cambridge University Press, 1989).

19. E.g., *Nippon fujin shinbun*, March 25, 1949; *Tokyo shinbun*, April 10, 1949; *Mainichi shinbun*, April 20, 1949; *Nihon keizai shinbun*, April 22, 1949; *Chūbu nippon shinbun*, April 25, 1949; see also Warren Thompson, "The Need for a Population Policy in Japan," *American Sociological Review* 15, no. 1 (February 1950).

20. June 6, 1949, memo, WNRC, RG No. 331, Box No. 9425, "Eugenics" file, SCAP PHW Section, Administrative Branch, Subject File; *Nippon Times*, July 2, 1949. See also a series of draft Birth Control Directives from General MacArthur, 1949, WNRC, RG No. 331, Box No. 9344, "Birth Control" file, SCAP PHW Section, Administrative Division, Nursing Affairs and Health Statistics.

21. See, e.g., Katō, *Aru josei seijika no hansei*, p. 154; see also an August 17, 1949, letter from birth control activist Fumiko Amano which states: "Even now, the Occupation will do nothing about it [birth control] because of the religious opposition from the States" (WNRC, RG No. 331, Box No. 9425, "Eugenics" file, SCAP, PHW Section, Administrative Branch, Subject File).

22. February 1950 letter to Kenneth Colegrove, WNRC, RG No. 331, Box No. 9425 "Eugenics" file, SCAP PHW Section, Administrative Branch, Subject File.

23. Oakley, "The Development of Population Policy in Japan," pp. 153–54.

24. National Archives, WNRC, RG No. 331, Box No. 9344, "Birth Control" file, SCAP PHW Section, Administrative Division, Nursing Affairs and Health Statistics.

25. Oakley, "The Development of Population Policy in Japan," pp. 192, 201.

26. Ibid., p. 201. The occupying forces in Germany turned down repeated German requests for permission to lift Himmler's 1941 Police Ordinance banning contraceptives, and birth control remained illegal in Germany for the duration of the occupation (Hans Harmsen, "Notes on Abortion and Birth Control in Germany," *Population Studies* 3, no. 4 (1950): 402–3.

27. Oakley, "The Development of Population Policy in Japan," pp. 156, 210. Although it should be noted that Yoshida was already personally in favor of birth control, according to Kenneth Colegrove, a political science professor who had several conversations with Yoshida on the subject in 1946 (January 17, 1950, letter from Kenneth Cole-

grove to Brigadier General Sams, WNRC, RG No. 331, Box No. 9425 "Eugenics" file, SCAP PHW Section, Administrative Branch, Subject File).

28. It is interesting to note that, in this case, economic growth was a means to an end (i.e., national independence), not just an end in itself. This supports the argument of Muramatsu and Krauss that the LDP used economic development to accomplish political goals during its long rule over Japan (Muramatsu and Krauss, "The Conservative Policy Line and the Development of Patterned Pluralism," pp. 553–54).

29. Oakley, "The Development of Population Policy in Japan," p. 216.

30. Amemiya, "The Road to Pro-Choice Ideology in Japan," pp. 165–66.

31. The draft article read, "[P]hysicians may freely (*jiyū ni*) take steps to [enable patients to] temporarily avoid reproduction." For the full text of the draft law, see *Proceedings of the House of Representatives Health and Welfare Committee*, no. 35 (February 1, 1947): 272–74. The *Yomiuri* interpreted the use of the word *jiyū* as an attempt to make it clear that choosing whether to contracept was an individual's prerogative (*Yomiuri shinbun*, August 22, 1947).

32. See the previous chapter for a more detailed discussion of the 1947 bill's failure and the changed emphasis of the 1948 bill. Taniguchi, the main sponsor of the 1948 bill, supposedly intended to include contraceptive services in the duties of Eugenic Marriage Consultation Offices (Oakley, "The Development of Population Policy in Japan," pp. 234–35).

33. WNRC, RG No. 331, Box No. 2508, *The Official Gazette Extra*, no. 26, the Fifth Session of the National Diet, May 14, 1949, pp. 11–14.

34. Ibid.; WNRC, RG No. 331, Box No. 9332, "EPL" file, SCAP PHW Section, Administrative Division, Publications File.

35. *Shūkan asahi*, May 29, 1949.

36. From Ōta, *Nihon sanji chōsetsu 100-nen shi*, cited in Nishiuchi, *Nihon no boshi hoken to Moriyama Yutaka*, pp. 221–22.

37. Whelpton, "The Outlook for the Control," p. 40. Ōta also notes that in the late 1940s and early 1950s the EPCOs "did not get government cooperation or support, and few had active [operations]" (Ōta, *Nihon sanji chōsetsu 100-nen shi*, p. 384).

38. Oakley, "The Development of Population Policy in Japan," pp. 240–41.

39. April 1950 memo from O. R. McCoy of the Rockefeller Foundation to General Sams, WNRC, RG No. 331, Box No. 9344, "Birth Control" file, SCAP PHW, Administrative Division, Nursing Affairs and Health Statistics.

40. For a description of the activities of an operational private EPCO in Sendai, see Hiroko Nagaike and Keiko Takahashi, eds., *10 nen no ayumi* (Sendai: Nagaike Yūsei Hogo Sōdanjo, 1984); and Mitsuo Fujiwara, ed., *Nagaike yūsei hogo sōdanjo: 20 nen no ayumi* (Sendai: Nagaike Yūsei Hogo Sōdanjo, 1993).

41. "A Draft of Law on Control of Contraceptive Appliances and Others," WNRC, RG No. 331, Box No. 9425, "Eugenics" file, SCAP PHW, Administrative Division, Subject File.

42. John Dower, "The Useful War," in Carol Gluck and Stephen R. Graubard, *Showa: The Japan of Hirohito* (New York: Norton, 1992).

43. Dower, *Embracing Defeat* (New York: Norton, 1999), p. 205.

44. April 27, 1948 memo from the Narcotics Control Division, WNRC, RG No. 331, Box No. 9425, "Eugenics" file, SCAP PHW, Administrative Division, Subject File.

45. Whelpton, "The Outlook for the Control," p. 39; Kato, *The Development of Family Planning in Japan*, p. 7. During the war, the police banned the use of the word *contraceptive*, so contraceptive manufacturers advertised their products as anti-venereal disease drugs or as drugs for menstrual disorders (Katō, *Aru josei seijika no hansei*, p. 152).

46. *Tokyo Times*, June 9, 1950.

47. Whelpton, "The Outlook for the Control," p. 38.

48. Supply Division memos, November 11, 1949, and December 3, 1949, WNRC, RG No. 331, Box No. 9387, "Contraceptives, 1948–51" file, PHW, Supply Division, Subject File.

49. *Kazoku keikaku*, October 1955; Hardacre, *Marketing the Menacing Fetus*, p. 65. See *Shin Tokyo*, June 16, 1949, for an editorial on tainted contraceptives; see also *Yomiuri shinbun*, June 14, 1949; *Mainichi shinbun*, June 15, 1949; and June 24, 1949 Memo from Chief of Inspection Section to Chief of Supply Division, RG No. 331, Box No. 9387, "Contraceptives, 1948–51" file, PHW Supply Division, Subject File.

50. G-2 Civil Censorship Detachment Special Report, WNRC, RG No. 331, Box No. 9332, "Birth Control" file, SCAP PHW Section, Administrative Division, Subject File.

51. Ibid. *Jiji shinpō* and *Asahi shinbun* opinion surveys conducted in the same year had roughly similar results. The *Jiji* survey, which was the larger of the two, found 68 percent of respondents in favor of birth control, 18 percent noncommittal, and 14 percent opposed. Of those who favored birth control, 54 percent cited economic and living problems, 24 percent cited "the population problem," 16 percent cited eugenic reasons, and 6 percent cited women's rights and health (Whelpton, "The Outlook for the Control," pp. 36–37).

52. Ibid.

53. Interview with Matsumoto Seiichi, Chairman, Japan Family Planning Association, June 13, 1995.

54. *Asahi shinbun*, May 20, 1949.

55. *Seinen shinbun*, May 17, 1949.

56. G-2 Civil Censorship Detachment Special Report, WNRC, RG No. 331, Box No. 9332, "Birth Control" file, SCAP PHW Section, Administrative Division, Subject File. Anti-birth control views were also expressed in the press. For example, an article in the April 2, 1949, *Shinkō shinbun* argued that "our present advocacy of population control . . . may ruin our race in the future. It is difficult for a race that has once begun to decline to be revived again. . . . [But] history shows that no race has been ruined by overpopulation." An article in the May 31, 1949, *Yūkan chūgai* expressed anxiety that widespread use of birth control might result in a large number of old people's homes in the future.

57. *Jiji Shimpō*, March 5, 1949; The Mainichi Newspaper's Population Problems Research Council, *The Population and Society of Postwar Japan*, pp. 173–79.

58. Yoshio Koya, *Pioneering in Family Planning* (New York: Population Council, 1963), pp. 18–19.

59. WNRC, RG No. 331, Box No. 9425, "Eugenics" file, SCAP PHW Section, Administrative Branch, Subject File, SCAPINS translation of *Recommendations of the Population Problem Council in the Cabinet*, November 29, 1949, Councillor's Room, Prime Minister's Office, pp. 21–22.

60. *Mainichi shinbun* (Tokyo edition), September 17, 1949. (This article was written after the first draft of the Council's recommendations were made public.)

61. WNRC, RG No. 331, Box No. 9425, "Eugenics" file, SCAP PHW Section, Administrative Branch, Subject File, SCAPINS translation of *Recommendations of the Population Problem Council in the Cabinet*, November 29, 1949, Councillor's Room, Prime Minister's Office, p. 22. MHW Minister Tsurumi made a statement similar in character several years later, at the outset of the 1954 family planning campaign. He said that the purpose of the campaign was to educate parents so that they could " 'take their own economic resources and our country's future into account' when deciding how many children to have" (Amemiya, "The Road to Pro-Choice Ideology in Japan," pp. 227–28).

62. WNRC, RG No. 331, Box No. 9425, "Eugenics" file, SCAP PHW Section, Administrative Branch, Subject File, SCAPINS translation of *Recommendations of the Population Problem Council in the Cabinet*, November 29, 1949, Councillor's Room, Prime Minister's Office, p. 7.

63. According to Oakley, all population policy Advisory Council reports written during the occupation were very similar in content to a 1930 report pointing to industrialization as the solution to the "already born" portion of the population problem that could not be "solved" by means of birth control (Oakley, "The Development of Population Policy in Japan," pp. 165–66).

64. June 13, 1949, memo, WNRC, RG No. 331, Box No. 9334, "Population Problems" file, SCAP, PHW, Administrative Division, Subject File; see also Thompson, "The Need for a Population Policy in Japan."

65. *Shin yūkan*, March 21, 1949. See also John Dower, "Peace and Democracy in Two Systems: External Policy and Internal Conflict," in Gordon, *Postwar Japan as History*, p. 12.

66. June 13, 1949, memo from P. K. Whelpton, "Lessening the Future Increase in the Ratio of Population to Natural Resources," WNRC, RG No. 331, Box No. 9334, "Population Problems" file, SCAP PHW, Administrative Division, Subject File. On the basis of talks with MHW officials, Whelpton concluded that "there may be a vigorous [birth control] campaign" comparable to the very successful campaigns to combat venereal disease and tuberculosis.

67. Koya, *Pioneering in Family Planning*, p. 20.

68. The reported number of abortions rose from 264,104 in 1949 to 805,524 in 1952 (*The Population and Society of Postwar Japan*, 1994, p. 116). The ratio of abortions to live births increased from 20.9 in 1950 to 67.6 in 1955 (Hardacre, *Marketing the Menacing Fetus*, p. 58).

69. According to Matsumoto, the government started to support family planning measures following the passage of the Eugenic Protection Law, as the abortion rate skyrocketed and abortion-related injuries and deaths began to increase. Interview with Matsumoto Seiichi, Chairman, Japan Family Planning Association, June 13, 1995. Some evidence suggests that although Health Ministry bureaucrats were concerned about overpopulation and its effects on economic development, they felt inhibited from openly advocating birth control as the solution to overpopulation, fearing that such an approach would have led to accusations that the MHW was again trying to force the Japanese to conform to a national birth control policy. Kunii, for example, writes that MHW Minister Kusaba's October 1954 statement that "the limitation of population growth should be the basic principle of Japan's population policy" was surprising since it made the MHW vulnerable to attack from opposition parties (Chojiro Kunii, *Humanistic Family Planning Approaches: The Integration of Family Planning and Health Goals* [New

York: U.N. Fund for Population Activities, 1983], p. 10; Minoru Muramatsu, ed., *Japan's Experience in Family Planning—Past and Present* [Tokyo: Family Planning Federation of Japan, 1967], p. 95).

70. Nishiuchi, *Nihon no boshi hoken to Moriyama Yutaka*, p. 223.

71. *Yomiuri shinbun*, October 26, 1951.

72. *Nihon keizai shinbun*, November 24, 1951.

73. See *Kazoku keikaku*, July 1955; August 1955; October 1955. Article 39 of the Eugenic Protection Law was written to be effective for only five years, so every five years, until the present day, Article 39 is reviewed and new legislation is passed that allows midwives and nurses to sell birth control for another five years.

74. *Kazoku keikaku*, November 1961, p. 4.

75. Nishiuchi, *Nihon no boshi hoken to Moriyama Yutaka*, 1988, p. 225.

76. Ōbayashi Michiko, *Josanpu no sengo* (Tokyo: Keisō Shobō, 1989), p. 216; Muramatsu, *Japan's Experience in Family Planning*, p. 92. In 1952 the government's family planning budget was ¥21.2 million ($59,000). The family planning budget peaked at ¥72.5 million ($201,000) in 1958 and declined steadily after that (Muramatsu, *Japan's Experience in Family Planning*, p. 93).

77. Calculated on the basis that there were 12 million women of childbearing age, and a ¥24 million family planning budget, at an exchange rate of $1 = ¥360 (*Yūkan yomiuri*, August 6, 1952).

78. Ibid.

79. Muramatsu, *Japan's Experience in Family Planning*, pp. 88–89.

80. Ōbayashi, *Josanpu no Sengo*, p. 214.

81. *Yūkan yomiuri*, August 6, 1952.

82. Some groups that formed after the war were, for example, Ōta Tenrei's Birth Control League (Sanji Seigen Dōmei), established in 1945; the Amano's Japan Pregnancy Control Institute (Nihon Ninshin Chōsetsu Kenkyūjo) and Yasukochi Hisashi's Society to Study Birth Control (Sanji Seigen Kenkyūkai), both formed in 1946; and, in 1947, the Society for the Study of Birth Control (Shussei Chōsetsu Kenkyūkai), the Japan Birth Control League (Nihon Sanji Chōsetsu Renmei), and the Japan Birth Control Popularization Society (Sanji Seigen Fukyūkai) headed by Katō Shizue (Ōta Tenrei, "Sanji chōsetsu no 10-nen," *Kazoku keikaku*, Nos. 206–14 [1971], cited in Amemiya, "The Road to Pro-Choice Ideology in Japan," pp. 157–58).

83. Ōta, *Nihon sanji chōsetsu shi*, pp. 392–93; Nihon Kazoku Keikaku Kyōkai, ed., *Yoakemae no wakai kikansha—Nihon kazoku keikaku kyōkai no 15-nen no ayumi* (Tokyo: Nihon Kazoku Keikaku Kyōkai, 1969), pp. 71–72; Hardacre, *Marketing the Menacing Fetus*, p. 51.

84. Chojiro Kunii, *It All Started from Worms: The 45-Year Record of Japan's Post–World War II National Health and Family Planning Movement* (Tokyo: The Hoken Kaikan Foundation, 1992), pp. 70–72.

85. Concerns about the relationship between overpopulation and economic development had changed slightly, however. With recovery well under way, the government shifted its attention to industry's ability to absorb the millions of already unemployed, as well as the almost one million new people who would be going on the job market every year for the foreseeable future.

86. For discussions of state delegation of authority, see Margaret McKean, "State Strength and Public Interest," and Frank Upham, "Privatizing Regulation: The Implica-

tions of the Large-Scale Retail Stores Law," in Allinson and Sone, *Political Dynamics in Contemporary Japan*. Amemiya also notes that "the MHW was involved in the creation of this national network of family planning organizations from the beginning, though it was quite willing to take a back seat in allowing private family planning organizations to do much of the work" (Amemiya, "The Road to Pro-Choice Ideology in Japan," p. 216).

87. *The Population and Society of Postwar Japan*, p. 76. Twenty-six percent of the population was *actually* practicing contraception in 1952; this figure rose to 42 percent in 1961 and ranged between 57 percent and 64 percent for much of the 1970s, 1980s, and 1990s (Hardacre, *Marketing the Menacing Fetus*, p. 61).

88. Amemiya, "The Road to Pro-Choice Ideology in Japan," p. 155. It should be noted, however, that abortion was equally, if not more responsible for the birth rate decline during this period. The number of abortions and ratio of abortions to live births did not begin to decrease significantly until the mid-1960s.

89. Muramatsu, *Japan's Experience in Family Planning*, p. 93; Koya, *Pioneering in Family Planning*, p. 24.

90. *Tokyo mainichi shinbun*, April 26, 1955.

91. Amemiya, "The Road to Pro-Choice Ideology in Japan," pp. 221–22.

92. Muramatsu, *Japan's Experience in Family Planning*, p. 97. One midwife complained that the ¥250 fee she received for giving instructions on birth control to a group of fifty did not even cover her bus fare (Kunii, *Humanistic Family Planning Approaches*, p. 17).

93. Ōbayashi, *Josanpu no Sengo*, p. 216.

94. *Tokyo mainichi shinbun*, February 22, 1957.

95. The Public Health Bureau was responsible for contraception policy until 1966; since then, contraception policy has been the province of the Mother and Child Health Section of the Children and Families Bureau.

96. Kunii, *Humanistic Family Planning Approaches*, p. 12.

97. Ibid., pp. 13–14.

98. Chojiro Kunii and Tameyoshi Katagiri, eds., *Basic Readings in Population and Family Planning in Japan* (Tokyo: Japan Organization for International Cooperation in Family Planning, 1976), p. 68; Coleman, *Family Planning in Japanese Society*, p. 45. According to Gelb, one-fourth of family planning groups' revenue is still derived from condom sales (Joyce Gelb, "Abortion and Reproductive Choice: Policy and Politics in Japan," in Githens and Stetson, *Abortion Politics*, p. 125).

99. See Article 15, Paragraph 2, of the Eugenic Protection Law.

100. Nishiuchi, *Nihon no boshi hoken to Moriyama Yutaka*, p. 226.

101. Ōbayashi, *Josanpu no Sengo*, p. 212; Kunii, *Humanistic Family Planning Approaches*, p. 19; Koya, *Pioneering in Family Planning*, p. 29.

102. *Kazoku keikaku*, October 1956; November 1956.

103. *Yoakemae no wakai kikansha*, p. 72.

104. *Kazoku keikaku*, February 1956; May 1956; July 1956.

105. In accordance with recommendations of the Population Problems Council, the government started funding the New Life movement in 1955 (Kato, *The Development of Family Planning in Japan*, p. 12).

106. Garon, *Molding Japanese Minds*, pp. 168–69; Gordon, "Managing the Japanese Household," p. 246.

107. Claude V. Kiser, ed., *Research in Family Planning* (Princeton, N.J.: Princeton University Press, 1962), p. 571.

108. Koya, *Pioneering in Family Planning*, p. 133; Gordon, "Managing the Japanese Household," p. 268.

109. Muramatsu, *Japan's Experience in Family Planning*, p. 99; Kato, *The Development of Family Planning in Japan*, p. 17; Gordon, "Managing the Japanese Household," p. 254. Not all companies embarked on intensive large-scale programs but instead initiated activities on a smaller scale, like selling condoms at the company store (Kato, *The Development of Family Planning in Japan*, p. 37).

110. According to Gordon, although there were similar movements in other countries, the focus on small groups was a distinctive feature of the Japanese New Life movement (Gordon, "Managing the Japanese Household," pp. 261, 263; Fumiyo Mitsui, " 'Hinin' o meguru nihon no kindai shi," *Human Sexuality*, no. 5 [November 1991]).

111. Gordon, "Managing the Japanese Household," p. 265.

112. Kato, *The Development of Family Planning in Japan*, pp. 27–28; Gordon, "Managing the Japanese Household," pp. 266–67.

113. Kato, *The Development of Family Planning in Japan*, p. 26; Gordon, "Managing the Japanese Household," pp. 255–56, 258, 269–70.

114. Amemiya, "The Road to Pro-Choice Ideology in Japan," p. 229.

115. Kato, *The Development of Family Planning in Japan*, p. 37.

116. See *The Population and Society of Postwar Japan*, 1994, for fifty years of surveys that show, among other things, the rise in birth control use over the postwar period. See also Nakatani Kinko, "The Status of Abortion in Japan and Some Issues," *Keio Law Review* (1985): 16.

117. Muramatsu, *Japan's Experience in Family Planning*, p. 99; Koya, *Pioneering in Family Planning*, p. 27.

118. Dower, "Peace and Democracy," in Gordon, *Postwar Japan as History*, p. 16.

119. The family planning movement's response to this repudiation of the economic imperative for contraception was to shift emphasis to the eugenic advantages of birth control. In 1961, articles began to appear in the JFPA's newsletter, *Kazoku keikaku*, discussing the need to redefine family planning, not as a means to achieving fewer children but as a way to produce better quality children. The family planners accomplished this switch from quantity to quality quite smoothly because of the long, respectable history of eugenic justifications for contraception. Although the family planning movement lost some of its dynamism and urgency in the 1960s, it actually adjusted quite well to the new climate of concern over the birth rate. See Amemiya, "The Road to Pro-Choice Ideology in Japan," chapter 10.

120. *Yoakemae no wakai kikansha*, p. 63.

CHAPTER SEVEN
THE POLITICS OF THE PILL

1. There are also some short articles on the subject, e.g., Misako Iwamoto, "Seishoku no jiko ketteiken no ima: Nihon ni okeru piru kaikin tōketsu o megutte," *Joseigaku* 2 (May 1994); Jitsukawa and Djerassi, "Birth Control in Japan"; Sumie Uno, "The Oral Contraceptive Pill in Japan," *Issues in Reproductive and Genetic Engineering* 5, no. 3 (1992); Takashi Wagatsuma, "History and Present Status of Contraceptive Practice in

Japan," in Masahiko Mizuno, ed., *Recent Advances in Hormonal Contraception*, Satellite Symposium of the Eighth International Congress of Endocrinology, Tokyo, 1988.

2. Coleman, *Family Planning in Japanese Society*, pp. 36–38. Until 1994 this group was called Nihon Bosei Hogo I Kyōkai; in English it is called the Japan Association of Maternal Welfare.

3. Ibid., p. 38.

4. Ibid., pp. 44–50.

5. These groups all submitted similar petitions to the MHW in 1985 and early 1986 requesting permission to do clinical tests on the low-dose pill. See, e.g., *Nichibo i hō*, October 1985.

6. Coleman, *Family Planning in Japanese Society*, pp. 210–15.

7. James Reed, *From Private Vice to Public Virtue: The Birth Control Movement and American Society since 1830* (New York: Basic Books, 1978), pp. 338–39.

8. She invested $2 million to $4 million in the project over a period of years (Bernard Asbell, *The Pill: A Biography of the Drug That Changed the World* [New York: Random House, 1995], pp. 9–12; Reed, *From Private Vice to Public Virtue*, p. 340).

9. Doctors and scientists had realized the therapeutic potential of hormones in the decades before World War II, but it was not feasible to develop hormone-based drugs at that time as hormones could only be extracted from animals in small quantities, very laboriously, and at great expense. In the late 1940s–early 1950s, however, a series of U.S. chemists (Russell Market, Karl Djerassi, and others) developed a process for synthesizing artificial steroid hormones using an inedible wild yam. Drug companies initially seized on this synthetic hormone technology to make cortisone and other corticoid drugs, which are used for treating arthritis and immune disorders (Asbell, *The Pill*, pp. 83, 103).

10. The pill also works by thickening cervical mucus, thus preventing sperm from reaching eggs that are released; additionally, the pill may prevent fertilized eggs from implanting in the uterus.

11. Reed, *From Private Vice to Public Virtue*, pp. 356–61; Asbell, *The Pill*, p. 133.

12. Asbell, *The Pill*, pp. 135–36.

13. *Kazoku Keikaku*, November 1955.

14. Reed, *From Private Vice to Public Virtue*, p. 344; Asbell, *The Pill*, p. 156.

15. Cited in Asbell, *The Pill*, p. 163.

16. Questions were also raised about whether healthy women would want to take medication with possible side effects every day, whether oral contraceptives would prove prohibitively expensive, whether religious objections to the pill would create problems for manufacturers, and whether legal problems would arise since contraception was still illegal in some states (ibid., pp. 156–60, 163).

17. Ibid., p. 304.

18. Ibid., pp. 166–68.

19. Deborah Anne Dawson, "Trends in Use of Oral Contraceptives—Data from the 1987 National Health Interviews Survey, *Family Planning Perspectives* 22, no. 4 (July/August 1990); Asbell, *The Pill*, pp. 166–68.

20. The failure rate is 3–6 percent with perfect use. The term *typical use* refers to the rate of accidental pregnancy during the first year of method adoption (not necessarily for the first time) among typical couples; the term *perfect use* refers to the rate of accidental pregnancy during the first year of method adoption (not necessarily for the first time)

among couples who use the method perfectly, that is, both consistently and correctly (*Contraceptive Technology Update* 17, no. 2 [February 1996]: 14).

21. Ibid. The failure rate is 0.1–0.5 percent. It should be noted that this source only gives the failure rate for the pill with "perfect use." The pill's failure rate with "typical use" (that is, when the user occasionally forgets to take the pill) is presumably higher.

22. Petchesky, *Abortion and Woman's Choice*, pp. 103–11, 170; Elizabeth Siegel Watkins, *On the Pill: A Social History of Oral Contraceptives, 1950–1970* (Baltimore: The Johns Hopkins University Press, 1998), p. 63.

23. Asbell, *The Pill*, pp. 307–8.

24. Gordon, *Woman's Body, Woman's Right*, pp. 421–22; Watkins, *On the Pill*, p. 3.

25. Gordon, *Woman's Body, Woman's Right*, p. 421; Kristin Luker, *Taking Chances: Abortion and the Decision Not to Contracept* (Berkeley: University of California Press, 1975), pp. 124–26.

26. Gordon, *Woman's Body, Woman's Right*, pp. 420–21.

27. Ibid., p. 430. For similar points, see also Petchesky, *Abortion and Woman's Choice*, p. 189, and Boston Women's Health Collective, ed., *Our Bodies, Ourselves: A Book by and for Women* (New York: Simon and Schuster, 1973).

28. Women who have early abortions and nonsmoking pill users under the age of thirty run about the same risk of health complications (Petchesky, *Abortion and Woman's Choice*, pp. 169, 186).

29. Ibid., pp. 171–73, 181.

30. Coleman, *Family Planning in Japanese Society*, chapters 5–7.

31. Japanese researchers were reproducing Pincus's experiments in 1956–57, and Japanese drug companies used their results to gain the Ministry of Health and Welfare's permission to sell hormonal drugs for gynecological problems (*Kazoku keikaku*, November 1957; interview with Matsumoto Seiichi, Chairman, Japan Family Planning Association, May 9, 1995. Shio Nogi received approval in 1957, and Dai Nippon Seiyaku in 1960. The American company Searle received similar approval from the FDA in 1957 (Kunii and Katagiri, *Basic Readings in Population and Family Planning in Japan*, p. 110; Asbell, *The Pill*, p. 156).

32. Chronology from personal communication, Mr. Katō, OC Liaison Committee Representative, Nihon Schering, May 8, 1995.

33. *Asahi shinbun*, April 18, 1961.

34. See the news clipping file entitled "*Suiminyaku asobi*" at the National Diet Library in Tokyo.

35. *Kazoku keikaku*, August 1964.

36. See the Thalidomide clipping file at the National Diet Library in Tokyo. Thalidomide was an over-the-counter sleeping medicine that was thought to be safe for pregnant women; before it was withdrawn from the market, it caused tens of thousands of babies to be born with severe deformities, particularly to their arms and legs.

37. *Asahi shinbun*, August 10, 1964.

38. Reich, "Resistance to the Pill in Japan," Keynote Address; see also Watkins, *On the Pill*, pp. 34–35, 41–42.

39. When the drug companies first put in their applications in 1961, they were required to do tests at two different hospitals on thirty patients each, which was the standard requirement at the time for all new drugs. The government changed the requirements for pill testing in July 1962 to tests at more than five hospitals on sixty

patients at more than two of those hospitals, including patients who had taken the pill for more than two years (*Asahi shinbun*, January 24, 1965).

40. Ibid., September 10, 1964.

41. Ibid., January 24, 1965.

42. *Kazoku keikaku*, August 1964; *Asahi shinbun*, September 10, 1964; *Yomiuri shinbun*, September 22, 1964; *Asahi shinbun*, January 24, 1965; interview with Matsumoto Seiichi, May 9, 1995.

43. The MHW planned to require that the pill be sold as a prescription drug not to be advertised outside medical journals and not to be used for more than two years at a time (*Asahi shinbun*, January 24, 1965).

44. Interview with Matsumoto Seiichi, May 9, 1995.

45. *Proceedings of the House of Councilors Budget Committee*, no. 8 (October 20, 1961): 27–28. Watkins notes that there was also a strong association in the American press between the pill and sexual promiscuity in the 1960s but that no research was done at the time to establish whether there was, in fact, any correlation (Watkins, *On the Pill*, pp. 53–56).

46. Ibid.; *Proceedings of the House of Councilors Budget Committee*, no. 17 (March 22, 1962): 3.

47. My interview with Matsumoto Seiichi, May 9, 1995, and Coleman, *Family Planning in Japanese Society*, pp. 36–37, confirm that MHW bureaucrats were wary of taking the blame if problems with the pill developed.

48. *Yomiuri shinbun*, September 22, 1964.

49. *Kazoku keikaku*, August 1964; *Asahi shinbun*, January 24, 1965; *Bosei hogo i hō*, October 1964; interview with Matsumoto Seiichi, May 9, 1995; personal communication, Shirota Kumeo, Vice President, Japan Behringer-Sohn, August 1, 1995. It should be noted that opposition to the pill *within* these groups was not completely unanimous, but pro-pill members were in the minority. Pro-pill respondents to the Japan Family Planning Association's 1964 opinion survey supported their position in a variety of ways. They argued that the pill had already been approved in Europe and the United States, that the pill had no proven negative side effects, that the pill was easy to use, and that it would prevent overpopulation as well as abortion. (*Yomiuri shinbun*, September 22, 1964; *Kazoku keikaku*, September 1964).

50. *Asahi shinbun*, September 10, 1964; January 24, 1965; *Yomiuri shinbun*, September 22, 1964.

51. *Kazoku keikaku*, August 1964; *Asahi shinbun*, January 24, 1965.

52. *Kazoku Keikaku*, August 1964; *Asahi shinbun*, January 24, 1965.

53. *Kazoku keikaku*, August 1964.

54. *Yomiuri shinbun*, September 22, 1964; *Kazoku keikaku*, September 1964.

55. Over the last fifty years there has been a complete changeover from midwives, who performed the majority of deliveries until the late 1950s, to doctors, who now dominate the field. In 1947, 92.1 percent of births were attended by midwives and only 3.5 percent by physicians. Midwives' share of deliveries decreased to 71.5 percent in 1957 and further decreased to 32.7 percent in 1964; meanwhile, physicians' share of deliveries increased to 25.1 percent in 1957 and then to 66.6 percent in 1964. This trend persisted over time so that, by 1990, midwives were attending the minority of births—only 2 percent—and physicians were attending the rest (*Maternal and Child Health in Japan*, compiled under the supervision of the Maternal and Child Health Divi-

sion, Children and Families Bureau, Ministry of Health and Welfare [Tokyo: Mothers' and Children's Health and Welfare Association, 1992], p. 60). The number of midwives in Japan has also declined dramatically during the postwar period, from 55,356 in 1955 to 22,690 in 1992 (Boshi Eisei Kenkyukai, ed., *Boshi hoken no omo naru tōkei* [Tokyo: Boshi Hoken Jigyōdan, 1994], p. 114).

56. Kunii and Katagiri, *Basic Readings*, p. 68; Coleman, *Family Planning in Japanese Society*, p. 45.

57. *Kazoku keikaku*, August 1964; *Asahi shinbun*, January 24, 1965; interview with Matsumoto Seiichi, May 9, 1995.

58. *Bosei hogo i hō*, October 1964.

59. Kunii and Katagiri, *Basic Readings*, p. 153; Coleman, *Family Planning in Japanese Society*, p. 38.

60. *Yomiuri shinbun*, September 22, 1964; *Kazoku keikaku*, September 1964.

61. *Asahi shinbun*, January 24, 1965.

62. In the same survey a few people did express pro-pill opinions. They argued that approving the pill would lower the abortion rate or mitigate overpopulation; that the pill had few side effects; that it was easy to use; and that it had been approved in the United States and Europe (*Yomiuri shinbun*, September 22, 1964; *Kazoku keikaku*, September 1964). But these views came mostly from professionals in nonmedical fields, and in any event, they were very much in the minority. See note 49, above.

63. *Kazoku keikaku*, August 1964.

64. *Asahi shinbun*, September 10, 1964.

65. See Steslicke, *Doctors in Politics*. As recently as the 1980s, Calder found that "the power of the JMA [Japan Medical Association] . . . contrasts strongly to the relative political weakness of the pharmaceutical firms" in struggles over a drug pricing and distribution system that benefits physicians (Kent Calder, *Crisis and Compensation: Public Policy and Political Stability in Japan* [Princeton, N.J.: Princeton University Press, 1988], p. 356).

66. Dorothy Robins-Mowry, *The Hidden Sun: Women of Modern Japan* (Boulder: Westview, 1983), p. 167, cited in Sandra Buckley, "Altered States: The Body Politics of 'Being-Woman,'" in Gordon, *Postwar Japan as History*, p. 351. For evidence of Satō's conservatism in the related area of abortion policy, see also Amemiya, "The Road to Pro-Choice Ideology in Japan," pp. 263, 271. Satō was Prime Minister from 1964 to 1971.

67. It is not clear who or what prompted Satō to make this call—nor is it even possible to verify whether he actually made it. It has been rumored that Satō's wife feared the pill would corrupt popular morals and asked him to intervene. But given that many members of the anti-pill interest groups had connections with the LDP (e.g., Japan Midwives Association and LDP Women's Bureau president Yokoyama Fuku), it is entirely possible that they asked Satō, or his wife, to come to their aid—or that the whole story is apocryphal.

68. In 1966 the Hormone Committee of the Japan Association of Obstetricians and Gynecologists performed clinical tests on the pill on fifteen hundred patients at thirty-five hospitals nationwide and found only minor side effects in 10 percent of cases (*Asahi shinbun*, January 23, 1970). But according to one source, concern among politicians over future labor shortages led to the suppression of the Committee's report

(Representative Suhara Shōji, *Proceedings of the House of Councilors Budget Committee*, part 4, no. 1 (April 5, 1973): 28.

69. "Piru nenpyō," Ribu Shinjuku Sentā publication, April 1974, reproduced in Akiyo Mizoguchi et al., eds., *Shiryō Nihon ūman ribu shi*, vol. 2 (1972–75) (Kyoto: Shōkadō, 1994), p. 76.

70. Ibid; *Asahi shinbun*, December 1, 1973.

71. Miho Ogino, "Abortion and Women's Reproductive Rights: The State of Japanese Women, 1945–1991," in Gelb and Palley, *Women of Japan and Korea*, p. 83.

72. See *Asahi shinbun*, May 26, 1973.

73. See comments made by Rep. Suhara Shōji, *Proceedings of the House of Councilors Budget Committee*, part 4, no. 1 (April 5, 1973): 29; and comments made by Rep. Doi Takako, *Proceedings of the House of Representatives Social Policy and Labor Committee*, no. 29 (May 23, 1974): 7. See also *Bosei hogo i hō*, November 1972; March 1974; *Nihon keizai shinbun*, November 22, 1974. An investigation conducted at the time found that, within three months of the MHW's decision, sales of one brand of pill had gone up 40 percent, and another had gone up 80 percent (*Ampo*, no. 17 [summer 1973]: 20).

74. *Asahi shinbun*, December 1, 1973.

75. The most notable exceptions were the involvement of mainstream women's groups in birth control promotion projects during the heyday of family planning in Japan in the mid- to late 1950s and in contests over revising the Eugenic Protection Law in the 1970s and 1980s. (See chapters 4 and 5.)

76. *Nihon keizai shinbun*, November 22, 1974.

77. This includes the family planning newsletter *Kazoku keikaku*.

78. Particularly Barbara Seaman's 1969 book, *The Doctor's Case against the Pill* (Alameda, Calif.: Hunter House, 1995, 25th ed.).

79. Akiyama Yōko, "Enoki Misako to Chūpiren—'ribu shishi nōto' yori—" *Joseigaku Nenpō* 12 (October 1991): 112. Also, my interviews with Matsumoto Seiichi, May 9, 1995; and Suga Mutsuo, Marketing Department, Nippon Organon KK, December 8, 1994.

80. *Yomiuri shinbun*, March 26, 1974.

81. Yūsei Hogo Hō Kaiaku Soshi Jikkō Iinkai publication, June 1973, reproduced in Mizoguchi et al., *Shiryō Nihon ūman ribu shi*, vol. 2, p. 175. My interview with Yonezu Tomoko (current Soshiren member and former member of the Ribu Shinjuku Sentā), June 20, 1995, confirmed that Japanese feminists made this connection between the pill, abortion rights, and doctors' and drug companies' financial interests. See also Yūsei Hogo Hō Kaiaku = Kenpō Kaiaku to Tatakau Onna no Kai, ed., *Yūsei Hogo Hō kaiaku to tatakau tame ni* (Tokyo: '82 Yūsei Hogo Hō Kaiaku Soshi Renrakukai, 1982), p. 13.

82. Akiyama, "Enoki Misako to Chūpiren," pp. 110, 114–15; Ehara, "Japanese Feminism in the 1970s and 1980s," p. 51; Onna no Tame no Kurinikku, ed., *Piru: watashitachi wa erabanai* (Osaka: Onna no Tame no Kurinikku, 1987), pp. 76–77; Ogino, in Gelb and Palley, *Women of Japan and Korea*, p. 85; Watashitachi no ima o tō kai, ed., *Zenkyōtō kara ribu e—Jūgoshi nōto 8 sengoken* (Tokyo: Impakuto Shuppansha, 1996), p. 220.

83. *Neoribu*, vol. 1 (July 1972), reproduced in Mizoguchi et al., *Shiryō Nihon ūman ribu shi*, vol. 2, p. 244. *Neoribu* was Chūpiren's newsletter.

84. Akiyama, "Enoki Misako to Chūpiren," p. 112.

85. Ibid., pp. 111–12; interview with Yonezu Tomoko, June 20, 1995; Mizoguchi et al., *Shiryō Nihon ūman ribu shi,* vol. 2, p. 246; Watashitachi no ima o tō kai, *Zenkyōtō kara ribu e,* p. 216.

86. That Enoki was a pharmacology major in college and that the pills she distributed to Urufu Kai members were marked "sample" could be interpreted as evidence to support that theory, and one source does assert that Enoki got the pills she distributed from pharmaceutical companies (interview with Yonezu Tomoko, June 20, 1995); Watashitachi no ima o tō kai, *Zenkyōtō kara ribu e,* p. 216.

87. Mizoguchi et al., *Shiryō Nihon ūman ribu shi,* vol. 2, p. 244–46.

88. Ibid., p. 244.

89. *Asahi shinbun,* March 14, 1973; October 24, 1973.

90. Ibid., October 24, 1973.

91. Akiyama, "Enoki Misako to Chūpiren," p. 114.

92. *Namae no Nai Gurūpu Aratame Josei Kaihō Sensen,* "Josei kaihō tōsō no hatten no tame ni Chūpiren hihan," *Josei Kaihō Sensen,* vol. 2, date unknown, reproduced in Mizoguchi et al., *Shiryō Nihon ūman ribu shi,* vol. 2, pp. 248–52. The Chūpiren members who left the group called themselves Namae no Nai Gurūpu.

93. Akiyama, "Enoki Misako to Chūpiren," p. 115.

94. Ibid., p. 114.

95. According to Steslicke, "as of 1960 only 14 percent of all Japanese pharmacies had actually filled a doctor's prescription more than once" (Steslicke, *Doctors in Politics,* p. 46–48).

96. *Asahi shinbun,* December 1, 1973. Other contemporary sources report that doctors sold the pill for between ¥1,800 and ¥2,000 per cycle (*Ampo* 17 [summer 1973]: 20).

97. *Proceedings of the House of Councilors Budget Committee,* part 4, no. 1 (April 5, 1973): 27–31; *Nichibo i hō,* March 1974.

98. See, e.g., *Asahi shinbun,* May 26, 1973; February 5, 1974; *Nichibo i hō,* March 1974; *Proceedings of the House of Councilors Budget Committee,* part 4, no. 1 (April 5, 1973): 28–30.

99. These representatives were Rep. Doi Takako (JSP), Representative. Ōhara (JSP), and Representative Yamashita (LDP). See *Proceedings of the House of Representatives Social Policy and Labor Committee,* no. 25 (May 16, 1974): no. 28 (May 22, 1974); and no. 29 (May 23, 1974).

100. *Proceedings of the House of Councilors Budget Committee,* part 4, no. 1 (April 5, 1973): 28.

101. *Bosei hogo i hō,* January 1973; November 1973.

102. E.g., that the pill had numerous side effects, that there had not been enough testing, and that the pill was different from other drugs because it was used by healthy women for long periods of time (ibid., November 1973; June 1973).

103. Interview with Ashino Yuriko, Deputy Executive Director, Family Planning Federation of Japan, January 10, 1995; interview with Wagatsuma Takashi, International Medical Center, International Medical Cooperation Bureau, November 17, 1994.

104. Moriyama's position on IUDs was not without precedent: when Nichibo referred the question of whether the IUD should be approved to thirty local chapters in February 1967, almost all responded that they supported approval only on the condition that insertion and follow-up care be restricted to designated doctors (*Bosei hogo i*

*hō*, January 1968). In other words, Nichibo members wanted to exclude even fellow doctors in other specialties from inserting IUDs.

105.  *Bosei hogo i hō*, June 1973; *Sanfujinka no sekai* 26, no. 2 (February 1974). And Nichibo did, in fact, devote more energy to lobbying for the IUD than for the pill. In March 1973, Nichibo petitioned the minister of health and welfare for speedy approval of the IUD, citing safety improvements, successful clinical trials in Japan, and the fact that the IUD was being widely used in other countries. In the same year the Drug Council (*Chūō Yakuji Shingikai*) set up an IUD Investigation Committee (*chōsakai*) to deal with the IUD question for the first time. The following spring the MHW Drug Bureau chief reported in Diet committee meetings that the Drug Bureau took a positive stance on the IUD, and in August 1974 the MHW approved two kinds of IUD (*Bosei hogo i hō*, June 1973; August 1974; *Nihon keizai shinbun*, May 17, 1974; Kunii and Katagiri, *Basic Readings*, p. 18). Two more kinds of IUD were approved in 1977, and another in 1980 (*Nichibo i hō*, December 1977; September 1980; *Kazoku keikaku*, December 1977).

106.  *Proceedings of the House of Councilors Budget Committee*, part 4, no. 1 (April 5, 1973): 29–30.

107.  Ibid.; *Asahi shinbun*, May 26, 1973. Steslicke comments that "there is . . . a surprising degree of fragmentation and lack of coordination between bureaus [at the MHW]" (William Steslicke, "The Japanese State of Health," in Norbeck and Lock, *Health, Illness, and Medical Care in Japan*, p. 50). There is evidence that at least one other agency within the MHW was in favor of legalizing the pill for birth control purposes, as the Population Problems Institute (*Jinkō Mondai Kenkyūjo*) of the MHW issued an opinion paper in March 1974 stating that the pill ban should be lifted ("Piru nenpyō," Ribu Shinjuku Sentā publication, April 1974, reproduced in Mizoguchi et al., *Shiryo Nihon ūman ribu shi*, vol. 2, p. 76).

108.  *Proceedings of the House of Councilors*, December 1, 1973; *Asahi shinbun*, February 5, 1974; *Nichibo i hō*, March 1974.

109.  *Asahi shinbun*, December 1, 1973.

110.  For a similar conclusion, see Yūsei Hogo Hō Kaiaku = Kenpō Kaiaku to Tatakau Onna no Kai, *Yūsei Hogo Hō Kaiaku to tatakau tame ni*, p. 13.

111.  Chūpiren noted that many doctors did not do a physical examination or discuss usage and possible side effects with patients before prescribing the pill (*Asahi shinbun*, December 1, 1973). In 1991, a reporter for the *Mainichi shinbun* found that such perfunctory practices were still the norm at private clinics, whereas at university and general hospitals doctors took women's health history, gave thorough physical examinations, and discussed the pill with patients (*Mainichi shinbun*, October 3, 1991).

112.  *Proceedings of the House of Councilors Social Policy and Labor Committee* no. 29 (May 23, 1974): 7.

113.  The low-dose pill has 77.4 percent less hormone content than the high-dose pills in use in Japan (Seiichi Matsumoto et al., "Results of a Clinical Study with Low-Dose Oral Contraceptives," *Current Therapeutic Research* 44, no. 1 [July 1988]).

114.  Two informants claim that despite the fact that the ob-gyn groups submitted the first petition, the family planning groups were actually more enthusiastic about the pill and more active in organizing clinical trials (interviews with Suga Mutsuo, December 8, 1994; and Honda Hiroshi, Japan Association of Maternal Welfare, June 13, 1995). This dovetails with the argument some make that although the organizations repre-

senting ob-gyns lobby for pill approval, rank-and-file members still oppose the pill as a threat to their abortion income (*Financial Times*, February 27–28, 1999).

115. Interviews with Wagatsuma Takashi, November 17, 1994; Ashino Yuriko, January 10, 1995; Matsumoto Seiichi, May 9, 1995; Honda Hiroshi, June 13, 1995.

116. See Jansson Yumiko, "Piru 'kaikin' o mae ni ima, hinin to kyōiku o mitsumenaosu," *Human Sexuality*, no. 5 (November 1991): 18; Jitsukawa and Djerassi, "Birth Control in Japan," *Japan Times*, September 7, 1991.

117. *Nichibo i hō*, October 1985.

118. *Kazoku to Kenkō*, February 1986.

119. Ibid., March 1986.

120. Ibid., January 1987.

121. *Nihon keizai shinbun*, April 9, 1992. Four of the applicants were American companies, one was Dutch, and four were Japanese (*The Washington Post*, July 11, 1996).

122. For example, in 1986, Drug Bureau chief Kobayashi remarked that one of the pill's merits was that it could prevent abortions (*Proceedings of the House of Councilors Budget Committee Meeting*, no. 14 [March 24, 1986]: 21).

123. See, e.g., *Asahi shinbun*, May 31, 1991; Iwamoto, "Seishoku no jiko ketteiken no ima," p. 196.

124. Interviews with Suga Mutsuo, December 8, 1994; and Matsumoto Seiichi, May 9, 1995; personal communication from Mr. Katō, May 8, 1995.

125. *Yomiuri shinbun*, March 18, 1992.

126. Ibid., December 21, 1991. It should be noted that this notion was not new to the medical and family planning communities: The July 1987 issue of *Kazoku keikaku* discusses the possibility that the pill would leave Japan "defenceless" against AIDS.

127. *Yomiuri Shinbun*, December 21, 1991.

128. *Nihon keizai shinbun*, April 9, 1992.

129. Katō outlines a scenario in which the section in charge of drug approval encountered interference from the section in charge of disease prevention after the release of the AIDS report (personal communication from Mr. Katō, Nihon Schering, May 8, 1995).

130. Iwamoto, "Seishoku no jiko ketteiken no ima," pp. 196–97; *Nihon keizai shinbun*, April 9, 1992.

131. This point is illustrated by the fact that seven days before the Drug Council went public with its decision (but a week or so after the decision had been made) a Kōmeitō politician made comments at an Education Committee meeting indicating that he believed the pill would be approved and go on sale in the fall (*Proceedings of the House of Councilors Education Committee*, no. 2 [March 10, 1992]: 16).

132. Frank Schwartz, "Of Fairy Cloaks and Familiar Tales: The Politics of Consultation," in Allinson and Sone, *Political Dynamics in Contemporary Japan*, p. 230.

133. See, e.g., Iwamoto, "Seishoku no jiko ketteiken no ima"; Takashi Wagatsuma interview with H. Minaguchi, "Keikō hininyaku no genkyo to tenbō," *Nihon Ishikai Zasshi* 110, no. 10 (1991); Uno, "The Oral Contraceptive Pill in Japan." Practically everyone I interviewed during the course of this research drew a connection between the declining birth rate and the 1992 freeze.

134. *Kazoku to Kenkō*, August 1997; *The Japan Times Weekly*, June 22–28, 1998.

135. Wagatsuma interview with Minaguchi, "Keikō hininyaku no genkyo to tenbō," p. 1285.

136. Iwamoto cites the Welcome Baby Campaign, the revision of the child allowance, the shortening of the legal abortion period by two weeks, and the fact that, under the 1990 consumption tax revisions, childbirth was made tax exempt but abortions, contraceptives, and contraceptive guidance remained taxable (Iwamoto, "Seishoku no jiko ketteiken no ima," p. 196).

137. Many condom users in Japan only use condoms during (what they believe to be) the woman's fertile period (*Far Eastern Economic Review*, April 14, 1994; Mission Statement, Professional Women's Coalition for Sexuality and Health; Reich "Resistance to the Pill in Japan," Keynote Address, March 5, 1999; *Financial Times*, February 27–28, 1999).

138. *Financial Times*, February 27–28, 1999; Reich, "Resistance to the Pill in Japan"; "Teiyōryō keikō hininyaku no sōki ninka ni kansuru yōbōsho," petition submitted to the health and welfare minister by the Japan Association of Obstetricians and Gynecologists, the Japan Association of Maternal Welfare, the Japan Family Planning Association, and the Family Planning Federation of Japan, May 12, 1993; personal communication, Suga Mutsuo, Marketing Department, Nippon Organon KK, December 8, 1994.

139. See, e.g., *Kazoku to kenkō*, April 1992; *Lancet*, April 2, 1992; *Nihon keizai shinbun*, April 9, 1992; "Teiyōryō keikō hininyaku no sōki ninka ni kansuru yōbōsho," petition submitted to MHW Minister Niwa Yūya by the Japan Association of Ob-Gyns, Nichibo, the FPFJ, and the JFPA, May 12, 1993. Studies done by the World Health Organization have shown that there is no connection between pill use and AIDS infection (*Far Eastern Economic Review*, April 14, 1994).

140. Interviews with Mr. Koyama at Yakuji Nippōsha, March 28, 1995; and Suga Mutsuo, December 8, 1994; personal communication from Mr. Katō, May 8, 1995; *Far Eastern Economic Review*, April 14, 1994. Powell and Anesaki report that "the research and development of a new drug is a lengthy and costly business anywhere in the world; in Japan it is more so as requirements for test data have increased or been added to . . . . It has been estimated that the cost of developing and introducing a new drug in Japan is in the order of $20 million and that it takes more than a decade to get the product from the research stage into use by the medical profession; for every single product that is approved, nine others will fail" (Powell and Anesaki, *Health Care in Japan*, pp. 183–84).

141. In a personal communication dated May 8, 1995, Mr. Katō at Nihon Schering estimated the market for low-dose oral contraceptives at $500 million to $5 billion, based on the number of fertile women between the ages of fifteen and forty-nine (31,000,000) and projected user rates ranging from 0.6 percent to 5.6 percent. In a December 8, 1994, interview, Mr. Suga at Organon estimated a market of $1.17 billion. And a Japanese trade journal, the *Pharma Journal*, estimated a $1 billion market (*The Washington Post*, July 11, 1996).

142. Personal communication from Ogawa Etsuyo, Nihon Schering Hormone Therapy Product Management Department, April 21, 1995.

143. Interviews with Ashino Yuriko, January 10, 1995; and Suga Mutsuo, December 8, 1994.

144. Yokomitsu submitted a *shuisho* to the Cabinet on October 19, 1993, inquiring about the progress of the Drug Shingikai's deliberations, the relationship between AIDS and the pill, and the abortion situation in Japan. He received a noncommittal reply on

November 9, 1993. Yokomitsu then addressed many of the same subjects in a June 1994 Lower House Budget Committee meeting. On March 6, 1995, he submitted another *shuisho* on the low-dose pill to the government, receiving another noncommittal reply on March 28; and in June 1995 he brought the subject up again in a Lower House Health Committee meeting.

145. See, e.g., a presentation put together by Organon's marketing department called "Why Does Japan Not Legalize the Use of Oral Contraceptives? Strange Country in the Orient." Mr. Suga of Organon also admitted that Representative Yokomitsu had asked the government questions about the low-dose pill at his request (interviews with Suga Mutsuo, December 8, 1994; March 8, 1995).

146. Interview with Rep. Yokomitsu Katsuhiko, March 8, 1995.

147. See *Proceedings of the House of Representatives Budget Committee*, part 4, no. 1 (June 7, 1994): 8–9; *Proceedings of the House of Representatives Health Committee*, no. 14 (June 6, 1995): 16; "Teiyōryō piru ni kansuru shitsumon shuisho," opinion paper submitted by Representative Yokomitsu to the Cabinet, March 6, 1995.

148. Personal communication from Mr. Katō, May 8, 1995; interview with Mr. Koyama, staff journalist, *Yakuji Nippōsha*, March 28, 1995.

149. Interview with Suga Mutsuo, March 8, 1995.

150. Government reply (*tōbensho*) to Representative Yokomitsu's written questions, March 28, 1995.

151. *Kazoku keikaku*, June 1993; Wagatsuma interview with Minaguchi, "Keikō hininyaku no genkyo to tenbō," p. 1284.

152. Joyce Gelb, "Abortion and Reproductive Choice: Policy and Politics in Japan," in Githens and Stetson, *Abortion Politics*, p. 129.

153. The percentage of women who said that they would want to take the pill if it were approved was 9.9 percent in 1990, 6.9 percent in 1992, 12.8 percent in 1994, 13.1 percent in 1996, and 7.2 percent in 1998 (The Population Problems Research Council, the Mainichi Papers, "Fertility Control in the Postwar Years," pp. 305–98; Muramatsu, *The Population and Society of Postwar Japan*, p. 56; the Population Problems Research Council, the Mainichi Papers, ed., *The Future of the Family: Beyond Gender. Summary of the Twenty-fourth National Survey on Family Planning* [Tokyo: Population Problems Research Council, the Mainichi Shimbun, 1998], pp. 212, 222). A 1998 survey of contraceptive behavior (n = 1,200 women), conducted by the Professional Women's Coalition for Sexuality and Health, shows slightly different numbers. According to the survey, 14 percent of women would use the pill if it were approved, 42 percent would not use it, and 41 percent do not know whether they would use it. Of those who say they would not use the pill, 52 percent cite side effects as their reason. It should be noted, however, that this survey was directed only at working women, high school students, and college students, so the results are not as representative of the national population as the Mainichi survey (*Women's Health and Sexuality* 5 [November 1998]).

154. *The Vancouver Sun*, September 1, 1999.

155. Ogino, "Abortion and Women's Reproductive Rights," pp. 84–85. Japanese women may also be less interested in the pill because it is costly and relatively inconvenient to acquire. Many doctors require women to make monthly or quarterly office visits to fill pill prescriptions, whereas in most other countries annual or biannual visits are the norm. This brings the annual cost of taking the pill up to at least ¥60,000 ($480

at ¥125 = $1) (*Mainichi Daily News*, December 4, 1996). In the United States the annual cost of taking oral contraceptives generally ranges between $100 and $250.

156. Calder, *Crisis and Compensation*, p. 354; Steslicke, "The Japanese State of Health," p. 46.

157. Malcolm Gladwell, "John Rock's Error," *The New Yorker*, March 13, 2000, pp. 55–57.

158. "Teiyōryō piru wa, hatashite josei no mikata ka," *Josanpu Zasshi* 45, no. 8 (1991).

159. Adopting a line of argument familiar to feminists in the United States and Japan, Jansson advocated condoms because they promote communication between men and women and protect against sexually transmitted disease (ibid.; Jansson, "Piru 'kaikin' o mae ni ima," p. 16; Onna no Tame no Kurinikku, *Piru: watashitachi wa erabanai*, 1987; Uno, "The Oral Contraceptive Pill in Japan"). In an interview on January. 10, 1995, Yuriko Ashino indicated that Jansson had recently softened her opposition to the pill.

160. For example, the feminist group Karada no Shaberikai opposed the pill, as did the Osaka Health Center (*Japan Times*, April 16, 1992). Onna no Tame no Kurinikku also opposed the pill, and wrote a book entitled *The Pill: We Do Not Choose It*, but urged women to decide for themselves (Onna no Tame no Kurinikku, *Piru: watashitachi wa erabanai*).

161. Iwamoto, "Seishoku no jiko ketteiken no ima," p. 197. In a group interview with five Soshiren members on June 20, 1995, three said that they thought the pill should be approved, two that it should not be approved, and all five that they personally would not use it. See also Ogino, "Abortion and Women's Reproductive Rights," p. 87.

162. Iwamoto, "Seishoku no jiko ketteiken no ima," p. 197.

163. *Mainichi Daily News*, November 5, 1996; November 3, 1997. By 1999 the Professional Women's Coalition had five hundred members (personal communication from Midori Ashida, former secretary of the Professional Women's Coalition for Sexuality and Health, December 1999).

164. In comparison, 66 percent of births are wanted or planned in France, and 15 percent are mistimed or unwanted; in the United States the figures are 43 percent and 28 percent, respectively (Mission Statement, Professional Women's Coalition for Sexuality and Health; Press Release, March 3, 1999, Professional Women's Coalition for Sexuality and Health; the Alan Guttmacher Institute, ed., *Hopes and Realities: Closing the Gap between Women's Aspirations and Their Reproductive Experiences* [New York: The Alan Guttmacher Institute, 1995], p. 25 [Chart 13]).

165. *Women's Health and Sexuality* 3 (May 1998); "Piru to josei no kenkō" (kentō shiryō), Sei to kenkō o kangaeru josei senmonka no kai, November 1998.

166. *Mainichi Daily News*, September 19, 1995.

167. MHW Minister Kan made this announcement in response to a BBC reporter's question at a meeting of the Foreign Correspondents' Club (*Kazoku to kenkō*, August 1996). In a May 9, 1995, interview and a May 8, 1995, personal communication, both Matsumoto Seiichi, chairman of the Japan Family Planning Association, and Mr. Katō of Nihon Schering also indicated that they thought the pill would be approved in 1996 or 1997.

168. *Daily Yomiuri*, June 17, 1997; *Japan Times*, June 17, 1997; July 3, 1997.

169. *Mainichi Daily News*, December 4, 1996.

170. *Soshiren nyūsu*, April 29, 1998; *Mainichi Daily News*, January 6, 1998.

171. Janet Raloff, "The Gender Benders," *Science News*, January 8, 1994; Janet Raloff, "That Feminine Touch," *Science News*, January 22, 1994. As JFPA director Kitamura Kunio points out, the hormone concentration in the urine of a woman in the late stages of pregnancy is ten thousand times higher than that of a pill user, so it is unlikely that pill users are causing hormonal imbalances (*Mainichi Daily News*, December 5, 1997).

172. *Kazoku to kenkō*, May 1998.

173. Press Release, March 3, 1999, Professional Women's Coalition for Sexuality and Health; *Financial Times*, February 27–28, 1999; *Japan Times*, March 5, 1999.

174. Hirai Toshiki, director of the Pharmaceutical Affairs Bureau of the MHW, initially made a vain attempt to defend the speed with which the Viagra decision was made by arguing that Viagra is a treatment for a disease—implying that the pill, by contrast, is not a treatment for a disease. But not long afterward, the MHW announced that Viagra would not be covered by health insurance because impotency is not a disease (personal communications from Midori Ashida, Secretary, Professional Women's Coalition for Sexuality and Health, February 9, 1999; March 10, 1999; *Japan Times*, March 5, 1999; Reich, "Resistance to the Pill in Japan," Keynote Address, March 5, 1999).

175. *Chūnichi shinbun*, February 16, 1999.

176. *Financial Times*, February 27–28, 1999.

177. *Mainichi shinbun*, June 3, 1999; Press Release, March 3, 1999, Professional Women's Coalition for Sexuality and Health.

178. Reich, "Resistance to the Pill in Japan," Keynote Address, March 5, 1999; personal communication from Midori Ashida, Secretary, Professional Women's Coalition for Sexuality and Health, February 9, 1999; *Financial Times*, February 27–28, 1999. The pill cost approximately ¥2,000 per month in 1999 ($18 at $1 = ¥110) (*Jiji Press Ticker Service*, September 1, 1999; *Los Angeles Times*, September 14, 2000).

179. *Los Angeles Times*, September 14, 2000.

180. In a study that traces the shifting fortunes of four professions over time in the United States, Britain, France, Germany, and Italy, Krause demonstrates how "as the number of Ph.D.s and graduates in medicine, law, and engineering began to far exceed the number of jobs available to them, the ability of professions to control their world hit a new low." Krause argues that the loss of "guild power" on the part of the professions is being compensated for by increases in state power and the power of "capitalists" (Elliott A. Krause, *Death of the Guilds: Professions, States, and the Advance of Capitalism, 1930 to the Present* [New Haven: Yale University Press, 1996], pp. 3–5, 280–83).

181. Some aspects of abortion policy are the exclusive domain of the Health Ministry, however. In particular, the MHW has the authority to determine and decree an administrative guideline (*tsūtatsu*) on the exact "period when the fetus cannot sustain life outside the mother's body," as it is not specified in Article 2, Paragraph 2, of the Maternal Protection Law (formerly the Eugenic Protection Law). The *tsūtatsu* is not legally binding, but because doctors fear being prosecuted for criminal abortion, they tend to behave as if it were, so, for all intents and purposes, the *tsūtatsu* dictates the cut-off period for legal abortions. In 1990, the MHW angered women's groups by shortening the period during which abortion is legal from twenty-four weeks to twenty-two weeks without first seeking the opinions of women, and after only three hours of deliberation in the Eugenic Protection Section of the Public Health Advisory Council (Iwamoto Misako, "Seishoku no jiko ketteiken to nihonteki seisaku kettei: 1990-nen ninshin chūzetsu kanō kikan nishūkan tanjuku o megutte," *Joseigaku* 1 [April 1992]).

182. Until about 1984 the approval rate for new drugs in Japan was comparable to that of Western countries, but since then it has fallen off dramatically, to a rate of less than 20 percent, versus 80–95 percent in the West. According to one critic, who labels the Japanese drug approval system "inefficient and opaque," little more than half of all "useful" (yūyō na) drugs widely used in other industrialized countries have received approval in Japan ("Piru to josei no kenkō" [kentō shiryō], Sei to kenkō o kangaeru josei senmonka no kai [Professional Women's Coalition for Sexuality and Health], November 1998).

183. For example, the Council on Population Problems released a report in late October 1997 describing the problems that the declining birth rate will generate, including a decline in the size of the labor force and lower rates of economic growth, a greater tax burden on current generations and lower take-home pay, and changes in the nature of families and communities. The report does note, however, that the declining birth rate may solve some of Japan's worst problems, such as overcrowding, traffic congestion, environmental pollution, and school competition. The report also discusses factors that discourage people from having children: the priority placed on work, long working hours, the high cost of education, and the relegation of all household and childrearing chores to women (*Mainichi Daily News*, November 4, 1997).

184. Reich, "Resistance to the Pill in Japan," Keynote Address, March 5, 1999.

CHAPTER EIGHT
CONCLUSION

1. Prof. Margaret McKean, Duke University, discussant for panel, "Citizen Activism in Postwar Japanese History," Annual Meeting of the Association for Asian Studies, Honolulu, Hawaii, April 12, 1996; personal communication, May 28, 1996. Professor McKean's comments focused primarily on the government's handling of the Minamata mercury poisoning case. As noted at the end of chapter 2, Campbell also points out that bureaucrats tend not to be very active in highly ideological policy areas (John Campbell, "Democracy and Bureaucracy in Japan," in Ishida and Krauss, *Democracy in Japan*, p. 129).

2. Ishii, "Yūsei Hogo Hō ni yoru datai gōhōka no mondaiten"; Iwamoto, "Seishoku no jiko ketteiken to nihonteki seisaku kettei"; Iwamoto, "Seishoku no jiko ketteiken no ima."

3. *Mainichi Daily News*, June 14, 1990.

4. According to Rogers Smith, American history reveals the influence of multiple philosophical traditions, including liberalism and republicanism, but also ascriptive and inegalitarian modes of thought that have been very hostile to individual and minority rights (witness the historical experiences of Native Americans, African slaves, women, and the landless poor) (Rogers M. Smith, *Civic Ideals: Conflicting Visions of Citizenship in U.S. History* [New Haven: Yale University Press, 1997], pp. 1, 3, 8–9).

5. See chapter 1.

6. The Alan Guttmacher Institute, *Hopes and Realities*, p. 25, Chart 13. It should be noted that aside from the enormous emotional distress that many women experience with an unintended pregnancy, significant health risks are also associated with pregnancy, such as preeclampsia, gestational diabetes, and anemia.

7. Garon, *Molding Japanese Minds*, p. 235.

8. Ibid., pp. 235–36.

9. Petracca, *The Politics of Interests*, pp. 7–11.

10. Of course, women have diverse interests in all policy areas, including abortion and contraception policy, so it would be impossible for any one group to represent the range of women's interests. One could argue that by representing the interests of some women and not others, these groups are guilty of the same sins as the professional and religious groups. But given that women were grossly underrepresented before the emergence of these women's groups, one could also argue that their entrance into the policy-making arena tends to make the environment favorable for other women's groups, representing other concerns, to do so as well.

11. Jane Jenson, "Changing Discourse, Changing Agendas: Political Rights and Reproductive Policies in France," in Mary Fainsod Katzenstein and Carol McClurg Mueller, eds., *The Women's Movements of the United States and Western Europe: Consciousness, Political Opportunity, and Public Policy* (Philadelphia: Temple University Press, 1987), p. 64.

12. In its 1997 White Paper on the national lifestyle, the Economic Planning Agency also took a "woman-friendly" stance, concluding that in order to stem the declining birth rate, the work and social environment needed to be made more amenable to raising young children. The White Paper called for improvements in the day care system, changes in the seniority-based pay system, and greater flexibility in the work culture to allow men to contribute more to the household and to childrearing (*Nikkei Weekly*, October 10, 1997).

# Bibliography

English Language Sources

Abe, Hitoshi, Muneyuki Shindo, and Sadafumi Kawato. *The Government and Politics of Japan*. Tokyo: University of Tokyo Press, 1994.

Alan Guttmacher Institute, The, ed. *Hopes and Realities: Closing the Gap between Women's Aspirations and Their Reproductive Experiences*. New York: The Alan Guttmacher Institute, 1996.

————, ed. *Sharing Responsibility: Women, Society, and Abortion Worldwide*. New York: The Alan Guttmacher Institute, 1999.

Allinson, Gary D., and Yasunori Sone, eds. *Political Dynamics in Contemporary Japan*. Ithaca: Cornell University Press, 1993.

Amemiya, Kozy Kazuko. "The Road to Pro-Choice Ideology in Japan: A Social History of the Contest between the State and Individuals over Abortion." Unpublished dissertation. University of California, San Diego, 1993.

————. "Woman's Autonomy within the Community: The Contextual Argument of Japanese Pro-Choice Women." *American Asian Review* 13, no. 2 (summer 1995).

Anderson, Stephen J. *Welfare Policy and Politics in Japan: Beyond the Developmental State*. New York: Paragon House, 1993.

Asbell, Bernard. *The Pill: A Biography of the Drug That Changed the World*. New York: Random House, 1995.

Atoh, Makoto. "An Era of Later Marriages, Fewer Kids." *Economic Eye* 15, no. 2 (summer 1994).

Baumgartner, Frank, and Bryan Jones. *Agendas and Instability in American Politics*. Chicago: The University of Chicago Press, 1993.

Bernstein, Gail Lee, ed. *Re-creating Japanese Women, 1600–1945*. Berkeley: University of California Press, 1991.

Bloom, David E., and Jeffrey G. Williamson. "Demographic Transitions and Economic Miracles in Emerging Asia." Cambridge, Mass.: National Bureau of Economic Research Working Paper 6268. November 1997.

Bock, Gisela. "Racism and Sexism in Nazi Germany: Motherhood, Compulsory Sterilization and the State." In Bridenthal, Renate, Gisela Bock, and Pat Thane, eds. *Maternity and Gender Politics: Women and the Rise of the European Welfare States, 1880s–1950s*. New York: Routledge, 1991.

Bridenthal, Renate, Atina Grossmann, and Marion Kaplan, eds. *When Biology Became Destiny*. New York: Monthly Review Press, 1984.

Buckley, Sandra. "Body Politics: Abortion Law Reform." In Gavan McCormack and Yoshio Sugimoto, eds., *The Japanese Trajectory: Modernization and Beyond*. Cambridge: Cambridge University Press, 1988.

————. *Broken Silence: Voices of Japanese Feminism*. Berkeley: University of California Press, 1997.

Butler, J. Douglas, and David F. Walbert, eds. *Abortion, Medicine, and the Law*, 4th ed. New York: Facts on File, 1992.

Calder, Kent. *Crisis and Compensation: Public Policy and Political Stability in Japan*. Princeton, N.J.: Princeton University Press, 1988.

Campbell, John. "Compensation for Repatriates: A Case Study of Interest-Group Politics and Party-Government Negotiations in Japan." In T. J. Pempel, ed., *Policymaking in Contemporary Japan*. Ithaca: Cornell University Press, 1977.

———. *How Policies Change*. Princeton, N.J.: Princeton University Press, 1992.

Cheng, Peter. "Japanese Interest Group Politics." *Asian Survey* 30, no. 3 (March 1990).

Chesler, Ellen. *Woman of Valor: Margaret Sanger and the Birth Control Movement in America*. New York: Simon & Schuster, 1992.

Cohen, Jean, and Andrew Arato. *Civil Society and Political Theory*. Cambridge, Mass.: MIT Press, 1992.

Coleman, Samuel. *Family Planning in Japanese Society: Traditional Birth Control in a Modern Urban Culture*. Princeton, N.J.: Princeton University Press, 1983.

Curtis, Gerald. *The Japanese Way of Politics*. New York: Columbia University Press, 1988.

Dahl, Robert. *Who Governs?* New Haven: Yale University Press, 1961.

David, Henry P., Jochen Fleischhacker, and Charlotte Hohn. "Abortion and Eugenics in Nazi Germany." *Population and Development Review* 14, no. 1 (March 1988).

Dawson, Deborah Anne. "Trends in Use of Oral Contraceptives—Data from the 1987 National Health Interviews Survey." *Family Planning Perspectives* 22, no. 4 (July/August 1990).

Dennery, Etienne. *Asia's Teeming Millions*. London: Jonathan Cape, 1931.

Dower, John. *Embracing Defeat: Japan in the Wake of World War II*. New York: Norton, 1999.

Ehara, Yumiko. "Japanese Feminism in the 1970s and 1980s." *U.S.–Japan Women's Journal* (English Supplement) 4 (1993).

Eisinger, Peter K. "The Conditions of Protest Behavior in American Cities." *American Political Science Review* 67 (1973).

Field, Marilyn Jane. *The Comparative Politics of Birth Control*. New York: Praeger, 1983.

Fujimura-Fanselow, Kumiko, and Atsuko Kameda, eds. *Japanese Women: New Feminist Perspectives on the Past, Present, and Future*. New York: The Feminist Press at The City University of New York, 1995.

Garon, Sheldon. "The World's Oldest Debate? Prostitution and the State in Imperial Japan, 1900–1945." *American Historical Review* 98, no. 3 (June 1993).

———. "Women's Groups and the Japanese State: Contending Approaches to Political Integration, 1890–1945." *Journal of Japanese Studies* 19, no. 1 (1993).

———. *Molding Japanese Minds: The State in Everyday Life*. Princeton, N.J.: Princeton University Press, 1997.

Gelb, Joyce, and Marian Lief Palley, eds., *Women of Japan and Korea: Continuity and Change*. Philadelphia, Pa.: Temple University Press, 1994.

George, Aurelia. "The Japanese Farm Lobby and Agricultural Policy-making." *Pacific Affairs* 54, no. 3 (fall 1981).

———. "The Comparative Study of Interest Groups in Japan: An Institutional Framework." Australia-Japan Research Centre Research Paper No. 95, December 1982.

George, Timothy. "Minamata: Power, Policy, and Citizenship in Postwar Japan." Unpublished dissertation. Harvard University, 1996.

Githens, Marianne, and Dorothy McBride Stetson. *Abortion Politics: Public Policy in Cross-Cultural Perspective*. New York: Routledge, 1996.

Gladwell, Malcolm. "John Rock's Error." *The New Yorker*, March 13, 2000.

Glendon, Mary Ann. *Abortion and Divorce in Western Law*. Cambridge, Mass.: Harvard University Press, 1987.

———. *Rights Talk*. New York: The Free Press, 1991.

Gluck, Carol. *Japan's Modern Myths: Ideology in the Late Meiji Period*. Princeton, N.J.: Princeton University Press, 1985.

Gluck, Carol, and Stephen R. Graubard. *Showa: The Japan of Hirohito*. New York: Norton, 1992.

Gordon, Andrew. "Managing the Japanese Household: The New Life Movement in Postwar Japan." *Social Politics* (summer 1997).

Gordon, Andrew, ed. *Postwar Japan as History*. Berkeley: University of California Press, 1993.

Gordon, Linda. *Woman's Body, Woman's Right: Birth Control in America*. New York: Penguin, 1990.

Grossmann, Atina. "The Debate That Will Not End: The Politics of Abortion in Germany from Weimar to National Socialism and the Postwar Period." In Manfred Berg and Geoffrey Cocks, eds., *Medicine in 19th and 20th Century Germany: Ethics, Politics, and Law*. Cambridge: Cambridge University Press, 1994.

———. *Reforming Sex: The German Movement for Birth Control and Abortion Reform, 1920–1950*. New York: Oxford University Press, 1995.

Hama, Hidehiko. *Population Problems and National Development Plans in Japan: Post-War Trends*. New York: United Nations, 1981.

Hane, Mikiso. *Modern Japan: A Historical Survey*. Boulder, Colo.: Westview, 1986.

Hardacre, Helen. *Marketing the Menacing Fetus in Japan*. Berkeley: University of California Press, 1997.

Harmsen, Hans. "Notes on Abortion and Birth Control in Germany." *Population Studies* 3, no. 4 (1950).

Hashimoto, Ryutaro. *Vision of Japan: A Realistic Direction for the 21st Century*. Translated by John Rossman. Tokyo: Bestsellers, 1994.

Havens, Thomas R. "Women and War in Japan, 1937–45." *American Historical Review* 80, no. 4 (October 1975).

Henshaw, Stanley K., and Evelyn Morrow. *Induced Abortion: A World Review*. New York: The Alan Guttmacher Institute, 1990.

Henshaw, Stanley K., Susheela Singh, and Taylor Haas. "Recent Trends in Abortion Rates Worldwide." *International Family Planning Perspectives* 25, no. 1 (March 1999).

Hodge, Robert, and Naohiro Ogawa. *Fertility Change in Contemporary Japan*. Chicago: University of Chicago Press, 1991.

Hopper, Helen. *A New Woman of Japan: A Political Biography of Kato Shidzue*. Boulder, Colo.: Westview, 1996.

Ishida, Takeshi. "The Development of Interest Groups and the Pattern of Political Modernization in Japan." In Robert Ward, ed., *Political Development in Modern Japan*. Princeton, N.J.: Princeton University Press, 1968.

Ishida, Takeshi, and Ellis Krauss, eds. *Democracy in Japan*. Pittsburgh: University of Pittsburgh Press, 1989.

Ishii, Ryoichi. *Population Pressure and Economic Life in Japan*. London: P.S. King and Son, Ltd., 1937.

Ishimoto, Shidzué. *Facing Two Ways: The Story of My Life*. Stanford: Stanford University Press, 1984.

Jenson, Jane. "Gender and Reproduction; or, Babies and the State." *Studies in Political Economy* 20 (summer 1986).

———. "Changing Discourse, Changing Agendas: Political Rights and Reproductive Policies in France." In Mary Fainsod Katzenstein and Carol McClurg Mueller, eds., *The Women's Movements of the United States and Western Europe: Consciousness, Political Opportunity, and Public Policy*. Philadelphia: Temple University Press, 1987.

———. "Representations of Gender: Policies to 'Protect' Women Workers and Infants in France and the United States before 1914." In Linda Gordon, ed., *Women, the State, and Welfare*. Madison: University of Wisconsin Press, 1990.

Jitsukawa, Mariko, and Carl Djerassi, "Birth Control in Japan: Realities and Prognosis." *Science* 265 (August 19, 1994).

Johnson, Chalmers. *MITI and the Japanese Miracle: The Growth of Industrial Policy, 1925–1975*. Stanford: Stanford University Press, 1982.

Kato, Toshinobu. *The Development of Family Planning in Japan with Industrial Involvement*. New York: United Nations, 1978.

Ketting, E., ed. *Contraception in Western Europe: A Current Appraisal*. Park Ridge, N.J.: Parthenon, 1990.

Kevles, Daniel. *In the Name of Eugenics: Genetics and the Uses of Human Heredity*. New York: Knopf, 1985.

Kiser, Claude V., ed. *Research in Family Planning*. Princeton, N.J.: Princeton University Press, 1962.

Kojima, Hiroshi. "Attitudes toward Population Trends and Policy in Japan." Tokyo: Institute of Population Problems, 1990.

———. "Attitudes toward Fertility Trends and Policy in Japan." Tokyo: Institute of Population Problems, 1993.

Koseisho (Japan Ministry of Health and Welfare). *Maternal and Child Health in Japan*, Tokyo: Mother's and Children's Health and Welfare Association, 1992.

Koven, Seth, and Sonya Michel. "Womanly Duties: Maternalist Policies and the Origins of Welfare States in France, Germany, Great Britain, and the United States, 1880–1920. *American Historical Review* 95 (1990).

———. *Mothers of a New World: Maternalist Politics and the Origins of the Welfare State*. New York: Routledge, 1993.

Koya, Yoshio. *Pioneering in Family Planning: A Collection of Papers on the Family Planning Programs and Research Conducted in Japan*. New York: Population Council, 1963.

Koyama, Shizuko. "The 'Good Wife and Wise Mother' Ideology in Post–World War I Japan." *U.S.–Japan Women's Journal* 7 (1994).

Krause, Elliott A. *Death of the Guilds: Professions, States, and the Advance of Capitalism, 1930 to the Present*. New Haven: Yale University Press, 1996.

Kunii, Chojiro. *Humanistic Family Planning Approaches: The Integration of Family Planning and Health Goals*. New York: U.N. Fund for Population Activities, 1983.

———. *It All Started from Worms: The 45-Year Record of Japan's Post–World War II National Health and Family Planning Movement*. Tokyo: The Hoken Kaikan Foundation, 1992.

Kunii, Chojiro, and Tameyoshi Katagiri, eds. *Basic Readings in Population and Family Planning in Japan*. Tokyo: Japan Organization for International Cooperation in Family Planning, 1976.

Kusano, Izumi, and Keiko Kawasaki. "Japanese Women Challenge Anti-Abortion Law." *Ampo: Japan-Asia Quarterly Review* 15, no. 1 (1983).

LaFleur, William. *Liquid Life: Abortion and Buddhism in Japan*. Princeton, N.J.: Princeton University Press, 1992.

Lebra, Takie Sugiyama. *Japanese Women: Constraint and Fulfillment*. Honolulu: University of Hawaii Press, 1984.

Lovenduski, Joni, and Joyce Outshoorn. *The New Politics of Abortion*. London: Sage, 1986.

Lowi, Theodore. *The End of Liberalism: The Second Republic of the United States*. New York: Norton, 1979.

Luker, Kristin. *Taking Chances: Abortion and the Decision Not to Contracept*. Berkeley: University of California Press, 1975.

———. *Abortion and the Politics of Motherhood*. Berkeley: University of California Press, 1984.

Madison, James, Alexander Hamilton, and John Jay. *The Federalist Papers*. New York: New American Library, 1961 [1788].

Maruyama, Hiromi, James Raphael, and Carl Djerassi. "Why Japan Ought to Legalize the Pill." *Nature* 379 (February 15, 1996).

Matsumoto, Y. Scott, Akira Koizumi, and Tadahiro Nohara. "Condom Use in Japan." *Studies in Family Planning* 3, no. 9 (September 1972).

McAdam, Doug. *Political Process and the Development of Black Insurgency, 1930–1970*. Chicago: University of Chicago Press, 1982.

McKean, Margaret. *Environmental Protest and Citizen Politics in Japan*. Berkeley: University of California Press, 1981.

———. "State Strength and Public Interest." In Gary D. Allinson and Yasunori Sone, eds., *Political Dynamics in Contemporary Japan*. Ithaca: Cornell University Press, 1993.

McLaren, Angus. *Sexuality and Social Order*. New York: Holmes & Meier, 1983.

Metraux, Daniel. *The Soka Gakkai Revolution*. Lanham, Md.: University Press of America, 1994.

Miyaji, Naoko, and Margaret Lock. "Monitoring Motherhood: Sociocultural and Historical Aspects of Maternal and Child Health in Japan." *Daedalus* (fall 1994).

Mohr, James. *Abortion in America*. New York: Oxford University Press, 1978.

Molony, Barbara. "Equality versus Difference: The Japanese Debate over 'Motherhood Protection,' 1915–50." In Janet Hunter, ed., *Japanese Women Working*. New York: Routledge, 1993.

Muramatsu, Michio, and Ellis Krauss. "The Conservative Party Line and the Development of Patterned Pluralism." In Kiichi Yasuba and Kozo Yamamura, eds., *The Political Economy of Japan*. Stanford: Stanford University Press, 1987.

Muramatsu, Minoru, ed. *Japan's Experience in Family Planning—Past and Present*. Tokyo: Family Planning Federation of Japan, 1967.

Muramatsu, Minoru. "Fertility Control in the Postwar Years—An Overview." In The Population Problems Research Council. *The Population and Society of Postwar Japan—Based on Half a Century of Surveys on Family Planning.* Edited by Mainichi Shimbun. Tokyo: The Mainichi Newspapers, 1994.

Murphy, John M. " 'To Create a Race of Thoroughbreds: Margaret Sanger and the Birth Control Review." *Women's Studies in Communication* 13, no. 1 (spring 1990).

Nagano, Yoshiko. "Women Fight for Control: Abortion Struggle in Japan." *Ampo* 17 (summer 1973).

Nakamura, Takafusa. *The Postwar Japanese Economy: Its Developments and Structure.* Tokyo: University of Tokyo Press, 1981.

Nakatani, Kinko. "The Status of Abortion in Japan and Some Issues." *Keio Law Review* (1985).

Nishikawa, Yuko. "Feminist Rhetoric and War Mobilization of Women." Paper presented at the Annual Meeting of the Association for Asian Studies, Chicago, March 1997.

Niwa, Akiko. "The Formation of the Myth of Motherhood in Japan." *U.S.–Japan Women's Journal* (English Supplement) 4 (1993).

Noakes, Jeremy. "Nazism and Eugenics: The Background to the Nazi Sterilization Law of 14 July 1933." In R. J. Bullen, H. Pogge von Strandman, and A. B. Polonsky, eds., *Ideas into Politics: Aspects of European History, 1880–1950.* Totowa, N.J.: Barnes & Noble, 1984.

Norbeck, Edward, and Margaret Lock, eds. *Health, Illness, and Medical Care in Japan.* Honolulu: University of Hawaii Press, 1987.

Norgren, Tiana. "Abortion before Birth Control: The Interest Group Politics behind Postwar Japanese Reproduction Policy." The Journal of Japanese Studies 24, no. 1 (Winter 1998).

Oakley, Deborah. "American-Japanese Interaction in the Development of Population Policy in Japan, 1945–52." *Population and Development Review* 4, no. 4 (1978).

———. "The Development of Population Policy in Japan, 1945–1952, and American Participation." Unpublished dissertation, University of Michigan, 1977.

Oaks, Laury. "Fetal Spirithood and Fetal Personhood: The Cultural Construction of Abortion in Japan." *Women's Studies International Forum* 17, no. 5 (1994).

Offen, Karen. "Depopulation, Nationalism, and Feminism in Fin-de-Siècle France." *American Historical Review* 89 (June 1984).

———. "Defining Feminism: A Comparative Historical Approach." *Signs* 14 (1998).

Ogino, Miho. "Abortion and Women's Reproductive Rights: The State of Japanese Women, 1945–1991." In Joyce Gelb and Marian Lief Palley, eds., *Women of Japan and Korea: Continuity and Change.* Philadelphia: Temple University Press, 1994.

———. "Abortion, Contraception, and Feminism: Reproductive Politics in Modern Japan." Paper presented at the Annual Meeting of the Association for Asian Studies, Chicago, March 1997.

Olson, Mancur. *The Rise and Decline of Nations: Economic Growth, Stagflation, and Social Rigidities.* New Haven: Yale University Press, 1982.

Outshoorn, Joyce. "The Stability of Compromise: Abortion Politics in Western Europe." In Marianne Githens and Dorothy McBride Stetson, eds., *Abortion Politics: Public Policy in Cross-Cultural Perspective.* New York: Routledge, 1996.

Palmer, Arvin. *Buddhist Politics: Japan's Clean Government Party*. The Hague: Martinus Nijhoff, 1971.

Pempel, T. J. "The Unbundling of 'Japan, Inc.': The Changing Dynamics of Japanese Policy Formation." *The Journal of Japanese Studies* 13, no. 2 (summer 1987).

Petchesky, Rosalind Pollack. *Abortion and Woman's Choice: The State, Sexuality, and Reproductive Freedom*. Boston: Northeastern University Press, 1990.

Peter, W. W. "Germany's Sterilization Program." *American Journal of Public Health* 24, no. 3 (March 1934).

Petracca, Mark P., ed. *The Politics of Interests: Interest Groups Transformed*. Boulder, Colo.: Westview, 1992.

———. "The Rediscovery of Interest Group Politics." In Mark P. Petracca, ed., *The Politics of Interests: Interest Groups Transformed*. Boulder, Colo.: Westview, 1992.

The Population Problems Research Council. *Family Planning in Japan*. Edited by *Mainichi shimbun*. Tokyo: Japanese Organization for International Cooperation in Family Planning, 1970.

———. *The Population and Society of Postwar Japan—Based on Half a Century of Surveys on Family Planning*. Edited by *Mainichi shimbun*. Tokyo: The Mainichi Newspapers, 1994.

———. *The Future of the Family: Beyond Gender, Summary of the Twenty-fourth National Survey on Family Planning*. Edited by *Mainichi shimbun*. Tokyo: The Population Problems Research Council, *Mainichi shimbun*, 1998.

———. *Toward a New Century of Equality and Symbiosis: Summary of the Twenty-third National Survey on Family Planning*. Edited by *Mainichi shimbun*. Tokyo: The Population Problems Research Council, *Mainichi shimbun*, 1996.

Potter, Joseph E. "The Persistence of Outmoded Contraceptive Regimes: The Cases of Mexico and Brazil." *Population and Development Review* 25, no. 4 (December 1999).

Powell, Margaret, and Masahira Anesaki. *Health Care in Japan*. London: Routledge, 1990.

Putnam, Robert. *Making Democracy Work: Civic Traditions in Modern Italy*. Princeton, N.J.: Princeton University Press, 1993.

Ray, Joyce M., and F. G. Gosling. "American Physicians and Birth Control, 1936–1947." *Journal of Social History* 18, no. 3 (1985).

Reed, James. *From Private Vice to Public Virtue: The Birth Control Movement and American Society since 1830*. New York: Basic Books, 1978.

Reich, Michael. "Resistance to the Pill in Japan: Money, Gender, and Culture." Keynote Address, Harvard Medical School's Conference on Health and Social Change in Asia, March 5, 1999, Cambridge, Mass.

Rolston, Bill, and Anna Eggert, eds. *Abortion in the New Europe: A Comparative Handbook*. Westport, Conn.: Greenwood, 1994.

Rosenberger, Nancy. "Gender and the Japanese State: Pension Benefits Creating Difference." *Anthropological Quarterly* 64 (October 9, 1991).

Rosenbluth, Frances. "Financial Deregulation and Interest Intermediation." In Gary D. Allinson and Yasunori Sone, eds., *Political Dynamics in Contemporary Japan*. Ithaca: Cornell University Press, 1993.

Rousseau, Julie. "Quantity and Quality: The Politics of Eugenic Discourse in Imperial Japan." Unpublished M.A. essay, Columbia University, Department of History, 1990.

Ruoff, Kenneth. "Reviving Imperial Ideology: Citizens' Movements from the Right." Paper presented at the Annual Meeting of the Association for Asian Studies, Honolulu, Hawaii, April 1996.

Samuels, Richard J. *The Business of the Japanese State: Energy Markets in Comparative and Historical Perspective.* Ithaca: Cornell University Press, 1987.

Sanger, Margaret, ed. *International Aspects of Birth Control.* New York: The American Birth Control League, 1925.

Saxton, Marsha. "Disabled Women's View of Selective Abortion: An Issue for All Women." *Journal of the American Medical Women's Association* 54, no. 1 (1999).

Schattschneider, E. E. *The Semisovereign People: A Realist's View of Democracy in America.* Hinsdale, Ill.: Dryden, 1975.

Schmitter, Philippe. "Still the Century of Corporatism?" In Philippe Schmitter and Gerhard Lembruch, eds., *Trends toward Corporatist Intermediation.* Beverly Hills: Sage, 1979.

———. "Interest Intermediation and Regime Governability in Contemporary Western Europe and North America." In Suzanne Berger, ed., *Organizing Interests in Western Europe: Pluralism, Corporatism, and the Transformation of Politics.* Cambridge: Cambridge University Press, 1981.

Schwartz, Frank Jacob. "Shingikai: The Politics of Consultation in Japan." Unpublished dissertation. Harvard University, 1991.

Seaman, Barbara. *The Doctor's Case Against the Pill.* 25th ed. Alameda, Calif.: Hunter House, 1995.

Shapiro, Thomas. *Population Control Politics: Women, Sterilization, and Reproductive Choice.* Philadelphia: Temple University Press, 1985.

Sievers, Sharon. *Flowers in Salt: The Beginnings of Feminist Consciousness in Modern Japan.* Stanford: Stanford University Press, 1983.

Skocpol, Theda. *Protecting Soldiers and Mothers: The Political Origins of Social Policy in the United States.* Cambridge, Mass.: Harvard University Press, 1992.

Smith, Rogers M. *Civic Ideals: Conflicting Visions of Citizenship in U.S. History.* New Haven: Yale University Press, 1997.

Smith, Thomas C. "Peasant Families and Population Control in Eighteenth-Century Japan." In *Native Sources of Japanese Industrialization, 1750–1920.* Berkeley: University of California Press, 1988.

Steinmo, Sven, Kathleen Thelen, and Frank Longstreth, eds. *Structuring Politics: Historical Institutionalism in Comparative Analysis.* Cambridge: Cambridge University Press, 1992.

Steslicke, William. *Doctors in Politics: The Political Life of the Japan Medical Association.* New York: Praeger, 1973.

———. "The Japanese State of Health." In Edward Norbeck and Margaret Long, eds., *Health, Illness, and Medical Care in Japan.* Honolulu, Hawaii: University of Hawaii Press, 1987.

Stetson, Dorothy McBride. *Women's Rights in France.* New York: Greenwood, 1987.

Stone, Clarence. "Group Politics Reexamined: From Pluralism to Political Economy." In Lawrence Dodd and Calvin Jillson, eds., *The Dynamics of American Politics: Approaches and Interpretations.* Boulder, Colo.: Westview, 1994.

Suzuki, Zenji. "Geneticists and the Eugenics Movement in Japan." *Japanese Studies in the History of Science* 14 (1975).

Taeuber, Irene B. *The Population of Japan*. Princeton, N.J.: Princeton University Press, 1958.

Tama, Yasuko. "The Logic of Abortion: Japanese Debates on the Legitimacy of Abortion as Seen in Post–World War II Newspapers." *U.S.–Japan Women's Journal* 7 (1994).

Teitelbaum, Michael S., and Jay M. Winter, eds. *Population and Resources in Western Intellectual Traditions*. Cambridge: Cambridge University Press, 1989.

Thompson, Warren S. "Population and Resources in Japan: A 1949 Forecast." Reprinted in *Population and Development Review* 7, no. 1 (March 1981).

Thurston, Donald. *Teachers and Politics in Japan*. Princeton, N.J.: Princeton University Press, 1973.

Tipton, Elise K. "Birth Control and the Population Problem in Prewar and Wartime Japan." *Japanese Studies Bulletin* 14, no. 1 (1994).

———, ed. *Society and the State in Interwar Japan*. New York: Routledge, 1997.

Truman, David. *The Governmental Process*. New York: Knopf, 1951.

Tsujinaka, Yutaka. "Interest Group Structure and Regime Change in Japan." Maryland/Tsukuba Papers on U.S.–Japan Relations, November 1996.

Tsuya, Noriko. "Proximate Determinants of Fertility Decline in Japan after World War II." Unpublished dissertation. University of Chicago, 1986.

Uno, Sumie. "The Oral Contraceptive Pill in Japan." *Issues in Reproductive and Genetic Engineering* 5, no. 3 (1992).

Upham, Frank K. *Law and Social Change in Postwar Japan*. Cambridge, Mass.: Harvard University Press, 1987.

Waldschmidt, Anne. "Against Selection of Human Life—People with Disabilities Oppose Genetic Counselling." *Issues in Reproductive and Genetic Engineering* 5, no. 2 (1992).

Watkins, Elizabeth Siegel. *On the Pill: A Social History of Oral Contraceptives, 1950–1970*. Baltimore, Md.: The Johns Hopkins University Press, 1998.

Weindling, Paul. "Fascism and Population in Comparative European Perspective." In Michael S. Teitelbaum and Jay M. Winter, eds., *Population and Resources in Western Intellectual Traditions*. Cambridge: Cambridge University Press, 1989.

Whelpton, P. K. "The Outlook for the Control of Human Fertility in Japan." *American Sociological Review* 15, no. 1 (February 1950).

White, James. *The Soka Gakkai and Mass Society*. Stanford: Stanford University Press, 1970.

JAPANESE LANGUAGE SOURCES

Agora, ed. *Umu umanai umenai: Yūsei Hogo Hō to yūsei shisō*. Tokyo: BOC Shuppanbu, 1983.

Akiyama, Yōko. *Ribu shishi nōto: onnatachi no jidai kara*. Tokyo: Impakuto Shuppankai, 1993.

———. "Enoki Misako to Chūpiren—'ribu shishi nōto' yori—" *Joseigaku Nenpō* 12 (October 1991).

Araki, Seishi. *Taniguchi Yasaburō den*. 1964.

Ashino, Yuriko. "Hinin ni onna no jinken to kenkō no shiten o." *Human Sexuality* 5 (November 1991).

Boshi Eisei Kenkyūkai, ed. *Boshi hoken no omo naru tōkei*. Tokyo: Boshi Hoken Jigyōdan, 1994.

"Chūzetsu mondai o mitsumeru." *Josanpu Zasshi* 18, no. 5 (1964).

Doi, Jūji. *Kokumin Yūsei Hō.* Tokyo: Kyōiku Toshosha, 1941.

Ehara, Yumiko. "Josei mondai to jinkō mondai—Joseigakuteki kanten kara—" *Kikan Shakai Hoshō Kenkyū* 28, no. 3, 1992.

———. *Sochi toshite no sei shihai.* Tokyo: Keisō Shobō, 1995.

'82 Yūsei Hogo Hō Kaiaku Soshi Renrakukai, ed. *Yūsei Hogo Hō kaiaku wa doko e itta?* Tokyo: '82 Yūsei Hogo Hō Kaiaku Soshi Renrakukai, 1984.

Fujime, Yuki. "Senkanki nihon no sanji chōsetsu undō to sono shisō." *Rekishi Hyōron* 430 (February 1986).

———. "Aru sanba no kiseki." *Nihonshi Kenkyū* 366 (February 1993).

Fujin Kyōdō Hōritsu Jimusho, ed. *Ima naze Yūsei Hogo Hō o kaiaku ka?* Tokyo: Rōdō Kyōiku Sentā, 1983.

Fujiwara, Mitsuo, ed. *Nagaike yūsei hogo sōdanjo: 20 nen no ayumi,* Sendai: Nagaike Yūsei Hogo Sōdanjo, 1993.

Furukawa, Seiji, et al., eds. *Bio jidai ni kyōsei o to: hanyūsei no ronri,* Tokyo: Zakushoku Shobō, 1988.

Gurūpu Bosei Kaidoku Kōza. *"Bosei" o kaidoku suru,* Tokyo: Yuhikaku Sensho, 1991.

Gurūpu Onna no Jinken to Sei, ed. *Repurodakutibu herusu o watashitachi no te ni,* Tokyo: Gurūpu Onna no Jinken to Sei, 1990.

Harada, Kunio. "Toki no hanrei." *Jūrisuto* 906 (April 15, 1988).

Hayakawa, Kiyo. "Senji taisei, yūsei shisō, jinkō seisaku—'Yūsei Hogo Hō' kaisei no ugoki o megutte—" *Rekishi Hyōron* 396 (April 1983).

Hirose, Yoshi. "Jinkō ninshin chūzetsu no dekiru kikan no tanjuku ni atatte." *Nihon Ishikai Zasshi* 106, no. 2, 1991.

Hiroshima, Kiyoshi. "Gendai nihon jinkō seisakushi kōron: jinkō shishitsu gainen o megutte (1916–1930)." *Jinkō Mondai Kenkyū* 154, (1981).

———. "Gendai nihon jinkō seisakushi kōron (2): Kokumin Yūsei Hō ni okeru jinkō no shitsuseisaku to ryōseisaku." *Jinkō Mondai Kenkyū,* 160 (1982).

Honda, Hiroshi. "Jutai chōsetsuho no shurui to jissai."*Josanpu Zasshi* 44, no. 2 (1990).

Ichikawa, Fusae. *Watakushi no fujin undō.* Tokyo: Akimoto Shobō, 1972.

———. ed. *Nihon fujin mondai shiryō shūsei,* vol. 2 (Seiji); vol. 6 (Hoken). Tokyo: Domesu Shuppan, 1978.

Inoue, Nobutaka, et al., eds. *Shinshūkyō jiten.* Tokyo: Kōbundō, 1990.

Inoue, Shiden. *Yūsei Hogo Hō kaisei o meguru mondai to iken.* 2 vols. Tokyo: Yūsei Hogo Hō Kaihatsu Kisei Dūmei, 1968–69.

Inoue, Teruko, et al., eds. *Nihon no feminizumu 5: Bosei.* Tokyo: Iwanami Shōten, 1995.

Ishihara, Tsutomu. "Yūsei Hogo Hō no rekishi." *Sanfujinka Chiryō* 53, no. 4 (1986).

Ishii, Michiko. "Yūsei Hogo Hō ni yoru datai gōhōka no mondaiten." *Shakai Kagaku Kenkyū* 34, no. 4 (1982).

———. *Jinkō seishoku no hōritsugaku: Seishoku iryō no hattatsu to kazoku hō.* Tokyo: Yuhikaku, 1994.

Ishizaki, Nobuko. "Seishoku no jiyū to sanji chōsetsu undō—Hiratsuka Raichō to Yamamoto Senji." *Rekishi Hyōron* 503 (March 1992).

Isō, Abe. "Sanji chōsetsu no shakaitei igi." *Taiyō* (November 1926).

Itō, Hiroto, and Eiji Marui. "Funin shujutsu no yūseigakuteki tekiyō no suii to mondaiten—seishin shōgaisha e no tekiyō o chūshin toshite—" *Minzoku Eisei* 59, no. 1 (1993).

Iwamoto, Misako. "Seishoku no jiko ketteiken to nihonteki seisaku kettei." *Joseigaku* 1 (1992).

———. "Jinkō ninshin chūzetsu seisaku ni okeru kettei, hikettei, meta-kettei: 1980 nendai nihon no nitōri no kesu o chūshin ni." *Gyōsei* (May 1993).

———. "Seishoku no jiko ketteiken no ima: Nihon ni okeru piru kaikin tōketsu o megutte." *Joseigaku* 2 (May 1994).

Jansson, Yumiko. "Piru 'kaikin' o mae ni ima, hinin to kyōiku o mitsumenaosu, *Human Sexuality* 5 (November 1991).

———. "Onna wa naze kodomo o umanai no ka." *Sekai to Jinkō* 238 (January 1994).

"Jinkō chūzetsu hō kaisei no noroshi." *Shūkan Shinchō* (June 15, 1962).

Jinkō Mondai Kenkyūjo, ed. "Fūfu no shussanryoku: umeyo fuyaseyo." *Shūhō* (June 25, 1941).

———, ed. *Jinkō mondai kenkyūjo sōritsu 50 shūnen kinenshi.* Tokyo: Jinkō Mondai Kenkyūjo, 1989.

"Jinkō ninshin chūzetsu o kangaeru shiten—'karada no jiko ketteiken' to iu messēji o tsutaeru ni wa—" *Human Sexuality* 13 (November 1993).

Joseigaku, Zemi. "Yūsei Hogo Hō ni kansuru futatsu no chōsa." *Joseigaku Nenpō* 8 (1987).

Kanai, Yoshiko, and Mikiyo Kano, eds. *Onnatachi no Shisen.* Tokyo: Shakai Hyōronsha, 1990.

Kanazawa, Fumio. "1) Tekitō na iryō kōi ni ataranai to sareshita jirei, 2) Yūsei Hogo Hō 28 jo no 'shujutsu' no imi." *Hanrei Taimuzu* 280 (1972).

Kaneko, Junji. "Danshu hō mondai kentō (1)." *Iji Kōron* 1345 (1938).

Kaneko, Takeharu, and Noriko Shiraishi. " 'Nihon ishikai zasshi' ni mirareru jinkō kankei ronbun, kiji ni tsuite." *Jinkō Mondai Kenkyūjo Nenpō* 22 (1977).

Katō, Shizue. *Aru josei seijika no hansei.* Kyoto: PHP Kenkyūjo, 1981.

Kikakuin. "Jinkō mondai o dō suru." *Shūhō* (February 12, 1941; February 19, 1941).

"Kojin toshite wa ii, kokka toshite wa imada shi." *Taiyō* (November 1926).

"Kokka mondai toshite mirareru sanji chosetsu." *Taiyō* (October 1926).

"Kono hito hi kiku: Katō Shizue San," *Agora* 28 (June 1983).

Kōno, Satoko, and Keiko Seikai. "Onna no 'jiko ketteiken' to seimei." In Sechiyama Kaku et al., eds., *Feminizumu Corekushon.* Vol. 1. Tokyo: Keisō Shobō, 1993.

Kōseishō. "Minzoku yūsei hōsaku." *Shūhō* 151 (September 6, 1939).

———. "Kokumin Yūsei Hō kaizetsu." *Shūhō* 244 (June 11, 1941).

Kōseishō Gojūnen Shi Shuiinkai, ed. *Kōseishō Gojūnen Shi.* Vols. 1–2. Tokyo: Chūō Hōki, 1988.

Kōseishō Imukyoku, ed. *Isei hyakunen shi.* Tokyo: Gyōsei, 1976.

Kōseishō Shōbōkyoku, ed. *Kokumin yūsei zukai.* Tokyo: Kōseishō Shōbōkyoku, 1941.

Machino, Saku. "Seitenkan shujutsu." *Bessatsu Jūrisuto* 33 (1971).

Mainichi Shimbunsha Jinkō Mondai Chōsakai, ed. *Atarashii Kazokuzō to Motomete: #22 Zenkoku Kazoku Keikaku Yoron Chōsa.* Tokyo: Mainichi Shimbunsha, 1994.

Maki. " 'Dataizai' ni tsuite no shisatsu (1)—keihōgakuteki shiten kara." *Nihon Fujin Mondai Konwakai Kaihō* 51 (1991).

———. " 'Dataizai' ni tsuite no shisatsu (2)—keihōgakuteki shiten kara." *Nihon Fujin Mondai Konwakai Kaihō* 52 (1992).

Marumoto, Yuriko. "Josei no karada to kokoro—dataitsumi, Yūsei Hogo Hō, Boshi Hoken Hō o megutte." *Jūrisuto Zōkan Sōgō Tokushū* 39 (summer 1985).

Marumoto, Yuriko. "Umu, umanai wa onna no ishi de kimeru koto." In Sechiyama Kaku et al., eds., *Feminizumu Korekushon*. Vol. 1. Tokyo: Keisō Shobō, 1993.

Matsumoto, Seiichi. *Boshi Hoken Gairon*. Tokyo: Bunkōdō, 1983.

———. "Wagakuni ni okeru jinkō ninshin chūzetsu no nenjiteki suii." *Sanka to Fujinka* 58, no. 1 (1991).

Minaguchi, H., and T. Wagatsuma. "Keikō hininyaku no genkyo to tenbō." *Nihon Ishikai Zasshi* 110, no. 10 (1991).

Mitsui, Fumiyo. " 'Hinin' o meguru nihon no kindai shi." *Human Sexuality* 5 (November 1991).

Miyahara, Shinobu. "Kazoku keikaku to tomo ni ayunda michi—Katō Shizue-san intabyu." *Josanpu Zasshi* 44, no. 10 (1990).

Miyaji, Tōru. "Jinkō ninshin chūzetsu jisshi kanō jiki no tanjuku ni tomonatte shōjiru shomondai." *Josanpu Zasshi* 45, no. 9 (1991).

Mizoguchi, Akiyo et al, eds., *Shiryō Nihon ūman ribu shi*, vols. 1–3, Kyoto: Shōkadō, 1992–1995.

Morikawa, " 'Umu, umanai wa onna ga kimeru' kangae," *Shinchihei* (August 1983).

Moriyama, Yutaka. "Yūsei Hogo Hō no kaisei mondai." *Sanka to Fujinka* 40, no. 9 (1973).

———. "Yūsei Hogo Hō to jinkō mondai." *Sanfujinka no Sekai* 25, no. 9 (1973).

———.*Sanfujinka no Sekai* 26, no. 2 (1974).

———. "Yūsei Hogo Hō to ichibu kaisei mondai." *Sanfujinka no Sekai* 27 no. 2 (1975).

Murakawa, Ichirō, et al., eds. *Gendai no seiji katei*. Tokyo: Gakuyō Shobō, 1982.

Nagaike, Hiroko, and Keiko Takahashi, eds. *10 nen no ayumi*. Sendai: Nagaike Yūsei Hogo Sōdanjo, 1984.

Nakajima, Kuni. "Kokkateki bosei—senjika no joseikan." In Joseigaku Kenkyūkai, ed., *Onna no imeiji*. Vol. 1: *Kōza joseigaku*. Tokyo: Keisō Shobō, 1984.

Nakagawa, Kiyoshi. "Toshi nichijō seikatsu no naka no sengo: minshū ni totte no jinkō ninshin chūzetsu." In Narita Ryūichi, ed., *Kindai nihon no kiseki: toshi to minshū*. Tokyo: Yoshikawa Kobunkan, 1993.

Nakatani, Kinko. "Datai zai." *Bessatsu Jūrisuto* 83. Keihō Hanrei Hyakusen II Kakuron (Dainihan), 1984.

———. "Datai ni yori shussei saseta mijukuji o hōchi shita ishi to hogosha iki chishizai no seihi." *Jūrisuto Rinji Zōkan: Shōwa 63 nendo jūyō hanrei kaisetsu* 935 (1989).

———. "Jinkō ninshin chūzetsu to seiiku genkai." *Shūsanki Igaku* 22, no. 12 (1992).

———. "Sanfujinka ryōiki ni okeru keiji jiken to saishin no kaigai jōhō." *Nihon Ishikai Zasshi* 113, no. 12 (June 1995).

Nihon Bosei Hogo I Kyokai, ed. and pub. *Shitei Ishi Hikkei*. 1992.

*Nihon Iji Shinpō*. "Danshuhō no seitei o megutte." *Nihon Iji Shinpō* 893 (1939).

Nihon Kazoku Keikaku Kyōkai, ed. *Yoakemae no wakai kikansha—Nihon kazoku keikaku kyōkai no 15-nen no ayumi*. Tokyo: Nihon Kazoku Keikaku Kyōkai, 1969.

Nihon Kazoku Keikaku Renmei, ed. *Kanashimi o sabakemasu ka*. Tokyo: Ningen no Kagakusha, 1983.

Nihon Kyōbunsha, ed. *Taiji wa ningen de nai no ka: Yūsei hogo hō no gimonten*. Tokyo: Nihon Kyōbunsha, 1982.

Nishiuchi, Masahiko. *Nihon no boshi hoken to Moriyama Yutaka: Subete no haha to ko ni hoken to iryō no onkei o*. Tokyo: Nihon Kazoku Keikaku Kyōkai, 1988.

Noma, Shinji. "Kenzen naru Dai Nihon Teikoku—Kokumin Yūsei Hō seitei o megutte—" *Hisutoria* 120 (September 1988).

Ōbayashi, Michiko. "Sanji chōsetsu undō to yūsei shisō." *Nihon Fujin Mondai Konwakai Kaihō* 46 (1987).

———. *Josanpu no Sengo.* Tokyo: Keisō Shobō, 1989.

Ochiai, Emiko. "Taiji wa dare no mono na no ka." *Gendai Shisō* 18, no. 6 (1990).

———. "Teiyōryō piru wa hatashite josei no mikata ka." *Josanpu Zasshi* 45, no. 8 (1991).

Ogino, Hiroshi. "Sengo no hinin shidō no rekishi." *Josanpu Zasshi* 44, no. 2 (1990).

Ogino, Miho. "Jinkō ninshin chūzetsu to josei no jiko ketteiken." In Hara Hiroko and Tachi Kaoru, eds., *Bosei kara jisedai ikuseiryoku e.* Tokyo: Shinyōsha, 1991.

———. "Ningen 'ryō' to 'shitsu'—birth control to yūsei shisō—." In Ueno Chizuko, et al., eds., *Kazoku no shakai shi.* Tokyo: Iwanami Shōten, 1991.

Ōhashi, Yukako. "Umu umanai wa watashi ga kimeru: Yūsei Hogo Hō kaiaku soshi undō kara miete kita mono." In Joseigaku Kenkyūkai, ed., *Onna wa sekai o kaeru: Kōza joseigaku 3.* Tokyo: Keisō Shobō, 1986.

Okazaki, Fumio. "Nihon ni okeru yūsei seisaku to sono kekka ni tsuite." *Jinkō Mondai Kenkyū* 61 (1955).

Okazaki, Yōichi. "Sengo nihon no jinkō mondai to Yūsei Hogo Hō." *Seikei Kenkyū* 28, no. 1 (1991).

"Onna no Jinken to Sei" Shinposhiumu Yushi. *Chinmoku o yabutta onnatachi.* Kyoto: Minerva Shobō, 1988.

"Onna no Jinken to Sei" Jikkō Iinkai, eds. *Chotto matte! "chūzetsu dekiru jiki no tanjuku"—onna kara no hatsugen—.* Tokyo: "Onna no Jinken to Sei" Jikkō Iinkai, 1989.

Onna no Tame no Kurinikku, ed. *Piru: watashitachi wa erabanai.* Osaka: Onna no Tame no Kurinikku, 1987.

Ōta, Tenrei. *Nihon sanji chōsetsu shi—Meiji, Taishō, Shōwa shoki made.* Tokyo: Nihon Kazoku Keikaku Kyōkai, 1969.

———. *Nihon sanji chōsetsu 100-nen shi.* Tokyo: Shuppan Kagaku Sōgō Kenkyūjo, 1976.

———. *Datai kinshi to Yūsei Hogo Hō.* Tokyo: Keieisha Kagaku Kyōkai, 1980.

Ōtani, Minoru. "Datai ni yori shussei saseta mijukuji o hōchi shita ishi ni tsuki. . ." *Hanrei Taimuzu* 670 (September 12, 1988).

"Piru 'kaikin' o mae ni ima, hinin to kyōiku o mitsumenaosu." *Human Sexuality* 5 (November 1991).

Saitō, Chiyo. "Mienai 'michi'—Yūsei Hogo Hō no keifu o tazunete mita koto kangaeta koto." *Agora* 28 (June 1983).

Saitō, Hikaru. "20 nendai nihon yūseigaku no ikkyokumen." *Gendai Shisō* 21, no. 7 (1993).

Sakamoto, Shōichi. "Piru to AIDS no kankei ni tsuite." *Boshi hoken jōhō* 28 (November 1993).

Sechiyama, Kaku, Katō Shuichi and Sakamoto Kazue, eds. *Feminizumu Korekushon.* Vol. 1. Tokyo: Keisō Shobō, 1993.

Seichō no Ie Honbu, ed. *Seichō no ie yonjūnen shi.* Tokyo: Nippon Kyōbunsha, 1970.

———. *Seichō no ie gojūnen shi.* Tokyo: Nippon Kyōbunsha, 1980.

Sensō e no Michi o Yurusanai Onnatachi Shūkai, ed. *Onna ni wa umenai toki mo aru.* Tokyo: Satsuki Sha, 1982.

Shakai Hyōronsha Henshūbu. *Onna no sei to chūzetsu: Yūsei Hogo Hō no haikei*. Tokyo: Shakai Hyōronsha, 1983.

"Shimbun kirinuki ni miru onna no 16-nen." *Agora* 136 (tokushū #35) (December 1988).

Shimizu, Katsumi. *Nihon kōshū eisei shi—Shōwa zenki hen*. Tokyo: Funi Shuppan, 1989.

Shinozaki, Nobuo. "Jinkō shishitsu to yūsei mondai." *Jinkō Mondai Kenkyūjo Nenpō* 13 (1968).

———. "Jinkō seisaku rongi no memo—Shōwa 2 nen no jinkō mondairon o chūshin toshite—." *Jinkō Mondai Kenkyūjo Nenpō* 19 (1974).

———. "Jinkō shishitsu ron—nihon jinkō no shishitsu to kankyō—mondai no shozai." *Jinkō Kenkyū Mondai* 154 (1981).

Suehisa, Toshihiko. "Taiji no sendensei ijō o riyū to suru jinkō ninshin chūzetsu (1)." *Tōhoku Gakuin Daigaku Ronshū (Hōritsugaku)* 43–44 (1994).

Suzuki, Naoko, ed. *Shiryō sengo bosei no yukue*. Tokyo: Domesu Shuppan, 1985.

Suzuki, Yūko. *Joseishi o hiraku: yokusan to teikō*. Vol. 2. Tokyo: Miraisha, 1989.

Suzuki, Zenji. *Nihon no yūseigaku—sono shisō to undō no kiseki—*. Tokyo: Sankyō Shuppansha, 1983.

Taguchi, Fukuji. *Shakai shūdan no seiji kitai*. Tokyo: Miraisha, 1969.

"Taiheiyō sensō zenya sokkuri kyōka sareru 'kenzen na ko' no shussan." *Agora* 78 (October 1983).

Takagi, Masashi. " 'Taishō demokurashii' ki ni okeru 'yūseiron' no tenkai to kyōiku—kyōiku zasshi no naiyō bunseki no shikaku kara—." *Nagoya Daigaku Kyōikugakubu Kiyo (Kyōiku Gakka)* 36 (1989).

———. "1920–30 nendai ni okeru yūseigakuteki nōryokukan—Nagai Sen oyobi nihon minzoku eisei gakkai (kyōkai) no kenkai o chūshin ni—." *Nagoya Daigaku Kyōikugakubu Kiyo (Kyōiku Gakka)* 38 (1991).

———. "Senzen nihon ni okeru yūsei shisō no tenkai to nōryokukan, kyōikukan—sanji seigen oyobi jinkō seisaku to no kankei o chūshin ni—." *Nagoya Daigaku Kyōikugakubu Kiyo (Kyōiku Gakka)* 40 (1993).

Takahashi, Hideyuki. "Nihon ishikai no seiji kōdō to ishikettei." In Minoru Nakano, ed., *Nihonkei seisaku kettei no henyō*, Tokyo: Tōyō Keizai Shinposha, 1986.

Takahashi, Katsuyo. "Yūsei Hogo Hō un'ei ni okeru todōfuken ishikai no yakuwari." *Nihon Ishikai Zasshi*, 90:1 (July 1, 1983).

Takashima, Manabe. "Seitankan shujutsu to Yūsei Hogo Hō 28 jō." *Bessatsu Jūristo*, 50 (1976).

Tama, Yasuko. "Chūzetsu no shakaishi." In Inoue Teruko et al., eds., *Nihon no feminizumu 5: Bosei*. Tokyo: Iwanami Shōten, 1995.

Taniai, Noriko. *Namida no senkyo—dokyumento Yūsei Hogo Hō*. Tokyo: Shio Shuppansha, 1978.

Taniguchi, Yasaburō. *Yūsei Hogo Hō shōkai*. Tokyo: Nihon Bosei Hogo I Kyōkai, 1952.

Taniguchi, Yasaburō, and Masako Fukuda. *Yūsei Hogo Hō kaisetsu*. Tokyo: Kenshin Shahan, 1948.

Tashiro, Mieko. "Kindai nihon ni okeru sanji seigen undō to seikyōiku—1920–30 nendai o chūshin ni—." *Nihon no Kyōikushigaku* 36 (1993).

Tsujinaka, Yutaka. *Rieki Shūdan*. Tokyo: Tokyo Daigaku Shuppansha, 1988.

Ueno, Chizuko et al., eds. *Kazoku no shakai shi*. Tokyo: Iwanami Shōten, 1991.

Yamada, Makoto. "Uchi naru yūsei shisō o utsu tame ni." *Nihon Fujin Mondai Konwakai Kaihō* 46 (1987).

———. "Warera no uchi naru yūsei shisō o tō." In Furukawa Seiji, et al., eds., *Bio jidai ni kyōsei o tō: Hanyūsei no ronri.* Tokyo: Soshoku Shobō, 1988.

Yamaguchi, Mitsuko. "Josei shodantai no josei seisaku ni taisuru gōi keisei katei—zenkoku soshiki 50 dantai no rentai to kōdō—." *Joseigaku to Seiji Jissen* 2 (1992).

Yamamoto, Katsumi. "Teach in 'ima, dō suru? Yūsei Hogo Hō' wa chikara ni haitta shūkai deshita." *Genba kara no repōto* (February 13, 1993).

———. "Nakusō Yūsei Hogo Hō, Datai Zai, kaeyo boshi hoken." *Genba kara no repōto* (October 14, 1994).

Yoneda, Taiko. " 'Shufu no Tomo' ni miru sanji chōsetsu—1920 nendai zengo no jidai ishiki—." *Ningen Hattatsu Kenkyū* 17 (1992).

" 'Yūsei Hogo Hō jiki kokkai teishutsu' wa 'mitei' to kiseisho." *Agora* 79 (November 1983).

Yūsei Hogo Hō Kaiaku = Kenpō Kaiaku to Tatakau Onna no Kai, ed. *Yūsei Hogo Hō kaiaku to tatakau tame ni.* Tokyo: '82 Yūsei Hogo Hō Kaiaku Soshi Renrakukai, 1982.

"Yūsei Hogo Hō kai'sei' to watashitachi no tachiba." *Fukushi Rōdō* (Tokushū) 21 (1983).

# Index

# STUDIES OF THE EAST ASIAN INSTITUTE

## Selected Titles

*Japan's Imperial Diplomacy: Consuls, Treaty Ports, and War with China, 1895–1938,* by Barbara Brooks. Honolulu: University of Hawai'i Press, 2000

*Japan's Budget Politics: Balancing Domestic and International Interests,* by Takaaki Suzuki. Lynne Rienner Publishers, 2000

*Cadres and Corruption: The Organizational Involution of the Chinese Communist Party,* by Xiaobo Lu. Stanford University Press, 2000

*Assembled in Japan: Electrical Goods and the Making of the Japanese Consumer,* by Simon Partner. University of California Press, 1999

*Nation, Governance, and Modernity: Canton, 1900–1927,* by Michael T.W. Tsin. Stanford: Stanford University Press, 1999

*Civilization and Monsters: Spirits of Modernity in Meiji Japan,* by Gerald Figal. Duke University Press, 1999

*The Logic of Japanese Politics: Leaders, Institutions, and the Limits of Change,* by Gerald L. Curtis. New York: Columbia University Press, 1999

*Trans-Pacific Racisms and the U.S. Occupation of Japan,* by Yukiko Koshiro. New York: Columbia University Press, 1999

*Bicycle Citizens: The Political World of the Japanese Housewife,* by Robin LeBlanc. Berkeley: University of California Press, 1999

*Alignment despite Antagonism: The United States, Japan, and Korea,* by Victor Cha. Stanford: Stanford University Press, 1999

*Contesting Citizenship in Urban China: Peasant Migrants, the State and Logic of the Market,* by Dorothy Solinger. Berkeley: University of California Press, 1999

*Order and Chaos in the Works of Natsume Sōseki,* by Angela Yiu. Honolulu: University of Hawai'i Press, 1998

*Driven by Growth: Political Change in the Asia-Pacific Region,* 2nd edition, edited by James W. Morley. Armonk, NY: M. E. Sharpe, 1998

*Japan's Total Empire: Manchuria and the Culture of Wartime Imperialism,* by Louise Young. Berkeley: University of California Press, 1997

*Honorable Merchants: Commerce and Self-Cultivation in Late Imperial China,* by Richard Lufrano. Honolulu: University of Hawai'i Press, 1997

*Print and Politics: 'Shibao' and the Culture of Reform in Late Qing China,* by Joan Judge. Stanford: Stanford University Press, 1996

*Troubled Industries: Confronting Economic Change in Japan,* by Robert Uriu. Ithaca: Cornell University Press, 1996

*Tokugawa Confucian Education: The Kangien Academy of Hirose Tansē (1782–1856),* by Marleen Kassel. Albany, NY: State University of New York Press, 1996

*The Dilemma of the Modern in Japanese Fiction,* by Dennis C. Washburn. New Haven: Yale University Press, 1995

*The Final Confrontation: Japan's Negotiations with the United States, 1941,* edited by James W. Morley. New York: Columbia University Press, 1994

*Landownership under Colonial Rule: Korea's Japanese Experience, 1900–1935,* by Edwin H. Gragert. Honolulu: University of Hawaii Press, 1994

*Japan's Foreign Policy after the Cold War: Coping with Change,* edited by Gerald L. Curtis. Armonk, NY: M.E. Sharpe, 1993